Seeing Through Religion

Seeing Through Religion is a cutting-edge textbook designed to help students in their study and research of the world's religious traditions. Providing the tools to learn this valuable subject theoretically, McGovern argues that religion isn't a thing out there in the world; it's the glasses on your face through which you see the world, shaped by Western history and, in particular, Christianity. By exploring the major religious traditions and comparing stereotypes about them to reality, this textbook establishes how the lens of "religion" systematically distorts our perception of the world. Topics covered include:

- What is religion?
- Colonialism and the two faces of Orientalism
- Islam: Does fear imply difference?
- Buddhism: A philosophy or a religion?
- Hinduism: A polytheistic or a monotheistic religion?
- Chinese religion: What is it, and where can we find it?
- Indian religions: How can one religion "include" another?
- Tibetan Buddhism: Is it still Buddhism?
- Judaism: A religion or an ethnicity?
- Indigenous traditions: What gets counted as a religion?
- Secularism: Can we put religion in a box?
- How is the way we think about religion influenced by the theology of Martin Luther?
- How does the Christian paradigm of religion distort our perception of Christianity itself?

This textbook not only provides a survey of important religious traditions but also guides the reader on how to study religion in a methodologically sophisticated way. This innovative volume is essential reading for those who want a contemporary and engaging approach to the study of world religions.

Nathan McGovern is Professor in the Department of Philosophy and Religious Studies at the University of Wisconsin-Whitewater, USA.

NATHAN McGOVERN

Seeing Through Religion

An Introduction to the Study of Religion and Religions

LONDON AND NEW YORK

Designed cover image: Getty Images

First published 2026
by Routledge
4 Park Square, Milton Park, Abingdon, Oxon OX14 4RN

and by Routledge
605 Third Avenue, New York, NY 10158

Routledge is an imprint of the Taylor & Francis Group, an informa business

© 2026 Nathan McGovern

The right of Nathan McGovern to be identified as author of this work has been asserted in accordance with sections 77 and 78 of the Copyright, Designs and Patents Act 1988.

All rights reserved. No part of this book may be reprinted or reproduced or utilised in any form or by any electronic, mechanical, or other means, now known or hereafter invented, including photocopying and recording, or in any information storage or retrieval system, without permission in writing from the publishers.

Trademark notice: Product or corporate names may be trademarks or registered trademarks, and are used only for identification and explanation without intent to infringe.

British Library Cataloguing-in-Publication Data
A catalogue record for this book is available from the British Library

Library of Congress Cataloging-in-Publication Data
Names: McGovern, Nathan, 1981- author
Title: Seeing through religion : an introduction to the study of religion and religions / Nathan McGovern.
Description: Abingdon, Oxon ; New York, NY : Routledge, 2026. | Includes bibliographical references and index.
Identifiers: LCCN 2025014776 | ISBN 9781032646398 hardback | ISBN 9781032646411 paperback | ISBN 9781032646428 ebook
Subjects: LCSH: Religion—Textbooks | Religions—Textbooks
Classification: LCC BL48 .M34 2026 | DDC 200—dc23/eng/20250516
LC record available at https://lccn.loc.gov/2025014776

ISBN: 9781032646398 (hbk)
ISBN: 9781032646411 (pbk)
ISBN: 9781032646428 (ebk)

DOI: 10.4324/9781032646428

Typeset in Berling
by codeMantra

For Nanda

CONTENTS

Preface   ix

PART I: REALIZE YOU ARE WEARING GLASSES   1

1 What Is Religion?   3

2 Colonialism and the Two Faces of Orientalism   29

PART II: TAKE THE GLASSES OFF   47

3 Islam: Does Fear Imply Difference?   49

4 Buddhism: A Philosophy or a Religion?   68

5 Hinduism: A Polytheistic or a Monotheistic Religion?   87

6 Chinese Religion: What Is It, and Where Can We Find It?   104

7 Indian Religions: How Can One Religion "Include" Another?   128

8 Tibetan Buddhism: Is It Still Buddhism?   149

9 Judaism: A Religion or an Ethnicity?   165

10 Indigenous Traditions: What Gets Counted as a Religion?   192

11 Secularism: Can We Put Religion in a Box?   211

PART III: LEARN HOW THE GLASSES WORK 231

12 You Are Martin Luther 233

13 How the Glasses Work 249

14 Christianity: Does It Look Different with the Glasses Off? 269

For Further Reading 295
Index 299

Preface

Religious Studies scholars who teach undergraduates are increasingly in a difficult position. We are called upon to teach survey courses like Intro to World Religions and Intro to Asian Religions, and such classes are unlikely to go away because K–12 education typically does not teach basic facts about world religions. There has been a shift in pedagogical philosophy in recent years, however, away from the coverage model, in which a specified number of disconnected topics must be covered at all costs, toward a more integrative approach in which topics covered serve the goal of a higher learning objective. This shift promises to be accelerated further by the rise of AI, which will render not only rote learning, but also routine intellectual tasks, obsolete as primary learning objectives. Increasingly, our students will need to acquire sophisticated metacognitive skills, and this will need to be the goal from the beginning of the learning process, rather than a distant hope for more advanced students. The difficulty this poses for religion teachers is that we need to teach these metacognitive skills, but we must do so within the context of classes set up as surveys, and we must do so with students who in a sense need the survey because they come in lacking a knowledge of basic facts.

Seeing Through Religion is the product of my decade of experience teaching a survey course (in my case, Intro to Asian Religions) and grappling with how to teach about a variety of unrelated religions with a higher theoretical goal in mind to avoid the course becoming just "one damn thing after another." It is an undergraduate textbook of world religions that allows the instructor to teach *about* particular religious traditions while also teaching *how* to study religion in a methodologically sophisticated way. It is also written with a linear argument that can fruitfully be followed by an educated reader in a non-classroom setting.

While the purpose of this book is to introduce readers to the major world religions while also teaching them how to study religion in a methodologically sophisticated way, it is not intended as a general introduction to religious studies theory. I do not introduce the major theories or theorists of religion, except in passing reference as relevant. Instead, I focus on a particular methodological framework, which is not associated with any one theorist but which many scholars of religion, especially those who study non-Western religions, make continual use of. This is the framework that sees religion as a Western concept, tied up with the history of Christianity, that was spread around the world by colonialism and is inflected by Orientalism. I present this methodology as an argument to the reader that is reflected in the title of the book: Religion is something we *see through* rather than look at. By getting the reader to understand this, I am helping them see through the illusion that religion is simply an objective given.

In pursuit of this argument, the book has three parts, which are built around a metaphor that compares the category religion to a pair of "Christian-tinted" glasses. In Part I, Realize You Are Wearing Glasses, I argue that religion is less some thing out there in the world than a lens through which we see the world. It is a Western concept, tied up with the history of Christianity, that was universalized and inflected by Orientalism over the course of the colonial period. Part II, Take the Glasses Off, is the meat of the book, in which I take up major religious traditions in turn. In each case I thematize the distinction between a popular misconception and reality, which is signaled by the question asked in the title of each chapter. Finally, in Part III, Learn How the Glasses Work, I explain how Christian assumptions, and in particular *Protestant* Christian assumptions, lead to the common misconceptions about various religious traditions and religion in general that we learned about in Part II. Parts I and III thus serve as methodological bookends to the introductions to particular religious traditions, which are mostly found in Part II.

To facilitate accessibility of the book to students and general readers, I have kept notes and citations to a minimum. Citations are given only in the case of very specific references, such as direct quotations. Most of the notes contain additional explanatory material that did not fit easily into the flow of the text. The "For Further Reading" section in the end matter provides a bibliographic reference divided by chapter. The books I have included in this section are those that I would recommend to instructors or motivated students or readers who wish to learn more about a particular topic.

One of the biggest challenges I faced in writing *Seeing Through Religion* was deciding how exactly to incorporate Christianity. On the one hand, Christianity is central to understanding the methodological framework of the book. On the other hand, Christianity is one of the religious traditions that deserves to be introduced on its own terms, like the others, but also without privileging it any more than the modern category of religion already does. My solution was to introduce just enough information about Christianity as needed over the course of the book to make the methodological argument. This is found primarily in chapters 1 and 12. I then provide a chapter dedicated specifically to Christianity at the very *end* of the book, in chapter 14. This approach might seem counterintuitive, but it allows me to first show how the "glasses" of religion work by focusing on the hegemonic Christian discourses that largely inform the "tint" of the glasses. This then puts me in the position at the end of the book to show that the glasses distort our understanding of Christianity itself, since Christianity is far more diverse than its most dominant voices (e.g., Nicene orthodoxy and Protestant theology) allow.

My approach to Christianity is reflective of my approach to all the religious traditions introduced in the book. Since the aim is to move away from the coverage model, I privilege the methodological arguments of the book and of each individual chapter over covering "everything" about a religious tradition. I therefore introduce facts on a need-to-know basis, to make the methodological point I want to make while also giving a reasonably rounded view of the tradition in question. The amount of content in each chapter is typically a bit more than I find through experience can be discussed in a week of a survey class but also a bit less than might be found in more encyclopedic treatments. Some instructors who are accustomed to more traditional textbooks may find this disconcerting at first. I would argue, however, that the urge to cover everything is one we should resist in order to move beyond the coverage model and update our teaching for the needs of the twenty-first century and education in the world of AI. My central focus is always on fostering critical evaluative skills, and the text provides facts primarily in support of this objective. Students can then acquire more facts on their own but equipped with the critical evaluative framework necessary to make productive use of those facts.

Although the book is written to be fruitfully read from beginning to end, each chapter is self-contained, with cross-references to other chapters as appropriate. The chapters introducing individual traditions in Part II are ordered in a way that I see as roughly progressing from more accessible methodological issues to more advanced methodological issues, but other instructors may wish to order them differently according to their needs or preferences. The book is thus adaptable to a variety of survey classes. The coverage is wide enough for an Intro to World Religions class, but it can also easily be adapted to a survey class with a narrower scope, such as Intro to Asian Religions, which is what I teach. I encourage the instructor to pick and choose chapters, or parts thereof, as needed and to supplement with other readings and multimedia.

In a similar vein, I strongly encourage instructors to emphasize to their students that they should not read this book as they would a traditional textbook. My voice as the author and as an instructor myself is strong throughout the book. I present individual chapters and the book as a whole as arguments, to model how practicing scholars communicate with one another. At times, I present my own opinion, just as I and other instructors do in the classroom as we grapple with the real-world implications of what we are discussing with our students. I encourage instructors to make use of this book in the classroom not merely as a source of facts but as an extended argument that one can think with, discuss, argue over, and potentially disagree with. The dawn of AI is shifting the needs of students up the levels of Bloom's taxonomy as lower levels of that taxonomy become automated. Although AI has fostered a great deal of fear and consternation among educators, it is important to remember that AI will never eliminate the need for citizens to critically evaluate the increasingly sophisticated opinions and analyses they will encounter throughout their lives. My hope is that this book will *both* model a useful way to critically evaluate popular narratives about religion *and* provide an opportunity for practicing critical evaluation in the classroom.

There are many people I would like to thank for their support and feedback as I have worked on this book, in various forms, over the past six years. Stephen Cooper, Lewis Doney, Jared Lindahl, Colleen Windham-Hughes, Rahuldeep Singh Gill, Adil Mawani, Miki Chase, and David Divalerio read and provided feedback on drafts of chapters. Jared Lindahl also provided an early suggestion that inspired the final title for the book. Jim Tranquada provided assistance with a question about the history of Occidental College. Amy Langenberg tested out the first chapter with one of her classes and provided feedback. Christina Tretter and Toei Talawat gave feedback on an earlier version of the manuscript from a non-scholarly perspective, and Taylor Hines and David McConeghy provided extensive scholarly feedback on the same manuscript. Alyson Prude also provided extensive feedback on that manuscript and, moreover, helped to inspire the approach of the book more than even I realized at first. I would particularly like to thank the dozens of anonymous readers who provided extensive and critical feedback on the chapters of this book as I was preparing it for publication. Writing outside of one's narrow specialization is a daunting task, and this book is much better for the broad range of expertise these readers brought with their feedback. Any errors, of course, remain my own.

Many thanks to my students over the years who have directly and indirectly played a central role in shaping my teaching methods and the approach taken in this book. The critical feedback from my students at

Franklin and Marshall College in 2012–2013, my first full-time teaching gig, gave me the kick in the butt that I needed to develop a more innovative and student-focused pedagogy. My students at Dalhousie University in 2015–2016, in turn, provided a warm and receptive audience for me to try out a new approach. Finally, my students at UW-Whitewater from 2016 on have helped me refine my approach to teaching religion as I continue to look for creative ways to move beyond the coverage model.

I am indebted to several people who gave me advice along the way as I grappled with how to market and publish this book. John Parsley, Sarah Smithline, and Theo Calderara gave advice from publishers' perspectives. Anya Foxen provided useful feedback on my book proposal and introduced me to Rebecca Clintworth at Routledge. Rebecca Clintworth and Fred Coppersmith provided a smooth and supportive process for publication and arranged the extensive anonymous review of the chapters.

Finally, I would like to thank all my family, friends, and colleagues for their support that has allowed me to become a successful scholar, teacher, and author. I'm appreciative of the support from my department at UW-Whitewater and especially from my Religious Studies mentor, David Simmons. My parents were of course my earliest teachers and fostered a love of learning and teaching. I'm also thankful to my aunt and uncle, Helen Collins and Frank Edgerton, who were themselves professional educators and served as some of my earliest models of professional pedagogy. Last but not least, I would like to thank my wife, Nanda Raksakhom, whose love and support over the last twenty years has helped me to become the successful teacher-scholar I am today. In particular, her encouragement enabled me to see my own gift for teaching at a time when I feared I lacked it. This book is dedicated to her.

Part I
Realize You Are Wearing Glasses

1 What Is Religion?

What is religion? How would you define it? "Isn't it obvious?" you might say. Well, is it? I want you to really think about this. If you were writing a definition of religion, what would it be? Now, be careful when you do this. You don't want your definition to be too broad, or else it will cover all kinds of random things that are not religion. And you don't want your definition to be too narrow, or it won't cover all the things that we *do* consider to be religion. Go ahead, put the book down, and try to come up with a definition of religion right now, before you read on.

Ok, so what did you come up with? If you are like many of my students, you probably came up with something like, "A set of beliefs about God or a higher power." In any case, it's highly likely that the word *belief*, or something closely related, showed up in your definition. This might seem obvious. By the end of this book, I will show you why it is *not* obvious that religion should be defined in terms of belief, as well as why it is so highly likely that you did so anyway. Of course, it hardly works to define religion solely as a system of beliefs; people believe all sorts of things, but not all of these beliefs are religious. So, it needs to be belief about something in particular, and it may seem obvious that this particular something is God, gods, the divine, a higher power, or whatever you want to call it. I'd argue that including gods, in some form, in a definition of religion indeed *is* more obvious than defining religion in terms of belief, but as we will see, even this gets complicated. In any case, doing so results in a common definition of religion like the one I gave above.

TESTING EXAMPLES

Let's approach the problem from a different angle. Remember I said that we need to make sure that our definition is neither too broad nor too narrow. This is harder than it looks at first glance. To see this, I'd like us to engage in a little mental exercise. Here's a list of several things: Christianity, Buddhism, communism, atheism, environmentalism, Boy Scouts, political parties, and football. Which of these are religions, and which are not? Again, the answer might seem obvious: Christianity and Buddhism are religions, and the rest are not. But why? Let's look at each of these things in turn and see if we can come up with an argument for why it is or isn't a religion.

We'll start with Christianity. This is an easy one: Of course Christianity is a religion. If you defined religion as "belief in God or a higher power," then Christianity certainly fits the bill because it is, indeed, a system of belief in a higher power, God. We could go on and on about what makes Christianity a religion. Christians follow a particular person, Jesus Christ, who effectively founded the religion and is understood to have a special place within it. (In this case, he is understood by most Christians to be God himself.) Christianity has a community of followers, called the Church, and these followers meet in places of worship called churches. There are clergy who lead Christians: priests and bishops in the Catholic and Orthodox Churches, ministers in the Protestant Churches. Christians look to a particular book or scripture for inspiration, known as the Bible. They believe in certain truths about God, Jesus, and the world as a whole based on their scripture and the teachings of their leaders. These beliefs include a belief in the afterlife and places of reward and punishment (heaven and hell) for one's actions in this life. Finally, Christians engage in various religious practices, including prayer, worship, and in some cases pilgrimage, rituals, and fasting.

What about Buddhism? Judging from common lists of world religions, this should also be easy, because Buddhism is always listed as a major world religion. But why is it? In one respect it is obviously very similar to Christianity: Like Christians, Buddhists follow a particular person, in this case the Buddha, who founded the religion and is looked upon as a special authority. What about God, though? The Buddha is not God in the Christian sense of the term. Sometimes people like to say that there is no God or gods in Buddhism. People also like to say Buddhism is very individualistic, doesn't have rituals, and is basically a philosophy or way of life. So then what is religious about it? Buddhists do strive to attain *nirvana*, a state of freedom from suffering. So maybe that's a little like going to heaven? And maybe Buddhism doesn't have God, but it does have the Buddha and *nirvana*. Maybe one of those is kind of like a higher power that one believes in?

Ok, now surely communism should be easy, but for the opposite reason, right? How can "godless communists" constitute a religion? They are explicitly *anti*-religion. Karl Marx wrote that religion is the "opium of the people,"[1] and he theorized that religion was an illusion used to oppress the common masses. Communist regimes have engaged in massive campaigns, at times violent, to suppress religion. But if you think about it, communism is in a lot of ways very similar to religion. Communists certainly hold strong beliefs. You could even say they believe in a higher power, whether communism itself, the proletariat, or the revolution. Communists have leaders, and in particular communist countries some leaders have taken on a cult-like status: Think Lenin, Mao, and the Kims of North Korea. In addition, in Marx's philosophy, the communist revolution was not simply something to strive for to institute communism; it was an *inevitable* event. According to Marx, history was inevitably leading to the communist revolution, in which the proletariat (working class) would violently revolt against the bourgeoisie (capitalists), ushering in a communist utopia that would mark the end of history. Sound familiar? Sounds to me a lot like the end times in Christianity, in which Jesus is supposed to return to Earth, destroy all of the earthly powers, and establish the kingdom of God on Earth, thus marking the end of history.[2]

If communism has elaborate beliefs and practices that might come across as religious, surely atheism can definitively be considered not religion? The word *atheism* comes from the Greek word for god, *theos*, but it has negative prefix *a-* in front of it (as also found in *a-moral*, meaning "without morals"). Atheism (nowadays) is the belief that there is no god. So how can that be a religion? Well, if it's just one's personal opinion, then perhaps it isn't a religion, any more than it is a religion to think that blue is the best color or that hamburgers taste better than hot dogs. Then again, it *is* a belief system, and ironically a belief system about God. There is actually a historical parallel here: It might surprise you to learn that in the ancient Roman Empire, Christians were called atheists because they denied all the gods worshipped by the Romans and their subject peoples. Moreover, atheists today, in particular those involved in what has been dubbed the New Atheism, are quite organized. They hold conferences and have respected leaders such as Richard Dawkins and Sam Harris. Moreover, their belief that there is no God is not some casually held opinion; one could go so far as to say that they are downright dogmatic about it. Many of them see religion not only as wrong or foolish, but as an evil that needs to be eradicated. They want to convert you to atheism. And although, like the ancient Christians before them, they deny the existence of the prevailing higher power (God today, the gods in ancient Rome), they replace this higher power with a new one: Nature or Science.[3]

Maybe communism and atheism are downright religious in their anti-religiosity, but surely the next few things I listed are too innocuous and mundane to be considered religions. But again, why? Environmentalists have strong beliefs and a code of ethics, and they are arguably devoted to a higher power, Mother Earth. In fact, some environmentalists have been fairly explicit in this religious devotion to Mother Earth, using the word *Gaia*, which is the name of the ancient Greek Earth goddess.[4] Boy Scouts, on the other hand, are highly organized with a leadership structure and even special garments. They hold to certain beliefs encoded in the Scout Law. They even have a scripture of sorts: the Scout handbook. And they have various rituals and a path that leads to an ultimate goal, like in Christianity and Buddhism: not heaven or *nirvana*, but the rank of Eagle Scout. Likewise, political parties are organized communities united by common beliefs, with leaders that can draw extremely devoted followings. (Think of political rallies.) The most devoted "believers" in a particular party's platform will often devote much time and energy to the party, making long treks to rallies, town halls, and conventions; volunteering and canvassing; and, in general, trying to "convert" others to their party's way of thinking.

I hope that by this point you can begin to see that many things can be looked at as religious. I'm sure you can think of a few examples yourself; maybe you have already. In fact, it's not all that uncommon for us to describe ordinary or mundane activities as religious or with other religiously inflected language, especially when they are done with great fervor or devotion. We even say things like, "He washes his hands religiously."

By far my favorite thing to present to my students as a religion is football. Obviously, we don't usually think of football as being a religion. But when I ask my students to think of football as a religion, they usually have a field day with it. Think about it: Football is organized into teams, each with their own fans, kind of like different religions have their own adherents. Fans can be extremely devoted to their teams, nowadays to a point that can even exceed ordinary religious devotion. There is a distinction in a sense between clergy and laity, insofar as some play and most watch. There is a place of worship, the stadium, and even a holy day of the week, when games are usually played. Some players reach a cult-like status and can be considered like saints or even gods within this religion. All players are supposed to play by the rulebook, which can constitute a sort of "scripture" or at least a code of ethics. Is there a higher power in football? To fans, probably the most popular players are, and to everyone, the team is a higher power insofar as it transcends all individuals and brings them together into a community.[5] Often someone will raise the issue of the afterlife or salvation. Isn't football totally this-worldly? But even in this case, I usually have a clever student who points to the Hall of Fame as an afterlife.

I hope you are thoroughly confused by now. If we're not sure why Buddhism is a religion and can't quite figure out what makes things that we obviously don't consider religions *not* religions, then how can we possibly define religion? What is religion, anyway? The academic field of Religious Studies, which I come from and to which this book is introducing you, is, if not exactly dedicated to answering this question, then in a very real sense built around the dilemma it poses. Religious Studies scholars don't, for the most part, sit around debating what religion "really" is. But we are constantly aware of the difficulties faced in defining it, and that awareness informs all our work. Religious Studies scholars come from a lot of intellectual perspectives, and so we all have different ways of thinking about the problem of religion's definition and to a certain extent have different working definitions that guide us in our research. What many of us have in common, however, is an acute awareness that *it is not obvious what religion "is"; religion is not some thing "out there," independent of the way human beings think about it.* Personally, I think this is a tremendous insight that has profound implications for the way we understand the world. Sharing that insight with you is what I hope to accomplish with this book.

APPROACHES TO DEFINING RELIGION

I'm not going to share with you every famous definition of religion that has been created. There are already good books out there that can do that.[6] In fact, like many Religious Studies scholars of my generation, I'm not particularly interested in defining religion at all. I'm much more interested in understanding why we talk about religion in the first place and why we talk about it in the way we do. This, I contend, not only helps us to understand religion better, but also illuminates the entire world we live in.

First, I do need to make a brief segue into some basic terminology used by scholars in tackling the problem of defining religion. When I first asked you to define religion, you probably came up with a statement that characterized it in a particular way, with a small number of specific characteristics. As I said then, many people define religion along the lines of "a system of belief in God or a higher power." This type of definition is called a *monothetic definition*. A monothetic definition is a black-and-white definition. If something has the characteristic or characteristics given by the definition, then it belongs to that word; otherwise, it doesn't. You can think of a monothetic definition as being like an impenetrable wall built around a word. It defines quite strictly what that word does and does not refer to. I think most of us tend to assume that definitions always work in this way. But for the purposes of defining religion, it is too rigid. It is difficult, probably impossible, to find any set of criteria that are shared by all religions but not shared by any nonreligions.

Another way of defining a word is with a *polythetic definition*. A polythetic definition does not strictly define what characteristics something *must* have to be properly described by a certain word. Instead, it just lists many (*poly*) characteristics that *tend* to be shared by those things described by a certain word. We can think of a polythetic definition as a diffuse boundary around a word, rather than an impenetrable wall. Monothetic definitions make words into fortresses with big walls, while polythetic definitions make them into leisurely estates with loose natural boundaries, such as an outcropping of trees, that mark their extent.

We already started experimenting with thinking about a polythetic definition of religion a minute ago when we asked ourselves if Christianity, Buddhism, communism, and the rest are religions. You'll notice that I sneakily started bringing up all sorts of comparisons to commonly understood characteristics of religion as I described each of the things we were discussing. By the end, you were probably making such comparisons on your own. This shows that there are lots of characteristics that we associate with religion, whether we consciously think about it or not. For example, we tend to associate religion with God, gods, the divine, or some sort of higher power. Religions tend to be organized into communities, which have places of worship and usually some sort of clergy or defined human leadership. These communities may have a codified set of beliefs and moral principles that they live by. Religions may have scriptures, texts that are held in high esteem and used to define the beliefs and moral principles of the community. Often these scriptures contain stories that are important to the religion, which may record history that is recognized even by outsiders, or else myths that are particular to the community. Religions have all sorts of practices, including prayer, fasting, pilgrimage, worship, and the like. The list could probably be expanded upon infinitely.

The beauty of a polythetic definition is that not all examples of a word have to share all of the characteristics. Thus, something need not have *all* the characteristics I just listed to be considered a religion. Buddhism doesn't have a God like Christianity? No problem! If it has other characteristics associated with religion, it can be considered a religion. On the other hand, the fact that football shares certain characteristics with religion doesn't mean that we *must* consider it a religion. I like to think of the characteristics in a polythetic definition of religion as those characteristics that make something feel "religion-y." This means that there is a certain playfulness to the way we use a polythetic definition of religion. It eliminates the problem of certain things ending up on the wrong side of the "wall" of a monothetic definition, but it also means that we can look at things not ordinarily considered religions *as religions* if we want. It is not uncommon for Religious Studies scholars to do exactly this, as for example by studying environmentalism through the categories of religion.

Defining religion polythetically does have one downside, however. It solves the problem of defining religion too broadly or too narrowly, but at the expense of basically giving up on any attempt to explain why we call certain things religions and not other things. It might be fun to play around with the idea of football being a religion, but the fact is that in real life, we simply don't consider football a religion. Christianity, Judaism, Buddhism, Hinduism, and Shinto are called religions, while communism, environmentalism, Boy Scouts, and the GOP are not. Why is this? Why do we have such a clear sense of what is and is not a religion when we are so bad at articulating what it is that makes something a religion?

THE HISTORY OF RELIGION

To answer this question, I think it is useful to approach the question of religion in an entirely different way. Instead of trying to define religion as if it is some timeless entity, we need to look at it as if it is a living being that has grown and changed over time. In other words, we need to understand religion *historically*. *Religion*, after all, is ultimately a word, and words change over time. You're probably aware of some words that have changed or added meanings in recent times. Slang is a great example of this. Words like *bad* and *wicked* have come to mean the precise opposite of their original meaning in slang. The word *gay* is now used almost exclusively as a synonym of (and preferred term for) *homosexual*. Originally, however, it just meant "happy." Similarly, *mad* is now used in American English almost always to mean "angry," but it is still used in British English in its more original meaning, which is "crazy" (think the Mad Hatter of *Alice in Wonderland*). These are just a few examples of the many ways that the meaning, usage, or nuance of words can change quite dramatically over time.

The word *religion* has a long and astounding history that profoundly affects not only the way that we look at and understand the world today, but also fundamentally the way in which the world *works*. Religion is not a word like *rock* or *water* that has a fairly precise synonym in every language at every stage of human history. It is a Western concept, with a long history and many dramatic changes over the course of over two millennia, that only relatively recently became a universal concept shared by cultures around the world. As a result, every time anyone today talks or thinks about religion, they are channeling a very specific set of historical circumstances, ideas, and ways of thinking about the world that are unique to Europe and, in many cases, to Christianity.

The English word *religion*, which is spelled the same or similarly in all Western European languages, comes from the Latin word *religio*. The etymology of this word is unclear, but it seems to have referred in ancient Rome to obligations held by human beings toward gods.[7] It is important to understand that the earliest use of the word *religio* does not correspond in a straightforward way to the modern use of the word *religion*, except insofar as it pertains to the gods. (That is why I said earlier that it makes *some* sense to define religion as having to do with the divine, but in modern usage, what exactly it has to do with the divine can get quite complicated, as in Buddhism, for example.) In ancient Rome, *religio* did not refer, as it does today, to discrete systems of belief, practice, or whatever other characteristics you want to take from the grab-bag of a polythetic definition of religion. There were many different ethnic groups in the empire, and each of them worshiped different gods in different ways. Nobody had any problem with that, as long as you paid appropriate obeisance to the Roman emperor.[8] Sometimes people would worship gods that came from different ethnic groups, and that was seen as okay, too. There were temples to Egyptian gods in Rome, for example, and temples to Roman gods around the empire. Sometimes gods from different ethnic groups would be identified with one another, as was the case with the Roman and Greek gods and goddesses (for example, Roman Jupiter equated with Greek Zeus, Roman Neptune with Greek Poseidon, Roman Juno with Greek Hera, Roman Mercury with Greek Hermes, and so on).

In many ways, *religio* was used in a manner akin to the word *language* today. Many people in the world speak only one language, which is associated with the community into which they are born. But many people speak two or more languages. Imagine someone asking the question, "Which language is true, English or French?" The question doesn't make sense. Languages are not a matter of truth or falsehood. Such was the case with *religio* in the ancient Roman Empire. Different ethnic groups had different languages, but also different *religio*, different gods and sets of obligations to those gods. And it was possible to become "bilingual" in *religio* by worshiping a god or gods from a different ethnic group.

All of this changed with Christianity. Christianity had its origins in Judaism, which was a bit of an outlier among the religions of the ancient Roman Empire in being monotheistic and rejecting the worship of other gods. While Jews were accorded a certain amount of respect by the Romans due to Judaism's antiquity, Christians had no such protection. Their refusal to make sacrifices to the emperor was interpreted as sedition, leading to the famous persecutions of Christians in the first few centuries after Christ. But Christianity's fortunes changed in the early fourth century when Constantine became emperor. This happened after a succession dispute in which Constantine had to go to war with rival claimants. As the story goes, he was preparing to go into battle with one of his rivals and had a vision in which he saw a sign in the sky with the words, "With this sign, conquer." Accounts differ on what exactly the sign was: either a cross-like standard known as the Labarum or the chi-rho symbol, which combines the first two Greek letters of the word *Christ*. Constantine took the symbol into battle and won. As a result, he became a Christian, and in the Edict of Milan issued together with

Figure 1.1 A modern depiction of Constantine's vision that led to his conversion to Christianity. This fresco is found inside the baptistry of the Lateran Basilica in Rome. It was painted by Giacinto Gemignani in the seventeenth century. © Getty Images

his co-emperor Licinius in 313, granted toleration to Christianity. The Roman Empire Christianized over the course of the fourth century, and in 380, the emperor Theodosius I declared Christianity the official religion of the empire.[9]

The conversion of the Roman Empire to Christianity marks a momentous change in the history of the word *religion*. While *religio* in its earliest usage did not imply truth or falsehood any more than the word *language* does, early Christianity made an audacious claim about itself: that it was the one *true* religion. This is not surprising given that Christianity is monotheistic. Christianity makes the claim that there is only one true God; all other gods are false, which is to say either that they do not exist or that they are demons and therefore not properly gods. This way of thinking about religion was quite different from the pre-Christian Roman one, in which it was assumed that there were many different gods worshiped by the various ethnic groups in the world.

The early Christian conception of itself as the one true religion still has a profound effect on the way in which religion is understood today. The modern concept of religion did not appear overnight, however. The way in which Christian Europeans understood religion in the Middle Ages, a period loosely defined as beginning with the fall of Rome and the collapse of the Western half of the Roman Empire in 476, was still quite different from the way we understand it today. Today, we tend to think of religion as an array of identities centered on belief: There are many religions throughout the world, all presumably making competing truth claims, that one can belong to. In medieval Christendom, however, *religion* referred mostly to intense practice and devotion to God, of the sort found in monasteries with their strict schedules of prayer and labor, within an assumed Christian context. We still preserve this sense of the word when we say that we do things, such as brush our teeth, "religiously"—that is, repeatedly and without fail.

Insofar as there was a sense of multiple religions in medieval Christendom, there were in theory just two: "true" religion (Christianity) and "false" religion (that of the "heathens"). Medieval Christians' knowledge of so-called heathens beyond the horizons of their world was limited, and they assumed that they were going to hell because they did not believe in the true religion. Medieval Christians were, however, aware of two other religions that were distinct from Christianity and yet somewhat distinct from the undifferentiated mass of heathens as well. First, there was Judaism. Christians were of course quite familiar with this religion: Christianity had emerged out of Judaism, the Jewish scriptures formed over half of the Christian Bible, and Jews lived alongside Christians throughout Europe. In the Middle Ages, Jews were despised by Christians as the erstwhile people of God who had rejected his Messiah. They were subjected to various slanders, including the false claim that they were "Christ killers"; repeatedly discriminated against; and subjected to periodic episodes of mob violence called pogroms. The treatment of Jews in medieval Christendom laid the groundwork for modern antisemitism, which found its culmination in the Holocaust, in which the Nazi regime industrialized the old practice of the pogrom to murder six million Jews. We will learn more about Judaism and antisemitism in chapter 9.

In addition to Judaism, many medieval Christians would have had some awareness of Islam. Islam, like Judaism and Christianity, is a monotheistic religion; Muslims believe that Muhammad was the last in a long line of prophets sent by God, including the prophets of the Jewish scriptures and Jesus Christ. An Arab Islamic Empire spread rapidly after the death of Muhammad in 632, conquering the Persian Empire as well as much of what had once been part of the Roman Empire. This included the Levant (the area around modern-day Syria, Lebanon, and Israel/Palestine), North Africa, and even much of Spain. Islam therefore existed right on the eastern and western flanks of European Christendom in the Middle Ages. The control of the "Holy Land" (the area in which Jesus lived) by Muslims was viewed with much consternation by medieval Christians, leading to a long series of mostly ill-fated Crusades to establish Christian kingdoms there. These Crusades laid the groundwork for much of the animosity that exists between the Western and Islamic worlds to this day. We will learn more about Islam and longstanding prejudices against it, which are known as Islamophobia, in chapter 3.

We can thus say that in medieval Europe (from a Christian perspective, at least), there was, in a sense, an awareness of four religions. First, there was Christianity, the one true religion. Second, there was Judaism, which was important to the Christian story, but whose members were understood to have been forsaken by God because they rejected his Son. Third, there was Islam, a religion on the margins of Christendom that was uncannily similar to Christianity but was based on the teachings of a false prophet. Finally, beyond the horizons of the European world, there were heathens, those who were totally ignorant of the one true God and thus subject to eternal damnation. To be clear, however, this fourfold scheme is just a simplified and somewhat anachronistic description of the awareness of religious diversity in medieval Europe, which would have varied according to the knowledge and viewpoint of any particular writer. In any case, medieval Christians were not interested in cataloguing religions on equal terms. For them, the most fundamental distinction was between true religion (Christianity, in whatever form one considered orthodox) and false religion (everything else).

Up until relatively recently, then, there simply was no concept of "world religions" in the modern sense. Much of what we now take as given about religion dates back only a few hundred years, to the Protestant Reformation. In 1517, Martin Luther issued his *Ninety-Five Theses*, setting in motion a chain of events that led to the birth of Protestant Christianity. In chapter 12, we will be looking at the Protestant Reformation in more detail and seeing how it played a pivotal role in shaping the modern world. Many of the common assumptions that modern people make about the nature of religion can actually be traced directly to ideas in Protestant theology, in many cases to the thought of Martin Luther himself.

Most importantly, as I mentioned at the beginning of this chapter, modern people have an overwhelming tendency to associate religion with belief. This is not an accident. Luther's main theological dispute with the Catholic Church was specifically over the matter of belief. Luther argued, based on his reading of the Bible, that there is nothing a human being can do to earn salvation. All of us are complete reprobates and deserve to go to hell. Salvation was earned for us by Jesus Christ through his death on the cross, and God gives it freely to us as a gift. We need only accept that gift by having faith in Jesus Christ. This emphasis on faith or belief[10] over what one actually does has become so ingrained in the popular consciousness that people today naturally assume that religion is mostly about belief.

One of the side-effects of the Reformation was the splintering of Christendom into hundreds or thousands of different denominations. There had already been a major split in Christianity in 1054, when a disagreement over whether the pope has special authority led to a separation between the Roman Catholic Church in Western Europe and the Eastern Orthodox Churches in Eastern Europe. With the Protestant Reformation, Christian identity was shattered even further. Martin Luther and the other Reformers rejected the centralized authority of the Catholic Church and encouraged ordinary people to read the Bible. The result was fairly predictable: As more and more ordinary people began to read the Bible, they interpreted it in different ways. This led to increasing disputes over theology, and since the precedent had now been set that one need not submit to the authority of Rome, every theological dispute could potentially lead to the formation of a new Church.

At about the same time that the disputes associated with the Reformation were raging in the sixteenth and early seventeenth centuries, Western Europeans also happened to be coming into closer contact with the outside world. This was the beginning of the age of colonialism. Beginning with the Portuguese in the fifteenth century, followed quickly by the Spanish and then, in succeeding centuries, by the Dutch, French, and British, European powers established extended maritime trading networks in Asia, Africa, and the Americas. Increasingly, the demands of trade led them to establish colonies in these far-away places. Colonialism was accompanied by a missionary fervor; Europeans were for the first time coming into close contact with so-called heathens, and Catholics and Protestants competed to convert these lost souls to the one true religion as they understood it.

To convert people to Christianity, missionaries found it useful to understand their native religious beliefs. The modern study of religion has its roots in this missionary enterprise. As Europeans studied the religious lives of far-away peoples, especially those in Asia, they came to realize they were not just an undifferentiated mass of heathens. They could be divided into several different religions that each had their own internal structure and were quite different from one another. It might seem like common sense now that a Buddhist is not the same as a Hindu, who is not the same as a Shinto, but this awareness in the Western consciousness came about relatively recently, as a result of the colonial encounter. At the same time as religious identity was becoming differentiated *within* Christianity due to the Protestant Reformation, the religious identities of non-Christians were becoming differentiated in the Western consciousness due to colonialism.

But here's the catch: Europeans didn't simply "discover" a bunch of religions "out there" during their colonial adventures. In a sense, they brought them into being. Of course, there have been Buddhists since the time of the Buddha 2,400 years ago, and Hindus have practiced their traditions for thousands of years. But they and the members of many other religions did not necessarily think of what they were doing as *religious*. The reason for this is simple: Prior to the colonial period, they were not familiar with the word *religion*, and *religion* was not a category with which they thought about the world. During the colonial period, languages around the world adapted to the growing prominence of Western ideas by creating new words, or adapting old ones, to translate a whole host of Western concepts. This included such concepts as *society*, *nation*, and *state*, but also *religion*.

To a certain extent, this process of translation was an arbitrary one. We can particularly see this in the way in which various languages in South and Southeast Asia came to translate *religion*. Many of these languages are either descended from the classical language of Sanskrit or else use Sanskrit as a prestige source of specialized vocabulary. In other words, they have the same relationship to Sanskrit that European languages have to Latin. Many languages in India use the Sanskrit word *dharma* to translate *religion*. The Southeast Asian languages of Thai, Lao, and Cambodian, on the other hand, use the Sanskrit word *shasana*. Both are reasonable choices for translating the word *religion*, but they have two completely different meanings in Sanskrit. Yet a third Sanskrit word, *agama*, is used to translate *religion* in the Sri Lankan language of Sinhala, as well as in the Malay and Indonesian languages of Southeast Asia. Ironically, this very same word is used in Thai not to translate *religion*, but rather to mean "magic." Burmese, on the other hand, uses the word *bhasa*, which in Thai means "language." All this goes to show that "religion" is not a universal human concept like "rock" or "sky"; when Western people *made* it universal during the colonial period, different languages adapted in a somewhat arbitrary way.

While Western religious identity was fracturing internally and Westerners were becoming increasingly cognizant of a diversity of religions in the world at large, there was a shift in Western culture away from intolerance of other religions to religious toleration. In large part, this shift was born out of necessity. The Protestant Reformation utterly destroyed Christian unity and laid the groundwork for religious war not only with non-Christians, as had been found in the Crusades, but between different Christians. This culminated in the Thirty Years' War, from 1618 to 1648, which began as a conflict between Catholic and Protestant states. It was the bloodiest conflict in Europe up to that time. The Peace of Westphalia that ended the war marked the first step in a progressive advance towards religious toleration in the Western world. Westerners increasingly found that toleration of religious difference was necessary to keep themselves from killing each other, and this was in time applied to non-Christian religions as well. Of course, there are many Western people even today who are not tolerant of different religions—some churchgoers may scoff, for example, at ecumenical outreach with other Christian denominations, and many (even non-churchgoers) look with disdain, fear, and hatred at Islam. But compared to the Middle Ages, religious toleration is structurally built into the public sphere, and a substantial portion of the population, including both those who do and those who do not see themselves as religious, personally support religious tolerance.

In a sense, then, the Western world has come full circle. Just as *religio* referred to a multitude of practices dedicated to a multitude of different gods that coexisted with one another in the ancient Roman Empire, so *religion* today has come to refer to a multitude of systems of belief around the world, and there is strong, if not ubiquitous, support for their mutual coexistence. It is not an uncommon sight, in fact, to see cars around the US sporting a bumper sticker that says "COEXIST," with the letters spelled using the symbols of major world religions. But it is a mistake to think that we have returned to an idyllic ancient past of religious toleration. We moderns have a chronic and nasty habit of idealizing the ancient world and then claiming that our modern world has overcome the deficiencies of the medieval world, thus returning to that idyllic past. We are not living in ancient Rome, nor should we want to. A lot has happened between now and then. *All* that history comes to bear in the way that we think, talk, and act regarding religion today.

CHRISTIANITY AND RELIGION

If religion is a concept that is inextricably tied up with the history of the West and, as such, particularly tied to the history of Christianity, then how is this reflected practically in our everyday perception of religions? To answer this question, it is useful to return to a polythetic approach to defining religion, which, as we saw, consists of listing various characteristics that we associate with religion. As it turns out, all the words that we use to describe aspects of religion are either Christian terminology (God, clergy, scripture, vestments, doctrine, etc.) or else generalizations of specific Christian terms ("higher power" instead of God, "community" instead of Church, etc.). I challenge you to think of any characteristic that you associate with religion that cannot be related in some way to Christianity. The bottom line is that things feel religion-y—even things like football—when they can be compared in some way to Christianity.

This implicit use of Christianity as a paradigm for religion poses a major problem. Nothing in the world other than Christianity is really quite like Christianity. So, viewing the world through a category that takes Christianity as its paradigm is inevitably going to lead to a lot of distortion. It's like looking at the world through "Christian-tinted" glasses. If you wear red-tinted glasses, everything appears as a shade of red: things that are actually red appear brightly, while things that are not red appear dark. Likewise, the modern concept of religion makes everything look like a shade of Christianity: things that are similar to Christianity will show up brightly, while things that are not like Christianity will just end up dark. You miss all the deeper nuances, the full spectrum of color, of the religion you're looking at.

To be clear, these Christian assumptions are built into the word *religion* itself, because of its history, and do not necessarily depend on your personal religious identity, if you have any. No matter whether you are Christian or non-Christian, religious or nonreligious, a religious seeker or a diehard atheist, you take as completely natural a whole set of assumptions about the world that are informed in large part by the history of

Christianity. These assumptions play out with every one of the characteristics found in a typical polythetic definition of religion. We could potentially discuss the distortions inherent in any number of characteristics associated with religion. Here, I would like to focus on just ten: higher power, holy persons, founder, stories, beliefs, scripture, soteriology, community, morality, and practice.

Certainly God, gods, or a **higher power** of some sort is one of the first things we think of when we think of religion. This is not surprising given that Christianity is focused on the worship of God. Accordingly, anything that involves belief in or worship of something like God is or can be perceived as religion. Of course, the Western concept of religion is older than Christianity and was originally tied not to the worship of one, all-powerful God, but rather to the worship of many gods. The worship of many gods is thus also perceived as religion today, but known specifically as polytheism, as opposed to the monotheism of Christianity. However, this dichotomization of religion into polytheism and monotheism, while reflective of the Western experience, is simplistic when applied more broadly. Daoists worship many gods, but they also believe that everything ultimately derives from the one Dao. So, are they polytheists or monotheists? Likewise, Hindus worship many gods, but many believe that one God is supreme. Again, are they polytheists or monotheists? Buddhists and Jains traditionally believe in and sometimes worship many gods, but their religions do not place ultimate importance on these deities. How do we categorize that? There seems to be a tendency to see as religious anything that has anything to do with or say about the gods. In that case, modern atheism must be seen as a religion that goes one step beyond the "atheism" of antiquity, Christianity, by denying the existence of *all* gods, not just all save one. Of course, even for modern atheists, there is a higher power: Nature, or the Science that studies it.

Things that are perceived as religions often have **holy persons** who are set apart from ordinary people. Usually, the terminology used for such people in English is borrowed from Christianity. Significant people from the history of the religion are usually referred to as saints in imitation of Christian practice. Religious leaders who are set apart from ordinary members of the religion are usually referred to as clergy. These clergy are usually referred to as either priests or monks/nuns depending on whether they more closely resemble the priests or monastics of Christianity. If they have a ritual/sacrificial function, like Daoist clergy and the Brahmans of Hinduism, they are referred to as priests. If they are celibate and live in an ordered community, like the clergy of Buddhism and Jainism, they are referred to as monks or nuns. While this use of Christian terminology is convenient, it can obscure the fact that the figures in other religions are often understood quite differently from their supposed Christian counterparts.

In addition, Christianity sets the paradigm for religions having a **founder**. In Christianity, this figure is of course Jesus Christ.[11] In some religions, this paradigm works quite well. Islam has Muhammad, Buddhism has the Buddha, Jainism has Mahavira, and Confucianism has Confucius. In other religions, it is difficult or problematic to identify a founder. Sometimes people point to Moses as the founder of Judaism, but Judaism wasn't really founded by Moses, or by anyone for that matter, in the same way that Christianity was by Jesus. Laozi is usually identified as the founder of Daoism, but Laozi was probably a mythical figure who didn't exist. Hinduism is, like Judaism, a very old religion with a complicated history, and it doesn't really make sense to talk about it having a founder. Even in the case of religions that do have a clear founder, the founder's role in the religion is usually quite different from that of Jesus Christ in Christianity. Confucius is understood by Confucians to be simply a wise teacher; Muhammad is understood by Muslims to be a prophet but not divine; and the Buddha and Mahavira are understood by Buddhists and Jains respectively to be human beings who escaped from the cycle of rebirth and thus are higher than the gods. Comparisons to Christianity, where the founder is understood to be God himself, are in all cases quite limited.

Religions usually have **stories** that are of particular significance to their adherents. I have chosen the word *story* here to be as broad as possible; in fact, the specific word typically used to refer to religious stories is *myths*. The word *myth*, however, is very much a loaded term in the context of the Western concept of religion. Think about it: What does the word *myth* imply in ordinary English? It implies that the story is made up, fictional, not true. We discredit things by saying, "That's just a myth." There even was an American TV show called *Mythbusters* that was dedicated to disproving things that people commonly believe. This pejorative use of the word *myth* goes back to ancient, pre-Christian times. The English word *myth* comes from the ancient Greek word *mythos*, which meant story. The ancient Greeks had stories about their gods, many of which are still well known today. Even in ancient Greece, there was a recognition among the intelligentsia that the myths about the gods were often fantastical. They dealt with this problem in different ways. Philosophers dealt with it by creating allegorical interpretations of the myths. Historians, on the other hand, expunged the fantastical elements to create a different type of story, *history* (or in Greek, *historia*).[12]

Since early Christianity developed in the Greek-speaking world of the eastern Mediterranean, it took advantage of the critique of myth that already existed in Greek discourse. Christian writers ridiculed the Greek myths as fantastical, impious, untrue, and therefore proving the falsehood of the pagan gods. They valorized their own story, the story of Jesus Christ, as *historical* and therefore demonstrating the truth of the Christian God. This dichotomy between myth and history is preserved in the way that we talk about stories valued in religions today. We talk about the *history* of Muhammad and the Buddha, since these are generally recognized as real human beings who actually lived. On the other hand, we talk about the *myths* of the Hindus, the stories about Vishnu, Shiva, Kali, and so forth, because these are not recognized universally as historical events. While making such distinctions is unavoidable insofar as the distinction between myth and history is fundamental to modern historiography, it can also have the unwarranted side effect of reproducing a uniquely Christian value judgment about religious storytelling in the perception of different religious traditions.

As we have seen, modern people tend to associate religion with **beliefs**. When modern Western people learn about different religions, they tend to focus on what members of other religions believe. Writing on religion, especially popular but also scholarly, has a marked tendency to focus on the beliefs found in various religions. This is not an accident; it is a direct result of the fact that Christianity is implicitly taken as paradigmatic of religion. Christians are, and always have been, obsessed with belief. Moreover, they are obsessed with *correct* belief, or *orthodoxy*.

Catholics and many Protestants recite a short text during their church services called the creed. The word *creed* comes from the Latin word *credo*, which means, "I believe." The creed is a succinct but detailed explanation of what Christians believe. There are different versions of the creed, but for our purposes they are all similar. The Nicene Creed (see Table 1.1) is based on the deliberations at the Council of Nicea in the early fourth century, with revisions made in later councils. Notice how *detailed* it is. It's basically a mini-essay! There's a paragraph about God the Father, a paragraph about Jesus (including a short biography), a paragraph about the Holy Spirit, and then a concluding paragraph on miscellaneous topics. Christians have been reciting this or something similar for over 1,500 years! Although most Christians today don't understand the nuances of what they are reciting, I can assure you that every word and phrase is imbued with a deep meaning that Christians in the past debated, fought, and even killed and died over. This is why I say that Christians are obsessed with belief.

I cannot emphasize enough that *no other religion on Earth is like this*. No other religion has dedicated so much energy to defining itself in terms of what it believes. The second-closest example is probably Islam. Islam does have a creed-like statement called the *shahada*, but it is very simple

Table 1.1 The Nicene Creed. This is a translation of the traditional Greek text used since antiquity, which was published in 1975 by the International Consultation on English Texts and was then adopted by several denominations for use in English-language liturgy. The text on which this translation is based is commonly known as the "Nicene Creed," but it differs in significant ways from the text adopted during the Council of Nicaea (325) and was not fully adopted in its current form until the Council of Chalcedon (451). The words "and the Son" are placed in brackets because they were added even later by Western churches and were not accepted by Eastern churches, eventually playing a role in the Great Schism of 1054. See https://www.englishtexts.org/the-nicene-creed.

> We believe in one God, the Father, the Almighty, maker of heaven and earth, of all that is, seen and unseen.
>
> We believe in one Lord, Jesus Christ, the only Son of God, eternally begotten of the Father, God from God, Light from Light, true God from true God, begotten, not made, of one Being with the Father; through him all things were made. For us and for our salvation he came down from heaven, was incarnate of the Holy Spirit and the Virgin Mary and became truly human. For our sake he was crucified under Pontius Pilate; he suffered death and was buried. On the third day he rose again in accordance with the Scriptures; he ascended into heaven and is seated at the right hand of the Father. He will come again in glory to judge the living and the dead, and his kingdom will have no end.
>
> We believe in the Holy Spirit, the Lord, the giver of life, who proceeds from the Father [and the Son], who with the Father and the Son is worshiped and glorified, who has spoken through the prophets.
>
> We believe in one holy catholic and apostolic Church. We acknowledge one baptism for the forgiveness of sins. We look for the resurrection of the dead, and the life of the world to come. Amen.

and only one sentence long: "There is no God but God, and Muhammad is his messenger."

Of course, you can identify things that people believe in any religion, but that does not mean that belief plays anything remotely similar to the role it plays in Christianity. In many cases, the things that one might identify as "beliefs" are not so much beliefs as they are basic assumptions about the way the world works. People in various religions do not necessarily believe in their gods so much as they assume that they exist because they interact with them (through sacrifice, ritual, stories, etc.) on a daily basis. Likewise, Buddhists, Jains, and Hindus do not so much believe in reincarnation as they simply assume that living beings are reincarnated when they die. In many cases, how you understand your religion may be far less important than what you *do*, the customs, rituals, and other practices you participate in. Modern scholars have dubbed this *orthopraxy* ("right practice") in contrast to the Christian emphasis on *orthodoxy* ("right teaching"). Of course, intellectuals in any religion may debate what constitutes the correct intellectual understanding of their tradition, but in no religion other than Christianity have such debates been so fundamental to defining the religion's identity.

Closely related to the issue of belief is the issue of **scripture**. For all Christians, but especially for Protestant Christians, orthodoxy is defined with primary reference to the Bible as authoritative scripture. This may lead to the perception that scripture is important to all religious traditions, a perception that is reinforced by the fact that in any religion that comes from a literate culture, there are texts that can be called scriptures insofar as they are held as particularly authoritative. But the implicit comparison to Christianity in talking about scripture in religions generally can be greatly misleading. In only a handful of religions is there a well-defined set of texts that can conveniently fit into one volume and that are uniquely held as authoritative. Jews have the Tanakh (which corresponds to the Christian Old Testament), Muslims have the Qur'an, and Sikhs have the Guru Granth. But in other religions, such as Buddhism, Daoism, and Hinduism, there is a vast literature, enough to fill up bookshelves, that is regarded as authoritative, and in many cases the limits of that authoritative literature may be ill defined.

In addition, ordinary people in most religions do not avidly read their scriptures. If your idea of scripture is based on people reading their Bible, thinking about it, discussing it at church and in study groups, and using it as a guide to live their life, then this will not be a good model for religions in general. In fact, it isn't even a very good model for Christianity in general. The practice of ordinary people reading the Bible is a very modern phenomenon; it began during the Reformation, and it remains far more common in Protestantism than in the other branches of Christianity. In most religions, authoritative texts are consulted and debated by elite intellectuals, and excerpts from them are used in prayers and rituals. But you won't necessarily see ordinary people keeping a copy of their scripture on their bookshelf or consulting it often or even ever.

The next characteristic often associated with religion is **soteriology**. This word comes from the Greek word *soter*, which means "savior" and, in the Christian context, refers to Jesus Christ. Religious Studies scholars use the word *soteriology* to refer to that aspect of a religion that has to do with salvation. The reference to a Christian paradigm here is very clear. Christianity offers human beings a plan for salvation. According to Christianity, human beings face an inherent problem: They are alienated from God and destined for death because of sin, in particular original sin (the sin inherited by all human beings because Adam disobeyed God).

Christianity then offers a solution: Jesus Christ died on the cross for our sins, and if we have faith in him, we will enjoy eternal life.

Insofar as we can identify a problem defined and a solution offered by a religion, then we can talk about the soteriology of that religion. But we must be clear about two things. First, no other religion has a soteriology exactly like Christianity's. And second, it is not clear that every religion has a soteriology or that soteriology plays the same central role that it does in Christianity. Probably two of the closest parallels are Islam and Buddhism. In Islam, the problem is that we deviate from God's will, and the solution is for us to submit to God's will and thus be rewarded with eternal life in paradise. In Buddhism, however, both the problem and the solution that human beings (and in fact all living beings) face is quite different. The problem is that we are stuck in a cycle of rebirth characterized by suffering, and the solution is to escape from that cycle and never be reborn again. In other religions, soteriology may look quite different if it can be identified at all. Judaism, for example, is not generally about personal salvation, although the salvation of Israel collectively is a common theme in the Jewish scriptures. Confucius similarly had little to nothing to say about the afterlife, but he did offer a plan for reuniting China and creating a more harmonious society. In Hinduism, you may subscribe to any number of plans for salvation, or none at all, depending on what particular type of Hinduism you follow. And if you think about the earliest layer in the history of the Western concept of religion, that of ancient Rome, then you will find that salvation was often not a concern at all.

It is fair to say that all religions have a sense of **community**. After all, there can't really be a religion unless there are people in it. Often the religious community is thematized and valorized. Christians have their Church (to be distinguished from *church*, which refers to a place of worship), Muslims have the *umma*, Sikhs have the *panth*, and Buddhists have the *sangha*. In most cases, however, religious communities are not nearly as centralized or institutionalized as the Christian paradigm would suggest. Early Christianity was not very centralized, and as a whole it is not very centralized today—but the Catholic Church specifically is, and the pope casts a long shadow over the history of Christianity and thus over the modern concept of religion. Western civilization was characterized by the increasing centralization of the Roman Catholic Church in the Middle Ages. Although this unity was shattered by the Reformation, Protestant denominations in many cases are fairly institutionalized, and many Protestants to this day still profess to believe in "one holy, catholic, and apostolic Church" in their creed. Religious communities in general, however, do not necessarily show much centralization. Authority in Islam, for example, is generally decentralized among a multitude of scholars who independently make pronouncements on Islamic Law, and the Buddhist *sangha* has historically spread through the travels of self-governing local communities of monks and nuns.

Often it is assumed that **morality** or ethics is a central concern of religions, and in many cases it is. Examples would include not only Christianity, but also Sikhism, Islam, Buddhism, Jainism, and Judaism. Ethics is a tricky thing, though, because it is often a concern of nonreligious systems. The word itself comes from ancient Greek and was originally a branch of Greek philosophy, not religion. (It remains a branch of study in modern philosophy as well.) Indeed, in the ancient Western world prior to the widespread adoption of Christianity, ethics was not a major concern of religion. Far more important was caring properly for the gods through sacrifice to ensure a harmonious relationship between them and human society. Christianity brought with it the idea, inherited from Judaism, that God was inherently good and demanded ethical behavior from human beings. It is probably best, then, to see ethics/morality as an autonomous field of human inquiry and activity that often overlaps with religion but is not necessarily central to it. This allows us to avoid overlooking aspects of religions around the world where morality is not the primary concern—especially in the way that human beings interact with gods in many religious traditions, which often follow the ancient Roman model more closely than the Christian one.

I leave **practice** for last because it, surprisingly, is often one of the last things people think about when they think about religion. Nevertheless, we all have a sense of practices that are considered religious. This would include prayer, ritual, sacrifice, pilgrimage, and fasting. Protestant Christianity theologically deemphasizes many types of religious practice because of its doctrine of salvation by faith alone, but in most religions, practice is incredibly important, even central. One can think of Jews keeping close to the provisions of Jewish Law, Muslims going on pilgrimage to Mecca and fasting during Ramadan, Hindus bathing in the Ganges, Buddhists giving alms to monks, and even Catholics abstaining from meat on Fridays during Lent. But the tendency to focus on religious belief more than practice entails more than simply forgetting that religious people *do* stuff too. It completely warps our view of what is important about religions, emphasizing things that may be of marginal importance to ordinary members of a religion and ignoring things that are centrally important. It also creates a perverse incentive for religions in the modern world to reinvent themselves, either in self-presentation or in actual practice, in order to conform to expectations of what a religion "should" be like. We'll return to these issues in chapter 13.

What Is Religion?

For you to see how Christianity serves as a hidden paradigm for the category religion, I want you to try out an analogy. Try to think of the word *religion* as being analogous to the word *cake*. *Cake* is a word that acts as a broad category including many subtypes below it. There is chocolate cake, carrot cake, angel food cake, upside-down cake, ice cream cake, red velvet cake—the list goes on and on. If you think about these cakes in terms of their ingredients, there are ingredients that are essential to making something a cake—like water, flour, and eggs—and others that are inessential—like chocolate, vanilla, frosting, and so forth. The inessential ingredients are the things that make a cake a particular type of cake, as opposed to the essential ingredients, which basically every cake (excluding exotic examples like gluten-free cake) has. Superficially, the word *religion* works the same way. It is a broad category that includes many subtypes—Christianity, Judaism, Islam, Buddhism, Hinduism, and so forth. And we can think of the characteristics of a typical polythetic definition—the things that make something feel religion-y—as being like the "ingredients" of religion.

But if we press on, as we have here, the analogy breaks down. It's not really possible to identify any essential ingredients that are neutrally shared by all religions and distinct from the incidental ingredients of any particular religion. At best, you find that every characteristic that fits a polythetic definition is a generalization of something specific in Christianity (see Table 1.2). That's because religions, in this respect, are not like cakes. They are not things intentionally created according to a fixed recipe with certain embellishments added. Instead, they are the result of looking at the pre-existing social life of human beings through the lenses of a particular paradigm. We use the word *cake* to describe things that we create according to a particular type of recipe. We use the word *religion*, conversely, as a pair of lenses through which to look at the world as it already exists.

What I want to demonstrate to you with this book is that religion is not simply something out there in the world for you to have an opinion about. The word *religion* itself is instead a particular way of looking at the world. It is like a pair of glasses through which we look at the world every time we use the word. And no matter what religion (if any) you follow or what your opinion about religion is, you did not design those glasses. They were forged over the course of more than 2,000 years, during most of that time by Europeans. And because Christianity is so dominant throughout the history in which these glasses were created, the result is a pair of Christian-tinted glasses. Just as red-tinted glasses make everything look like various shades of red, so too does the word *religion*

Table 1.2 Why religions are not like cakes. There are many ways one could set up such a table of correspondences; this is simply one possibility using the ten terms discussed in this chapter. The point is that one cannot separate "essential" and "incidental" ingredients of religion. The terms used in a polythetic definition of religion are always generalizations of specific terms used in Christianity.

General Characteristic of Religion	Specific Christian Terms
Higher power	God
Holy persons	saints, clergy (pope, bishops, priests, ministers, monks, nuns)
Founder	Jesus Christ
Stories	Genesis, the Passion of Christ, etc.
Beliefs	the Creed, orthodoxy
Scripture	the Bible
Soteriology	salvation through Jesus Christ
Community	the Church
Morality	the Ten Commandments, the Beatitudes, etc.
Practice	liturgies, monastic rules, etc.

make everything that we call by that term look like a different "shade" of Christianity.

But this Christian tinting is not the only thing that distorts our view of world religions. The image of various religions is also refracted to produce an image that, on the surface at least, will either appear positive or negative. This refraction is the product of a set of powerful ideological forces that scholars refer to as Orientalism. In the next chapter, we will see how events in the last several centuries—in particular, the incredible global imbalance of power that manifested itself through colonialism—summoned Orientalism and baked it into the modern concept that we call religion.

DISCUSSION QUESTIONS

1. How would you define *religion*? Try to be as precise as possible; be sure to avoid a definition that is too narrow (excludes certain religions) or too broad (includes things that we don't consider religions).

2. Come up with your own polythetic definition of religion by listing as many characteristics associated with religion as you can think of.
3. Where does the word *religion* come from? How was it used differently in its original context than it is used today?
4. In what ways did Christianity contribute to the evolving meaning of the word *religion*?
5. What role did colonialism play in the formation of the modern concept of religion?
6. Look back at the polythetic definition of religion you created in question 2. How can each of the characteristics you included in your list be understood as a generalization of something found in Christianity? Try to give specific correspondences between the general words you included in your list (e.g., *scripture*) and specific words from Christianity (*Bible*).

NOTES

1 Karl Marx, "Contribution to the Critique of Hegel's *Philosophy of Right*: Introduction," in *The Marx-Engels Reader*, ed. Robert C. Tucker (New York: W. W. Norton, 1978), 54.
2 This is not an accident. Early in his philosophical career, Marx was a member of the Young Hegelians, a radical leftist group that adopted aspects of the thought of G. W. F. Hegel, whose philosophy was based on the Christian conception of history. The concept of an "end of history" thus passed from Christianity into Hegel's philosophy and from there into Marxism.
3 For a provocative history of atheism, including the New Atheism, see John Gray, *Seven Types of Atheism* (New York: Farrar, Straus and Giroux, 2018).
4 As with communism, the religious overtones of environmentalism are not entirely an accident. Evan Berry studies the Christian underpinnings of the modern environmental movement in *Devoted to Nature: The Religious Roots of American Environmentalism* (Oakland: University of California Press, 2015).
5 This idea actually points to an interesting point of comparison. The famous sociologist Émile Durkheim argued that in all religions, the higher power, in whatever form it takes, is a stand-in for the actual power that society takes over all human individuals. Society transcends any one human individual but can also be felt *within* that individual due to social conditioning. Durkheim argued that all religions are attempts to make sense of the awareness of this power that society has.

6 A particularly useful book in this regard is Daniel L. Pals, *Ten Theories of Religion* (Oxford: Oxford University Press, 2021), along with its companion anthology of classical theorists of religion, Daniel L. Pals, ed., *Introducing Religion: Readings from the Classic Theorists* (Oxford: Oxford University Press, 2009).

7 James B. Rives, *Religion in the Roman Empire* (Malden, MA: Blackwell Publishing, 2007), 13–14. The full history of the different uses of the word *religio* in Latin is quite complex, both in its use by ancient non-Christian authors and even well into the Middle Ages by Christian authors. The history I give in the next few pages is quite simplified, focusing on discrete turning points that led to the modern conception of *religion*, rather than the history of the word *religio* and its vernacular cognates in full detail. For such a detailed history, see Brent Nonbri, *Before Religion: A History of a Modern Concept* (New Haven: University of Yale Press, 2013), 26–34.

8 This is actually a somewhat complicated issue because *living* emperors were generally not considered divine, although they were worshiped in certain contexts, especially in the provinces by noncitizens, and the *de facto* cult of the emperor was charged with political valence. On the complexities of the imperial cult, see Rives, *Religion in the Roman Empire*, 148–156.

9 On the conversion of Constantine and the subsequent Christianization of the Roman Empire, see Bart D. Ehrman, *The Triumph of Christianity: How a Forbidden Religion Swept the World* (New York: Simon and Schuster, 2018), 217–253.

10 *Faith* and *belief* do not necessarily refer to exactly the same thing. *Belief* can, and often does, refer to accepting the validity of certain propositions (such as the existence of God) without direct evidence. *Faith*, however, usually refers to a more specific type of belief in which one *trusts* another person or, in the context of Christianity, God. Nevertheless, believing a set of propositions and faith in God have been intertwined in Christianity throughout its history. This is even more true since the questioning of the existence of God in the Enlightenment, because having faith in God necessarily entails believing that he exists. Therefore, for our purposes in this book, we will be treating *faith* and *belief* as functionally equivalent.

11 To be clear, when I speak of a founder, I do not mean that that person necessarily intended to found a religion. It is unlikely, for example, that Jesus had any such intention. What I mean by founder is a human being whose life and/or teachings historically led to the formation of the religion and whom that religious community looks back to as authoritative.

12 Paul Veyne, *Did the Greeks Believe in their Myths? An Essay on Constitutive Imagination*, trans. Paula Wissing (Chicago: University of Chicago Press, 1988), 59–65.

Colonialism and the Two Faces of Orientalism

As we saw in chapter 1, religion is not just some obvious thing out there in the world; it is a way of seeing the world, a Western concept that was universalized during the colonial period when Western countries established political, military, economic, and cultural dominance. To understand how the modern concept of religion came about, we need to know a bit about the history of colonialism. Moreover, to understand why colonialism continues to be relevant today even though most colonies have gained independence, we will need to learn about *Orientalism*, a form of prejudice that both served to justify colonialism and continues to structure our ways of thinking about the world today. Understanding the legacy of colonialism and Orientalism will give us the tools we need to understand why there is so often a disconnect between popular perceptions of world religions and their actual practice, which we will dive into in Part II.

A BRIEF HISTORY OF COLONIALISM

Colonialism has taken many forms over the course of history, but it generally involves the settlement or domination of people from one country in another country or countries that are separated from the home country by a sea or ocean. In this respect, it is distinct from ordinary imperialism in which one country conquers neighboring countries to create a contiguous land-based empire. Defined in this way, colonialism existed on a small scale even in the ancient world. For example, both the Phoenicians (whose home was in modern-day Lebanon) and the Greeks established colonies far from their home countries around the Mediterranean Sea. Later, during the Middle Ages, Western Europeans, hoping to "retake" the Holy Land from Muslims in a series of Crusades, established a series of Crusader States in the Levant (the region along the eastern shore of the Mediterranean Sea). These Crusader States can also be considered an early form of colonization.

When people talk about colonialism today, however, they are usually referring to a modern period of colonization that took place on a global scale, beginning in the fifteenth century and continuing until the middle of the twentieth. Portugal was the first major modern colonial power, establishing colonies in South America, Africa, and Asia in the fifteenth and sixteenth centuries. It was spurred to do so by recent advances in Western Europeans' seafaring technology, as well as a desire to reestablish trade routes for spices from the East when traditional routes were cut off after the old Byzantine capital of Constantinople was conquered by the Ottoman Empire in 1453. By the standards of later colonialism, Portuguese colonialism was less invasive and totalizing. Most Portuguese colonies consisted of small enclaves around forts that were built on coasts and served to protect and advance Portuguese trading interests in the surrounding area. The major exception was Brazil, which was a large, inland colony, along with a few colonies in Africa where Portugal sought inland domination in the nineteenth century.

The second major modern colonial power was Spain, which was active mostly in the Americas. After the discovery (from the Europeans' perspective) of the Americas by Christopher Columbus in 1492, Spanish *conquistadores* conquered two major American empires: the Aztec Empire, in what is now Mexico, by Hernán Cortés in 1521, and the Inca Empire, in South America, by Francisco Pizarro in the 1530s. Spain then established a vast empire in the Americas that stretched from northern California to the southern tip of South America and from the Pacific coast in the West to Florida and the Caribbean islands in the East. Although the degree of colonial control varied across this enormous territory, Spain possessed a major inland power due to its defeat of the two largest inland empires, and it clearly aspired to complete control of all the territories it laid claim to. Two of its major goals within its colonies were the conversion of native peoples to Catholic Christianity and the extraction of resources to enrich the home country. Although Spain was less active as a colonial power in other parts of the world, it did establish a major colony in the Philippines, in Southeast Asia.

The third major modern colonial power was the Netherlands. The Dutch rose to prominence as a colonial power in the seventeenth century, largely supplanting the Portuguese in controlling trade through a network of forts and trading posts around the coasts of Africa and Asia. Although their empire was like that of the Portuguese in seeking mostly to control trade rather than land, the Dutch introduced a significant innovation to colonialism: capitalism. The earlier colonial empires of the Portuguese and Spanish were driven and controlled by their respective monarchies. Dutch colonialism, conversely, was driven by private enterprise. The Dutch East India Company (known by its Dutch acronym VOC), the first joint-stock company in the world, was established in 1602, and it spearheaded the effort to attack and capture Portuguese colonial forts, as well as build new Dutch forts, to establish and maintain control of trade around the world. Because the focus of Dutch colonialism was trade, only a few countries were subjected to total Dutch domination, the most significant of which was Indonesia in Southeast Asia.

The fourth and fifth major modern colonial powers were France and England. These two countries first became major colonial players in the seventeenth century, when they established settler colonies in North America. During the same century, joint-stock companies in imitation of the Dutch East India company were established in England and France to enter the competition for trade with Asia. Although the Dutch achieved supremacy in this sphere in the seventeenth century, French and British interests rose in the eighteenth and nineteenth centuries as Dutch fortunes waned. Although their interests began mostly with controlling trade, like the Dutch and Portuguese before them, competition between the two increased to such a point that there was ultimately a scramble for direct control of entire countries in Africa and Asia in the decades just before and after the turn of the twentieth century.

France established a large overseas empire in this later period, including about a third of Africa, Syria in the Middle East, a large portion of mainland Southeast Asia (Vietnam, Laos, and Cambodia), and numerous other smaller holdings (mostly islands), around the world. But it was the British who undoubtedly were the winners of this colonial scramble, establishing the geographically most expansive empire in the history of the world. Like the French, the British established colonial dominion over a significant portion of Africa, but it also had much larger holdings in Asia than the French, and it maintained a certain degree of authority over its semi-autonomous settler colonies in Canada, Australia, and New Zealand. Britain's most significant direct colonial holding was India—a country whose colonial history is particularly important for this book because it is home to many of the major world religions recognized today. Colonial rule over India was established slowly by the British East India

Company over the course of the eighteenth century, but in 1857, after a failed rebellion by Indians against Company rule, the British Crown took direct control of the colony, which continued until independence in 1947.

Although the modern colonial period was dominated by these five powers—Portugal, Spain, the Netherlands, France, and England—there were other countries involved, especially as the mass colonization of the world came to a head around the turn of the twentieth century. Italy, Germany, and Belgium, for example, established colonies in Africa, while the United States engaged in several overseas colonial ventures, including in the Philippines, Cuba, and Hawai'i. In addition, Japan established several overseas colonies in Asia, including Korea and Taiwan, and in the early twentieth century it pursued an aggressive effort to conquer much of East and Southeast Asia until it was ultimately defeated by the Allied Powers in World War II.

World War II, in fact, proved to be a turning point that led to the end of modern colonialism. Japan was forced to relinquish its colonies at the end of the war, but even Britain and France, though victors, had had their control over their colonies severely disrupted by the war. Just as importantly, the war, which had seen the defeat of the naked imperial ambitions and violence of Germany and Japan, made it less tenable for Britain, France, and other colonial powers to continue to defend the virtue of their own colonial practices. As already mentioned, India won independence from Britain just a couple years after the end of the war, in 1947, and over the course of the next three decades nearly every major colony gained independence from its previous colonial master. Today, most overseas colonies that remain are small islands and enclaves.

Different countries have been affected in different ways by colonialism. First, there are settler colonies in which the local population was subjected to genocidal policies and ultimately overwhelmed demographically by the colonizing settlers. The former English colonies of the United States, Canada, Australia, and New Zealand are the primary examples of this type. Second, there are countries in which the colonizers imposed their culture on the local population but also intermarried with them, creating a new, hybrid culture. Many of the former Spanish and Portuguese colonies of Latin America are of this type. Third, there are colonies that were controlled politically for a certain amount of time by a colonial power, during which time they were depleted of resources, but without large-scale settlement by the colonizers. Many of the (mostly French and British) former colonies of Africa and Asia are of this type. Finally, there are certain countries that were not directly colonized but were forced during the colonial period to sign unequal treaties that subjected them to unfair trading conditions, gave colonial powers special rights within their borders, and otherwise impinged upon their sovereignty. The most important example of this type is China, which was carved up by the colonial powers into "spheres of influence" in the nineteenth century. The Ottoman Empire was subjected to similar treatment and, being on the losing side of World War I, was ultimately dismantled, leaving the modern nation-state of Turkey without its former imperial holdings in Europe, the Middle East, and North Africa. Siam (now Thailand) was never directly colonized, but only because it served as a buffer between British colonies (Burma and Malaysia) and French colonies (Laos and Cambodia), and the ever-present threat of colonization forced it to change itself to fit colonial norms. Overall, the entire world was profoundly impacted by colonialism, even those few countries that avoided being directly colonized.

People who identify with countries that have a history of being colonizers rather than with countries that have a history of being colonized sometimes suggest that there were benefits to colonialism. This approach to colonialism is deeply insensitive and misses the point. Nobody asks to be colonized. The citizens of France, Britain, the United States, Japan, and other colonial powers would be outraged by the suggestion that another country simply take over theirs. Moreover, there are clear ways in which much of the world suffered under colonialism: slavery, cultural destruction, and theft of resources, not to mention the simple loss of autonomy and the dignity of self-rule while under a colonial regime. While one can point to certain so-called benefits of colonization (e.g., industrialization, democratization, etc.), casting these as purely benefits ignores the fact that colonialism completely reshaped the world in ways that made them both possible and beneficial. They were not gifts from a superior civilization to an inferior one but rather products of the totality of the colonial world.

ORIENTALISM

You're probably aware that nowadays referring to people as "Oriental" is considered offensive. You may not exactly be aware of why, however. *Oriental*, after all, is not a straightforward slur in the same sense as the n-word or any other number of epithets for various ethnic groups. Slurs such as those really have no purpose in the English language other than to intentionally denigrate someone because of their race or ethnicity. *Oriental* certainly *can* be used as a slur, but of course any word can be if the person wielding it so chooses. Although it is increasingly seen as problematic, the word *Oriental* is still used in ways that are clearly not meant as slurs: to refer to a type of rug, in the names of hotels and academic institutions, and so forth. This is because the original meaning of *Oriental* is simple and not offensive. It is an archaic way of saying "Eastern." *Oriental* is an adjective derived from the noun *Orient*, which comes from the Latin for "East." There is an equivalent archaic word for "West." That word is *Occident*, and it also comes from Latin. The corresponding adjective that means "Western" is *Occidental*. The words *Occident* and *Occidental* are not used nearly as much in English today as *Orient* and *Oriental*, but they exist. President Obama, in fact, began his college studies at a school called Occidental College, which is so named because it is on the West Coast of the United States.

In 1978, a Palestinian-American professor named Edward Said (pronounced *sah-eed*) published a book that both explains why *Oriental* is a problematic term and has played a significant role in bringing about its current un-PC status. This book, called *Orientalism*, has been enormously influential in academia, across the Humanities and Social Sciences. In it, Said defines what he calls *Orientalism* (thus the name of the book): a whole set of attitudes, institutions, and power relations that are evoked by the word *Oriental*. This word is not considered appropriate for referring to Asian people or people of Asian descent precisely because of the Orientalist attitudes it has come to stand for.

What is Orientalism? Although Said does not describe it in this way, a simple explanation is that Orientalism refers to prejudice against Asians. In practice, this is one of the primary ways in which the word is now used. There are all sorts of words that refer to different types of prejudice: *racism* for prejudice against people because of their race, *sexism* for prejudice against women, *homophobia* for prejudice against gay people, *Islamophobia* for prejudice against Muslims, *antisemitism* for prejudice against Jews. *Orientalism* has come to fill the same role for prejudice against Asians. Yet as Said originally defined it, Orientalism is far broader and more complex than this. It is not simply a matter of being prejudiced against Asians, or even about Asia *per se*, although these are central to Orientalism. According to Said, Orientalism permeates people's attitudes, the power structure of the world, even knowledge itself.

In his book, Said identifies Orientalism as referring to three distinct but interlocking phenomena. The first of these is an academic institution, and it is from this, in fact, that Said borrows the term *Orientalism*. When the major disciplines of the modern university were coalescing in the nineteenth century, it was common to refer to the academic study of Asia as Orientalism, and those academics who studied Asia for a living as

Orientalists. This is far less common today, but there are still some academic institutions that retain *Oriental* in their names. The word *Oriental* is found in several departments and academic institutions in Europe, which typically date to the colonial era. It is less common in the United States, where departments focusing on the study of Asia were mostly founded later, during the Cold War, and are referred to as Asian Studies departments.

It might not be clear to you yet what racism against Asians has to do with schools and academic departments. I promise we will get back to this in a minute. First, let us turn to Said's second definition of Orientalism. According to Said, "Orientalism is a style of thought based upon an ontological and epistemological distinction made between 'the Orient' and (most of the time) 'the Occident.'"[1] This is a fancy way of saying something simple, something so simple that it might seem too obvious to be worth mentioning. Said here is using the word *Orientalism* to refer to *the very idea* that there is a difference between the East (the Orient) and the West (the Occident). Like I said, this might seem obvious. After all, we talk about "the West," "Western civilization," and "the East" all the time. But this way of looking at the world is not at all obvious. The world does not have any natural borders marking the difference between "East" and "West." Indeed, there is no absolute way to mark any part of the world as being to the east or west of any other, since if you travel in either direction, you will eventually end up right back where you started. The idea that there is a distinction between East and West is based on European experience and a Euro-centric view of the world. Historically, Europeans have seen themselves as being to the west of a great eastern landmass, Asia, which was known to be home to great civilizations, but about which Europeans until recently knew little. Europeans have been making distinctions between themselves and the peoples to their east for pretty much all of their recorded history, going all the way back to the ancient Greeks and their attitudes toward their eastern rivals, the Persians.

This binary distinction between East and West is where prejudice against Asians comes into play in a direct way. Once the distinction between East and West is made, characteristics begin to be attributed to each. Since Orientalism refers to attitudes coming out of the Western world, these characteristics inevitably make the West compare favorably to the East. This phenomenon is found in every type of prejudice. Homophobia involves attributing positive characteristics to straight people and negative ones to gay people. Sexism involves attributing positive characteristics to men and negative characteristics to women. And so forth. Orientalism involves a particular set of binary characteristics attributed to Westerners and Asians that systematically denigrate Asians in comparison to Western people. Although they are unpleasant, I will describe them explicitly here because they show how Orientalism works. These binary characteristics used to be attributed to Westerners and Asians quite explicitly by Western elites; although that is less common now, they still inform Western attitudes toward Asia and the non-Western world in general.[2]

One binary attributed to Asians and Westerners is that Asians are irrational, while Westerners are rational. This prejudice might seem out of date now that it is common, in the United States at least, for Asians and Asian-Americans to be perceived as excelling at school and particularly at math and science. This "positive" stereotype (which is equally pernicious) notwithstanding, there is a very old assumption that Western culture is uniquely rational compared to non-Western cultures. It is perhaps less often articulated now that Western culture, values, and forms of knowledge are so widely accepted around the world. We still see it live on, however, insofar as people in the West often look to Asia when they seek an escape from rationality because they find it oppressive or stifling. New Age movements and frequently popular culture fantasize a "mystical East" that supposedly operates differently from the rationality of the West.

Another classic Orientalist binary is that Asians are depraved, while Westerners are virtuous. This again may seem a bit out of date as a blanket stereotype against Asians. During the colonial period, however, Westerners' conceit that they were the most rational and virtuous people in the world served to justify their colonial assertion of dominance over non-Western peoples. You may be familiar with Rudyard Kipling, the author of *The Jungle Book*, which is now a beloved children's story, with multiple movie adaptations. But Rudyard Kipling, who was born in British India, was also a notorious racist. He wrote a poem called "The White Man's Burden" in which he argued that the "white man" had the duty to civilize the other, supposedly less civilized, peoples of the world. Arguably, Western people continue to hold this smug sense of superiority even today, although it plays out a bit differently than it did during the colonial period. Whereas then it took the form of direct control of colonies around the world, today it takes the form of domineering foreign policy, misbegotten and paternalistic humanitarian efforts, and a patronizing attitude toward non-Western cultures. With respect to religion, Islam is probably the most frequent target of the Orientalist assumption that non-Westerners are depraved. Despite the West's own history of violence and misogyny, Westerners delight in constantly pointing out and condemning the violence and misogyny that is found in Islamic cultures.

A third binary found in Orientalism is that Asians are childlike, while Westerners are mature. This stereotype is still quite operative today. This is particularly true for East Asians and those of East Asian descent, who are often treated patronizingly because they are perceived as small, young-looking, and thus childlike. Western norms of maturity are constructed so rigidly—and Westerners are so oblivious to their cultural contingency—that innocuous features of Asian cultures are often treated as signs of a childlike quality. For example, in Thai culture, it is common to smile in situations where it might not be considered "normal" to do so in Western culture. Often, I have found, Westerners perceive this as a sign of childishness. In fact, Thai people smile (aside from usual happiness) to be polite in socially awkward situations. Socially awkward situations arise often when dealing with foreigners—especially when they unthinkingly talk a mile a minute in English—so Westerners often see Thai people smile, then completely misinterpret it. Likewise, there is a culture of cuteness in East Asia, emanating from Japan (where it is known as *kawaii*), that often is perceived as childish in the West. Hello Kitty is probably the most well-known example of this culture. While cute culture can certainly be critiqued, like any aspect of culture, I think it says more about the West than it does about Asia that Westerners are so hostile to childhood that they perceive cute culture as inherently ridiculous.

Closely related to the third binary is a fourth, which posits that Asians are intrinsically feminine, while Westerners are comparatively masculine. This is what we could call an intersectional form of prejudice because it combines racism with sexism. The perception of Asians as feminine or effeminate is very old and still very prevalent today, and it affects both Asian women and Asian men, albeit differently. On the one hand, it affects Asian women by hypersexualizing them. The prime example of this is the Dragon Lady, the stereotype of Asian women, especially East Asian women, as exotic, mysterious, and deceitful. It also plays out in the fetishization of Asian women by non-Asian (often white) men, a phenomenon sometimes referred to as "yellow fever." On the other hand, the perception of Asians as feminine affects Asian men by making them appear effeminate. In popular media, Asian men are often portrayed as weak and less "manly"—or if they are strong, as in say martial arts, then that is treated as a curiosity. Even in ordinary dating culture, Asian-looking men are often considered less desirable because they are perceived as too "feminine." Overall, the stereotype of Asians as feminine contributes to the patronizing way in which Asians and people of Asian heritage are often treated.

One last Orientalist binary is the root of all the others: The West is normal, while Asia is different. This binary should not be surprising at all, since some variation of it is the basis of all prejudices: the perception that one's own group is normal and the denigration of all deviations from that norm. *Different* is a word with a neutral connotation, but there are synonyms for *different* that have stronger connotations. Most of these are negative: *strange, weird, odd, bizarre.* Western perceptions of the difference of non-Western cultures have often taken such negative valences in the past, and sometimes they still do so today. In polite society, one is less likely now to hear non-Western cultures blatantly dismissed as "strange," both because such attitudes are considered uncouth and for the simple reason that there is a broader awareness of the diversity of world cultures, and thus non-Western cultures are less likely to be perceived as strange. There is another synonym for *different*, however, that has a positive connotation. That word is *exotic.* Although it is now frowned upon in Western cultures to dismiss other cultures as "strange," it has become almost second nature to embrace them as "exotic."

The word *exotic* has a positive connotation, but is it really such a positive thing, especially when applied to people and human cultures? Think about what sorts of things get labelled exotic. Probably the sorts of things that come to mind are food, travel destinations, and animals. What makes these things exotic? The fact that they deviate from a Western norm—but in a good way, at least according to some people. Exotic food is usually spicy—different from Western food, but delicious. Exotic travel destinations are usually tropical—great for a vacation when it is snowing back home. Exotic animals are not deer, rabbits, and squirrels that (in a Western country) you might see by the side of the road, but magnificent animals like elephants, giraffes, and tigers. Where do you see such animals? Unless you travel to Asia or Africa, you see them . . . in a zoo. This, I hope, gives you a hint as to what is problematic about the word *exotic*. Zoos have been reformed in recent years, but in the classic zoo, exotic animals were kept in cages.

This is the dark underbelly of the word *exotic*: It is superficially positive, but it always implies a power relationship. Exotic foods and exotic animals come from exotic places, which are usually poor or only recently developed, often formerly colonies. All three of these things imply some sort of consumption on the part of the Westerner: literally with the mouth in the case of food, economically in the case of travel, and with the eyes in the case of animals. Consumption of another sort is also implied in another word that is often paired with *exotic*: *women*. Women are frequently described as exotic to imply that they are sexually appealing precisely because they are different in appearance (darker and with different features) than white women. Also implied, in many cases, is that they will be more subservient to men, in parallel to the subservient position of their countries of origin in the colonial world order. This, of course, ties back into the previously mentioned binary that casts the Asian as feminine in contrast to the masculine West.

So far, we've looked at two distinct definitions of *Orientalism*. The third and final definition that Said gives is this: "a Western style for dominating, restructuring, and having authority over the Orient."[3] First and foremost, this refers to colonialism. As we saw, colonialism was a defining feature of the last several centuries, but in the decades after World War II, most former colonies gained their independence. For this reason, scholars usually refer to the period we are living in now as the "postcolonial" period. Now, you might ask, if colonialism is over, then why does Said even mention it? What does something that happened in the past have to do with Orientalism today? Said explains why with one very key word: *hegemony*.

Hegemony comes from a Greek word that means "leadership," and as such it can be understood to mean "power," but it refers to a very particular type of power. Imagine that you're a kid going to school and a bully comes up to you and says, "Give me your lunch money!" You say no, so the bully beats you up. Then you give him your lunch money. That's one type of power—the power of brute force. On a social scale, the equivalent to this is military force. One country wants another country's land, so it sends in its military. If the other country puts up a fight, then the first country fires bullets, drops bombs, and kills people. Eventually, assuming the first country is stronger, it gets the land that it wants. This is what we can call *hard power*. Such hard power was of course involved in establishing colonies and squashing independence movements during the colonial period.

Hegemony does not refer to this kind of power. It refers instead to various forms of *soft power*—power that might be backed up by military force or the threat thereof but does not itself involve direct physical violence. We see this in the hegemonic power of the world today, which is the United States. The United States is the most powerful country in the world in part because it has the largest and most powerful military, but it does not exercise its power primarily through military force. Instead, America's power is mostly exerted through cultural, social, and economic means. This is hegemony: the power of cultural leadership.

One great example of this phenomenon is McDonald's. McDonald's is found all around the world, and it doesn't just sell hamburgers: It sells, in a sense, a packaged and consumable form of American culture. There are of course many American restaurant chains that are found around the world, including KFC, TGI Fridays, and Burger King, as well as, most recently, Starbucks, which is just about as ubiquitous in non-American cities as it is in American ones. Another example is Hollywood. There are many regional movie industries that serve various markets around the world, but the one whose movies can be seen in just about any country is Hollywood. Hollywood doesn't just disseminate movies; it disseminates culture. In large part because of movies, people in other countries often know a lot more about American culture than Americans know about any other culture.

One of the best examples of American hegemony is English. English is the lingua franca of the world today. All international airports conduct business in English. Business and diplomatic transactions between people speaking different languages, even if neither is English, are usually conducted in English. Most travel destinations, regardless of the country, have people who speak English to be able to serve international clientele. If you are a native speaker of English, you have automatic access to opportunities that people who are not native English speakers struggle to attain. In many countries where English is not the primary language, students nevertheless study English as a subject in school, and often they will engage in extracurricular study of English to gain proficiency in the language that is the key to social advancement.

Of course, American hegemony did not come out of nowhere. In large part, it emerged out of the Allied victory in World War II and America's subsequent success in the Cold War. If Germany had won the war, we probably would all be eating at an international bratwurst chain instead of McDonald's, and we would all be desperately trying to learn German to gain access to greater opportunities in life. American hegemony also piggy-backed on the broader hegemony of Europe through the colonial period and in particular the hegemony that the United Kingdom enjoyed at the height of colonialism in the late nineteenth and early-twentieth centuries. The universality of English as a means of communication was established through the massive extent of Britain's empire and then confirmed and entrenched by the superpower status gained by one of Britain's former colonies, the United States, after World War II. American hegemony today also tends to universalize broader Western norms. This includes various political and social ideas that have become so pervasive that we take them for granted today: democracy, capitalism, human rights, the rule of law, and the whole international system of diplomacy are based on European norms that were universalized through colonialism and continue to be enforced today because of the hegemonic power of the United States.

To summarize, then, the three distinct aspects of Orientalism that Said identifies are (1) an academic institution, (2) the binary distinction between East and West, and (3) a system of domination. What do these three things have to do with each other? Although at first glance they might seem to be completely unrelated, they are in fact closely intertwined and mutually dependent. I like to think of them as being like the three legs of a tripod. In a well-constructed tripod, the three legs both lean on and support each other, without the need for any additional support.

Let us first consider the first and second definitions of Orientalism. Orientalism as an academic field was very much informed by a binary way of thinking about East and West. On a very basic level, the distinction between East and West served as the basis for considering the Orient (that is, the East) as a field of study. In addition, early Orientalist scholarship—in the eighteenth, nineteenth, and even into the twentieth century—was riddled with racist assumptions about the innate nature of Asian people. At the same time, Orientalists reinforced racist binary thinking about the East and West by promoting such ideas under the guise of science or knowledge. If this surprises you, it shouldn't. Racism was part and parcel of mainstream academic thought at the height of the colonial era. It wasn't just the ignorant views of uneducated hicks; it was considered a respectable academic paradigm for vast swaths of the Western academy. It is only more recently, in the twentieth century, especially after World War II, that Western academic opinion turned conclusively against racism. Orientalist scholarship thus both was informed by the binary way of thinking about East and West and reinforced that way of thinking. Scholars who study Asia and other non-Western cultures today are still struggling to extricate themselves from the Orientalist biases of our intellectual forebears.

Consider next the second and third definitions of Orientalism. Why did Europeans pursue their colonial project? There were of course many reasons, including a Christian missionary impulse and simple greed, but one reason was a belief in the innate superiority of European civilization. The binary thinking about East and West, which goes all the way back to the time of the ancient Greeks, gave Europeans a motive for conquering the peoples of the East. At the same time, once colonial dominance was established, that very situation of domination over non-Western peoples tended to reinforce racist views about them.

Think about it: Let's say you are introduced to two people. One of them is free, independent, and wealthy, while the other has been held in captivity and deprived of their possessions. If you are not told which is which, who will give you a more positive impression, in say a job interview? Probably the one who is free, independent, and wealthy. A similar thing happened when Europeans traveled to Asia and other colonized lands in the colonial period. They of course came primed with racist views, but these views were often reinforced when they saw the state that the colonized peoples were in. This was particularly true at the height of the colonial period, in the late nineteenth and early twentieth centuries. Unlike the early colonial period, when Europeans were still fairly evenly matched with the rest of the world, by the late colonial period much of the non-Western world had lost its independence to Western powers, and Europe had grown rich and more developed on the backs of its colonies. Individual Westerners who already harbored racist views would have those views reinforced upon seeing the inequalities between the East and West, ignoring the broader system of domination that had brought those inequalities about in the first place.

Finally, how do the first and third definitions of Orientalism relate? Here we are talking about Orientalism as an academic institution and Orientalism as a system of domination (colonialism). These might seem unrelated, but they are actually related quite closely. How and why do you think scholars came to intensively study Asia? Precisely because of colonialism. Prior to the colonial period, Europeans did not know much about Asia or the rest of the world. How could they? There was no internet, radio, or TV at that time. Travel and transportation were difficult, and although certain goods might travel long distances by passing through the hands of multiple merchants, it was quite rare for people to travel to distant lands and then return home to report what they saw. Marco Polo is famous because he did so at a time, in the twentieth century, when Europeans knew next to nothing about the Far East.

Colonialism changed all this. It created links between East and West that made it possible for Europeans to learn about Asia. It also gave Europeans the *power* to create knowledge about the East. You've probably heard the slogan "Knowledge is power." Usually, people assume this just means it is good to get an education. But really it should be taken more literally. Knowledge really is a form of power. It is gained through power, and it creates power. Orientalists were able to create knowledge about the East because they operated under colonial regimes that gave them access to the peoples, locations, and literatures of Asia. At the same time, the knowledge they created was used by colonial regimes to exercise power over their colonies and justify the colonial project itself.

Orientalism thus is a complex machine of interlocking parts. It was largely built in the colonial period, but it lives on today because the legacy of colonialism is far from a thing of the past. We may live in a postcolonial era, but the inequalities that colonialism created still exist. Western hegemony still exists. And Western attitudes toward Asia and the non-West more generally, although they may have morphed and become less overtly antagonistic, still reflect old Orientalist binaries.

RELIGION AND THE JEKYLL-AND-HYDE NATURE OF ORIENTALISM

As already explained above, Orientalism lives on largely through the hegemonic power of the West today. The West might not control the world directly in the same way it did during the colonial period, but it still exercises a great deal of soft power, or cultural influence. Western norms are taken as universal norms. Religion itself is one of these norms. As we already saw in chapter 1, the very idea of religion is a Western concept that became universalized through colonialism. That is why we have the concept of world religions today—a concept that did not exist anywhere in the world in premodern times. In addition, because the Western concept of religion is so tied up with Christianity, Christianity has become the implicit paradigm for world religions. By using the word *religion*, we see the world's religions through Christian-tinted glasses.

The chapters of Part II will help you to take off those glasses and see how they distort the way you look at the world. Each chapter will focus on a particular religion or religious sphere and illustrate the disconnect between common misunderstandings about that religion and the reality of it. In chapter 3, we will look at Islam and the prejudices that exist against it, which are known as Islamophobia. How is it that a religion that is so similar to Christianity is dogged by such hatred and misunderstanding? Chapter 4 introduces Buddhism and asks whether it is better understood as a philosophy or a religion. Many people in the West see Buddhism as less a religion than a philosophy, but this involves ignoring many of the more religion-y aspects of traditional Buddhist practice. In chapter 5, we will turn to Hinduism and ask whether this religion is monotheistic or polytheistic. Many non-Hindus in the West perceive it as polytheistic, but many Hindus themselves would say that it is monotheistic. Chapter 6 introduces Chinese religions. The three main religions of China are Buddhism, Confucianism, and Daoism, but contrary to what one would expect from the Western experience of religion, all three of these religions can and usually are practiced by the same people at once. Chapter 7 then turns to India to illustrate a similar phenomenon: inclusivism. Although Indian religions typically have distinct identities, they historically have competed with one another not by rejecting each others' gods or main figures, but rather by including them in a subordinated role. Chapter 8 looks at a particular form of Buddhism, Tibetan Buddhism. This form of Buddhism has sometimes been looked down upon as "not real Buddhism" because it involves a form of practice, called Tantra, that on the surface violates Buddhist principles. As we will see, though, it represents a form of Buddhism that, yes, evolved nearly a millennium after the time of the Buddha but nevertheless is based on traditional Buddhist philosophy. Finally, chapters 9, 10, and 11 will examine the limits of what religion includes. In chapter 9, we will look at Judaism and ask whether it is a religion or an ethnicity. We will see that this ambiguity in Jewish identity has been exploited to create modern racism against Jews, which is known as antisemitism. Chapter 10 will examine the vast category of "indigenous religions"—religions that are not considered major world religions and challenge our understanding of religion as something distinct from culture. And chapter 11 will look at secularism and question whether it makes sense to refer to religion as a separate sphere of life at all.

As we look in Part II at the misconceptions and prejudices about world religions that are mediated by Orientalism, it is important to keep in mind that Orientalism is not reducible simply to a set of negative stereotypes. Orientalism, especially in today's world, is a lot like Dr. Jekyll and Mr. Hyde. Sometimes Orientalism manifests itself in an overtly negative way, but at other times, just as or even more often, it manifests itself more subtly through stereotypes and perceptions that are superficially positive. With respect to religion, overtly negative Orientalist perceptions were most common at the beginning of the colonial period and have become less common with time. Conversely, superficially positive Orientalist perceptions have become increasingly common and nowadays often are the primary lens through which Asian religions are seen in the West. Overtly negative stereotypes are most common with Islam, the product of over 1,000 years of Christian animosity toward that religion and the recent dominance of popular discourse by media portrayals of terrorism. While negative stereotypes still exist with respect to other Asian religions, especially within conservative Christian communities, popular discourse often is filled with nice sounding but vapid stereotypes about these religions, which often serve to draw the interest of the "spiritual but not religious" crowd. This is particularly true of Buddhism, Daoism, and (somewhat more ambiguously) Hinduism.

Awareness of the dangers of Islamophobia is widespread among the West's creative class, even if Islamophobia itself is on the rise. But superficially positive stereotypes of the East—the Dr. Jekyll of Orientalism—is still Orientalism. It still denigrates, perhaps even more perniciously because of its pleasant mask, the lived experience of billions of people. And it is far more powerful than the overt hostility of Islamophobia because it has the ability, over time, to recast the lived experience of billions in its own image. In this respect, the glasses we are trying to slough off in this book are not just like red-tinted glasses that make all the paintings in an art gallery look like they are painted in shades of red.

They are like magic glasses that, when enough people wear them for a long enough time, *actually make the paintings turn red.*

DISCUSSION QUESTIONS

1. What were the major powers of the modern colonial era? When was each most dominant, and where were they most active?
2. How did colonialism change as it progressed over time?
3. What is Orientalism? What are the three definitions of Orientalism given by Edward Said, and how do they relate to one another?
4. What does the word *hegemony* mean? What are some examples of hegemonic power in the world today?
5. In what way is Orientalism like Dr. Jekyll and Mr. Hyde?

NOTES

1 Edward W. Said, *Orientalism* (New York: Random House, 1978), 2.
2 Although Said originally used *Orientalism* to refer to a relationship between the West and Asia, and in particular the Middle East, nowadays it is common to use it to refer to relationships between the West defined in some way and virtually any geographic and cultural other. If we define the West as Europe and its major settler colonies (most importantly the US), then that other can be Asia, but also Africa, the indigenous peoples displaced by white settler colonialism, and (by extension) even Latin America. Orientalist attitudes are arguably at work even in Europe itself. Eastern Europe is Orientalized in the gaze of Western Europe, and even the attitudes of northern Europeans and their cultural descendants (such as in the US) toward southern Europeans (such as Italians) can mimic Orientalist tropes.
3 Said, *Orientalism*, 3.

//
Part II
Take the Glasses Off

3

Islam

Does Fear Imply Difference?

In this book I am aiming to show the way that most religions do not fit a Christian paradigm of religion well, but if any comes close to fitting a Christian paradigm, Islam is it. In this chapter, I will describe Islam, starting with its founding figure, the prophet Muhammad, and showing the ways in which it is broadly similar to Christianity, while differing in certain details. Unfortunately, there is a great deal of ignorance in society about Islam, as well as fear and malignment of it. The word for prejudice against Islam and Muslims is *Islamophobia*, which literally means "fear of Islam." Considering the Christian heritage of the West and the fact that many of those doing the fearing, maligning, and hating are committed Christians, it is deeply ironic that Islam is more similar to Christianity than any other world religion. So then where does Islamophobia come from? To answer this question, I will finish the chapter by exploring the history of Islamophobia and argue that it is ironically precisely the similarities between Islam and Christianity that lie behind Islamophobia.

THE PROPHET MUHAMMAD

The word *Islam* means "submission," and it comes from the same root as the word *salam*, which means "peace"; as such, *Islam* refers to the peace that comes from submission to the one true God. People within the religion of Islam are referred to as *Muslims* because they submit to God.[1] Within the Islamic worldview, Islam is as old as the world itself and refers to the proper worship of the one true God. Historically speaking, however, Islam as an organized religion began in the

DOI: 10.4324/9781032646428-5

seventh century with the rapid rise of an Arabic-speaking empire. That empire organized itself ideologically around the teachings ascribed to a man named Muhammad, who was also considered to be the founder of the empire. Muhammad is thus effectively the founder of Islam, although Muslims consider him simply to be the last in a long line of prophets proclaiming the truth that God is one. What we know about the prophet Muhammad comes solely from a vast literature known as the *hadith*, which are stories and sayings of the prophet Muhammad that were circulated in the early Islamic community. Early on in Islam's history, people recognized that many of the *hadith* were spurious, and thus they made an effort to separate early, trustworthy *hadith* from later fabrications. There thus arose a traditional consensus about Muhammad's life, which I will relate here, some of which is disputed by modern scholars but which in any case has been authoritative for Muslims over the centuries.

According to the traditional account, Muhammad was born in 570 in the city of Mecca, which is located in modern-day Saudia Arabia. At that time, the Arabs were mostly polytheists, although there were some Jews and Christians among them as well, so Muhammad would have been familiar with the monotheism and stories associated with these religions. Muhammad had a pensive character and would frequently go into the wilderness outside the city to contemplate. According to Islamic tradition, in 610, when Muhammad was forty years old and was secluded in a cave called Hira outside the city, the angel Gabriel appeared to him. This Gabriel was the same angel who appeared to Mary in the Gospel of Luke to tell her that she would bear a son even though she was a virgin, an event Christians call the Annunciation. Gabriel commanded Muhammad to recite. Muhammad protested that he could not recite because he was illiterate. Gabriel then told him to recite the following verses:

> Read, in the name of your Lord who created,
> Created humans from a clinging clot.
> Read! And your Lord is the Most Generous,
> Who taught by the pen,
> Taught humanity what they knew not.[2]

These verses became the first of many verses Muhammad received from God over the course of the rest of his life. They were later collected into a book called the Qur'an, which Muslims consider to be a divine revelation, quite literally the word of God. The first verse to be revealed plays on the ambiguity of a word in Arabic that can mean to recite but also to read, in the sense of reading out loud. In the story, the word-play prompts Muhammad to bring up the fact that he is illiterate. Muslims consider this to be proof that the Qur'an must be of divine origin, for how could an illiterate man devise such beautiful verses on his own?

The message of the revelations collected in the Qur'an is consistent: Submit to the will of the one true God and turn away from the worship of false idols. As Muhammad first started receiving these revelations, he was entrusted with spreading this message as a prophet, a messenger sent by God. He initially made only a few converts: his wife Khadija and a few relatives and friends. They were known as *Muslims* because they "submitted" (the meaning of the word in Arabic) to the one true God. Muhammad's message overall was not popular in Mecca, however. Mecca was the location of a temple, the Kaaba, where people from a wide area would come to worship the various Arab gods. While in Mecca, these pilgrims would naturally spend money. Polytheism, in other words, was big business in Mecca. Tensions between the Muslims and the powerful families in Mecca rose to the point that they were forced to leave the city. They left in 622 and migrated to the nearby city of Medina, an event known as the *hijra*.

The *hijra* may seem to have been a setback for the Muslims, but it was considered by later Muslims to be of such significance that the Islamic calendar counts from that year. The reason for the significance of the

Figure 3.1 Muslim pilgrims around the Kaaba during the hajj. © Getty Images

hijra is that Muhammad was invited by the tribes of Medina to serve as a city administrator. There were disputes among the tribes of the city, most of which were polytheistic but some of which were Jewish, and they needed a neutral outside figure to resolve the disputes. Muhammad agreed to become leader of the city, and fragments of a document establishing a communal alliance between the tribes of the city, known as the *umma*, still exist, which make reference to God and Muhammad as his prophet. The *umma* was a community, like many in its day, that was simultaneously political and religious.

Medina under Muhammad's leadership made a peace treaty with Mecca, but tensions between the two cities grew until finally war broke out. The Medinan forces led by Muhammad ultimately conquered Mecca in 630. When Muhammad entered the city, he destroyed the idols found in the Kaaba, and most of the people of Mecca converted to Islam. From there, the Islamic *umma* grew rapidly through warfare and diplomacy to encompass the western part of the Arab peninsula by the time of Muhammad's death in 632. Over the course of the next century, under the leadership of leaders called caliphs who were considered successors of the prophet Muhammad, the *umma* grew into an empire, conquering the Persian Empire and large portions of the Byzantine Empire in the Levant and North Africa, as well as conquering much of the Iberian Peninsula. This empire fragmented in the tenth century and was fully brought to an end by a Mongol invasion in the thirteenth, but in its short duration it established a religious culture that became the basis for the endurance and spread of Islam as a world religion.

THE TWO MAIN BRANCHES OF ISLAM

Although, at the beginning, the Islamic community, or *umma*, was a unified political community, that has not been the case since the Islamic Empire fragmented in the tenth century. The vast majority of Muslims today identify as belonging to one of two major branches, whose differences are primarily defined by the way in which they interpret the succession to the prophet Muhammad and the growth of the original Islamic Empire. These two groups are the Sunnis and the Shi'ites. Both Sunnis and Shi'ites agree that the Islamic Empire became corrupt early in its history, but they disagree on when and why.

Most Muslims are and have throughout history been Sunnis. Close to 90% of Muslims today are Sunni. Sunnis believe that the first four caliphs of the Islamic Empire—Abu Bakr (632–634), 'Umar (634–644), 'Uthman (644–656), and 'Ali (656–661)—were "righteously-guided"; that is, they ruled in keeping with the traditions (in Arabic, *sunna*) of the prophet Muhammad that serve as an example for Muslims. These first four caliphs were not chosen on a hereditary basis but by consultation in the *umma*. When 'Ali was elected caliph, however, Mu'awiya, the governor of Syria, opposed his election and challenged his rule, leading to a civil war that lasted from 657 to 661. It ended with 'Ali being assassinated and Mu'awiya assuming the caliphate, founding a hereditary dynasty known as the Umayyads, who ruled from Damascus in Syria as their capital. This dynasty ruled over the Islamic Empire until 750, when a revolt led by Abu al-Abbas resulted in the founding of the Abbasid Dynasty. The Abbasids moved the capital to a new city, Baghdad (in modern-day Iraq), from which they ruled until the city was sacked by the Mongols in 1258. The Umayyads and Abbasids, though historically important for having taken the original Islamic Empire to its largest extent and cultural efflorescence, are not considered by Muslims of either branch, Sunni or Shi'ite, to be models of righteous rule.

Just over ten percent of Muslims today are Shi'ites. They form a majority of Muslims in Iran, Iraq, Azerbaijan, Bahrain, and Lebanon, with minorities found elsewhere. Shi'ites hold that the succession of caliphs after the death of Muhammad was corrupt from the very beginning. They believe that only God can name his prophet's successor, and that Muhammad announced before his death that God had named 'Ali. Thus, in theory, 'Ali should have been the first caliph. The Shi'ites derive their name from this fact, since they call themselves the "party of 'Ali," or in Arabic, *shi'at 'ali*. Since in reality the caliphs did not follow the (in the Shi'ite view) proper succession, Shi'ites refer to the *proper* successors of Muhammad, all of whom come from his family, as Imams.[3] These Imams are understood by Shi'ites to have special knowledge and divine authority that they possess as descendants of Muhammad. There are different subsects of the Shi'a that vary in who they hold to have been the proper lineage of Imams. The largest subsect of the Shi'a are Twelvers, who accept a lineage of twelve Imams, starting with 'Ali. All of these Imams were persecuted and most of them were also assassinated by the ruling caliphs. According to the Twelvers, the twelfth Imam, Muhammad al-Mahdi, went into hiding in 874 and will return with Jesus in the future on the Day of Judgment to restore the righteous rule of Islam to the earth.

THE FIVE PILLARS OF ISLAM

Within Sunni Islam there developed a concept of "Five Pillars of Islam" to describe the most important, obligatory elements of Islamic faith and practice. Although Shi'ites describe their practices in slightly different terms, they also practice what the Sunnis call the Five Pillars in mostly similar ways. The Five Pillars of Islam thus give a good overview of what being a Muslim consists of.

The first of the Five Pillars is the *shahada*, or profession of faith. It plays a role similar to the Christian Creed, but in comparison with the Creed, it is quite simple: "There is no God but God, and Muhammad is his messenger." The *shahada* thus defines Muslims as those who accept Muhammad as a prophet of God, both as such and in terms of his message, which is that there is only one true God. There is no elaborate conversion ceremony in Islam. Instead, to become a Muslim one must simply recite the *shahada*, with intention to convert, in front of two witnesses.

The remaining four Pillars detail what one is supposed to *do* as a Muslim. The second Pillar is *salat*, or prayer. Muslims are supposed to pray five times a day. They do this in a ritualized fashion, at particular times of the day, and always facing Mecca, whatever direction that might be given their location in the world. Unlike Christianity, Islam does not have a monastic tradition, but the Islamic style of prayer follows a pattern similar to the Christian Liturgy of the Hours[4] to organize the day of ordinary Muslims around remembrance of God.

Most of these prayers are performed by Muslims individually or with their family at the specified prayer times. However, it is customary for Muslims to gather as a community to perform the midday prayer on Fridays at a worship center known as a *mosque*. An *imam*, who serves a role similar to a Protestant minister, gives a sermon and then leads the congregation in the midday prayer. Mosques can be as simple as a room but in Islamic countries are often quite large and ornate, rivaling in size and beauty the cathedrals of Europe. The central structure of a mosque is a room or open space where people can line up to perform their prayers. Since Muslims always pray facing Mecca, the direction of Mecca, known as the *qibla*, is indicated permanently by an alcove in one of the walls, known as the *mihrab*. Near the *mihrab* is often a *minbar*, or pulpit, from which the imam gives his sermon.

Muslims are required to wash certain parts of their body (the face, arms, head, and feet) prior to performing *salat*, so mosques have special facilities for performing these ablutions. In addition, mosques in Islamic countries usually have minarets, special towers from which vocalists known as *muezzins* can give the call to prayer, or *adhan*. The *adhan*, like the prayers themselves, is performed in Arabic, but its words translate as follows:

> God is most great! God is most great!
> God is most great! God is most great!

I testify that there is no god but God.
I testify that there is no god but God.
I testify that Muhammad is the messenger of God.
I testify that Muhammad is the messenger of God.
Come to prayer! Come to prayer!
Come to success! Come to success!
God is most great! God is most great!
There is no god but God.

Muezzins recite the *adhan* in different styles, many of which are quite beautiful. (I recommend checking it out on YouTube.) The purpose of the minaret originally was to allow the muezzin to project his voice around a village or a neighborhood of a city served by a particular mosque. Nowadays, however, loudspeakers are usually mounted from minarets. The *adhan* is thus a ubiquitous part of the soundscape of Islamic countries, as it is projected from the minarets of mosques at the various prayer times throughout the week.

Mosques can be quite large and beautiful, but unlike Catholic and Orthodox Christian churches they are almost never decorated with pictorial art. Instead, they are usually decorated with geometric designs and calligraphy of verses taken from the Qur'an. The reason for this is that

Figure 3.2 Muslims listening to an imam's sermon at a mosque. The imam is giving his sermon from the *minbar* on the right. Note also the alcove to the left, which is the *mihrab*, indicating the *qibla*, or direction of Mecca. © Getty Images

Islam has a strong *iconoclastic* tradition. The word *iconoclastic* comes from Greek and literally means "destroying images." It refers to the opinion, which has been influential to varying degrees throughout the Abrahamic traditions, that one should not make use of religious images. In Islam, this means that one certainly should not depict God as an anthropomorphic image; in addition, many Muslims throughout history have extended this prohibition to depictions of Muhammad and the other prophets. This practice contrasts sharply with Catholic and Orthodox Christianity, but it is similar to that of Judaism and many denominations of Protestant Christianity, which also eschew images of God, prophets, and saints.

The third Pillar of Islam is *zakat*, or alms. Muslims are expected to give a certain amount of their money to the poor. Usually, this amount is 2.5% of one's total wealth every year, provided that one surpasses a certain minimum threshold of wealth. The purpose of *zakat* is to redistribute wealth within the *umma*, in order to promote a more egalitarian community since all are equal in the eyes of God. Historically, *zakat* was collected by the state like a tax, and there are a few Islamic countries that still follow this practice. Nowadays, however, for most Muslims the payment of *zakat* is done on a voluntary basis.

The fourth Pillar of Islam is *sawm*, or fasting. Muslims are expected, unless they are sick or infirm, to abstain from food, drink, and sex from sunrise to sunset during the month of Ramadan in the Islamic calendar. The Islamic calendar is lunar and floats against the solar calendar, so Ramadan falls at different times of the year from year to year. The purpose of this month of fasting is to renew the individual Muslim's commitment to God. It serves a similar purpose to fasting found in many religious traditions, and as a set month in the annual calendar, it serves a similar purpose to Lent in Christianity in being a period of annual recommitment to one's faith. To be clear, while the rules of *sawm* are quite strict *within daylight hours*, Muslims are certainly not expected to go without food and drink for an entire month. They break their fast every evening at dusk with a great feast called an *iftar*. *Iftars* can be quite elaborate and festive occasions through which Muslims bond together with their family or larger community over their shared commitment to the Ramadan fast. The end of the month of Ramadan is then celebrated with a great festival called Eid al-Fitr, which also features an exuberance of food and eating.

Finally, the fifth Pillar is the *hajj*, or pilgrimage to Mecca. All Muslims are expected to make this pilgrimage at least once during their lifetimes if they have the financial means. The *hajj* takes place once a year, during the Islamic lunar month of Dhu al-Hijja. (Muslims can also make a pilgrimage to Mecca at other times of the year, but that is not considered a *hajj*.)

During the *hajj*, all pilgrims wear simple white clothing, symbolizing purity as well as the equality of all Muslims before God. Over the course of several days, they perform a series of rituals at and around the Kaaba, a cube-shaped temple that Muslims believe was originally built by the prophet Abraham and then cleansed of idols and rededicated to the worship of the one true God by Muhammad when he conquered Mecca in 630. The *hajj* ends with a four-day festival, simultaneously celebrated by Muslims around the world, called Eid al-Adha, which commemorates Abraham's willingness to sacrifice his son to God.[5]

Many Muslims who make the *hajj* find it to be a profoundly transcendental and life-transformative experience. People who have been on the *hajj* are called *hajjis* and are often quite respected in their communities. Although it is only obligatory to perform the *hajj* once in one's lifetime, and even then, only if one is able, some people of sufficient means make a point of performing the *hajj* multiple times or even every year.

ISLAM AND CHRISTIANITY

As I already noted above, Islam is very similar to Christianity. To begin with, Muslims and Christians (as well as Jews) share in a common tradition about a monotheistic God. There is a common misconception that Allah is the name of the Muslim God, as if that God were different from the God referred to in English. This is not the case. *Allah* is simply the Arabic word for God. (Literally *Allah* means "the God," with the article *the* indicating the monotheistic God rather than one god out of many, since Arabic doesn't have capital letters to make this distinction.) There are Arabic-speaking Christians and Jews, and when they talk about God in Arabic, they also refer to him as *Allah*.

The entire Islamic worldview is based upon, but seen as superseding, that of Judaism and Christianity that preceded it. In this respect, its relationship to Judaism and Christianity is similar to the relationship of Christianity to Judaism. This extends to its view of scripture, but in a somewhat different way. Christians accept the Jewish scriptures in their existing form and simply add additional scriptures of their own to them to make a larger Bible—the Jewish Bible being called by Christians the "Old Testament," with the newer Christian additions being called the "New Testament." Muslims do accept both the Jewish scriptures and the later Christian scripture as authentic revelation, but they hold that these texts have been corrupted by later tradition and thus do not accept them in their extant form. The Qur'an consists solely of revelations believed to have been received by Muhammad from God in Arabic; they are not attached to the Jewish and Christian scriptures to make a larger "Bible."

Nevertheless, Muslims accept many of the stories that are found in the Bible, and well-known figures such as Adam, Noah, Abraham, Moses, and Jesus are referred to in the Qur'an. Muslims accept these and other biblical figures as prophets sent by God, with Muhammad being the last prophet. Muslims refer to Muhammad as the "seal of the prophets" because they believe that he is the last prophet that will be sent by God. Muhammad brought with him the perfect revelation of God's will, the Qur'an, and thus there is no need for further prophets to be sent.

This means that Muslims differ from Christians in accepting one additional prophet (Muhammad), and Muslims differ from Jews in accepting two additional prophets (Jesus and Muhammad). All three religions worship one God and are built around a common view of history beginning with God's creation of the world and the first man, Adam, followed by a series of prophets whose primary message was that there is one true God. These are the stories that are found in the Jewish Bible, or what Christians call the Old Testament. Given the close relationship between Judaism, Christianity, and Islam, it is common to refer to them as the "Abrahamic religions."

In the Biblical book of Genesis, Abraham had a son named Isaac, who in turn had a son named Jacob. Jacob was given a new name by God, Israel, and he in turn had twelve sons, who were the progenitors of the Twelve Tribes of Israel. Abraham, Isaac, and Jacob are known as the three patriarchs, and Jews trace their lineage back to Abraham through Isaac and his son Jacob. Christians, insofar as they see themselves as the "spiritual" heirs of the Jews, also trace their lineage back to Abraham through Isaac. According to the Bible, however, Abraham had another son named Ishmael, whose mother was not the same as Isaac's. Abraham had his son Isaac after great difficulty with his wife Sarah, but he had earlier had Ishmael with his concubine Hagar. Muslims hold that the Arabs are descended from Ishmael, and thus they trace their lineage back to Abraham through Ishmael. The term "Abrahamic religions" thus refers to the fact that Judaism, Christianity, and Islam all trace their "lineage," at least rhetorically, back to a common ancestor, Abraham.

As I have already mentioned, Muslims accept Jesus as one of the prophets sent by God. He figures prominently in the Qur'an, which even uses the word *messiah* to describe him. The Qur'an also refers to John the Baptist and Jesus' mother Mary, and it says that Jesus was born miraculously to her while she was still a virgin, just as Christians believe. Muslims do not, however, regard Jesus as the Son of God or as God incarnate, and they reject the Christian doctrine of the Trinity—all of these Christian teachings they regard as blasphemous deviations from monotheism. God, according to Islam, is one, and he is radically beyond any human form. Muslims also deny that Jesus really died on the cross and believe rather that God saved him, so that Jesus is still alive. Like Christians, they believe that Jesus will come back at the end of time to battle an Antichrist and that at that time there will be a final judgment of all souls. Islam thus has a conception of history very similar to Christians: a linear one stretching from God's creation of the world in the past to the Final Judgment in the future.

ISLAMOPHOBIA

So why is there so much fear and loathing of Islam within the Western world when it is in fact so similar to Christianity? I find there is a common misconception among my students that Islamophobia started with 9/11. While it is true that Islamophobia spiked after the 9/11 attacks, it was certainly nothing new. There is a long history of Islamophobia, touching on many of the same themes as today, stretching back over a thousand years to the first centuries of the expansion of the Islamic Empire. Islamophobia, in fact, was one of the primary forces driving the Crusades, in which Christians from Western Europe, urged on by the pope or individual kings, organized armies to march east and "liberate" the Holy Land—Jerusalem and its environs—from Muslim control.

One of the primary themes of Islamophobia, then and now, is the association of Islam with violence. Nowadays, that association is amplified by Islamist[6] terrorist groups. This is in part an unfortunate side-effect of the fact that many people in the West know nothing about Islam other than what they hear in the news, which is reports of violence perpetrated by radical Islamist organizations. Popular culture then amplifies this association by depicting Muslims mostly as terrorists. Islamist terrorist organizations, such as Al Qaeda and ISIS, represent a miniscule fraction of Muslims and are no more representative of Islam than are Christians who commit violence in the name of Christianity.

Sometimes you will hear Islamophobes say, "Ok, maybe not all Muslims are terrorists, but all terrorists are Muslims." This is also not even remotely true; it only seems true because it has become increasingly common in public discourse to arbitrarily reserve the word *terrorism* for violence committed in the name of Islam, when in fact there are many more such acts of violence committed by non-Muslims. (Think, for example, of the epidemic of gun violence in the United States, overwhelmingly committed by non-Muslims.) In fact, there are terrorist organizations and acts of violence committed in the name of all sorts of religions. The KKK, for example, is a Protestant terrorist organization. The Irish Republican Army is a Catholic terrorist organization. No one seems to have trouble recognizing that they are not representative of Protestants, Catholics, or Christians writ large.

More sophisticated (if that is the right word) fear-mongers will point to the history of Islam to argue that it is a religion inherently prone to violence. It is true that Muhammad was not simply a prophet; he was simultaneously a political leader who engaged in military activity. In the first hundred years or so of Islam's existence, Muslims engaged in warfare that allowed them to establish an Islamic Empire stretching from the Iberian Peninsula in the west to the Indus River in the east. Because modern people have a tendency to focus on the origins of a religion as establishing its "true" identity (an issue we will explore in chapter 9), people point to these historical facts as evidence that Islam is an inherently violent religion. This argument is specious because it takes the early Islamic Empire out of its historical context. To begin with, Islam arose in a world already dominated by two religious empires. To its northwest was the Byzantine Empire, which was a Christian empire; to its northeast was the Persian Empire, which was a Zoroastrian[7] empire. There was no conception of a separation between religion and politics at that time, and empires that were backed by religious ideologies simultaneously engaged in warfare, as empires are wont to do.

It is often claimed that when Islam first expanded, it did so by forcing people to convert "by the sword." While establishing a far-flung empire did of course create strong incentives for the various peoples conquered to convert, there is little evidence that Muslims routinely forced conquered people to convert to Islam under penalty of death. Indeed, many Muslims would argue that to do so is itself un-Islamic; there is a verse in the Qur'an that says, "There is no compulsion in religion" (2:256). In addition, religious minorities were arguably treated better under Islamic rule in the Middle Ages than they were in Christendom. Islamic Law provided for the free exercise of religion by Christians, Jews, and certain other religious minorities as "people of the book" (i.e., those who had a revealed scripture), so long as they paid a special tax. Meanwhile, Jews were severely persecuted by Christians in medieval Europe.

The second most common theme within Islamophobia is the characterization of Islam as uniquely patriarchal or misogynistic. Islamophobes will often point to the practice of polygamy within Islam, including by Muhammad himself, as well as the practice of *hijab*, which is the use of a veil by women as a modest form of dress. To be sure, Islamic societies today and throughout history have generally been patriarchal and as such have engaged in the oppression of women. That, however, does not make them even remotely unique, as nearly every society in recorded history, including modern Western society, has been patriarchal and engaged in the oppression of women. What Islamophobes do is point to particular aspects of Islamic culture that will be perceived by Western audiences as exotic—most notably, polygamy and *hijab*—in order to falsely paint Islamic societies as *uniquely* patriarchal and oppressive of women. This is often done cynically, as these Islamophobes are seldom interested in engaging in feminist critique of their own cultures' systems of patriarchy and misogyny.

The Islamophobic portrayal of polygamy and *hijab* in Islam is characteristically taken out of context. It is true that, according to the traditional story, Muhammad took multiple wives after the death of his first wife Khadija. In addition, a verse of the Qur'an states that Muslim men may take up to four wives. This practice of polygamy, however, does not make Islamic societies unique. Many societies around the world, including Buddhist, Hindu, and Chinese, have historically practiced polygamy, although polygamy has been outlawed in many of the societies where it was once practiced due to the spread of modern conceptions of human rights. Muhammad was also not unique among the prophets of the Abrahamic religions in practicing polygamy; according to the Bible, several prophets practiced polygamy, including Abraham himself.

In addition, most Muslims today do not practice polygamy. Some Islamic countries ban polygamy altogether, while others restrict it, and even in places where it is legal, it is not necessarily common. The issue of polygamy is and has long been controversial within Islam, as the Qur'anic verse sanctioning it (1) states unequivocally that a man may only marry multiple wives if he can support all equally and (2) implies that the purpose of polygamy is so that families who have lost their husband/father to war will not be left destitute. Many Muslims argue that the first criterion is almost impossible to meet, while the second criterion makes polygamy an outdated practice meant to protect widows and orphans in the early years of Islam that is no longer relevant today.

The Islamic practice of *hijab* is also frequently taken out of context and treated monolithically. Several Qur'anic verses enjoin modest forms of dress and deportment for men and women in public to prevent lust that will encourage illicit sexual relations. Most Islamic schools of interpretation hold that modest dress for women consists of covering the body except for the hands and face, as well as covering the hair. The most common form of *hijab* therefore consists of a veil to cover the hair.[8] As an article of clothing for women, a veil covering the hair has historically been quite common in many cultures around the world, not just Islamic ones. At various times and in particular circumstances it has been common in Christian societies. Indeed, until the Second Vatican Council in the 1960s, it was a *required* article of clothing for Catholic women attending Mass.

A common misconception is that Muslim women are universally "forced" to wear the *hijab*. Only two countries, as of the time of writing, require women by law to wear *hijab*: Iran and Afghanistan. Many Islamic societies have a mixture of women, some of whom wear *hijab* and some of whom do not. In addition, some Muslim women, including some who would consider themselves feminists, quite pointedly insist that they *choose* to wear the *hijab* as an expression of their culture and values. Ultimately, *hijab* is an article of clothing like any other, and although it was common just a few decades ago for Western feminists to decry *hijab* as a form of oppression, there is an increasing consensus among feminists around the world today that the only truly *feminist* style of dress is a style of dress of the individual woman's own choosing.

Closely related to Islamophobic stereotypes about violence and misogyny in Islam is a great deal of fear-mongering about so-called Shariʻa Law. Islamophobes like to cite draconian punishments like stoning and the cutting off of limbs that they misleadingly claim are representative of Shariʻa Law to paint Islam as barbaric. They then, without any evidence whatsoever, claim that Muslims want to implement Shariʻa Law in their own countries to justify persecuting and stirring up hatred against Muslim minorities.

To begin with, the term "Shariʻa Law" is a misnomer. The word *shariʻa* in Arabic refers in the abstract to God's law or divine will, something that is ultimately beyond human beings' ability to fully comprehend. Such a concept is found in all the Abrahamic religions and therefore is not particularly unique to Islam. Islam does, however, like Judaism but unlike Christianity, have a system of religious law—a set of rules that in theory covers everything from criminal law to personal rules of morality and dietary restrictions. In Judaism, this system of religious law, known as *halakhah*, is based on the Torah, the first five books of the Bible. In Islam, the system of religious law, as concrete rules rather than God's will in the abstract, is known as *fiqh*, which can be translated as "jurisprudence." The rules that have been produced by Islamic *fiqh* are similar to those found in Jewish *halakhah* and probably are historically related to them—for example, Muslims, like Jews, are not supposed to eat pork, and Muslim men, like Jewish men, are supposed to be circumcised—but the system is separate and conceptualized differently.

The Islamic theory of *fiqh* is that God's will, *shari'a*—what he would want a good Muslim to do in a particular situation—is not fully knowable, but it can be approached by human minds through reason. Islam for most of its history has had a decentralized structure, and it does not have an ordained clergy. There are, however, certain men who are trained in *fiqh* known as *muftis*, or jurists. If a Muslim has a question about whether something is permissible or impermissible, or what to do in a particular situation, they go to a *mufti* and ask for a *fatwa*, or legal opinion. The most important authority that a *mufti* consults in making his decision is the Qur'an, because it is the literal word of God. The Qur'an specifically prohibits the drinking of alcohol, for example, so the general consensus in Islamic jurisprudence is that Muslims should not drink alcohol. There are many questions, however, that the Qur'an does not have a specific answer to. The second most important authority a *mufti* consults after the Qur'an is *hadith*. *Hadith* are stories about the life and sayings of the prophet Muhammad. Not all are considered equally authentic, and none are considered divine revelation, so they require critical analysis. Using these two main sources, as well as general Islamic tradition and his own reasoning, the *mufti* issues his *fatwa*. This *fatwa* is simply a legal opinion. By itself, it has no binding force, and two *muftis* may issue contradictory *fatwa*s on the same question.

The relationship between the world of *fiqh* and the actual criminal justice system in the Islamic world has varied widely over the centuries. Historically, *muftis* have been called upon to issue *fatwa*s on matters of criminal law. In the grand totality of the history of *fiqh*, there are punishments, such as stoning and the cutting off of limbs, that do not meet modern conceptions of humane punishment, as Islamophobes love to point out. This Islamophobic narrative is disingenuous, however. To begin with, *fiqh* consists entirely of legal opinions, issued at particular times and in particular places over history. It is not immutable scripture. It is true that historically *muftis* have issued *fatwa*s calling for punishments that today we might consider inhumane, but it is important to remember that *all* human cultures, including Western cultures, had laws and punishments in the past—often in the not-so-distant past—that today we would consider inhumane or barbaric. Judging Islam in its totality based on the fact that certain punishments might have been common in the Middle Ages makes about as much sense as judging Christianity in its totality based on the fact that it was common to burn heretics at the stake in medieval Europe.

In addition, in the modern world, with a few notable exceptions, Islamic jurisprudence is no longer involved with matters of criminal law. Most Islamic countries have secular systems of law that operate much like those in any other country in the world, with punishments that are in line with international norms, such as fines, incarceration, and in some cases the death penalty. Islamic jurisprudence is then limited to certain matters of civil law, such as marriage and divorce, as well as answering general questions about personal morality and religious practice that are not enforced by the state. Although there have been some high-profile cases, often sensationalized by the media, in which radical Islamist groups, in some cases exercising state power, have returned to the use of draconian historical punishments, this is the exception, not the norm.

The Islamophobic obsession with Shari'a and Islamic law, moreover, distorts the Western perception of Islamic culture by completely ignoring another equally important institution, the Sufi traditions. Many religions have a mystical tradition, a tradition that seeks a closer connection with the divine through a deeper, more internalized, and often esoteric interpretation of that religion's scripture or traditional teachings. Sufism is the Islamic mystical tradition, and it historically has played a very important role in Islam, perhaps more so than the mystical tradition within any other religion. Sufism does not form a separate branch of Islam; rather, Sufis are ordinary Muslims, usually Sunnis, who seek a closer connection to God through the Sufi path. Sufis are concerned with cultivating an *inner* state of perfection and closeness with God, which they call *ihsan*. They often contrast this to the *outer* practices of Shari'a and are critical of overly legalistic interpretations of Shari'a. This does not necessarily mean that Sufis do not follow the practices of Shari'a as determined by *fiqh*, but they consider the inner cultivation of *ihsan* to be of greater importance.

Islamic Sufism is organized a bit like Christian monasticism, insofar as Sufis belong to different orders, each with its own lineage and individual traditions. Each order is led by a *shaykh*, a teacher in a lineage that is said to go back to the prophet Muhammad himself. Unlike Christian monks, however, Sufis are married, since Islam does not valorize celibacy and in fact considers marriage preferable. Different Sufi orders follow various practices to cultivate *ihsan*, but most involve some form of *dhikr*, which is the practice of the remembrance of God. Islam in general is structured in such a way as to cultivate the remembrance of God among Muslims—for example, through the five daily prayers—so the Sufi practice of *dhikr* is simply an extension of this principle with the goal that the Sufi will be totally oriented toward God, remembering him during every waking moment. Practices of *dhikr* can be quite meditative, inducing a trancelike state in which the Sufi becomes totally absorbed in the remembrance of God.

The Sufi orders also played an important role in the spread of Islam as missionaries. In practical terms, Islam became a religion of world-historical importance through the rapid spread of the Islamic Empire, making it quite similar to Christianity, which also rose to world-historical importance through the Christianization of the Roman Empire. Most of the spread of Islam after the initial expansion of the Islamic Empire, however, was accomplished through trade and missionary activity. Sufis originally organized in response to what they saw as the corruption of the Umayyad Dynasty, and over the centuries they traveled beyond the borders of the original Islamic Empire with their message of deep devotion to God to bring Islam to new peoples in sub-Saharan Africa, Central Asia, and Southeast Asia. A common Western stereotype is that all Muslims are Arabs, but most Muslims today are not Arabs, in part because of the efforts of Sufi missionaries. The most populous Islamic country in the world today is Indonesia, in Southeast Asia.

The Western portrayal of Islam spreading through violent conquest is thus deeply hypocritical. After its initial military expansion in the first century or so of its existence, warfare had little to do with the expansion of Islam. Indeed, the Western accusation of Islam spreading through violence, as with all Islamophobic tropes, is clearly an act of projection. If I ask you, "Which religion tried to take over the world and make everyone convert?" Christianity fits this description much better than Islam. Over the course of the past five hundred or so years, Europeans engaged in a massive project of colonization that encompassed nearly the entire world, often with explicit missionary aims, and at times converting indigenous peoples to Christianity by force.

Without a doubt, there are problems within the Islamic world today. These include, as Islamophobes are all too quick to point out, extremist violence, repressive governments, and discrimination against women. There are two important points that we need to remember, however. The first is that the Islamic world is incredibly diverse, and conditions vary from country to country. Often Westerners hear about repressive conditions in one part of the Islamic world and just assume that they pertain to the Islamic world as a whole or somehow to Islam intrinsically.

The second point that we need to remember is that conditions in the Islamic world today are in large part the product of colonialism and contemporary geopolitics. A case in point: Unlike most of the Islamic world, Saudi Arabia is ruled by an autocratic monarchy that supports an extremely conservative interpretation of Islam and concordantly places severe restrictions on its citizens, especially women. Many of the stereotypes Westerners hold of repression in Islam actually come specifically from Saudi Arabia and are not representative of the Islamic world as a whole. But Saudi Arabia and its monarchy are actually *allies of the United States*. The United States has a military base in Saudi Arabia and supports the current Saudi regime. The other two most repressive regimes in the

Islamic world, the Islamic Republic of Iran and the Taliban of Afghanistan, also came to power inadvertently as a result of covert operations perpetrated by the CIA. Other stereotypes about violence or repression of women in Islam usually come from very particular circumstances, including extremist groups like ISIS, that are even less representative of Islam as a whole.

Why do Islamophobic tropes persist? If people feel the need to project anxieties about troubling patterns in their own religion or civilization onto another religion/civilization, why Islam, especially considering how similar Islam is to Christianity? I would argue that it is precisely *because of* this similarity that Islamophobia has proved so enduring, from the Middle Ages until today. There seems to be a human tendency to find fault in the small differences in those who are similar to us more so than the large differences in those who are obviously different from us. Likewise, looking at another person who is similar to us is like looking into a mirror. It forces us to confront the flaws we have in ourselves but provides the convenient excuse that those flaws are *really* in the other person, not in ourselves.

A quotation from George W. Bush explains perfectly what is so wrong-headed about Islamophobia. He was speaking about a different issue, but I think his words apply just as well to the fear and hatred of Islam that has become far too common today. He said, "Too often, we judge other groups by their worst examples, while judging ourselves by our best intentions."[9] Before we in the West judge Islamic civilization for violence, repression, and misogyny, we really should reflect on and reckon with the violence, repression, and misogyny in our own.

DISCUSSION QUESTIONS

1. In what ways is Islam closely similar to Christianity? What are some key differences?
2. Why are Islam, Christianity, and Judaism referred to as "Abrahamic religions"? Explain the significance of Abraham in some detail.
3. Explain in brief the five pillars of Islam and how they encapsulate the key practices and beliefs of Islam.
4. What is the main dividing line between Sunni and Shi'ite Islam, and how does it relate to Islam's early history?
5. What are the key themes of Islamophobia, and how do they paradoxically relate to the close relationship between Islam and Christianity?

NOTES

1. Take care to distinguish between these two terms. *Islam* refers to the religion and is only used in the singular. *Muslim* refers to a member of the religion of Islam. The more correct adjective to use in reference to something other than a person that has to do with Islam is *Islamic*, although it is not uncommon to see people use the word *Muslim* in English as a general adjective.
2. Q. 96:1–5 (Khattab, 597).
3. All Muslims, including Sunnis, use the word *imam* in a broader sense to refer to a man who leads public prayers at a mosque. The use of the word Imam here is a special sense used only by Shi'ites. It is usually distinguished in English by being capitalized.
4. The Liturgy of the Hours or Divine Office is a set of prayers, largely derived from the Book of Psalms in the Bible, recited at set times of the day by many monastics and clergy in various Christian Churches, especially in the Roman Catholic and Orthodox traditions.
5. This story is also found in the Bible, in the Book of Genesis. In that version, the son that God asks Abraham to sacrifice is Isaac. Many Islamic versions of the story say that the son in question was Ishmael, reflecting the fact that Muslims trace their lineage to Abraham through Ishmael, as opposed to Jews, who trace their lineage through Isaac. In either case, an angel stops Abraham at the last minute and substitutes a ram for the son in the sacrifice.
6. *Islamist* is not the same as Muslim or Islamic. It is a technical term that refers specifically to modern political movements that believe that the state should be run on fundamentalist Islamic principles.
7. Zoroastrianism is an ancient religion involving the worship of a God named Ahura Mazda. It was once the national religion of Persia, prior to conversion of that country to Islam after the Islamic conquest. There are a small number of Iranians today who still practice Zoroastrianism, as well as a small religious group in India known as Parsees, who are descended from Persian Zoroastrians.
8. There are some more extensive forms of *hijab*, such as the *niqab* and *burka*, which are intended to cover the face as well, but these are found only in certain Islamic societies and are far less common.
9. https://www.vox.com/2016/7/12/12164176/george-bush-dallas-shooting-speech-video

4

Buddhism
A Philosophy or a Religion?

Buddhism, at about half a billion followers, is among the smaller of the major world religions, but it has a long and expansive cultural influence in Asia, and in the West it is often perceived as emblematic of Asian religion. Buddhism began in India about 2,500 years ago, and although it mostly died out in that country in the early second millennium, it spread to other countries in East, Southeast, and Central Asia where it is still practiced by millions of people today. In addition, in the past hundred or so years, Buddhism has become increasingly popular in Western countries, making it a truly global religion. This popularity of Buddhism in the West has also led to new ways of understanding Buddhism that are shaped by modern Western sensibilities.

Buddhism, like Christianity and Islam, is a founded religion—it was founded in a particular time and place, by a particular human being. That person was the Buddha, a man who lived in what is now northern India and Nepal, probably in the fifth century BCE.[1] Like *Christ, Buddha* is not a name but a title; the Buddha's name, according to tradition, was Siddhartha Gautama. Gautama is referred to as the Buddha—and from there the religion gets its name—because Buddhists believe that he "woke up" to reality. The term *buddha* literally means "awakened." The Buddha's waking up to reality occurred while he was sitting under a tree in meditation. In English, it has become common to refer to that event as the Buddha's *Enlightenment*. The Buddha's Awakening or Enlightenment bears the same central importance in Buddhism as the Resurrection does in Christianity.

There is a standard story about the Buddha's life that, although it was probably not developed until a few centuries after his death, nevertheless has become accepted in all major Buddhist cultures. According

DOI: 10.4324/9781032646428-6

Buddhism: A Philosophy or a Religion?

Figure 4.1 The Mahamuni Buddha image in Mandalay, Myanmar (Burma). Photo by the author.

to this story, Siddhartha Gautama was a prince, born to Shuddhodana, king of a people called the Shakyas, with their capital at Kapilavastu in what is now Nepal. When Siddhartha was born, experts in physiognomy (a form of divination in which one makes predictions about a person's life based on signs in their body) declared that the baby Siddhartha was destined to become a "Great Man" who would fulfill one of two destinies. He would either become a great, world-conquering monarch, or he would become a Buddha, an "Awakened One" who renounced the world and penetrated the mysteries of existence. King Shuddhodana, like many fathers today, wanted his son to follow in his footsteps—that is, to become a king. He therefore raised Siddhartha in total luxury, giving him three palaces, the best food, and a harem of women to serve him. He also strove to make sure that Siddhartha would know nothing about suffering so that he would not be inclined toward abandoning kingship in favor of a more spiritual vocation. He therefore swept the palace grounds of all who were sick, old, or dead so that Siddhartha would not know of the existence of sickness, old age, and death.

Siddhartha thus grew up in the palace not knowing about the suffering inherent to life. When he was a young man, however, shortly after he had married and had a son, he became restless and curious about life outside of the palace. He therefore arranged for his charioteer, Channa, to help him sneak out of the palace several times. On each occasion, he encountered something he had never seen before: first a sick man, then an old man, and finally a corpse. Each time, he had to get Channa to explain what he was seeing, and Channa informed him that illness, old age, and death are forms of suffering that all human beings must experience. Siddhartha was shocked and distressed to learn this, and he became disenchanted with his life of luxury in the palace, which seemed shallow and pointless in light of the suffering we all must ultimately endure. In some versions of the story, Siddhartha then went out for a fourth time, during which he encountered a holy man, a person who had renounced everything and was living as a beggar, but who nevertheless seemed serene and content. In any case, Siddhartha decided to leave his family and life of luxury. With Channa's help, he snuck out for good in the middle of the night; after he was well away from the palace, he cut off his hair, exchanged luxurious clothes for rags, and sent Channa back.

Siddhartha then spent the next six years wandering as a religious mendicant seeking a penetrating insight into reality. He studied with two meditation teachers, but he did not feel that the highest meditative attainments they had reached represented the ultimate goal he sought. He then started performing extreme forms of *asceticism* with five other wandering religious seekers. (*Asceticism* is a word used in Religious Studies to refer to any sort of religious practice in which one deliberately denies oneself ordinary pleasures or comfort in pursuit of a religious goal.) The men he was practicing with engaged in various forms of asceticism, like standing motionless for long periods of time and exposing themselves to extreme heat, but Siddhartha himself chose to practice extreme fasting. According to the story, he ate only one grain of rice per day, and he became so emaciated that he could reach from the front of his abdomen and grab hold of his spine.

Obviously, at this point Siddhartha was suffering greatly because he was close to death. Yet he was still no closer to the goal he sought. So, one day he decided to give up and eat normally again. The five men he had been practicing with ridiculed him as weak in his practice and abandoned him. He then wandered for a bit until he found a tree that he thought would provide reasonable shelter; he sat down under the tree; and he vowed not to get up until he had achieved the penetrating insight into reality that he sought.

Over the course of that night, Siddhartha meditated, and he attained his goal. In Sanskrit, this goal is known by two metaphorical terms. The first is *bodhi*, which means "Awakening," and it is from this term that Siddhartha got the title Buddha, the Awakened One. Siddhartha "woke up" to ultimate reality, as if from a dream. The second term is *nirvana*,

Buddhism: A Philosophy or a Religion?

which means "blown out" (like a flame). This refers to the idea that the Buddha has blown out all passions, becoming cool and serene. In addition, it is common in English to refer to the ultimate goal in Buddhism as *Enlightenment*, which provides a third metaphor in which a light is turned on in the darkness. All three of these terms—Awakening, *nirvana*, and Enlightenment—refer to the same thing.

At this point, the Buddha wanted to teach his Awakening to others, so he decided to seek out the five men he had been practicing asceticism with. At first, they didn't want to even acknowledge him because they thought he was pathetic for giving up his hard-core asceticism, but then they saw that he was so serene that they could not help but offer him a seat. The Buddha then proceeded to teach them what he had learned, and they became the first five Buddhist monks. The Buddha spent the rest of his life wandering around north India, ordaining more monks, establishing an order of nuns, and gaining many lay followers as well before his death at age eighty. When he died, he did not appoint an individual successor. Instead, he made his teaching, known as the *dharma*, his successor, and he entrusted the Buddhist community, known as the *sangha*, with teaching it. To this day, these three things: the Buddha, the *dharma*, and the *sangha*, are known as the "three jewels" in Buddhism. Although there is no specific ceremony for becoming a Buddhist, Buddhists traditionally

Figure 4.2 Buddhist monks on their morning alms round in Luang Prabang, Laos. Photo by the author.

acknowledge themselves as such through a short recitation in which they "take refuge" in the three jewels.

From the beginning, Buddhism was a missionary religion: Buddhists travelled and sought to spread the *dharma* as widely as possible, because anyone according to Buddhism is capable of achieving the Awakening that the Buddha achieved. In addition, the first emperor who conquered nearly all of India, King Ashoka (r. 268–232 BCE), was a Buddhist, and his missionary efforts spread Buddhism quickly throughout the Indian subcontinent and to some neighboring countries. In the following centuries, Buddhist missionaries spread the *dharma* and set up local *sanghas* (communities of monks and sometimes nuns) in countries throughout East, Southeast, and Central Asia.

As already mentioned, Buddhism mostly died out in India in the early second millennium, but it remains a major religion in three Asian regions outside of India, each of which practices a different form of Buddhism. In the Southeast Asian countries of Burma, Thailand, Laos, and Cambodia, as well as the island country Sri Lanka, a majority of people practice a form of Buddhism called Theravada ("the Doctrine of the Elders"), which uses the very oldest Buddhist texts as their scriptures. These scriptures are known collectively as the *Tipitaka*, or "Triple Basket." They are so called because they have three parts: the *Sutta Pitaka*, which contains texts called *suttas* that recount episodes and teachings from the Buddha's life; the *Vinaya Pitaka*, which contains the rules and regulations for the Buddhist monastic institution, the *sangha*; and the *Abhidhamma Pitaka*, which contains more systematic philosophical explications of the Buddhist *dharma*.

In the East Asian countries of China, Japan, Korea, and Taiwan, as well as the Southeast Asian country Vietnam, another form of Buddhism called Mahayana ("the Great Vehicle") is practiced. This form of Buddhism is based on texts called Mahayana *sutras* that were written a few centuries after the time of the Buddha and claim to teach a superior Buddhist path that allows one to become a fully Awakened Buddha. Finally, in Tibet, Mongolia, Nepal, and Bhutan, people practice Vajrayana ("Thunderbolt Vehicle") Buddhism, which is a subsect of Mahayana Buddhism. These Buddhists follow the Mahayana *sutras* but also another set of scriptures, written a few centuries later, known as *tantras*, that provide instructions for various rituals, including rituals that claim to provide a shortcut to Awakening. Theravada, Mahayana, and Vajrayana thus represent the three major traditional branches of Buddhism.

In addition to the three traditional forms of Buddhism, there is a fourth form of Buddhism emerging in the modern world that scholars refer to as "Buddhist Modernism." This form of Buddhism tends to present Buddhism as a religion unlike all other religions, one that is uniquely scientific and rational, more of a philosophy than a religion. There is nothing intrinsically wrong with this, but it does represent a significant departure from traditional forms of Buddhism, and yet it is typically the only form of Buddhism that people in the West hear about. When Westerners hear about or become interested in Buddhism, they often are presented—by the media, by popular culture, by popular books, and so forth—with Buddhist Modernism, but as if that simply were what Buddhism *is*. In fact, it is quite possible that if you have heard about Buddhism from Western popular culture, what you have actually heard about is this new form of Buddhism. Therefore, I am going to start in the next section by outlining Buddhism as it is presented within Buddhist Modernism. Then, I will explain what aspects of traditional Buddhism this leaves out and how they fit together. Finally, at the end of the chapter we will see how Buddhist Modernism came about and how it represents one but by no means the only form of Buddhism practiced today.

BUDDHIST MODERNISM: BUDDHISM AS A PHILOSOPHY OF LIFE

As I already mentioned above, after he attained Awakening, the Buddha went back to the five men he had been practicing with and taught them what he had learned. The contents of this teaching, the Buddha's first sermon, are found in an old Buddhist scripture called "Turning the Wheel of Dharma into Motion" (*Dhammacakkappavattana Sutta*). In it, the Buddha begins by explaining why he gave up his extreme fasting and started eating normally again. He says that he has discovered the "Middle Way"—a religious path between two extremes. These two extremes are hedonism—indulging one's every pleasure—and extreme asceticism—punishing the body through harsh practices like fasting. Note that these two extremes are reflected in the Buddha's traditional biography: He spent his childhood and young adult life in the palace indulging his sensual pleasures, and he spent his years with the five ascetics doing the exact opposite. He tells them that both these extremes are worthless because they lead to suffering. The Middle Path that he has discovered, however, avoids these two extremes and leads to the end of suffering.

The Buddha then turns to his second teaching, which is known as the Four Noble Truths. The Four Noble Truths can be understood as *the* central teaching of Buddhism. They outline the basic Buddhist worldview, the goal of Buddhism, and the path for reaching that goal.

The first Noble Truth is that life is thoroughly characterized by suffering. We are all aware that we suffer in life. Sometimes we get sick, we get injured and experience pain, or we experience mental anguish during a breakup or when a loved one dies. Ultimately, we all die. So, there are certainly times in life when we obviously suffer. But the Buddha is making a stronger claim than this. He says that suffering thoroughly suffuses life as we ordinary beings live it. Even when we think we are happy, we are suffering on a deeper level.

This might sound overly pessimistic at first, but bear with me for a minute. The reason for this insistence on life being suffering is that, according to Buddhism, everything we experience is impermanent. We can see impermanence in the weather, in the seasons, in rivers that are constantly flowing, and even in the mountains that over millions of years are pushed up out of the ground and then worn down by erosion. But most importantly, we see impermanence in ourselves. Obviously, we see this in our bodies. If you are old enough to read this book, then you certainly are much bigger than you were when you were born. Assuming you live to an old age, you will look much different when you die.

Even more importantly, our mental/emotional lives are impermanent. Our thoughts and emotions are constantly changing. I'm sure you can think back to something you said or did ten years ago or so that, when you think about it in retrospect, you can't believe that you said or did. It's like you were a different person. That's because, in a sense, you were a different person. You're not the same person you were when you were born; you're not the same person you were ten years ago; you're not the same person who woke up this morning; you're not even the same person you were when you started reading this sentence. Everything, then, according to Buddhism, is impermanent. Buddhism does not appeal to things like God or a soul that are considered eternal but beyond the reach of ordinary sensory experience. And since everything is impermanent, even the ordinary happiness we feel is suffering, because it will not last.

This leads to the second noble truth, which is that the cause of suffering is craving. Craving here is of two types. The first type is what we usually mean by craving: desperately wanting something you don't have. Maybe you'd like to eat some chocolate now, but you don't have any. You're not suffering because you don't have chocolate; you're suffering because you crave it. The other type of craving is a negative sort of craving; it's a craving that pushes away. Let's say there's someone at work you can't stand. You really hate working with them, and you feel miserable every time you have to interact with them. You're not suffering because of that person per se, but rather because of your reaction to them. You "crave" having them out of your life. In all cases of craving, you are acting as if things are permanent even though they are not. Your state of not having chocolate is not permanent. But even if you get chocolate, the happiness you get from chocolate won't be permanent either. So why are you worrying so damn much about chocolate? The same goes with your lousy coworker. Having to work with them is not permanent, and being rid of them in your life won't bring permanent happiness either—so what is all the fuss about? The Buddha is basically saying that we live our lives in an addictive sort of way, constantly clinging to this or that in an effort to gain a happiness that can never be gained from impermanent things.

The third noble truth follows logically from the second. It states simply that if you stop craving, you will stop suffering. You have to let go and not cling to impermanent things anymore. This is the goal of Buddhism, which is called *nirvana*, a state of bliss and freedom from suffering born of non-attachment. Reaching this state is easier said than done, however. We can't just snap our fingers and stop craving. We have deeply inborn habitual tendencies that lead us to crave. The fourth noble truth therefore provides a path to end craving and thus end suffering. It is the Noble Eightfold Path: right view, right intention, right speech, right action, right livelihood, right effort, right mindfulness, right concentration. The eight limbs of this path lead from an acknowledgment of the predicament of our existence, through basic tenets of morality, and finally to meditative practices that are intended to uproot the habitual tendencies that cause us to crave and thus suffer.

Buddhism presented in this way, as encapsulated in the Four Noble Truths, has become increasingly attractive in the last hundred years or so to Western people who are disenchanted with the religious tradition they grew up in, usually Christianity or Judaism. All of us recognize that we suffer in life, and Buddhism provides a way out of this. But it does so without appealing to God, some divine being or beings we can't see, or the need for faith. There's no need for rituals that seem pointless and boring. You don't have to believe in heaven or hell, God, angels, or any of the things that seem so unscientific about Western religions. In fact, many have claimed that Buddhism is a uniquely scientific religion.[2] The Four Noble Truths are in any case very logical principles that one can apply in one's everyday life. Life is suffering, that suffering has a cause, and if you eliminate that cause, you will no longer suffer. For this reason, some have claimed that Buddhism is more a philosophy than a religion.

TRADITIONAL BUDDHISM

As we saw in chapter 1, *religion* is a Western concept that only got applied worldwide in the colonial period, so Buddhism, until recently almost completely confined to Asia, was not traditionally conceived of as a religion. Nevertheless, in the modern world, there are very good reasons for calling Buddhism a religion. The claim that Buddhism is a philosophy, not a religion, is deeply misleading. The account of Buddhism I just gave above, while completely authentic with respect to traditional Buddhism, also leaves a whole lot out. Indeed, all we have to do is read the end of the "Setting the Wheel of Dharma into Motion" scripture to see that what we are dealing with here is not simply a philosophy for living a better life. After the Buddha finishes telling the five ascetics about the Four Noble Truths, he says that upon realizing these truths, he also realized that this would be his last birth, that he would no longer be reborn. Then, a variety of gods in multiple heavens called out and rejoiced at the Buddha's teaching. The entire universe shook and a bright light surpassing that of the gods was seen.

What's going on here?! What happened to the rational philosophy that Buddhism is so often presented as being? Western portrayals of Buddhism as rational and scientific are right to focus on the Four Noble Truths, but they also leave out a key element of traditional Buddhism: the overall Buddhist worldview. According to Buddhism, all living beings are trapped in a cycle of rebirth called *samsara*. Often people in the West think that rebirth is cool, but this is not how it is conceived of in Buddhism or any Asian religions. Rebirth is characterized by old age, sickness, and death—that is, constant suffering. We are trapped in this cycle of rebirth because of karma. *Karma* literally means "action," but in Buddhism it refers first and foremost to our moral intentions to do good or evil, which in turn affect what happens to us in the future, including how we are reborn. Good actions can bring us a better rebirth, but all forms of rebirth are characterized by impermanence and thus suffering. The goal of Buddhism, *nirvana*, is not simply to end suffering in this life, but to bring an end to rebirth and thus suffering altogether. When the Buddha attained *nirvana*, he never was reborn again.

The concept of rebirth obviously points to a conception of life after death that is at odds with modern science. It also entails a world inhabited by what modern people would call supernatural beings. According to Buddhism, there are six major realms of rebirth. One of them is the human realm. But you can also be reborn as an animal if your karma is characterized particularly by ignorance. If you are greedy, you may be reborn as a hungry ghost. These are ghosts who are doomed to wander about constantly hungry. If you are a hateful person and commit sins like murder, you will be reborn in hell. Vivid depictions of the torments of hell, rivaling the fiery sermons of Jonathan Edwards or the descriptions of Dante's *Inferno*, are common in Buddhist temples. The only difference between Buddhist hell and Christian hell is that Buddhist hell is impermanent. You will be tormented there for a long time, but eventually you will die and be reborn somewhere else.

If you do good deeds in your life, you could be reborn as a god. Buddhism, like Christianity, arose in a world where the worship of many gods was common. Unlike Christianity, however, Buddhism did not deny the existence of the gods or reduce them to demonic status. According to Buddhism, the gods are real, but they (like everything else) are impermanent. So, if you are reborn as a god, that's great, and it may last many millions of years (the gods live a long time), but it won't last forever. It's still not *nirvana*, escape from the cycle of rebirth, which is the ultimate goal.[3]

Although the Buddha was a human being and is not generally considered to be God in the Christian sense, traditionally he is considered to be what we might call a supernatural being by virtue of his Awakening. The Buddha, according to the Buddhist scriptures, could remember his past lives and see how people are going to be reborn; he could walk on water, levitate, and walk through walls; he had the ability to see and hear things at long distances; he routinely had conversations with the gods and other supernatural beings; and he could perform miracles. The Buddha is worshiped by Buddhists in much the same way one might worship a god. Most traditional Buddhist temples have a central statue of the Buddha before which Buddhists bow and make offerings of flowers, candles, incense, and the like.

All the supernatural elements that I have described so far are found in all traditional forms of Buddhism. In Mahayana Buddhism, practiced in East and Central Asia, there are additional elements that are even more reminiscent of things we associate with religion. Mahayana Buddhism is premised on the idea that all of us can and should strive to become Buddhas. This is a subtle distinction from earlier non-Mahayana Buddhism, which holds that all can and should strive for *nirvana*, but that Buddhas are rare beings, appearing only once every cosmic eon, who possess a special form of Awakening. In all forms of Buddhism, a being that is on the path to becoming a Buddha is called a Bodhisattva, which literally means, "Being of Awakening." Since Mahayana Buddhism advocates for all to strive to become Buddhas, it is also referred to as the Bodhisattva Path.

Mahayana Buddhism's Bodhisattva Path has two logical implications: (1) There should be a lot of Buddhas in the cosmos, even right now, and

(2) there should be many Bodhisattvas who are very advanced on the path and close to Buddhahood. The belief in advanced Bodhisattvas is a commonplace in Mahayana Buddhist societies. These Bodhisattvas are considered to be so advanced on the path that they have special powers beyond those of normal beings. You can pray to them, and they can help you, both with ordinary problems in your life and with the path to *nirvana*. In this way, they serve a role very similar to gods or saints in other religions. By far the most well-known and popular Bodhisattva in Mahayana Buddhist societies is Avalokiteshvara, the Bodhisattva of Compassion. Avalokiteshvara has a thousand arms, and each hand has an eye in it so that he can look for people to help with his compassion. Originally, Avalokiteshvara was conceived of as male, but in East Asia he was transformed into a woman and is known, in Chinese, as Guanyin. Guanyin is a popular focus of devotion in China and throughout East Asia. In Tibet, the Dalai Lama, the highest Buddhist leader and king, is understood to be a reincarnation of Avalokiteshvara.

The other corollary of the Bodhisattva Path is that there should be many fully Awakened Buddhas in the world, even right now. We haven't had any in our visible world since Siddhartha Gautama lived in India over 2,000 years ago, so where are they? Mahayana Buddhism has for this reason developed a belief in "Pure Lands"—special faraway lands that have been purified by Buddhas to make it easier for people to attain Awakening. The most popular Pure Land Buddha is Amitabha. He has created a Pure Land in the West (a mythical West by modern geographical understandings) called Sukhavati. If you pray to him, chant his name, and are devoted to him, he will bring you to his Pure Land after you die, and it will be easy to attain *nirvana* there. Devotion to Amitabha is incredibly popular throughout East Asia, to the point that Amitabha has arguably become more important in those Buddhist countries than the historical Buddha who founded Buddhism in India. Pure Land Buddhism, as it is called, is essentially a salvation religion like Christianity in which devotion to a savior brings about salvation.

Mahayana Buddhists have also developed conceptions of the Buddha that transform him into a supernatural being rather than simply a human being who reached the highest attainment. According to a key Mahayana Buddhist theory, the Buddha has three bodies. The first, the Dharma Body, is reality itself. *Dharma* originally referred to the teaching of the Buddha or the reality it points to, but in Mahayana Buddhism it is seen as the Buddha in his form as a cosmic principle. The second body of the Buddha is the Enjoyment Body. The Enjoyment Body is the Buddha's form as a supernatural cosmic being, which exists in a perpetual state of Awakening. In this form, the Buddha has something like the status of a god or God in other religions. The third body is the Buddha's Emanation Body. This is the form in which the Buddha appears as a human being who is born, undertakes the path, attains Awakening, teaches the *dharma*, and establishes a *sangha* of disciples. But this is simply a phantasm, a show put on by the eternal Buddha to provide an example of how to attain *nirvana*. Mahayana Buddhism thus flips the script on what the Buddha is. In the oldest Buddhist scriptures, the Buddha was simply an exemplary human being who escaped from *samsara*. In Mahayana Buddhism, he becomes a cosmic being, the essence of Awakening itself, who projects an image (an emanation) into the world to show beings the way to realizing their true nature.

There is one last aspect of traditional forms of Buddhism that differs markedly from Buddhist Modernism: ritual. In contrast to the frequent portrayal of Buddhism in the West as being without ritual, all traditional forms of Buddhism are full of rituals. This is particularly true of Vajrayana Buddhism, a subdivision of Mahayana Buddhism that is practiced in Central Asia. As we will learn in more detail in chapter 8, this form of Buddhism is based on a set of scriptures called *tantra*s, all of which are dedicated to establishing elaborate rituals—rituals to help one with worldly concerns and rituals to help one attain Awakening. Until relatively recently, many Westerners, even those who were sympathetic to Buddhism, were disdainful toward Vajrayana Buddhism because of the centrality of ritual within it, seeing this is a corruption of the Buddhist tradition. But, in fact, all traditional forms of Buddhism, including also Theravada and Mahayana Buddhism, have rituals. The idea that rituals are meaningless, pointless, or lacking in power is a modern prejudice that is not reflected in traditional ways of thinking about the Four Noble Truths and the Buddhist path.

HOW THEY FIT TOGETHER

Sometimes people in the West who think that Buddhism is a rational, scientific philosophy are shocked and even disdainful when they hear about the aspects of traditional Buddhism that do not fit into their preconceived notions of what Buddhism is. They then go on to rationalize the supernatural aspects of Buddhism as simple marketing tools that were used to make Buddhism appealing to the ignorant masses in the past. So, for example, Buddhist scriptures may depict the Buddha conversing with gods not because he believed in or taught about gods but to cast the Buddha in a favorable light in front of people who believed in and worshipped the gods.

This way of looking at traditional Buddhism is, to begin with, condescending, and it reflects the imperious attitude of Westerners towards Asians that characterized the colonial period. Given that millions of Asian Buddhists over the course of over two millennia have believed in, worshipped, and aspired to become gods, it is astoundingly arrogant for a person from outside of those cultures to suddenly come in and say that traditional Buddhists don't understand their own religion. This is why I said in chapter 2 that exotifying forms of Orientalism (such as the idea that Buddhism is just a philosophy) are just as harmful as overtly negative forms of Orientalism (such as Islamophobia).

But a dismissive attitude towards the supernatural aspects of traditional Buddhism is not only condescending; it also represents a misunderstanding of the close way in which they are integrated with Buddhist philosophy. Yes, Buddhism accepts the existence of the gods and other supernatural beings, but it does not accept that the gods are immortal. The gods may live for a long time, even millions of years, but like all beings trapped in *samsara*, they will eventually die and be reborn. They thus reflect the key Buddhist principle of impermanence. In addition, the entire Buddhist cosmos, populated as it is with both natural (humans and animals) and supernatural (gods, demons, and ghosts) beings, is governed by the law of karma. Karma in traditional Buddhism does not only explain what happens to us in this life; it also explains what happens to us after we die. Supernatural beings in Buddhism are thus not simply "superstitious" holdovers from earlier religions; they are manifestations of the central Buddhist emphasis on moral causality.

The more supernatural understanding of the Buddha in Mahayana Buddhism also has its roots in Buddhist philosophy. Buddhists have developed a variety of philosophical schools and perspectives over the centuries, but one of the most influential of these philosophical schools in Mahayana Buddhism is called Yogachara. Although Yogachara is a unique philosophical perspective found only in Mahayana Buddhism, it is based on earlier ideas in Buddhist philosophy. One of the earliest teachings of Buddhist philosophical thought is that there is no such thing as a self. Many teachers in the Buddha's day taught that at our core, each of us has a true "self," or in Sanskrit *atman*, and that it is this true self that moves from body to body in the process of rebirth. If we realize our essential *atman*, then we will be liberated from *samsara*, the cycle of rebirth. This idea, in fact, became important to Hinduism.

Buddhists, however, rejected this idea. The Buddha taught that all things—and in particular our bodies and minds—are *anatman*, or "not self." This is because he also taught that all things are impermanent, and the teachers of the *atman* believed that this self is eternal and unchanging. Buddhists of course do believe in rebirth, but they understand this as a natural process in which different causes and conditions come together in the right way to create a link from one life to the next. There is no permanent "thing" that moves from one body to the next.[4]

Nearly all Buddhists accept the philosophical position of *anatman*, but Mahayana Buddhism particularly emphasizes it with a concept that they call *shunyata*, or "emptiness." Indeed, the earliest Mahayana scriptures are structured around a central emphasis on understanding emptiness. Emptiness means that not only living beings, but in fact all things in the universe, no matter how great or small, lack a permanent essence. They are empty of self-existence. This might sound quite heady and abstract, but it really is just a reemphasis of the Buddhist idea of impermanence—that there is no such thing as a permanent entity. Everything changes.

Yogachara philosophy developed in part to expand upon the Mahayana concept of emptiness. Yogachara philosophers asked, what is going on when you are aware of a sense object—that is, when you see, hear, smell, taste, or feel something? Is there really some "thing" out there that you are seeing, hearing, or otherwise sensing? According to the principle of emptiness, the answer should be no. So, then what is happening when we see and hear things and so forth, if those things are not really there? The Yogachara philosophers answered this question by saying that all these things are "just mind." For this reason, Yogachara is also referred to as the "Mind-Only" school.

From a technical philosophical perspective, the Yogachara position is that there is no distinction between the subject that is aware of sense objects and the objects of that awareness. But even if the technical philosophical position seems difficult to grasp, the practical import of it is quite simple. Yogachara philosophers are saying that reality is like a dream. In a dream, we see and hear things, but they are not separate things "out there." They are just manifestations of our mind. Likewise, the proponents of this philosophical school say that all of reality as we experience it is like a dream. There is no world out there; it is just a projection of our mind. This position, incidentally, works quite well with Buddhism's central metaphor of waking up. The Buddha, the Awakened One, according to Yogachara, woke up from ordinary existence, which is like a dream in which we think that the external world is real, when in fact all of this is just a trick of mind.

To be clear, Yogachara philosophy does not think of the mind as the ultimate self. This would go against foundational Buddhist principles. Mind is an ever-changing process, and a complex one at that, as it results in the creation of not just one but billions upon billions of intertwined subjectivities (i.e., all the beings trapped in *samsara*). What Yogachara rejects is dualism: the assumption that there is a fundamental distinction between mind, which is aware of external objects, and matter, which comprises the objects that mind is aware of. It is all just mind.

Yogachara has some pretty useful side benefits for explaining Buddhist ideas. Buddhists always believed that Buddhas and other people with high meditative attainment could perform miracles like levitation, walking through walls, walking on water, remembering past lives, and so forth. Yogachara has a simple explanation for this: Buddhas and others with high attainment have sufficient insight into the mind-only nature of reality that they are able to manipulate it, just as ordinary people can manipulate their own minds through acts of imagination. Yogachara also has a ready explanation for the law of karma. Why is it that someone is born in hell after committing murder in a previous life, for example? Since everything is just mind, committing the act of murder plants a "seed" in mind that comes to fruition in the form of experiencing the torments of hell later on. Hell is not a place that you go to after you die; it is your own mind tormenting you because of the evil deed you committed in the past.

The Mahayana doctrine of the Three Bodies of the Buddha developed out of this same mind-only philosophical outlook. Buddhists from an early date had talked about two bodies of the Buddha—his physical body and the body of his teachings, the *dharma*. Originally this was mostly a metaphor, a way of saying that the Buddha, although he has died and is no longer reborn, nonetheless lives on through the *dharma*. But Mahayana Buddhists began to rethink this metaphor in light of the Yogachara philosophical outlook. If physical objects (including bodies) are ultimately just manifestations of mind, then maybe it is not best to understand the Buddha as merely a human being who discovered the *dharma*. Maybe it is better to look at it the other way round: The Buddha's most fundamental body is the *dharma* itself, with his human body a manifestation emerging from it. That would make the manifestation of the Buddha's earthly career an act of compassion emerging from the *dharma*, with the "Buddha" a conventional term for a cosmic being (the Enjoyment Body) who displays that compassion for us ordinary beings.

I have delved a bit deeply into Buddhist philosophy here not because it is necessary for the introductory student to understand the intricacies of such philosophy but because I want to make a point. All the supernatural elements of traditional Buddhism are grounded in and often motivated by deeply philosophical concerns. It is not faithful to the tradition to separate Buddhist "philosophy" from Buddhist "religion." We have an ethical responsibility to take traditional forms of Buddhism seriously and not adopt a condescending attitude that regards them as corruptions of the pure Buddhist teachings. But this condescending attitude is also just wrong on the facts. Buddhist philosophy has always been intertwined with the supernatural and in fact generative of evolving Buddhist ideas about how the world works that, while unique, are quite similar to those of other religions.

THE ORIGINS OF BUDDHIST MODERNISM

Having said this, I want to make clear that there is nothing intrinsically wrong with being a Buddhist Modernist. You yourself may have an interest in Buddhism but prefer to understand Buddhist ideas within a modern, rational, scientific framework. In other words, you may find the Four Noble Truths meaningful and the Buddhist Path appealing as a way to address suffering in this very life but have no interest in developing new beliefs about supernatural beings or devotional practices toward them. Many people in the West become interested in Buddhism precisely because they are dissatisfied with their own religious traditions, or Western religions in general, and they find Buddhist ideas meaningful *without* appeal to the aspects of Western religions, especially Christianity and Judaism, that may seem incompatible with the modern scientific worldview. In fact, I was one such person myself when I was in high school and college.

It is useful in this respect to understand a bit about how Buddhist Modernism came about. Buddhist Modernism was not simply a racist conspiracy by Westerners to steal the Buddhist tradition and remake it in an image that they found acceptable. In the nineteenth century, at the height of the colonial period, Buddhist leaders in Asian countries often faced competition and even outright hostility from Christian missionaries who sought to convert Asian Buddhists. In so doing, the missionaries relied on typical Orientalist themes to paint Buddhism as irrational, unscientific, immature, evil, and the like.

Buddhist leaders, however, also found allies in other Westerners who had learned about Buddhism and were interested in and sympathetic toward it. Given their modern Western sensibilities, these Buddhist sympathizers tended to be more interested in certain aspects of Buddhist philosophy that could be understood in a modern scientific framework. Some Asian Buddhist leaders, in concert with these Western sympathizers, started to flip the script on the Christian missionaries. They pointed to the aspects of Buddhist philosophy that were appealing to modern, rationalistic Westerners and contrasted this Buddhist philosophy with aspects of the Christian tradition that could be considered irrational, unscientific, immature, and evil.

In this respect, they were striking at exactly the right time, as Europe had just gone through an intense period of intellectual change known as the Enlightenment, in which prominent European thinkers began questioning many of the key tenets of Christian faith—including the supernatural, the possibility of miracles, and even the existence of God—and labeling them as irrational. (Incidentally, the rebranding of Buddhist Awakening as "Enlightenment" is a result of the encounter with ideas associated with the European Enlightenment.) Not all Asian Buddhist leaders participated in this thoroughgoing rethinking of the Buddhist tradition, and even those who did participate did not always agree with their Western sympathizers on what parts of traditional Buddhism should be discarded, but the cumulative effect was a movement in which both Westerners attracted to Buddhist teachings and Asian Buddhists themselves developed new ideas about how the Buddhist *dharma* could best be understood within the modern scientific worldview. The result was Buddhist Modernism, a new form of Buddhism adapted for the modern world.

The rise of Buddhist Modernism is not unique or unusual. It is not unique within the history of Buddhism, and it is not unique within the context of world religions. Over the course of the past two and a half millennia, as Buddhism spread to various countries beyond its homeland of India, it has always adapted to local culture and given rise to new forms of Buddhism. Tibetan Buddhism, Chinese Buddhism, and Thai Buddhism, to name just a few examples, are all unique and different from one another, in part, because of the cultural sensibilities in those countries that shaped how Buddhism was received and understood. Buddhist Modernism is simply another manifestation of this phenomenon, albeit a less geographically bound one. It is not the result of the spread of Buddhism to a specific place, but rather of the encounter between Buddhism and an emerging global culture of modernity that is typically represented by highly educated cultural elites who live in cities around the globe.

The rise of Buddhist Modernism is also not unique to Buddhism. All religions, including Christianity, have rethought key elements of their worldview in light of the discoveries of modern science and new intellectual sensibilities associated with the Enlightenment. For example, whereas premodern Christians might have understood heaven and hell as existing quite literally as physical places "up there" in the sky and "down below" the surface of the earth, modern Christians typically understand these "places" more abstractly, as modes of existence after death. Of course, not all Christians are equally committed to rethinking traditional Christian teachings in light of the modern scientific worldview; many Christians, in fact, are quite committed to belief in angels, demons, miracles, and the supernatural in general. This can create an optical illusion for Westerners who are attracted to Buddhism. They know from their own cultural experience in the West, or even their own upbringing in Western religious communities, that Christianity historically and even today for many involves things that they see as conflicting with modernity. But if all these Western sympathizers know about Buddhism is the portrait painted by Buddhist Modernism, they have no way of knowing that Buddhism is really no different from Christianity in this respect.

There is therefore nothing intrinsically wrong with Buddhist Modernism or with being a Buddhist Modernist. Where it becomes problematic is when a Westerner attracted to Buddhism assumes that the only real form of Buddhism is Buddhist Modernism and that any form of Buddhism that does not conform to the modern rationality of Buddhist Modernism is ridiculous, corrupt, or simply not real Buddhism. This attitude is not only ignorant of the Buddhist tradition but also condescending and Orientalist.

DISCUSSION QUESTIONS

1. Who was the Buddha? When/where did he live? In broad strokes, what is the traditional story about his life?
2. What are the Four Noble Truths? How do they identify the problem inherent in living existence and the solution to it?
3. Why is it misleading to say that Buddhism is a philosophy, not a religion? What are some of the religion-y aspects of traditional forms of Buddhism?
4. What are the three major branches of Buddhism? How do they differ from one another?
5. What is Buddhist Modernism? How did it come about?

NOTES

1 The abbreviation BCE means "Before the Common Era." Many scholars today, especially Religious Studies scholars, prefer to use this abbreviation instead of BC, which means "Before Christ." The abbreviation BC clearly reflects a specifically Christian perspective, while BCE is more neutral. The corresponding replacement for AD (from the Latin *anno domini*, "in the year of our Lord") is CE, which means "Common Era." None of this change in nomenclature changes

the actual dates we use, or the fact that our modern calendar was based on a (probably inaccurate) calculation of Jesus Christ's birth.

2   For a history of this idea that Buddhism is scientific, see Donald S. Lopez, *The Scientific Buddha: His Short and Happy Life* (New Haven: Yale University Press, 2012).

3   I said that there are six realms of rebirth, but I have only discussed five here. The sixth is the realm of the *asuras*. The *asuras* are demi-gods; they have a role in Indian mythology somewhat akin to the Titans in Greek mythology. Their inclusion in traditional Buddhist depictions of the cycle of rebirth is mostly for mythological completeness.

4   The traditional Buddhist view is that it is the consciousness that moves from one body to the next and thus maintains the continuity of personality across rebirth. But the consciousness is a process, not a permanent self like the *atman*.

# 5

Hinduism
A Polytheistic or a Monotheistic Religion?

If you are not yourself Hindu, you may not know much about Hinduism, but you probably know one thing for certain: Hindus worship many gods. Indeed, this is one of the common ways Hinduism is portrayed in the West. Aside from giving us Yoga, the greeting *namaste*, and the sacred syllable OM, Hinduism is seen as an exotic Indian religion in which people worship many gods, many of whom have many arms (like Vishnu) or the characteristics of animals (like the monkey-god Hanuman or the elephant-headed god Ganesh). Hinduism is, simply put, the quintessential polytheistic religion of the modern world.

It may surprise you, then, that if you ask Hindus about their religion, many of them will tell you that it is monotheistic. According to a 2019–2020 survey by the Pew Research Center, the world's premier institution for demographic research about religion, a whopping 90% of Hindus say that they believe in one God, while only 7% say that they believe in multiple gods.[1] In 2005–2006, Hindu groups in the United States protested the depiction of Hinduism in proposed textbooks for schoolchildren in the state of California, with one of their objections being that the religion is monotheistic, rather than polytheistic as stated in the proposed text.[2]

Indeed, many Hindus have been trying to tell Western audiences that Hinduism is not polytheistic for well over a hundred years. In 1893, an event called the World's Parliament of Religions was held in Chicago. Held in conjunction with the World Columbian Exhibition, it was intended to foster dialog between the different religions of the world. Scholars today now see this 1893 Parliament as a pivotal moment in shaping the discourse on religion in the United States and around the world in the twentieth century and beyond. Representing Hinduism

DOI: 10.4324/9781032646428-7

at the Parliament was Swami Vivekananda, a disciple of the Hindu mystic Ramakrishna and a prominent Hindu reformer in his own right. His appearance at the Parliament was a sensation and played an important role in fixing Hinduism as a world religion in the Western consciousness and even in promoting Hinduism among Westerners as a religious option.

During one of his speeches to the Parliament, one that was intended to introduce Hinduism to his listeners, Vivekananda said,

> Descend we now from the aspirations of philosophy to the religion of the ignorant. At the very outset, I may tell you that there is no *polytheism* in India. In every temple, if one stands by and listens, one will find the worshippers applying all the attributes of God, including omnipresence, to the images. It is not polytheism, nor would the name henotheism explain the situation. "The rose called by any other name would smell as sweet." Names are not explanations.
>
> . . . Superstition is a great enemy of man, but bigotry is worse. Why does a Christian go to church? Why is the cross holy? Why is the face turned toward the sky in prayer? Why are there so many images in the Catholic Church? Why are there so many images in the minds of Protestants when they pray? My brethren, we can no more think about anything without a mental image than we can live without breathing. By the law of association, the material image calls up the mental idea and *vice versa*. This is why the Hindu uses an external symbol when he worships. He will tell you, it helps to keep his mind fixed on the Being to whom he prays. He knows as well as you do that the image is not God, is not omnipresent. . . .
>
> As we find that somehow or other, by the laws of our mental constitution, we have to associate our ideas of infinity with the image of the blue sky, or of the sea, so we naturally connect our idea of holiness with the image of a church, a mosque, or a cross. The Hindus have associated the idea of holiness, purity, truth, omnipresence, and such other ideas with different images and forms. But with this difference that while some people devote their whole lives to their idol of a church and never rise higher, because with them religion means an intellectual assent to certain doctrines and doing good to their fellows, the whole religion of the Hindu is centred in realisation. Man is to become divine by realising the divine. Idols or temples or churches or books are only the supports, the helps, of his spiritual childhood: but on and on he must progress.[3]

Although this is only an excerpt of the speech Vivekananda gave introducing Hinduism to the delegates at the World's Parliament of Religions, it is characteristic of his message as a whole. Vivekananda does not refer, except obliquely, to the many gods worshipped by Hindus, not even the major ones such as Vishnu, Shiva, or the Goddess. Instead, his message is clear: *Hinduism is* not *polytheistic. The central teaching of Hinduism is the oneness of God and the oneness of all the universe. Multiplicity, not only of gods, but of forms in general, masks a deeper unity which is the ultimate reality.*

In this chapter, we will have to contend with a situation that may be difficult to understand at first. There *are* many gods in Hinduism. They have individual names, individual appearances, and individual stories. Insofar as it makes sense to call any religion polytheistic, Hinduism is as polytheistic as it gets. Yet Vivekananda was not perpetrating a subterfuge when he denied that Hinduism is polytheistic in his speech to the World's Parliament of Religions. Likewise, Hindus today are not lying or confused about their own tradition when they say that it is monotheistic. Vivekananda's philosophical approach to explaining Hinduism is not representative of the totality of the Hindu tradition, and modern-day Hindus may have a variety of different *reasons* for calling themselves monotheists (if and when they do), but none of this obviates the inherent legitimacy of their self-representation or the ways they can appeal to Hindu tradition to justify it. To understand what is going on here, we will have to delve a bit more deeply into the culture and history of Hinduism and then ask ourselves what we even mean by polytheism and monotheism to begin with.

THE MANY GODS AND GODDESSES OF HINDUISM

The Hindu tradition itself states that there are 330 *million* gods. This number is obviously not meant to be taken literally but nevertheless gives a sense of the sheer multiplicity of deities within the Hindu tradition. This section will give a brief overview of some of the more well-known gods and goddesses in the Hindu tradition, ones that a typical Hindu would likely be familiar with and have some interaction with in the worship they engage in over the course of their lives.

I will begin with three gods, Brahma, Vishnu, and Shiva, who are often spoken of together and are referred to as the *Trimurti* ("three forms") in the Hindu tradition. Sometimes accounts written in English like to refer to them as the "Hindu Trinity," but the comparison to the Christian Trinity is not very close and probably obscures more than it illuminates. The three are often referred to together in Hindu mythology, and they are in a sense important as such, but they are not of equal practical importance in the Hindu tradition. Vishnu and Shiva each have large followings, but Brahma is hardly worshipped at all. His importance today is mostly as a figure within the mythology of the other two.

Brahma is the Creator god of Hinduism. He is usually depicted as an old man, with white hair and beard, signifying his grandfatherly status over creation. Or, rather, *beards*—as Brahma is almost always depicted as having four faces, one facing in each direction. Out of these four faces Brahma spoke the four Vedas, the oldest scriptures of Hinduism, at the beginning of time. There are different stories in Hindu mythology about how Brahma himself came into being before creating the universe. One is that he was born of a golden egg at the beginning of time, and for this reason he is known as the Self-Existent. Another story holds that he was born from Vishnu. In this story, Vishnu was reclining on a serpent floating in a cosmic sea of milk. A lotus blossom sprouted from Vishnu's navel, and out of that lotus blossom Brahma was born. For that reason, Brahma is also known as the Lotus-Born. As already mentioned, Brahma is mostly known from mythological stories such as these and is not a particularly popular object of worship among Hindus today. In fact, there is only one major temple dedicated to him in all of India, in the city of Pushkar.

Vishnu is known as the Preserver in the context of the *Trimurti*. He is usually depicted with four arms, holding a conch, a discus, a club, and a lotus flower. He is dressed like a traditional Indian prince, and his overall appearance is regal and socially affirming. He is often depicted riding on a mythical bird named Garuda. One of the unique aspects of Vishnu's mythology is that he is said to have incarnated on Earth as various animals and human beings to intercede at important points in history. The concept of incarnation here is much the same as the idea in Christianity that God incarnated as the human being Jesus, who lived at a particular point in history—the main difference being that Vishnu is said to have many incarnations, not just one. These incarnations are called *avatars*. You may know this word because it has entered English and has even been used as the title for a successful Hollywood movie franchise directed by James Cameron. The logic of the English use of the word is that you take a particular form—your avatar—when you enter into a computer game, in much the same way as Vishnu has taken various forms when entering into the mortal realm. There are many stories about Vishnu's avatars, but these have coalesced into a fairly standard list of ten. Of these, nine have already come, while the tenth, Kalkin, is a savior who is predicted to come in the future. Among the more popular of Vishnu's past avatars are Rama, the hero of the Hindu epic *Ramayana*, and Krishna, who is a major character in the other Hindu epic, the *Mahabharata*.

Shiva is the Destroyer of the Hindu *Trimurti*. His physical appearance can be contrasted to that of Vishnu. While Vishnu's dress is that of a traditional Indian prince, Shiva's is that of a person who dresses against social norms. He is usually depicted as living out in the wilderness of the Himalayas, and he wears a loose-fitting animal skin, as well as a snake around his neck. His hair is long and unkempt. In it is lodged a crescent moon, and the Ganges River flows out from it. Shiva is often portrayed holding a trident, which is one of his characteristic symbols. He is sometimes depicted with Nandin, a bull that he rides upon. In another popular form, Shiva is depicted dancing while throwing balls of fire. This is the form Shiva takes at the end of a cosmic age, when he destroys the universe. The destruction of the universe is not understood as a bad thing in the Hindu tradition but rather as a natural part of the cosmic cycle. With each cosmic age, Brahma creates the world, Vishnu preserves it, and Shiva destroys it, so that it can be renewed. Time is not linear in Hinduism but cyclical.

Although Shiva has a well-known human-like form as just described, this is not the form in which he is most commonly worshipped. Instead, Hindus typically worship Shiva in an aniconic form known as a *linga*. A *linga* is a short cylinder, usually made of stone, that symbolizes or instantiates Shiva's power. It is fixed on a base called a *yoni* that usually has a groove around the *linga* leading to a drainage spout. This allows worshippers to perform *puja*, or worship, of the *linga* by pouring milk over it. This milk is then drained through the groove in the *yoni* and can be collected. The symbolism of the *linga* and *yoni* is at least partially sexual. In Sanskrit, *linga* and *yoni* refer to a man's and a woman's sexual organs, respectively. There are moreover historical precedents in the mythology and worship of Shiva that support the sexual interpretation of the *linga*. However, for many Hindus today, the sexual aspect of the *linga* is not at the forefront of their minds. The *linga* is for them simply a non-anthropomorphic form in which one typically worships Shiva.

There are many other gods that perhaps do not have as much importance in Hindu mythology as the members of the *Trimurti* but nonetheless are popular objects of worship. One of these is Shiva's son Ganesh. Ganesh is easily recognizable as having a slightly overweight human body and the head of an elephant. The most common story about how he got his elephant head is that Shiva's wife Parvati created him to guard her while she took a bath. When Shiva went to see her, he got angry at Ganesh for preventing him from entering and cut off his head with his trident. Parvati was distraught, so Shiva sent his followers to bring back the head of the first creature they found, which happened to be an elephant, and he used that to replace Ganesh's head. Ganesh is known as the god of

Figure 5.1 A Shiva-linga with a picture of the god Ganesh in the background. From the Brihadeshwar Temple in Tanjavur, Tamil Nadu, in India. Photo by the author.

prosperity and the remover of obstacles. Not only Hindus, but many people around Asia, pray to Ganesh when they want help getting more money, getting a better job, or anything else in their everyday lives, making him one of the most popular gods in the world.

Another popular god is Hanuman. Hanuman is a monkey; in the Hindu epic *Ramayana*, he leads an army of monkeys to help the hero Rama defeat the demon-king Ravana, who has taken Rama's wife Sita hostage. Due to his character in the *Ramayana*, Hanuman is valued for his courage, devotion, and loyalty. He is also well-known around Asia because of the popularity of the *Ramayana* beyond the Hindu cultural sphere.

There are several important goddesses in Hinduism, who can be roughly divided into two types depending on whether they have a peaceful or a ferocious character. Among the more important peaceful goddesses are Saraswati, Lakshmi, and Parvati (also known as Uma). These correspond to the three members of the *Trimurti*, as Saraswati is the wife of Brahma, Lakshmi is the wife of Vishnu, and Parvati is the wife of Shiva. They are similar in appearance: All three are depicted as attractive women, wearing beautiful saris, and corresponding in traditional Indian cultural terms to the model of an ideal wife. They do have differences in iconography that reflect their fields of patronage. Saraswati is worshiped as the goddess of learning and the arts, and she is often portrayed holding a traditional Indian stringed instrument called the *veena*. Lakshmi is worshiped as the goddess of prosperity; she is often portrayed with a pile of coins and being showered with water by two elephants. Parvati/Uma is often portrayed together with her husband Shiva and their two sons, Ganesh and Skanda, and as such she is taken as paradigmatic of the ideal wife and mother.

Two goddesses with more ferocious characteristics are particularly popular in Hinduism. The first of these is Durga, who is a warrior goddess. She is portrayed as beautiful, like the peaceful goddesses, but she has many arms in which she holds an array of weapons, and she is depicted sitting on either a lion or a tiger while going into battle. The story behind Durga is that there was a buffalo-demon named Mahishasura who had received a boon from Brahma that no man could kill him. He used his immunity to terrorize the earth, so the gods took advantage of a loophole to defeat him. No *man* could defeat the demon, but a *woman* could. So, the gods combined their power—which in Sanskrit is a feminine noun, *shakti*—to create the goddess Durga. Durga then went into battle with Mahishasura and ultimately defeated him. She is thus celebrated as representing divine power over evil.

The second ferocious goddess is Kali. Kali's appearance is shocking, and deliberately so. She is portrayed as bold, defiant, and violent, in gross violation of feminine norms. She is nearly naked, wearing only a skirt made from severed human arms and a garland of severed human heads. She has a fierce look in her eyes, a lolling tongue, and long, unkempt hair. In one of her many arms, she holds a severed human head, and in another of her arms, she holds a skullcap to catch the blood dripping from the head. She has extremely dark skin, reflecting one of the meanings of her name Kali, which is "black." In many depictions, she is stomping upon the corpse of her husband Shiva.

Many Western Orientalist depictions of Hinduism have had a field day with Kali, making her out to be a demonic figure and her devotees to be devil-worshipers. The most famous example of this is the Indiana Jones film *Temple of Doom*. Nothing could in fact be further from the truth. Most devotees of Kali are very ordinary people who live ordinary lives. They consider Kali to be a beneficent, maternal figure. This might seem at odds with her appearance, but as with Durga, the ferocity of Kali is symbolic of divine wrath against evil. Some Hindus have made a useful comparison: Christians talk about the wrath of God, which is righteous and just and directed against evil. Imagine giving that divine wrath an anthropomorphic and feminine form. That is the idea behind Kali.

A BRIEF HISTORY OF HINDUISM

On the surface, the vast array of gods and goddesses in Hinduism, with their different appearances and individual personalities and stories, would seem to quite obviously be polytheism. To better understand what those Hindus who say that they are monotheistic are drawing from in their tradition, we need to look a bit at the history of the religion. Hinduism is difficult to define. It is not structured in the same way as religions such as Christianity, Islam, and Buddhism, each of which were founded by a particular person in history, who taught specific things that are recorded in a scripture. There is no Mr. Hindu who founded Hinduism because Hinduism does not have a founder. The word *Hindu* comes from a Persian word that was used by Muslim rulers in India in the second millennium to refer to their subjects who were not Muslim. Etymologically, *Hindu* means "Indian," and thus Hinduism is most broadly defined as the religion of Indians that do not belong to another specific religion (e.g., Islam, Buddhism, Jainism, Sikhism, Christianity, or Judaism). In this sense, Hinduism is much like Judaism—an ethnic religion, rather than a religion founded by a person and spread by missionaries—but it is practiced by a much larger group of people—over a billion as of 2020—and thus shows much more diversity in belief and practice.

Although there is no founding figure in Hinduism, and there is no centralized institution to enforce uniformity in practice or even basic beliefs, historically Hinduism has been structured by the teachings of a group of people called Brahmans.[4] Nowadays, Brahmans are a hereditary caste, representing a small fraction of the total number of Hindus, but they were the priests of ancient India, and throughout Indian history they have served as the intellectual class. In ancient India, going back about 3,000 years, Brahmans were priests who performed sacrifices to the gods, much as priests did in many ancient cultures. They believed in a variety of gods who were associated with various natural powers. The king of the gods was Indra, a sky god who corresponded to the Greek sky god Zeus and the Roman sky god Jupiter. The Brahmans made sacrifices to Indra and the other gods by offering food into a sacred fire, who was also considered a god, Agni. Agni would then carry the offerings up to the gods in the form of smoke.

The ancient Brahmans used oral texts known as Vedas to perform their sacrifices. The Vedas contain a variety of hymns and sacred formulas to be used in the sacrifice itself, as well as commentarial texts that speculate about the nature, purpose, and structure of the sacrifice. In the later parts of the Vedas, these texts became increasingly philosophical. Certain texts suggested that there might be one ultimate principle or one God behind the multiplicity of gods worshiped in the sacrifice. Certain texts likewise asked questions about what happens to us after we die, suggesting that sacrifices might build a place for a person in heaven. It seems that Brahmans were unsure as to whether a place in heaven built through sacrifice would be permanent, and certain late Vedic texts introduce the concept of reincarnation—the idea that we are born over and over again in various forms (human, animal, perhaps even gods) according to our *karma*—that is, the good or bad deeds that we perform. This idea of a cycle of rebirth, known in Sanskrit as *samsara*, became foundational to the worldview of Indian religions from then on.

Around the fifth century BCE, there was a split in approaches to the ideas found in the Vedas. A group known as *shramanas* arose that advocated a radical approach to seeking liberation from the cycle of rebirth. This radical approach involved a renunciation of normal ways of living in the world. Although different *shramana* groups conceived of renunciation in different ways and practiced it to varying degrees, it typically involved at minimum giving up the normal comforts of a home life, including marriage and sexual relationships of any kind. *Shramanas* took a very negative view of *samsara*: They saw it as full of suffering and as driven by the various mundane desires—epitomized by sexual desire—that ordinary people indulge in. The point of renunciation was to overcome desire and transcend the cycle of karma and rebirth. Originally, there was probably much diversity among *shramana* groups, but they quickly coalesced into a few major groups, two of which survived into modern times as world religions: Buddhism and Jainism.

Conservative Brahmans in ancient India were troubled by some of the more radical claims of the *shramanas*. In particular, they did not agree with the claim that one should practice lifelong celibacy to attain liberation from *samsara*. This did not mean that they totally rejected renunciatory practices—these, after all, had a basis in the Vedas—but they also saw marriage and the production of children as a duty that was required by the Vedic texts. More broadly, they clearly had a commitment to maintaining the traditions of the Vedas that *shramanas* were less concerned with. The Brahmans were interested in maintaining study of the Vedas; promoting the language they were written in, Sanskrit; continuing the performance of Vedic sacrifices; and showing the relevance of the Vedic gods in a world where *shramanas* claimed to transcend even the gods themselves by attaining liberation from rebirth. These Brahmans wrote many new texts to promote their worldview in the face of the *shramana* movements, but of these the most important is the *Mahabharata*, an epic poem about a great war that took place in the distant past. The *Mahabharata* is the longest epic poem ever written anywhere in the world, and the universe of gods and human characters it created became the basis for many if not most of the traditions we associate with Hinduism today.

The *Mahabharata* is long and complex, but one part of it, the *Bhagavad Gita*, has been enormously influential. The *Mahabharata* as a whole is about a war between two sides in a succession dispute—the Pandavas (the good guys) and the Kauravas (the bad guys). After many adventures in trying to settle the dispute over which side would get to rule over the kingdom, the Pandavas and Kauravas prepare for war. Just before the battle begins, Arjuna, who is one of the Pandavas, asks his chariot driver, Krishna, to drive his chariot to the center of the battlefield. (Arjuna is the Pandavas' best archer, and he has Krishna, who is an ally of the Pandavas, drive his chariot so that he is free to shoot arrows during the battle.) Once Krishna drives the chariot to the middle of the battlefield, Arjuna tells him that he doesn't want to fight. The Kauravas are the cousins of the Pandavas, so fighting means that he will end up killing his own relatives, and the battle will cause much destruction in general. In response, Krishna tells Arjuna that he must fight, that it is his duty to fight as a member of the warrior class. But as Krishna continues speaking, it becomes clear that he is talking about much deeper philosophical and religious issues than just the question of whether to fight. The chapters of the *Mahabharata* that follow, in which Krishna gives this long speech to Arjuna on the eve of the battle, have become revered in the Hindu tradition and are known as the *Bhagavad Gita*—the "Song of the Lord."

In the *Bhagavad Gita*, Krishna describes three religious paths, which are usually referred to as the "three *yogas*." (*Yoga* here refers to a religious path, not the spiritual/physical exercise we associate with the word today.) The first is *karma-yoga*, the path of action. This refers to action in the world in general, but most importantly making sacrifices to the gods. Krishna says that engaging in action is inevitable and that sacrifices are useful, but they are ultimately of limited value because (just as the *shramanas* would say) they don't lead to liberation from rebirth. The second path is *jñana-yoga*, the path of knowledge. This doesn't refer to book knowledge but rather to the knowledge one can obtain through meditation. It is, if one reads between the lines, precisely the path advocated by *shramanas*, such as the Buddhists. Krishna says that this is a perfectly valid path, but it is hard. He therefore advocates a third path, *bhakti-yoga*, the path of devotion. In this path, you simply devote yourself to God, and God saves you from the cycle of rebirth.

At this point, Krishna reveals to Arjuna that *he himself* is God! He transforms into his divine form as Vishnu, and Arjuna sees the entire universe, with all its living beings, including all the individual gods and goddesses spoken of in the Vedas, inside of God's body. Arjuna unsurprisingly finds this sight of God himself to be blinding and terrifying, and so he asks him to return to his human form, which Krishna does. Krishna finishes his speech, and Arjuna goes back to fight in the battle on the side of the Pandavas, who ultimately win the war and secure the kingdom.

The *Bhagavad Gita* is the most well-known Hindu scripture that contains ideas that inform the modern self-identification of many Hindus as monotheists. According to the *Bhagavad Gita*, there is one God, and much like the Christian God, he has the power to bring us mortals to salvation—although salvation here is conceived of as liberation from the cycle of rebirth rather than rescue from eternal damnation in hell. This one God, however, *contains* the universe, including the multiplicity of gods and goddesses, within himself. This is different from the monotheism of the Abrahamic traditions, in which God transcends the world and there exists no class of beings given the name gods and goddesses.

The *Bhagavad Gita* might seem to settle the matter in favor of Hinduism being monotheistic, but it is only one Hindu scripture out of many, and it is not interpreted in the same way or regarded with the same level of importance by all Hindus. It is true that many Hindus consider there to be one Supreme Deity—but they do not necessarily agree on who that is. In fact, there are three major sects within Hinduism who have three different opinions on the identity of the Supreme Deity. The first and largest of these are the Vaishnavas. These Hindus, inspired in large part by the *Bhagavad Gita*, consider Vishnu to be the Supreme Deity. The second sect is the Shaivas. They believe that Shiva is the most supreme form of God. They are inspired by parts of the *Mahabharata* other than the *Bhagavad Gita*, in which Shiva has an important role, and they also have many other scriptures of their own. Finally, there is a third sect known as the Shaktas. Shaktas worship the Goddess (known in Sanskrit as Devi) as the Supreme Deity. The Goddess is ultimately one, but she takes many forms, including the peaceful and ferocious forms that we learned about in the previous section. Many Hindus may consider themselves to be monotheists, but they do not agree on the identity of the one God nor even whether that God is male or female.

Even within each of these three major sects, there is yet *another* complicating factor in applying the label of monotheism: Not all Hindu theologians agree on the nature of God and his (or her) relationship to the

Figure 5.2 A gopuram (gateway) at Chidambaram, a famous temple to Dancing Shiva in Tamil Nadu, India. Photo by the author.

world and us within it. Although there are many differences between theologians in the Abrahamic religions, all three Abrahamic monotheisms tend to regard God as a transcendent figure who created the world and human beings, who are therefore separate in being from him. Hindu theologians, on the other hand, have had a variety of opinions on the nature of God, the world, and us. Some have argued that God and living beings like us are fundamentally separate, and that salvation consists of living with God or in a state that is like God but still fundamentally separate from him. This is the dualist position. Others have argued that God and the world (including us) are fundamentally identical—that all things are one, and multiplicity is an illusion. Salvation therefore consists of realizing one's oneness with the world and thus with God (or the Goddess). This is a nondualist, or monistic, position. Still others have argued that the relationship between God and the world is some combination of these two extremes. All of this means that there has been a great deal of diversity in Hinduism in understanding what one really means when one talks about God. A nondualist Shaiva thus might have more in common with a nondualist Vaishnava than with a dualist Shaiva, even though the Shaiva and the Vaishnava externally appear to be quite different in the scriptures they follow, the mythologies they appeal to, and the way they address God in worship.

Hinduism is fundamentally a very diverse religion. Of course, all religions are diverse, but the diversity of Hinduism is structured in a different way. Christians, Muslims, and Buddhists each have a founder whose teachings they appeal to for a sense of their identity. They may disagree on the interpretation of those teachings, but there tend to be certain non-negotiables that most within each religion can agree on. For Christians, that might be that Jesus Christ is the Messiah sent by God to bring the gift of salvation. For Muslims, it might be that there is one God and that Muhammad was a prophet sent by God. For Buddhists, it might be that the Buddha attained Awakening and showed the way for all beings to attain Awakening as well. Hindus are not held together by allegiance to a single founder in the same way. But they are held together by a common culture. On the surface, that culture is polytheistic, in the literal sense of "many gods," because it consists of a common set of stories about a variety of gods and goddesses, who in turn are instantiated and worshiped in temples around India (and increasingly the world). But that culture also includes a fairly widely held belief that there is a Supreme Deity behind the multiplicity of gods. Who exactly that God is, how exactly he or she should be understood, what manners of worship are to be used, have all been open to greater interpretation and contestation.

WHAT EVEN IS POLYTHEISM?

In the end, what is the answer to the question of this chapter? Is Hinduism polytheistic or monotheistic? In a sense, the answer is both. Hinduism does have many gods, which is what *polytheism* literally means. But many Hindus believe these gods are forms of a single divine being and therefore identify as monotheists. But not all Hindus identify as monotheists, and even those who do will not agree on who God is—and some recognize the Goddess as the one supreme divinity. How can we make sense of this situation from a neutral Religious Studies perspective? Perhaps the best way to answer the question would be to simply reject it as being based on a false premise. Can the world's religions easily be divided into two categories—polytheistic religions and monotheistic religions? I would argue that the example of Hinduism, along with others like Buddhism (which also has multiple gods but does not make them the focus of the religion), shows that the answer is no.

This is the thing: *Polytheist* is a word invented by monotheists to describe other religions that they do not consider to be monotheistic.[5] Although it is not in itself pejorative, it is reflective of a distinction that historically was. In earlier times, it was quite common for members of the Abrahamic monotheisms to use words that were more obviously pejorative: words like *pagan* and *idolater*. In modern times, Western thinkers created the categories monotheistic and polytheistic to classify religions in a more neutral sounding, "scientific" way, but this did not change the fact that the basic distinction between the two was derived from the disdain displayed by members of Abrahamic religions toward the worship of many gods. This led to the widespread assumption that polytheism is more "primitive" than monotheism. Even as some modern thinkers began to question the existence of God and embrace atheism, they tended to view history as a linear progression from "primitive" polytheism to the middle step of monotheism, then finally to modern rationality that does away with the divine altogether.

In part, this assumption that polytheism is somehow more primitive is a reflection of Western historical experience. The ancient Greeks, Romans, and Germanic peoples were all polytheists, and then they progressively converted to Christianity. Obviously, this was considered to be an improvement from the medieval Christian perspective, but modern Westerners have largely forgotten that ancient polytheists were grappling with many of the same questions as Jews and Christians did, just answering them in a slightly different way. The ancient Greek philosophers Plato and Aristotle, who lived centuries before the time of Christ, developed a branch of philosophy that they called theology, which was dedicated to understanding God (or, in Greek, "the god"), whom they considered to be ultimately a singular and good being. They lived in a culture with elaborate myths and practices surrounding a multiplicity of gods and goddesses, but they argued that behind this multiplicity there must ultimately be one supreme being. In this way, they were quite similar to Hindus.

If *polytheist* can be considered a euphemistic put-down, then why would anyone want to identify as a polytheist? This is not an abstract question for Hindus, especially when we think about the recent history of India. Prior to Independence in 1947, India was ruled for about two centuries by the British. Britain is a historically Christian country, and India's modern experience with British culture involved a mixture of Christian missionary attacks on Hindu polytheism and emerging atheist thought that would have similarly seen Hindu polytheism as even more primitive than Christianity. Prior to British rule, much of India was ruled for centuries by Muslims. The Delhi Sultanate was founded in 1206 and ruled over North India; this was followed by the Mughal Empire, which was founded in 1526 and at its height ruled over the entire Indian subcontinent. Muslims of course also took a dim view of polytheism, and different Muslim rulers had different degrees of toleration or intolerance of Hindu traditions depending on whether they interpreted Hindus as polytheists or as "people of the book."

Therefore, for nearly a millennium Hindus have lived in a world in which Abrahamic monotheists have held power over them, sometimes quite directly and other times more indirectly through cultural influence. Throughout this long period of time, they have experienced *polytheist* and words like it primarily as an insult. Their sensitivity to the term is thus quite understandable. But as we have seen in this chapter, this sensitivity is not simply a matter of an accurate description framed as a put-down. Hindus' sensitivity to being labeled polytheists is also rooted in the fact that the label, when used unproblematically, can lead to an overly simplistic understanding of Hindu traditions. It treats them superficially on the basis of the multiplicity of gods, without acknowledging the widespread belief in one divine power behind this multiplicity.

Before concluding this chapter, I would be remiss if I did not mention that not all Hindu protests against Western stereotyping of Hinduism are unproblematic. There is a powerful political, social, cultural, and intellectual movement in India today known as Hindutva. This movement is right-wing and religious nationalist. That is, subscribers to Hindutva see India as a fundamentally Hindu country, and they are generally intolerant of religious minorities, especially Muslims. They also tend to ignore diversity within Hinduism itself. They are usually Vaishnava in sectarian orientation and philosophically oriented to a nondualist interpretation of God and the world. When they say that Hinduism is monotheistic rather than polytheistic, they are often promoting a view of Hinduism that deliberately ignores the actual diversity of the Hindu tradition.

In fact, during the controversy over depictions of Hinduism in California textbooks that I mentioned at the beginning of this chapter, American Hindutva groups were at the vanguard of the protests. Their objections to the portrayal of Hinduism in the proposed textbook was not limited to the question of whether the religion is polytheistic or monotheistic; it also proposed many other revisions, some of which were historically questionable. This led to a counterprotest by a group of scholars who study Hinduism, some of Hindu heritage and others not, who argued that these Hindutva groups were trying to force their own political agenda into the depiction of Hinduism in California textbooks. All of this goes to show that words do indeed matter. Whether to categorize Hinduism as polytheistic or as monotheistic is fraught with a deep history of the power behind these terms and is tied up with a host of other issues that continue to have profound political salience to this day.

DISCUSSION QUESTIONS

1. Why do most Hindus consider themselves to be monotheists rather than polytheists? There may be more than one way to answer this question.
2. If we call Hinduism a monotheistic religion, how does that monotheism differ from the monotheism of the Abrahamic religions?
3. How does Hinduism model different approaches to or figurations of the divine through its gods and goddesses? Refer to and describe at least three gods and/or goddesses in your answer.
4. What are the three religious paths described in the *Bhagavad Gita*? Which one, according to Krishna, is the best, and why?
5. How does the binary division of world religions into monotheistic religions and polytheistic religions reflect a Western/Christian perspective?

NOTES

1 Note that the 90% who say they believe in one God includes two groups: 29% percent agree with the statement "There is only one God," while 61% agree with the statement, "There is only one God with many manifestations." The heavy preference for the second, qualified option points to the complexity of the issue that we will

be exploring in this chapter. Neha Sahgal, Jonathan Evans, Ariana Monique Salazar, Kelsey Jo Starr, and Manolo Carichi, "12. Beliefs about God," https://www.pewresearch.org/religion/2021/06/29/beliefs-about-god-in-india/.

2 For a thorough description of this controversy and its political background, see Purnima Bose, "Hindutva Abroad: The California Textbook Controversy," *The Global South* 2, no. 1 (Spring 2008): 11–34.

3 Vivekananda, "Paper on Hinduism," read at the Parliament of Religions, Sept. 19, 1893, http://www.ramakrishnavivekananda.info/vivekananda/volume_1/addresses_at_the_parliament/v1_c1_paper_on_hinduism.htm.

4 This word can be a source of confusion, as it is similar to two other words that are significant to Hindu traditions. Brahmans (sometimes also spelled as *Brahmins*) are people, members of the historically priestly class who for many centuries have been restricted within closed hereditary social groups called *castes*. The word *brahman* is a neuter noun that in some schools of Hindu philosophy is considered to be the ultimate reality behind the world of multiplicity. It is always used in the singular. Finally, Brahma is the name of the creator god in Hinduism.

5 The word *polytheism*, which comes from Greek, meaning "many gods," was coined by the Hellenistic Jewish philosopher Philo of Alexandria in the first century. It was revived in modern Western discourse by the sixteenth-century French philosopher Jean Bodin. See Francis Schmidt, "Polytheisms: Degeneration or Progress?" *History and Anthropology* 3 (1987): 9–60.

6
Chinese Religion
What Is It, and Where Can We Find It?

So far in this book, I have been presenting one new religion at a time, highlighting in each case a popular misconception or prejudice about the religion and how that contrasts with reality. This chapter will be a bit different. Instead of one new religion, we will be looking at two new religions—Confucianism and Daoism—and instead of one misconception about these specific religions, we will be looking at two misconceptions that people in the modern West typically have about religion in general. The first is that religions are always mutually exclusive, and the second is that the essence of a religion is a set of beliefs laid out in scripture.

In the West, we tend to take for granted that religions are mutually exclusive. This is just a fancy way of saying that religions don't overlap. You're either a Christian or a Muslim or a Jew, not some combination thereof. Even within a particular religion, we think of branches or denominations as mutually exclusive. You're either a Lutheran or a Catholic, a Baptist or a Presbyterian, a Sunni or a Shi'ite. We don't typically talk about Lutheran Jews, or Catholic Protestants, or Mormon Muslims. These combinations don't make sense because the identities are mutually exclusive—they are not supposed to overlap.

Of course, nowadays some people get married across religious boundaries, and their family or children might have a mixed identity. But there is still the sense that this identity is *mixed*, drawing from identities that are normally kept separate. Indeed, most Western religious

DOI: 10.4324/9781032646428-8

communities have historically been hostile to such "mixed marriages," and some conservative religious communities still are. In any case, the logic of most Western religions is one that makes them mutually exclusive: Each claims to worship God in the proper way and rejects the authorities and truth claims of the others. Thus, for example, Jews reject Jesus as the Messiah, both Christians and Jews reject Muhammad as a prophet, Protestants reject the authority of the Catholic Church, and so forth.

Religion in China is completely different in this respect. Traditional Chinese culture has three different religions[1]: Buddhism, Confucianism, and Daoism. One of these religions—Buddhism—came from India, while the other two—Confucianism and Daoism—originated in China itself. Each of these religions appeals to a different authoritative founding figure: the Buddha for Buddhism, Confucius for Confucianism, and Laozi for Daoism. Each of the three religions has its own separate set of scriptures, and each has its own elite "clergy"—Buddhist monks/nuns, Daoist priests, and Confucian scholars—who act as leaders of that particular religion. But if you ask what percentage of ordinary Chinese people "belong" to each of these three religions, that is not an easy question to answer. The reason is that in Chinese culture, most people are influenced by, and in a sense practice, all three religions at once.

Now, you might ask, what does that mean? What does it look like to be a Buddhist *and* a Confucian *and* a Daoist? As it happens, having multiple identities of this sort is not as unfamiliar as it might seem. All of us exercise multiple identities, usually in the same day, and sometimes even simultaneously. I, for example, exercise identities as a husband, as a man, as a teacher, as a colleague, as a son, as a friend, as a mentor . . . and many more. I live each of these identities regularly, many on a daily basis, and I do so without thinking consciously about it as the situation arises. So having multiple identities is not at all unusual in modern Western life; in fact, it is quite normal. What is unusual, or at least perceived as unusual, is having multiple *religious* identities.

To illustrate how having these three simultaneous religious identities works in Chinese culture, I will begin by treating the religions in isolation and then show how this contrasts with the lived experience of Chinese religion in practice. This might seem circuitous—why not just cut to the chase and explain what Chinese religion is *really* about?—but I do so for two reasons. The first is that Buddhism, Confucianism, and Daoism are legitimately autonomous entities that contribute to Chinese religion as a whole in different ways. Buddhism, for example, is originally from India and exists in many cultures other than China, so it obviously has an existence independent from its embeddedness in Chinese religion.

Confucianism and Daoism, likewise, while inextricable from each other and Chinese religion in general, each have their own elite specialists and scriptures.

The second reason I am taking this approach is that I want to make a point. Following a Western paradigm for religion, it can be easy to think that if you can simply identify the founder of a religion and learn about what they taught as recorded in the religion's scripture, you will understand that religion. But as we will see in this chapter, although there is much to be learned from a religion's "original scripture," you won't really understand what the religion is like *in practice* unless you look at what people in that religion do...*in practice*. The point is that religion is not just about belief. It is not just a set of ideas, teachings, or principles that are recorded in a holy book, which can be mastered simply by reading that book. Religion is something that people *do*. Beliefs may play a role in what people do, but religion is ultimately a matter of practice, not just belief.

We already learned about Buddhism, which originated in India, in chapter 4. The next two sections of this chapter will take up the other two major religions of China in turn, focusing on their founding figure and his teachings as recorded in the "original scripture" of each religion: Confucius and his teachings recorded in the *Analects*, Laozi and his (Daoist) teachings recorded in the *Daode Jing*. The fourth section will then describe what Chinese religion looks like in practice. By contrasting the two we will see in the conclusion that Chinese religion is more than just the sum of its three constituents, and more generally that religions are not just systems of belief embodied in scriptures.

CONFUCIUS, THE ANALECTS, AND CONFUCIANISM

The founder of Confucianism was a man named Confucius, who lived in what is now northern China from around 551–479 BCE. His Chinese name was Kongzi, or in a more formal form, Kongfuzi. When Jesuit missionaries were active in China in the sixteenth and seventeenth centuries, in a failed attempt to convert the Chinese emperor to Catholicism, they learned about the teachings of Kongzi and were sufficiently impressed that they wrote about him for audiences back home in Europe, giving him the Latin name Confucius. The Jesuits' admiration for Confucianism, which they saw as compatible with Catholicism, earned them enemies back home, but the Latin name they bestowed on this great ancient Chinese philosopher stuck and continues to be the one used in English and other European languages to this day.

Confucius lived near the end of a long period in ancient Chinese history known as the Zhou (pronounced like the nickname "Joe") Dynasty. The Zhou Dynasty was a kingdom that was founded around 1050 BCE and lasted (at least in name) until 221 BCE. It encompassed roughly what is now the northeast quadrant of China, around the Yellow River, which was the cradle of Chinese civilization. At first, the Zhou Dynasty was a unified kingdom, but over the centuries it became disunified as the kings of Zhou practiced a form of feudalism in which they parceled out land to nobles known as *gong* (usually translated as "dukes" in English). By the time of Confucius, these dukes were effectively more powerful than the king of Zhou, and they ran their fiefdoms like independent kingdoms. These small kingdoms became increasingly quarrelsome, fighting over land, resources, and power. This was a situation that would last for several hundred years, until China was reunited by the ruler of one of the warring kingdoms, Qin (pronounced "Cheen"), known in Chinese as Qin Shi Huang (the "First Qin Emperor"). We get the English word *China* from this Qin kingdom that played a pivotal role in creating a united Chinese civilization.

Confucius was the first and ultimately most influential of several philosophers who were active in China during the chaotic final centuries of the Zhou Dynasty. These philosophers all sought a *dao*, or "way," that would lead China out of its sorry state of violence and strife and back to a state of peace, unity, and prosperity. Confucius, in particular, idealized the "former kings" or "sage kings"—the kings who had ruled over China at the beginning of the Zhou Dynasty. He believed that they provided a perfect example of the way (*dao*) to follow, and that it was because people had deviated from that way that China had become so chaotic. China, Confucius argued, was full of, and in particular led by, what he called "petty people" (*xiao ren*), selfish people who were concerned only about their own pleasure and profit. He wanted to train them in the way of the sage kings, to transform them into "gentlemen" (*junzi*). Unfortunately, Confucius was unsuccessful in his lifetime. He wandered around China, attracting disciples to himself but failing to find any rulers who were willing to adopt his teachings. It was only several centuries after Confucius' death, with the founding of the Han Dynasty in 202 BCE, that Confucianism was adopted as the official ideology of the Chinese state.

Confucius did not write anything himself, but his disciples wrote down many short anecdotes about things he said or encounters he had with various people and collected them into a book called the *Analects* (*Lunyu*). In these anecdotes, Confucius claims that he is not teaching anything new, just advocating a return to the way of the sage kings at the beginning of the Zhou Dynasty. The way of the sage kings, according to him, is not some abstract or mystical path but a concrete set of rules about how to act in specific social situations. These rules are known in Chinese as *li*, usually translated into English as "ritual."

Ritual here doesn't just mean what we mean by ritual—elaborate ceremonies, although it includes that—it also refers to the small rules of etiquette you follow in everyday life. This might include how you greet someone or how you prepare a seat for a guest at dinner. Although the content of these rituals was specific to ancient China, all of us can relate to them because all cultures have rituals of this sort. For example, in modern Western culture, it is typical to shake hands when meeting someone for the first time, or even someone you already know after some absence. Likewise, in English we use words like *please* and *thank you* at the appropriate times to convey politeness and gratitude.

Contrary to modern thinking, which tends to view rituals as arbitrary and meaningless, Confucius saw ritual as deeply connected to ethics and social order in general. This is not such a crazy thought even if we consider the modern examples I just gave. Imagine that you offered your hand to someone, and they refused to shake it. How would you feel? Probably offended, hurt, and slighted. We also judge people by their handshakes. If someone has a limp handshake, we see them as cold, distant, or untrustworthy. If someone has too strong of a handshake, we see him (it is always a man) as trying too hard to assert his dominance.

Words like *please* and *thank you* are in many cases optional, but deft use of them in various situations signals certain qualities to others. Saying *please* signals polite acknowledgment of your debt to the other person for doing you a favor, especially if the favor is a big one. Overusing the word *please*, however, especially for routine requests or requests involving someone's job, can come across as curt or obsequious. *Thank you*, on the other hand, can be applied liberally (at least in English-language culture, less so in other cultures). There are certain cases where a *thank you* is obligatory, such as when someone gives you a gift. Failure to say "thank you" is rude and conveys a lack of appreciation. Liberal use of the words *thank you*, such as when service workers perform routine tasks, conveys a magnanimous and generous spirit not only to the service worker in question but also to others around you, such as a date.

All of this is to say that the routine rituals of everyday life are not meaningless. They play a real social function that affects how people relate to one another. Confucius went a step further and said that they are what *make us* into good people. Ritual, in other words, is not something done for its own sake. It is used to cultivate an inner sense of goodness, which he called *ren*. This Chinese word is usually translated into

English as "humaneness," in part to convey a pun in the original Chinese: the Chinese character for this concept sounds exactly like the Chinese character for "person" (also *ren*) and incorporates that character into its written form. But "goodness" gives a reasonable sense of the Chinese word *ren*. It is an inner disposition, in distinction to the outer form of the ritual (*li*).

All of these important concepts from the *Analects* fit together to form Confucius' overall program. According to Confucius, China was in a state of disarray in his day because it was led by petty people (*xiao ren*) who did not follow the way (*dao*) of the sage kings, the early kings of the Zhou Dynasty. His remedy to this situation was to follow the rituals (*li*) that had been taught by the sage kings, to cultivate an inner sense of goodness or humaneness (*ren*). Once petty people cultivated an inner sense of goodness by following the proper rituals, they would be transformed into gentlemen (*junzi*), and these gentlemen would return China to its prior state of unity, peace, and prosperity.

Confucius' program was directed toward the specific state he found China in 2,500 years ago, and China *did* become united only a few hundred years after his death, so neither that program nor the specific rituals he taught as being set down by the sage kings are the most enduring legacy of Confucianism. What *is* an enduring legacy is the broader principle of understanding social relationships as ritually governed. Traditionally, Confucianism demands the proper maintenance of five types of relationships. All of these are conceived hierarchically: between a king and a subject, between a parent and a child, between a husband and a wife, between an older and younger brother, and between an older and younger friend. Each of these pairs has reciprocal duties toward each other. The lower-ranked member of the pair is obligated to serve and show proper respect to the higher-ranked member, while the higher-ranked member is obligated to protect and care for the lower-ranked member.

Among the five relationships, the duties of a child to a parent, referred to as filial piety (*xiao*), are of particular importance. One of the greatest legacies of Confucianism is the emphasis placed in East Asian cultures on respect for elders. Within Chinese families, it is common for multiple generations to live in the same home so that the younger generations can take care of the oldest generation. The Western practice of putting elderly parents in retirement communities or nursing homes is far less common and is controversial because it is seen as a sign of disrespect. Even after the elders die, the living perform ritual obligations of filial piety toward them. It is common for Chinese families to record long genealogies so that they can maintain their duties of filial piety toward their ancestors going back many generations.[2]

LAOZI, THE *DAODE JING*, AND DAOISM

According to legend, Daoism[3] was founded by a man named Laozi, who supposedly was an older contemporary of Confucius. He became utterly disenchanted with Chinese society and journeyed off to the west, never to be seen again. As he was leaving China, he wrote a short book called the *Daode Jing*, which he left behind as his legacy. Or so the story goes. According to modern scholars, Laozi, unlike Confucius, probably never existed. *Laozi* isn't really a name; it literally just means "old man." The *Daode Jing* is real—you can read it in any number of translations available in just about any bookstore or online—but it probably was compiled by an author or authors unknown.

The *Daode Jing* is philosophical like the *Analects* of Confucius, but it takes a completely different approach to life, and thus Confuciansim and Daoism are often contrasted with one another. The central principle of the *Daode Jing* is the *Dao*, which as we already saw literally means "the Way" in Chinese. Every ancient Chinese philosopher was interested in finding this Way, and for Confucius, it was a set of rituals set down by the sage kings, which, if followed properly, can be used to cultivate inner goodness and thus become a gentleman.

The *Daode Jing* understands the Dao in a completely different way from Confucius. Its opening chapter makes it immediately clear that we are entering a very different world from the Confucian world of tradition and ritual:

> A Way that can be followed is not a constant Way.
> A name that can be named is not a constant name.
> Nameless, it is the beginning of Heaven and earth.
> Named, it is the mother of the myriad creatures.
> And so,
> > Always eliminate desires in order to observe its mysteries;
> > Always have desires in order to observe its manifestations.
> These two come forth in unity but diverge in name.
> Their unity is known as an enigma.
> Within this enigma is yet a deeper enigma.
> The gate of all mysteries![4]

There was nothing mysterious at all about the Confucian Way: follow the proper rituals; show honor to one's elders. But this Way seems at first glance to be shrouded in double-talk! A closer look at the words of the *Daode Jing* shows that they do indeed make sense, but they point to a conception of the Way that is difficult to put into words. The Dao, the

Way, is not something that can be followed or named. It is something that is ultimately beyond language.

This is not to say that language is not useful or that there are not ways that can be followed. (You probably followed some set way to get to class this morning.) But the world of language, the world of precise instructions on where to go and what to do, is the world of multiplicity and change, the world as we ordinarily experience it. The point the *Daode Jing* is making is that there is a deeper reality, one that is constant and unified. This reality is beyond the ability of language to talk about it and cannot be followed in the ordinary sense. It is a mystery that can only be observed, as the text says, by "eliminating desires." Both aspects of reality—the one characterized by unity, constancy, ineffability, and desirelessness, the other characterized by multiplicity, change, language, and desire—are manifestations of the Dao.

All ancient Chinese philosophers were interested in defining the Dao, including Confucius, but the *Daode Jing* did so in a manner so unique and enigmatic that the term *Dao* became virtually synonymous with the tradition coming out of this text. That is why the tradition that traces its lineage back to the *Daode Jing* and its putative author, Laozi, is known as Daoism. Usually, when people talk about the Dao, they are referring to the Dao of Daoism, not of Confucianism or any other ancient Chinese philosophy.

A second important key term introduced by the *Daode Jing*, closely related to the Dao, is *wuwei* (pronounced "oo way"). This word literally means "nonaction," but it doesn't mean standing still or doing nothing; it means acting in such a way that you do not make a deliberate effort. For this reason, *wuwei* is often translated "actionless action." It's acting in a way that is effortless. The classic example of *wuwei* was given by an ancient Chinese philosopher named Zhuangzi. He compared *wuwei* to the work of a butcher. A skilled butcher knows just where to cut the ox, so he's not struggling to cut it; it's like he's cutting through butter.[5] This is in contrast to an unskilled butcher, who must saw and hack away at the dead carcass because he doesn't know what he is doing.

If you're not a butcher, that example may not resonate with you, but have you ever been "in the zone" before? It could be while doing almost anything—playing a sport, exercising, playing a musical instrument, singing, or doing a hobby. You're doing something, something amazing, in fact, but it feels like you're doing nothing at all, it's so effortless. That's actionless action. It is, to use the language of the *Daode Jing*, acting in accordance with the Dao.

The *Daode Jing*'s conception of the Dao and *wuwei* is implicitly a criticism of Confucianism. This criticism becomes particularly clear in chapter 38 of the text:

> Those of highest Virtue do not strive for Virtue and so they have it.
> Those of lowest Virtue never stray from Virtue and so they lack it.
> Those of highest Virtue practice nonaction (*wuwei*) and never act for ulterior motives.
> Those of lowest Virtue act and always have some ulterior motive.
> Those of highest benevolence act, but without ulterior motives.
> Those of highest righteousness act, but with ulterior motives.
>> Those who are ritually correct act, but if others do not respond, they roll up their sleeves and resort to force.
>> And so,
>> When the Way was lost there was Virtue;
>> When Virtue was lost there was benevolence;
>> When benevolence was lost there was righteousness;
>> When righteousness was lost there were the rites.
>
> The rites are the wearing thin of loyalty and trust, and the beginning of chaos.[6]

Although Confucius is never named here, it is clear that he and his followers are the ones being criticized. Confucius loved ritual and saw following proper ritual as the path to becoming a good person.

According to the *Daode Jing*, the opposite is true: ritual is "the beginning of chaos." The reason for this is that it sees ritual as a stopgap measure that people employ when they are not acting in accordance with the Dao. If you were truly acting in accordance with the Dao, you wouldn't need artificial conceptions of virtue, benevolence, or righteousness, much less the rigid rules of ritual. The image of "ritually correct" people who "roll up their sleeves and resort to force . . . if others do not respond" is particularly vivid and one that I think we all can relate to. You probably know someone in your life, perhaps a family member, who demands that everyone follow the rules as they conceive them and gets angry if any of those rules are broken. The disconnect between such a person's supposed commitment to propriety and their inability to control their own anger can often be quite jarring.

A third key concept that is found in the *Daode Jing* is the concept of *yin* and *yang*. You've probably seen the symbol of it even if you didn't know what it means: It's a circle composed of what looks like two commas chasing one another. One is black, the other white, and each contains a dot of the other color within it. In the West today, this symbol is quite popular as a tattoo and in New Age jewelry.

Yin and *yang* are complementary principles whose combination characterizes everything in the universe. *Yin* literally means "shadow" and is associated with darkness, moisture, heaviness, passivity, and femininity. *Yang* literally means "sun" and is associated with light (as opposed to darkness), dryness, lightness (as opposed to heaviness), activity, and masculinity. It is not the case that *yin* is evil and *yang* good or vice versa. Ideally, the two should be in balance. If anything is bad, it is that there is too much *yang* or too much *yin*. Traditional Chinese medicine, in fact, explains ill health in part as an imbalance of *yin* and *yang*.

The point of *yin* and *yang* is that they are complementary principles whose ebb and flow can explain just about any natural phenomenon. Much of what we observe in nature is cyclical. Every twenty-four hours we experience a cycle between *yang* (day) and *yin* (night). The year is marked by seasons that likewise can be conceived of as the ebb and flow of *yang*, most pronounced in the summer with its light and warmth, and *yin*, most pronounced in the winter with its darkness and cold. The symbol for *yin* and *yang* represents this typical pattern by having the two chase one another. It also represents their complementarity by having a dot of *yin* in the middle of *yang* and a dot of *yang* in the middle of *yin*. The sun (*yang*) casts shadows (*yin*) in the middle of the day, and amid the darkness (*yin*) of night the moon shines light (*yang*). The two are ultimately inseparable.

One final important Daoist concept found in the *Daode Jing* is *qi* (pronounced *chee*). *Qi* literally means "air," but it refers to a fundamental energy/substance that flows through everything in the universe, including your body. *Qi* is the substance through which *yin* and *yang* operate and propagate. A useful comparison is to a body of water. Water can be calm and clear, with a flat surface or small ripples and gentle waves flowing across it. Or it can be violent and turbid, with large, erratic waves crashing into one another. In the same way, *qi* can have two modes: it can flow in the mode that manifests as *yin* or in the mode that manifests as *yang*.

Certain Daoist practices are intended to manipulate *qi* for various purposes. One such practice that has a popular following is called *qigong*. If you have ever been to a park in a big city and seen people that look like they're exercising, except that they are moving their arms very, very slowly, then you have seen people practicing *qigong*. The purpose is to manipulate the *qi* flowing through the body to promote good health. Some *qigong* masters claim to have the ability to manipulate *qi* to such an extent that they can perform superhuman feats.

A chapter of the *Daode Jing* ties *yin* and *yang* as modes of *qi* back to the Dao:

> The Way produces the One.
> The One produces two.
> Two produces three.
> Three produces the myriad creatures.
> The myriad creatures shoulder *yin* and embrace *yang*,
>   and by blending these *qi*, "vital energies," they attain harmony.[7]

These lines are cryptic and can be interpreted in different ways, but typically the "two" that are produced from the "one" of the Way are understood to be *yin* and *yang*. These two complementary principles thus represent a splitting of the original unity of the Dao. They then recombine in various ways to produce the multiplicity of the world as we observe it. And thus, we find the connection between the two aspects of the Dao described in chapter one of the *Daode Jing*. The unified, ineffable aspect of the Dao is connected to the world of multiplicity and language by the fundamental split into *yin* and *yang*, two complementary principles whose oppositions represent the logic of language itself.

CHINESE RELIGIONS IN HISTORY AND PRACTICE

If we follow a Western paradigm of religion, we should now, based on what we learned in chapter 4 about Buddhism and in this chapter about Confucianism and Daoism, have all we need to know to understand religion in China. There are three main Chinese religions: Confucianism, Daoism, and Buddhism. Some Chinese people are Confucians. They promote traditional families, with patriarchal structures and strong respect for the eldest generation. They are also sticklers for ritual and work hard to preserve rituals both great and small. Other Chinese people are Daoists. They are practically the opposite of Confucians. They completely reject rituals and advocate going with the flow, acting naturally in accord with the Dao, a state that they call actionless action. They seek peace, harmony, and good health by balancing the principles of *yin* and *yang*, and they perform simple exercises to smooth out the flow of *qi*, the energy through which *yin* and *yang* flow. Yet another group of Chinese people are Buddhists, who are like the Daoists but follow a different set of teachings that came to China from India. In accordance with the Buddha's teaching of the Four Noble Truths, they are disenchanted with the suffering inherent to life, and they follow the Eightfold Path to attain *nirvana*, a state free from suffering. All three of these Chinese religions are more like lifestyles than religions in the Western sense of the word. They are not focused on the worship of God or gods; instead, they are philosophical and ethical systems that tell their followers, in different ways, how best to live their lives.

But of course, this picture is completely wrong. It is wrong because it places the three Chinese religions into separate little boxes, and it is wrong because it mischaracterizes the way that the three religions are experienced in Chinese religious life, even insofar as they can be separated. But how did we go so wrong? We learned about the teachings of the founders of these religions from their oldest scriptures, did we not? They speak to three very different religious systems that look pretty much as we just described. How could Chinese people mix the three religions up and practice religion in a way that looks different from what we've come to expect?

As a first step to answering this question, we need to look at history. The Chinese religious landscape didn't emerge fully formed over two thousand years ago once Confucius' disciples wrote down his saying in the *Analects*, once the *Daode Jing* was written, and once Buddhism came to China. Many things have happened since then that have played a role in forming Chinese religion as it is experienced today.

CONFUCIANISM

As I already indicated, Confucius was unsuccessful in his lifetime in finding a ruler who would implement his ideas. He did, however, attract a following to himself, and Confucianism became one of the most influential intellectual movements of the late Zhou Dynasty. Two other Confucians, in fact, became prominent philosophers in their own right. The first was Mengzi (known in the West by a Latin name given him by the Jesuits, Mencius), who lived from 372 to 289 BCE. The second was his younger contemporary Xunzi, who lived from about 310 to 238 BCE. These two philosophers were followers of Confucius, but they disagreed in their interpretation of Confucius' teachings, especially on the question of human nature. Xunzi believed that human nature is evil and must be forced into a good form by ritual, while Mencius believed that human beings have the seeds of goodness within them, which should be cultivated to make one into a gentleman. Both men were wandering scholars much like their master Confucius, but Xunzi's career brought him a bit closer to the political influence Confucius had sought in ways that would help secure Confucianism's wider influence after his death.

The era of Chinese chaos and disunity finally ended in 221 BCE when the state of Qin conquered the other Chinese states and Qin Shi Huang became the first Chinese emperor. Two of Xunzi's students—neither of whom, however, are remembered as Confucians—played a role in the unifying reforms implemented by the Qin. The first, Han Feizi, was considered the primary thinker of a philosophical school known as Legalism, which like Confucianism sought to bring political unity to China but, unlike Confucianism, saw ethics as at best irrelevant and at worst an impediment to achieving this goal. Another of Xunzi's students, Li Si, became prime minister of the state of Qin and was the chief architect of the imperial reforms once Qin conquered China. He effectively put into practice the principles of Legalism, including by conspiring to have Han Feizi executed since he perceived him to be a dangerous rival.

The Qin Dynasty did not last long, and it was replaced in 202 BCE by the Han Dynasty. It was under this dynasty that Confucianism became official state ideology, a status it held for over two thousand years, until the fall of the Qing Dynasty in 1911. It is important to realize, however, that there were political reasons for the Han to give an elevated status to Confucianism. Legalism had become discredited by the perceived brutality of the Qin Empire, so valorizing Confucianism was a way of distancing the Han Dynasty from its predecessor. But that does not mean that the Han or any subsequent dynasty formed policy purely on Confucian principles or was uninfluenced by Legalism. Indeed, Xunzi, the Confucian philosopher whose writings held the most influence up until the Tang Dynasty (seventh to tenth centuries), was himself a synthesizing thinker who drew from many of the philosophical schools of his day, and his own students Han Feizi and Li Si were the chief architect and implementor of the Legalism that Confucians later decried.

Starting in the Han Dynasty, imperial examinations based on study of the Confucian classics were implemented for those entering civil service.[8] This might give the impression that Confucianism somehow became the state religion, in the same sense that Christianity was made the official religion of the Roman Empire in the fourth century by the emperor Theodosius. In fact, knowledge of Confucianism was seen primarily as a tool for proper statecraft and was not necessarily deemed incompatible with either Buddhism or Daoism. Chinese emperors themselves frequently patronized Daoist and Buddhist institutions.

Moreover, a revolution in Confucian thought, beginning in about the ninth century, known as Neo-Confucianism, in many ways synthesized Confucian ideals with ideas taken from Buddhism and Daoism. Many of the Neo-Confucian scholars were hostile to Buddhism and Daoism and resentful of their popularity among the court and the common people, but to successfully combat the threat that the other two teachings posed, they had to adapt to them. The result was a new synthesis that was much more in conversation and integrated with Buddhist and Daoist ideas. At the same time, Neo-Confucians switched their preference between the great ancient successors of Confucius from Xunzi to Mencius.[9] Mencius' emphasis on the innate capacity of human beings for goodness was better suited for constructing this synthesis, insofar as it found sympathetic resonance with the Buddhist concept of Buddha Nature, the innate capacity of all human beings to become Buddhas.

BUDDHISM

Buddhism, as we know, originated in India, and it first came to China in the mid- to late-Han Dynasty, that is, in the first couple of centuries CE. Buddhism had already been spreading into Central Asia along trade routes known as the "Silk Road," and it is likely that Chinese people first became aware of the religion through their role as the easternmost destination in those trade routes. Central Asian monks played a pivotal role in transmitting Buddhist teachings to China, and as monastic communities were established in China itself, Chinese monks periodically would travel to India in search of Buddhist scriptures to bring back and translate into Chinese. The most famous of these was the seventh-century monk Xuanzang, whose journey to India in search of scriptures was memorialized (in highly mythologized form) in the sixteenth-century novel *Journey to the West*, one of the great classics of Chinese literature.

The process by which Chinese people learned about Buddhism was quite slow compared to today's standards, taking many generations as scriptures were brought to China—either in manuscript form or in the minds of monks—and translated into Chinese. Moreover, most of the scriptures that became most popular in China were not the oldest Buddhist scriptures, in which the Buddha is portrayed as a human being who attained *nirvana* and established an order of monks and nuns to learn the Four Noble Truths and follow the Eightfold Path to attain *nirvana* for themselves. Instead, they were new Buddhist scriptures, or *sutras*, that were being composed in India in Sanskrit at about the same time that Buddhism was being transmitted to China. These scriptures were the heart of a new movement in Buddhism called the Mahayana.

As we learned in chapter 4, Mahayana Buddhism is distinguished from non-Mahayana Buddhism by its commitment to the Bodhisattva Path, the idea that all people should strive to become Buddhas. The Bodhisattva Path did not change the basic principles or values of Buddhism, but it did have a profound effect on the way that Mahayana Buddhists understood the Buddhist universe. First, if the Bodhisattva Path is open to all, then that means that there should be lots of Bodhisattvas all around us, some of them quite powerful. Mahayana Buddhists developed myths about many such Bodhisattvas, but by far the most popular was Avalokiteshvara, the Bodhisattva of Compassion. He is understood to be a godlike being who has a thousand arms, and in each of his palms he has an eye, so that he can constantly inspect the universe in all directions looking for ways to spread his compassion. According to the *Lotus Sutra*, which would become one of the most popular Mahayana Buddhist *sutras* in China, Avalokiteshvara can take many forms, including that of a woman. Over time, a female form of Avalokiteshvara known as Guanyin became extremely popular. She is depicted as an elegant woman in a white robe and is one of the most popular images within Chinese religion to this day.

We also saw in chapter 4 that Mahayana Buddhism developed a belief in multiple Buddhas who reside in Pure Lands, special realms that have been purified by their great merit. Although there are a few accounts about different Pure Land Buddhas in the Mahayana scriptures, by far

Figure 6.1 Buddha images at Fo Guang Shan Buddhist temple in Taiwan. Photo by Nanda Raksakhom.

the one who became most popular among Mahayana Buddhists, including in China, was Amitabha. He is said to reside in a Pure Land to the West called Sukhavati. One of the vows he made before becoming a Buddha was that he would create this Pure Land as a refuge for beings eager to attain Awakening and that anyone who invoked his name with pure intention would be reborn in that Pure Land in their next life and attain Awakening there.

Buddhism has a long and complex history in China, with vigorous debate in the monastic community over the proper interpretation of the Buddhist scriptures and the development of several properly Chinese Buddhist sects. One of these, known as Chan in Chinese culture but better known in the West by its Japanese name, Zen, put a great deal of emphasis on meditating to attain Awakening. But by far the most influential mode of Buddhism within Chinese was and continues to be simple Pure Land devotion. Amitabha, known in Chinese as Amituo Fo, is by far the most popular Buddha in China, more popular even than the Buddha Shakyamuni who founded the religion in India. Buddhism has had its most widespread popular influence in Chinese culture in the form of chanting the name of Amituo Fo in the hope of being reborn in his Pure Land after death and praying to Guanyin and other Bodhisattvas for help in one's everyday life.

DAOISM

Daoism arguably underwent the greatest change over the course of its history. Although legendarily Daoism began with Laozi writing the *Daode Jing*, this story is misleading from a historical perspective. Laozi probably never existed, and we do not really know who wrote the *Daode Jing* or whether it was a single person. There was a historical person in the late Zhou Dynasty who wrote with an outlook similar to the *Daode Jing*, namely Zhuangzi, who gave the metaphor of the skilled butcher cutting up an ox to explain *wuwei*, as we saw above. Zhuangzi and the mythical Laozi were retrospectively considered to be the founding figures of Daoism, but Daoism didn't really become organized until centuries later. Moreover, as Daoism did become organized, it probably did so largely in response to Buddhism, which first came to China from India during the Han Dynasty. That is, as the Buddhist monastic community entered China and laid roots there, some people were wary of its foreign origins but saw similarities with strands of Chinese thought deriving from Zhuangzi and the *Daode Jing*. They then sought to organize in response to the Buddhists' institutionalized monastic order.

Perhaps the most pivotal event in the transformation of Daoism into an organized "religion" was the establishment of the Way of the Celestial Masters in 142 CE. In that year, a man named Zhang Daoling received a revelation from Taishang Laojun, who was Laozi in the form of a god. Taishang Laojun bestowed on Zhang Daoling the title of "Celestial Master" and told him to create a state for a chosen people to rid the world of decadence. Zhang Daoling built a community of followers around himself based around the idea that they could balance their *qi* to attain immortality and thus survive a coming apocalypse. They created a breakaway state in the Chinese region of Sichuan, which survived for a few decades before being conquered by a Chinese warlord, causing the Celestial Master community to disperse. The lineage of Celestial Masters descended from Zhang Daoling, however, survived until modern times, with the last lineage holder escaping to Taiwan after the communist victory in mainland China in 1949.

The Way of the Celestial Masters became the prototype for several Daoist sects that emerged over the subsequent centuries. Although all took inspiration from the concept of the Dao found in the *Daode Jing*, these Daoist sects continued in the more "religious" direction taken by the Way of the Celestial Masters. They wrote a large body of scriptures that built upon but went far beyond the teachings of the *Daode Jing*. These scriptures were often heavily influenced by the Buddhist scriptures that were being translated into Chinese. They borrowed and gave new meanings to Buddhist terms; they drew from the Buddhist concept of rebirth; but above all, they mimicked the Buddhist propensity for giving elaborate descriptions of the cosmos full of gods. Daoist descriptions of the gods, however, tended to have a more Chinese character and were often designed to parallel the hierarchy of the imperial bureaucracy on earth. At the same time, Daoists established lineages of priests to perform elaborate rituals in the worship of these gods. All of this represented a sharp contrast from the *Daode Jing*, which makes little reference to gods and is openly suspicious of ritual.

In the Middle Ages, Daoist sects were also interested in alchemy. Many societies around the world, including European, took an interest at that time in alchemy, which purported to be able to find a way to transform a common substance into a valuable substance, such as lead into gold. Chinese Daoists, however, extended these alchemical principles into what they called "internal alchemy," the quest to transform the mortal body into an immortal body. This is slightly different from the Christian concept of eternal life, as it involves not eternal life with God after death but rather attaining such perfect health in this life that one never dies at all. Daoists developed legends about *xian*, or immortals, who had attained this state and had associated supernatural powers. Although distinct from the gods, the immortals were often thought of and worshiped together with them, and the Daoist quest for immortality was in a sense a quest to become, or become like, a god.

Internal alchemy was built on Daoist philosophical and cosmological ideas. In principle, perfect health and thus immortality was predicated on the purification of *qi* and balancing of *yin* and *yang*. Medieval Daoist principles made this process far more concrete than it might sound to the modern ear, however. Daoists understood the body to be a microcosm: a "small world" that was correlated directly with the "big world," the universe at large. That meant that by manipulating the body, whether through meditation or through physical exercises, one could tap into great cosmological powers, including heavenly bodies, gods, *yin* and *yang*, and even the primordial principle of the Dao itself. In addition, Daoists believed that the body was a substance that could be transformed alchemically like any other. Alchemists around the world were particularly interested in mercury, which they believed to have special powers because it is the only naturally occurring metal that is liquid at room temperature. Many alchemists thought mercury might be the key ingredient to turning lead into gold, and medieval Daoists thought that it might be key to attaining immortality, even feeding concoctions including mercury to some Chinese emperors who were interested in attaining immortality themselves. (Needless to say, this did not work out, as we now know that mercury is highly poisonous to humans.)

***

Given the history of Confucianism, Buddhism, and Daoism in China I have traced here, it became common in China, long before the introduction of the modern Western concept of religion, to refer to Three Teachings (*san jiao*)—Buddhism, Confucianism, and Daoism—which were seen as pillars of Chinese society. By the middle of the second millennium, the complementarity of these three within Chinese culture had become sufficiently widely recognized that a common saying arose: *san jiao he yi*, "The Three Teachings are one." Thus, many Chinese people recognized that Buddhism, Confucianism, and Daoism are complementary and equally contribute to a uniquely Chinese religious culture.

This is not to say that Buddhism, Confucianism, and Daoism have no autonomous existence in China or have never been antagonistic to one another. After all, there are specifically Buddhist, Daoist, and Confucian institutions and elites associated with them who have often come into conflict with one another. There are Buddhist monastic institutions with their ordained monks and nuns. There are Daoist sects with their lineages of priests. And until the educational reforms of the early twentieth century, there were Confucian scholars incorporated into the imperial bureaucracy. Moreover, at various times in Chinese history, different emperors have sought to favor one of the Three Teachings and suppress the other two. But in the aggregate, all three simultaneously have historically influenced and continue to influence the religious practice of ordinary Chinese people. They also have tended to exert a great deal of influence *on one another*, even and perhaps especially when the elites of each tradition fought with and tried to outdo one another. Some scholars of China have created a metaphor that I think explains this situation quite clearly. Imagine that Chinese religion is like a three-peaked mountain. At the top, the elite level, there is a differentiation between separate traditions. But the bulk of the people are in the base, which is united and draws from all three elite traditions above.[10]

What might "the Three Teachings are one" look like in the life of an ordinary Chinese person?[11] First, their life will almost certainly be structured by certain Confucian values, most importantly filial piety. They will be taught from a young age to respect their elders; their home will likely have a shrine where they will pay honor to their dead ancestors; and every spring during the Qingming Festival they will visit the tombs of their ancestors to clean them and make ritual offerings. At various times during their life, they may employ the ritual services of a Daoist priest, and they may go to temples with images of gods whose identity and cult are informed by Daoist mythology and ritual to ask for divine protection and favor. They may avail themselves of traditional Chinese medicine or practice *qigong*, which are structured around the principles of *yin* and *yang* and *qi*. They may also seek the protection of Buddhist Bodhisattvas, especially Guanyin, and they may make a vow to be vegetarian for a time to seek her favor. If they are concerned about their mortality, they may chant the name of Amituo Fo in the hope of being reborn in his Pure Land. At death, their family may seek the ritual services of either Daoist priests or Buddhist monks to perform the funeral and ensure their happiness in the next life.

One of the most tangible instantiations of the principle that "the Three Teachings are one" is the community temple. There are many different types of temples in Chinese religion, and some of them are dedicated specifically to Confucian, Daoist, or Buddhist worship. But many Chinese temples are not affiliated with one of the Three Teachings; they are built by a local community committee and typically draw from all three traditions. That is, they may have statues of Daoist gods, images of Buddhas and Bodhisattvas, and name plates for prominent community ancestors. The focus of such temples is the wellbeing of the community, by any means deemed efficacious, rather than allegiance to any one religion.

Chinese Religion: What Is It, and Where Can We Find It?

Figure 6.2 A typical Chinese community temple in Taiwan. Photo by Nanda Raksakhom.

RELIGIONS ARE NOT JUST SYSTEMS OF BELIEF EMBODIED IN SCRIPTURES

The big point I want to make in this chapter is that you cannot understand a religion just by reading its "original scripture" to find out what they believe. Doing so for the three religions of China simply does not work. If all you knew about Chinese religion came from reading the *Analects* of Confucius, the *Daode Jing*, and the first sermon of the Buddha, you wouldn't really know much about Chinese religion at all. You wouldn't know, first, that these three religions are not mutually exclusive. You also wouldn't know exactly which Confucian ideals continue to have influence today, that a whole pantheon of gods and goddesses are an everyday part of Chinese religion, that there are Daoist priests who perform elaborate rituals, or that Buddhism's influence takes the form of Bodhisattvas and Pure Land Buddhas more often than meditation and the Eightfold Path. To really understand religion, you have to look at what people *do*, not just what a scripture says that they *believe*.

To be sure, the ideas or beliefs that are found in the foundational scriptures of Buddhism, Confucianism, and Daoism are a part of Chinese religion. Most ordinary Chinese religious practitioners, even if they haven't received any deep education in a particular tradition, will be familiar with the concept of the gentleman and filial piety, the Dao, *qi* and *yin* and *yang*, the cycle of rebirth and Buddhist Awakening. These concepts will inform much of what they do in their religious lives and even in many cases in aspects of their life that they might not consider particularly religious, such as going to a traditional Chinese doctor for medical treatment. But you cannot guess what religious practice will look like from the beliefs alone. Practice is built around values, ideas, and beliefs, but it is shaped by history and tradition.

The fact that religious practice is not derived in a straightforward way from belief is exemplified by Western appropriations of Daoism. In a manner very similar to the Buddhist Modernism we learned about in chapter 4, Daoism has been avidly taken up by Westerners as a New Age religion. These Western "Daoists" see it as a religion without rules or rituals, without dogmas, myths, or superstitions, something more spiritual than religious that lets you follow your own individual path. Like the Western perception of Buddhism, this Daoism is more a philosophy than a religion, and it is praised as such. It teaches you to find the Dao, the natural Way, through actionless action and balancing *yin* and *yang*. Unsurprisingly, this Western understanding of Daoism is based almost exclusively on reading the *Daode Jing* (and also the *Zhuangzi*), without giving any consideration to the later history and practices of Daoism. Translations of the *Daode Jing* into English and other languages are extremely popular, and there are any number of popular books that claim to be based on Daoist principles, from *The Dao of Pooh* to *The Dao of Physics*.[12] The resulting Western image of Daoism gives a very misleading image of the tradition. First, it treats Daoism as a separate religion when it traditionally has been practiced alongside Buddhism and Confucianism. Second, it completely ignores the bulk of Daoist practice—its gods, its priests, its elaborate rituals—and moreover claims that what makes Daoism special is that it lacks those very things.

The modern Western concept of religion has certainly played a pivotal role in this Western (mis)perception of Daoism, but it has also had an influence on Chinese perceptions of their own traditions as well. For example, modern Chinese now distinguishes between philosophy and religion, with different suffixes used for philosophies (*jia*) and religions (*jiao*). Confucianism is now typically referred to as a philosophy (*rujia*), while Buddhism is usually referred to as a religion (*fojiao*). Daoism, on the other hand, is said to have two forms: philosophical Daoism (*daojia*) and religious Daoism (*daojiao*). The language can thus accommodate the modern perception that there is a disconnect between the philosophy of the *Daode Jing* and the religious practices of the Daoist sects that began with the Way of the Celestial Masters. In modern Chinese communities, some people, influenced by the modern identification of Buddhism as a discrete religion, choose to identify specifically as Buddhists if they take a particular interest in Buddhist practice and frequent Buddhist monasteries. There is also a trend among some rationally minded Chinese people of disdaining aspects of Chinese tradition they don't like or see as superstitious by calling it "Daoist" (by which they mean religious Daoism, not philosophical Daoism). The principle that "the Three Teachings are one" certainly continues to structure the overall field of Chinese religious practice, but Western ideas about what constitutes religion and what religion should or should not look like increasingly are fracturing the Three Teachings, at least in the way some people talk about them.

DISCUSSION QUESTIONS

1. What are the three major religions of China, and in what ways can they be said to not be mutually exclusive? Please give specific examples.
2. Would you say that the teachings of the *Analects* of Confucius and the *Daode Jing* are opposed to one another, or complementary? Be sure to refer to specific philosophical principles used by each text in your response.
3. In what ways does the Mahayana Buddhism that is popular in China show continuities and discontinuities with early Buddhism, as we learned about in chapter 4?
4. What might you expect Confucianism, Buddhism, and Daoism to look like if you only understood them by reading their "original scriptures"? How does that differ from the reality?
5. How is Daoism often portrayed in the West? How does that differ from the reality of Daoism in its Chinese context?

NOTES

1 To be clear, in modern China there are many more than just three religions, in part because modern China includes ethnic groups other than the Han Chinese majority. The most predominant of these that possesses a different religious culture is the Uyghurs, found in northwest China, who are predominantly Muslim. The Tibetans, found in southwest China, follow their own form of Buddhism that

is different from the Han Chinese, which we will explore in more detail in chapter 8. There are also other religions, such as Nestorian Christianity, that have historically had some influence in China. My point here is that the culture of the Han Chinese ethnic majority has been historically dominated by three religions: Buddhism, Confucianism, and Daoism. This is the religious culture we will be examining in this chapter.

2 These practices have often been referred to in English as "ancestor worship." The living, however, do not really worship their ancestors; rather, they in a ritualized way maintain a relationship with their ancestors out of filial piety.

3 You may also find the word *Dao* spelled *Tao* and the word *Daoism* spelled *Taoism*. The reason for this is that there are two different systems for representing the sounds of Chinese in the English alphabet. One of these systems is called Wade-Giles, which was created by two Western scholars named Wade and Giles. This is the system in which the spelling is *Tao*. The second system is called *pinyin*; it was created by the communist government in China to teach children how to read and to represent Chinese words in English. In this system, the spelling is *Dao*. Wade-Giles used to be the standard in Western scholarship about China, and it is still used in (noncommunist) Taiwan. Western scholars are increasingly switching to *pinyin*, however, and the emergence of (mainland) China as a global power means that *pinyin* is much more visible than the older Wade-Giles system. For that reason, I use *pinyin* spellings in this book, but you should be aware that you may see old Wade-Giles spellings sometimes, especially the words *Tao* and *Taoism*. Please be aware that whatever system is used, the correct pronunciation is closer to a *d* than a *t*; this is another reason to prefer the *pinyin* system.

4 Philip J. Ivanhoe and Bryan W. Van Nordern, eds., *Readings in Classical Chinese Philosophy* (Indianapolis: Hackett Publishing Company, 2005), 163.

5 For a translation of this famous passage of Zhuangzi, see Ivanhoe and Norden, *Readings*, 224.

6 Ivanhoe and Norden, *Readings*, 181.

7 Ivanhoe and Norden, *Readings*, 183.

8 The history of imperial examinations in China is complicated, and it was only in later dynasties that passing these exams became a more universal tool for entering the imperial bureaucracy. Nevertheless, the roots of the system lie in the Han Dynasty.

9 This, incidentally, is why we now have a Latinized name for Mengzi (Mencius) but not for Xunzi. When the Jesuits were in China, they

encountered Neo-Confucians who considered Mengzi the true successor of Confucius, while Xunzi had fallen into relative obscurity.
10 Peter N. Gregory and Patricia Buckley Ebrey, "Chapter 1: The Religious and Historical Landscape," in *Religion and Society in T'ang and Sung China*, ed. Patricia Buckley Ebrey and Peter N. Gregory (Honolulu: Hawai'i University Press, 1993), 12.
11 To be clear, this is simply an idealization. Chinese culture is quite broad and variegated, being found not only in mainland China but also in Taiwan, Malaysia, Singapore, and beyond. Mainland Chinese culture has been profoundly influenced by communist rule and the legacy of the Cultural Revolution in ways that Chinese cultures outside of mainland China have not. Moreover, as in any culture, especially in the modern world, different people choose to engage with the religious traditions around them to different degrees and in different ways.
12 Benjamin Hoff, *The Tao of Pooh* (New York: Penguin Books, 1982); Fritjof Capra, *The Tao of Physics* (Boston: Shambhala Publications, 1999).

7

Indian Religions

How Can One Religion "Include" Another?

In the last chapter, we saw that the Western assumption that religions are mutually exclusive totally breaks down in China. The three main religions of China are Buddhism, Confucianism, and Daoism, but these three religions are typically practiced together, often in the same temples and by the same people. Not all religious cultures outside of the West are quite so open to the simultaneous practice of multiple traditions, but another instructive example is that of India. Indian religions historically have dealt with one another through a strategy that we can refer to as *inclusivism*, a term that was coined by a scholar named Paul Hacker specifically to describe Indian religions.[1]

Inclusivism is a strategy for dealing with religious difference that contrasts with the exclusivism found in the Abrahamic traditions. The Abrahamic traditions are monotheistic, which means that they *exclude* the worship of all gods other than the one true God. The significance of this exclusion may not be entirely apparent in the modern world, in which monotheism is the norm in many cultures, but it would have been immediately apparent to a person in the ancient Roman empire who was considering becoming a Christian. Becoming a Christian at that time would have meant that you would have to refrain from worshiping *any* other god—of which there were many. This would set the newly converted Christian apart from most people in the society of their day. Indeed, in ancient Rome, Christians were disparaged as atheists because they rejected most of the gods—indeed, all of the gods except one.

DOI: 10.4324/9781032646428-9

This chapter is ordered roughly chronologically. We'll start with the earliest evidence for religion in India and then explore the way in which new religious identities formed over the centuries according to the logic of inclusivism. This history will involve three religions we have already learned about in this book: Hinduism, Buddhism, and Islam. It will also involve two additional religions that we have not encountered yet: Jainism and Sikhism.

THE VEDIC PERIOD

The earliest evidence we have for religion in India comes from the Vedas, the oldest part of which was composed about 3,000 years ago. The Vedas describe a culture of many gods and goddesses very similar to that found in other parts of the ancient world, including Greece and Rome. Various divinities were associated with different natural forces. The king of the gods is Indra, a sky god similar to the Greek Zeus, the Roman Jupiter, and the Nordic Thor. As a sky god, Indra wields a lightning-producing diamond scepter called a *vajra*—the equivalent of Zeus's thunderbolt or Thor's hammer. Similarly, Surya is the sun god, Prithivi is the earth goddess, Ushas is the goddess of dawn, Vach is the goddess of speech, Vayu is the god of wind, Agni is the god of fire, and Yama is the god of the dead. Certain gods have special roles that are unique to ancient Indian culture. For example, Soma is associated with the moon but is also embodied on earth as a plant that can be pressed to make a juice with stimulating properties that was drunk by warriors going into battle. Likewise, Rudra is a dark god associated with the wild and general chaos, considered both the instigator of disease and a curer of disease. Several gods are associated with creation, including Vishnu, who is said in the Vedas to have measured out the "triple world" (earth, atmosphere, and sky) with three giant strides. Many Vedic texts, however, refer to Prajapati—not a name but a title meaning "lord of creatures"—as the being who was ultimately responsible for creating the universe and all the other gods within it.

Ancient Indian religion, as attested in the Vedas, consisted, as in other ancient religions, of making sacrifices to the gods to ensure proper harmony in the universe. Sacrifices included animals, vegetable offerings, and the plant-derived drink called *soma*. These would be offered into a ritual fire, which would consume them and convert them into smoke to be conveyed up to the gods. These sacrifices were not performed in permanent temples. They were instead performed outside in the open air, using temporary ritual enclosures that would be constructed for a sacrificial session and then destroyed.

In the distant past, sacrifices to the gods were likely guided by a somewhat informal and creative culture of norms that were shared by various seminomadic groups who spoke similar dialects of a language we now call Sanskrit and who called themselves Aryas.[2] Over time, however, the rituals involved in performing the sacrifices were codified, and a more professional class of people known as Brahmans arose who were responsible for learning and performing the sacrifices, as well as for passing down orally the Vedas, which contained the hymns and sacred formulas used in the sacrificial rituals. Others could still perform sacrifices to the gods, but they would do so as a patron, hiring Brahmans to perform the sacrifice on their behalf.

The Vedas, as an oral tradition, were not static. They evolved and were added to over the centuries. In particular, Brahmans became increasingly interested in speculating about *why* various sacrifices were performed in the ways that they were. They added to the Vedic tradition with commentaries that tried to explain how the rituals of the sacrifice connected to the gods and the universe as a whole. The last layer of these commentaries, known as Upanishads, became concerned not just with the sacrifice narrowly, but with the nature of the universe as a whole. The Brahmans thus became a class of intellectuals very similar to the philosophers of ancient Greece. Indeed, once Greeks encountered Indian civilization at the edge of Alexander the Great's empire in the fourth century BCE, they used the word *philosophers* to describe the Brahmans.

The Upanishads, the latest layer of the Vedic tradition, contain many types of philosophical speculation within them, but one of the most common is about the *atman*, which literally means "self." Many passages of the Upanishads ask questions about what one's true self is, looking increasingly deeper within—deeper than the body, deeper than the breath, deeper even than the mind—to find it. Some passages of the Upanishads also speculate about what happens to the *atman* when you die, suggesting that it goes through a process whereby it returns to another body—a rudimentary theory of reincarnation. This process is not random, but is guided by one's actions, or *karma*, in this life, determining whether one has a good rebirth or a bad one.

THE BUDDHA AND MAHAVIRA OUTDO THE GODS

Starting around the fifth century BCE, a time when the region around the Ganges River in North India was becoming increasingly urbanized, a class of individuals known as *shramanas* emerged. These *shramanas* engaged in practices of renunciation to pursue liberation from the cycle of rebirth, known as *samsara*. The word *shramana* means "one who toils"; these were religious ascetics. The *shramanas* were not originally a separate group from the Brahmans, but over time the two groups became increasingly separate and antagonistic toward one another. In particular, Brahmans and *shramanas* fought over the issue of celibacy. *Shramanas* generally saw celibacy—total abstinence from sex—as an ascetic practice necessary to attain liberation from rebirth. More conservative Brahmans, on the other hand, argued that the Vedas command that one must produce children to repay a debt to the ancestors. They were not necessarily opposed to ascetic practices, even including celibacy, but they believed that one must repay one's debt to the ancestors by producing children first.

The *shramanas* at first were a loosely defined community of ascetics who engaged in a wide variety of practices taught through a network of ever-changing teacher-student relationships. In other words, a *shramana* might practice with one group or under one teacher for a while and then move on to another who appeared to have better teachings or attainment. Over time, however, two particular groups of *shramanas* became organized and survive to this day as major world religions. These two groups are the Buddhists and the Jains.

We already learned about Buddhism in chapter 4, so there is no need to go into detail about that religion again here. Jainism is similar in many ways to Buddhism, but it has some key differences. Like Buddhism, it was founded by a particular person, in this case a man named Vardhamana. Vardhamana is often referred to by a title, Mahavira, which means "great hero," and by the title Jina, which means "victor." It is from this latter title that Jainism gets its name. Mahavira, like the Buddha, was a *shramana* who wandered about practicing asceticism in search of liberation from rebirth. Unlike the Buddha, however, he remained committed all his life to the harshest ascetic practices. He renounced all possessions, including clothing, and wandered about naked. He also taught a very strict principle of *ahimsa*, or nonviolence. Because all actions—even walking, breathing, and eating—have the potential to cause violence to small creatures, Mahavira saw it as necessary to bring an end to action altogether.

In later centuries, Jains developed a more consistent philosophy to explain how liberation, which they call *moksha*, can take place. Every living being is in essence a *jiva*, which literally means "life" but can be understood to be similar to the Western concept of the soul. This soul is eternal, although not exactly unchanging, and it is intrinsically omniscient (all-knowing) and blissful, characterized by pure awareness.

Figure 7.1 An image of Mahavira from South India. Photo by the author.

The soul is trapped in *samsara* (the cycle of rebirth) because of *karma*. Jains, unlike other groups in India, understand *karma* to be an actual physical substance that sticks to the soul, obscuring its bliss and omniscience and trapping it in a succession of bodies. That is, whenever you perform an action, *karma* "leaks in" and sticks to your soul, weighing it down and preventing it from being liberated. *Karma* associated with violence is particularly bad, but really all actions are problematic from the Jain perspective. To attain *moksha*, it is therefore necessary to do two things: Stop the leakage of *karma* into the soul by ending action and get the *karma* that is already stuck to the soul to "fall off" by performing austerities. This is why Mahavira performed harsh asceticism, such as fasting. Although Mahavira himself did not do so, Jain scriptures suggest that a person can end their life, under very specific circumstances (such as terminal illness), with a fast to the death—an act that Jains most vigorously do not understand as suicide but instead regard as "religious death,"[3] which furthers the elimination of accumulated *karma*. When *moksha* is achieved—that is, when the soul is fully cleansed of all *karma*—the soul naturally floats to the top of the universe and experiences its intrinsic bliss and omniscience.

Jainism survives to this day as a minority religion in India through communities of monastics and their lay supporters who are divided into two major groups. The larger of these two groups are the Shvetambaras, which literally means "white-clad." They are thus called because the monks and nuns of this tradition wear white robes. In this respect, they are not as thoroughgoing in their renunciation as the founder Mahavira was, but they maintain a strong commitment to *ahimsa*, nonviolence. Often, Shvetambara monks and nuns will wear face masks to prevent microorganisms from being killed when they breathe, and they will use a whisk to brush the path ahead of them to prevent small insects from being killed when they walk. The smaller group of Jains are the Digambaras, which means "sky-clad." The monks of this tradition (there are no nuns) go completely naked as Mahavira himself did.

Structurally, Jain communities are similar to Buddhist communities. Monastics are celibate and engage in practices (to varying degrees, as we have just seen) traced back to the founder, and they are supported in their lifestyle by laypeople who live lives like those of non-Jains around them. Jains today do not generally believe that liberation is possible for ordinary human beings, so the hope, even among monastics, is to attain a better rebirth, rather than to engage in the harshest austerities to attain *moksha* here and now. That said, some Jains, including laypeople, do undertake religious death, but they usually do so only in old age and when death is imminent anyway (such as with a terminal cancer diagnosis). Unlike

Buddhism, Jainism never spread beyond India's borders, except among small immigrant communities, in large part because Jain monastics were forbidden to travel long distances. Jainism today is thus a relatively small religion by global standards but remains an important part of India's overall religious history and contemporary religious culture.

Ultimately, Jainism and Buddhism, as well as the broader *shramana* movement that they emerged from, represent a pivotal change in Indian religion. They are *soteriological* religions—that is, like Christianity they are religions that identify a problem intrinsic to the human condition and offer a solution to that problem, a path of salvation. The problem, according to both, is *samsara*, a cycle of rebirth in which we are all trapped. People in the modern West who are into such things often think that rebirth is cool, but that is not at all the way it is viewed in Indian religions. It is understood to be a thing of horror, forcing us to endure the suffering of life over and over again. We should want to escape from it, and Buddhism and Jainism offer different paths for attaining this goal. The key innovation over the Vedic religion that preceded is that these religions are about something more than simply maintaining good relations with the gods.

Unlike Christianity, however, Buddhism and Jainism did not deny the gods' existence or their divinity. They accepted that the gods existed and had all the powers usually attributed to them. They only denied one thing about the gods: that they are immortal. According to Buddhism and Jainism, gods live for a very long time (on the order of millions of years), but they are trapped in *samsara* just like the rest of us. Eventually, they too will die and be reborn in another form according to their *karma* or actions. This attitude toward the gods is the earliest example of inclusivism in the history of religion in India. Notice that while the gods and their worship are not denied by this strategy, they are significantly demoted. Now that the goal is to escape from *samsara*, the gods are not so special because they themselves are still trapped within it. Those who have escaped from *samsara*, exemplified by the Buddha (in Buddhism) or Mahavira (in Jainism), are in fact greater than the gods. In fact, these religions promise that you too can become greater than the gods if you attain liberation from rebirth.

THEISTIC RESPONSES TO THE BUDDHA, MAHAVIRA, AND EACH OTHER

At about the same time that Buddhism and Jainism arose, it seems that the belief arose among the Brahman priests of ancient India that there was one God who was greater than all the rest, even Indra, who created the universe and should be people's ultimate goal after they die. This god was Brahma. In many ways, Brahma was a continuation of the Vedic concept of Prajapati, a "lord of creatures" who was the ultimate source of the entire universe. The name Brahma comes from a neuter noun in Sanskrit, *brahman*, that had long had great significance in Vedic thought. *Brahman*, first and foremost, refers to sacred speech—that is, the speech that is uttered in the Vedas. The Brahmans, the priests who transmitted the Vedas and used them to perform sacrifices to the gods, also take their name from this word. In the speculations of the later parts of the Vedas, especially the Upanishads, the word *brahman* was elevated to the status of a cosmic principle: ultimate reality itself. Many passages in the Upanishads go further and say that the *atman* (the personal self) is identical with *brahman* (ultimate reality). The goal then becomes to recognize that one's true self is identical with *brahman* and thus attain liberation from rebirth. Brahma is a personification of this ultimate reality who thus can serve both as a creator God and as the goal one seeks in liberation.

Early Buddhists enjoyed making fun of this God. According to the early Buddhist scriptures, Brahma is not a single God; instead, there are many Brahmas who live in the higher levels of heaven but are still subject to rebirth like everyone else. There is a story in the Buddhist scriptures (*Majjhima Nikaya* 49) that says that one Brahma, named Baka, stupidly thought that he was the creator of the universe. The reason for this is that the universe naturally expands and contracts. As it expands, beings are born in various forms to populate the different levels of the universe. Baka was born first and then saw the universe expand below him with beings being born in the lower levels, so he thought he had created it all. The Buddha knew that Baka had this foolish notion and so went to heaven to tell him he was wrong—and demonstrate his own superiority through a show of miraculous power. Other stories in the Buddhist scriptures talk about Brahma visiting the Buddha and showing deference to him as a disciple—a common theme, incidentally, in Buddhist art. These stories are examples of what scholar Alexis Sanderson has called *super-enthronement*—a type of inclusivism in which the top figure of one religion's rivals is acknowledged to exist and be important but is shown to be subordinate to the top figure of one's own religion.[4] In these stories, the Buddha "super-enthrones" Brahma.

Super-enthronement became a common strategy in Indian religions, and Brahma was frequently a victim of it. The most important example of this is in the *Mahabharata*, an epic poem written by Brahmans in Sanskrit that became foundational to the religion we now know as Hinduism. There is a lot of debate among scholars about when the *Mahabharata* was written or if it was even written all at once, but most would agree that at least the original core of it was written in the second or first century BCE.

As it comes down to us, the *Mahabharata* is about a war in the distant past that was orchestrated by God to relieve the earth of its overpopulation and harassment by demons. How God is portrayed in this epic, however, is quite different from how he is portrayed in earlier sources. The story begins with Brahma, referred to as the "Grandfather," sending the other gods to incarnate as human beings to take part in the war. So seemingly Brahma is the "God" figure in this narrative, as we would expect. We soon find out, however, that one of those gods, Vishnu, who has incarnated as a human being named Krishna, is the ultimate being who created even Brahma. (Krishna's identity as God is revealed most famously in the *Bhagavad Gita*, a section of the *Mahabharata* at the beginning of the final battle in which Krishna urges Arjuna to fight.) As Krishna, Vishnu advises the Pandavas—the "good guys" in the war—and leads them to victory. At the same time, however, a third god, Shiva (better known in the Vedas as Rudra) also plays an important role, particularly in the destructive aspects of the war, and it is frequently intimated that he is the ultimate God.

Scholars have debated the significance of different passages of the *Mahabharata* and whether they could have been written by the same person or group of people. Regardless of one's opinion on these debates, the effect of the *Mahabharata* as a whole was to effectively demote Brahma from a singular representation of God to an aspect of some greater conception of God, who takes the role especially of Vishnu but also at times of Shiva. In this respect, the *Mahabharata* practices super-enthronement toward Brahma in much the same way as early Buddhist literature did.

The Puranas, later Hindu scriptures that all are based on the worldview painted by the *Mahabharata*, continue the trend of super-enthronement found in the epic. One example is a story, found in the *Mahabharata* but further elaborated in the Puranas, that shows the superiority of Vishnu to Brahma. According to this story, Brahma did indeed create the world, just as had earlier been claimed of him. But he didn't do it on his own. Vishnu is in fact the supreme God, and at the beginning of time he reclined on a serpent in a primordial sea of milk. As he reclined, a lotus blossom grew from his navel. Brahma was then born from that lotus blossom, and he created the world on Vishnu's behalf. Another story is intended to show the superiority of Shiva to both Brahma and Vishnu. According to this story, the three gods had an argument about who was the greatest. Now, Shiva is often not worshiped in anthropomorphic form, but in the form of a *linga*, a cylindrically shaped stone that is phallic-looking and represents fertility. So, in the story, Shiva converts himself into an infinitely long *linga* and challenges Brahma and Vishnu to find his end. One of them goes up, the other goes down, but neither can find the end. Thus, the superiority of Shiva is established.

Ultimately, more dedicated sectarian movements emerged out of the culture of the epics and Puranas. As we saw in chapter 5, there are three major sectarian groups in Hinduism: Vaishnavas, who regard Vishnu as the highest God; Shaivas, who regard Shiva as the highest God; and Shaktas, who worship the Goddess as the highest form of divinity. All these sectarian movements are inclusivistic toward one another. They do not regard the other two divine figures as nonexistent; rather, they consider them, along with all other gods and goddesses, to be creations of or alternate forms of whichever one they consider to be the ultimate form of the divine. Inclusivism was practiced so thoroughly against Brahma that no major sectarian movement emerged regarding him as the supreme form of God.

Although the bulk of theistic inclusivism was practiced by Hindus with respect to each other, Vaishnavas also used super-enthronement against the Buddhists, who, as we saw, had earlier used it against Brahma. Building upon the *Mahabharata* story of Vishnu incarnating as Krishna, Vaishnavas developed a theology in which Vishnu has, at multiple key moments in history, incarnated as a human being or an animal to have an influence on human events. It is a concept very similar to the incarnation of God as Jesus Christ in Christianity, except that Vishnu does it over and over, not just once. According to some Vaishnava texts, one of Vishnu's incarnations was the Buddha! They thus acknowledge the existence and importance of the Buddha but subordinate him to their own God by making him merely an incarnation of that God.

REORDERING UNDER MUSLIM INFLUENCE

Starting in the late tenth century CE, Turkic nomads began raiding into India. This was not something particularly new, as India had faced invasions from outside groups repeatedly since ancient times. What was new was that these invaders happened to be Muslim. These raids culminated in 1206 with the foundation of the Delhi Sultanate, a kingdom spanning much of North India that was ruled by an ethnically Turkic elite that had adopted Persian language and culture and followed the Islamic faith. This kingdom was then followed by the Mughal Empire, founded in 1526, which was similarly ruled by Persianized Muslims and which at its height around the year 1700 ruled over most of the Indian subcontinent.

Much has been made, both inside and outside of India, about this period of rule by Muslims. Often, the history has been told as part of a broader

Islamophobic narrative, in which Muslims, zealous to conquer the world and convert it to Islam, conquered India and destroyed much of its indigenous religion and culture. While it is certainly true that the Delhi Sultanate, Mughal Empire, and other smaller kingdoms ruled by Muslims in India during this period were oppressive and destructive in certain ways, the same could be said for several other kingdoms ruled by outsiders prior to the period of Muslim rule, the British Raj that followed the period of Muslim rule, and frankly any major empire anywhere in the history of humankind.

Second, the Muslims who ruled over these kingdoms in India were not trying to create a unified Islamic empire; in fact, they were the product of the *breakup* of the original Islamic empire. The Turkic people who founded the Delhi Sultanate came to power as the original Islamic empire broke apart; they chose Persian rather than Arabic as their court language; and they generally sought an increased separation between religious scholarship and royal power.

Finally, while the period of Muslim rule did result in a large number of people in South Asia converting to Islam—with the result that Islam is the majority religion in what is now Pakistan and Bangladesh and a large minority in India as well[5]—it is hardly the case that these Muslim rulers forced the wholesale conversion of their Indian subjects to Islam. Indeed, Hinduism flourished during the period of Muslim rule. In addition, the very sense of a unified Hindu identity is largely the product of Muslim rule. As we saw in chapter 5, the word *Hindu* comes from Persian, and it was used by Muslim rulers (who used Persian as their court language) to refer to their Indian subjects who did not convert to Islam.

I make these extensive caveats because the very discussion of Islam in Indian history has become utterly entangled with Islamaphobia. In modern India, Islamophobia has even given rise to a political movement known as Hindutva, which literally means "Hindu-ness." Hindutva is a religious nationalist movement that valorizes Hinduism (or rather a very particular type of Hinduism), regards India as properly and intrinsically Hindu, and engages in rhetorical and even physical violence against religious minorities, especially Muslims.

That being said, we should not go to the other extreme and pretend that the period of Muslim rule did not have a profound effect on Indian culture and Hinduism. It most certainly did, not least of all in providing the conditions for the arising of the consciousness of a common Hindu culture. But, additionally, the several centuries of Muslim rule served to valorize monotheism as intrinsically superior to polytheism. As we saw in chapter 5, the words *monotheism* and *polytheism* are too black and white to describe how Hinduism works. There we focused on the distorting effect Christian monotheism has on perceptions of Hinduism, but the first major experience Hindus had with the dichotomizing logic of monotheism came not from Christians but from Muslims.

As we have already seen, Indian religion has had important strains that are reminiscent of monotheism. The Vedas contain speculations about a supreme God, often referring to him as Prajapati. Many Brahmans around the time of the rise of the *shramana* movements worshiped Brahma as a supreme God. The epic *Mahabharata* made a concept of God, albeit somewhat paradoxically, central to its narrative, and this narrative became the basis for much of Hindu culture, including Vaishnavism, Shaivism, and Shaktism, that followed.

Yet in other respects, the Indian religion that Muslims encountered was quite different from monotheism, especially as conceived by Islam. Due to their inclusivism, even those Hindus who worshipped a supreme God (or the Goddess) recognized the existence and power of numerous other gods and goddesses. Moreover, Indian religion was replete with the use of imagery, both in the form of ordinary art and in the form of temple statues, called *murtis*, that Hindus understand as being imbued with the sacred power of the gods. These aspects of Indian religion obviously clashed with the Islamic *shahada*, which states that there is no god but God, as well as Islam's strict iconoclasm and rejection of idolatry.

In part due to the influence of Islam, Hindus under Muslim rule came to increasingly emphasize a virtue known as *bhakti* in Sanskrit. *Bhakti* means "devotion," and it is a key term in the *Bhagavad Gita*, in which Krishna tells Arjuna that the best path to liberation from rebirth is to have devotion to God (i.e., himself), and God will save you. Several important holy men and women, usually known in English as *"bhakti* saints," became famous during the period of Muslim rule for their devotion to God, and their devotion was transmitted throughout India in the form of songs of devotion that they composed. These saints came from and operated within a variety of sectarian traditions, but many of them were Vaishnava. At the same time, these *bhakti* saints served as agents for communication between Hindu and Muslim society. In particular, Hindu *bhakti* saints and Sufis representing the tradition of Islamic mysticism entered into dialog as they sought common ground between their two religious cultures.

Over time, the *bhakti* tradition was sorted into two broad types: *saguna bhakti* and *nirguna bhakti*. *Saguna* means "with qualities." *Bhakti* saints who were in the *saguna* camp leaned a bit more toward traditional Hindu culture, emphasizing a personal, anthropomorphic conception of God, following descriptions found in Hindu texts like the *Mahabharata*.

This does not mean that they did not see God as ultimately transcendent; they just emphasized the need for human beings to relate to God in a personal form. *Nirguna*, conversely, means "without qualities." Those in the *nirguna* camp leaned a bit more toward conceptions of God like those found in Islam, emphasizing that God is totally transcendent and does not ultimately have an anthropomorphic form or any human qualities whatsoever.

Historically, the most influential of the *bhakti* saints was a man named Guru Nanak. His teachings became the basis of a new religion, Sikhism, which is now the fifth largest religion in the world. Guru Nanak lived from 1469 to 1539 in a region known as the Punjab, which today straddles the border between Pakistan and India. In Nanak's day, the Punjab was already a very religiously diverse region, with large numbers of both Hindus and Muslims. Nanak himself was born to Hindu parents, but, according to the traditional account of his life, he refused to undergo *upanayana*, the rite of initiation for upper-class Hindus. After reaching adulthood, Nanak married and took a job in Sultanpur in a shop owned by a local Muslim landlord. Every day, he would take a bath in the River Bein, but one day he did not return from the bath. People found his clothes on the riverbank and assumed he had drowned. On the third day after his disappearance, however, Nanak reemerged. The first words he spoke were these: "There is no Hindu, there is no Muslim."

According to the traditional account, Nanak spent the days during his disappearance directly in the divine presence. God presented him with a cup of *amrit* (literally, "immortality") and told him, "This is the cup of my name." After Nanak drank from the cup, God ordered him to recite, and he recited his first *bhakti* hymn in praise of the divine name. After his reemergence from the river, Guru Nanak composed numerous hymns in his native tongue of Punjabi praising what he called *Ik Ongkar*, the one God, who, in alignment with the *nirguna* tradition, was completely beyond all qualities and who furthermore transcended all divisions between Hindu and Muslim. Nanak attracted disciples, of both Hindu and Muslim background, who became known as *Sikhs*, literally "students."

Before his death, Guru Nanak appointed one of his disciples, Angad, as his successor. Thus was initiated a series of ten Gurus, or teachers, whose leadership of the Sikh community lasted until 1708. The fifth Guru, Arjan, compiled the Sikh scripture, known as the Guru Granth Sahib. It was a collection of *bhakti* hymns by Guru Nanak, later Sikh Gurus, and even other *bhakti* saints and Muslims who preceded Nanak. The principle for inclusion lay not in sectarian identity but in thematic adherence to the principle of one God who is without qualities. He then placed the

Indian Religions: How Can One Religion "Include" Another?

Figure 7.2 The Golden Temple (Harmandir Sahib) at Amritsar, in India. © Getty Images

scripture in a special temple, the Harmandir, which is today known as the Golden Temple of Amritsar.

The early Sikh community was able to flourish in part because of the policy of religious tolerance followed by the Mughal Emperor Akbar. This policy changed with his death and the accession of Jahangir (reigned 1605–1627). In 1606, Jahangir, intolerant of the Sikhs' teachings that brought converts even from the Muslims, had Arjan captured, tortured, and killed. Arjan's martyrdom led to a stronger sense of Sikh identity and militancy to protect it. Arjan's son, Guru Hargobind, raised a small armed guard and built a fortress to protect Amritsar. Then, in 1675, the ninth Guru, Tegh Bahadur, was executed by the Mughals for protesting a policy, introduced by the Mughal Emperor Aurangzeb (reigned 1658–1707), that would force Hindus to convert to Islam. His son, Guru Gobind Singh, was thus forced again to protect Sikh autonomy and identity in the face of a religiously intolerant ruler.

In 1699, Guru Gobind Singh inaugurated a special fraternity of Sikhs called the Khalsa. This fraternity began at a large gathering of Sikhs in which he asked for five men who were willing to lay down their lives in devotion. He pretended to kill them one by one, as if making human sacrifices, but in reality, he initiated them into the new order by having them drink from a common cup of *amrit*. The Khalsa still exists today, and entry into it serves as a sort of confirmation ceremony for Sikhs that shows their equality before God regardless of social class. To show this equality, all Sikh men who enter the Khalsa receive the surname Singh, and all Sikh women who enter it receive the surname Kaur. Male members of the Khalsa also adopt certain standard elements of attire, known as the "five *ks*" because all five begin with a *k* sound in Punjabi. Of these five, the most publicly visible is that male Sikh members of the Khalsa keep their hair long and therefore customarily wrap their hair in a turban.

Unfortunately, this conspicuous mark of Sikh identity has frequently made Sikhs the target of racist attacks. In part, racists have attacked Sikhs simply for being different, but frequently in attacking them they are driven by Islamophobia. Popular culture in the West (such as the animated Disney film *Aladdin*) has tended to associate turbans with Muslims, so ignorant racists who see Sikhs wearing turbans often think that they are Muslims. A particularly deadly example was a mass shooting by a white supremacist at a *gurdwara* (Sikh temple) in Oak Creek, Wisconsin, in 2012, in which six people were killed.

When the Mughal Emperor Aurangzeb died in 1707, he was succeeded by Bahadur Shah, who was more open to religious diversity. Unfortunately, not all were happy about the return to religious tolerance. While Guru Gobind Singh was traveling with the new Mughal emperor, he was stabbed on the orders of a Muslim noble who was jealous of the Sikh leader's access to the emperor. Guru Gobind Singh lived until the next year, but he eventually died of his wounds. Before dying, he made a unique decision about his successor: Instead of naming a human successor, he named the Sikh scripture, the Guru Granth Sahib, as his successor. Thus ended the lineage of human Sikh Gurus but also began the basis for a truly global world religion. Today, Sikhs around the world gather as local congregations in temples called *gurdwaras*. They hold services in these *gurdwara*s in which the Sikh scripture and readings from it take center stage.

In sum, the period of Muslim rule in India served to reorient the already existing tendency toward inclusivism in Indian religion. During this period, Indians grappled in different ways with their preexisting religious traditions in a world that gave monotheism—the idea that there is one God, and belief in many gods is inferior—a certain hegemonic power. The *bhakti* saints drew upon sectarian traditions with their roots in the *Mahabharata*'s depiction of God to espouse a more monotheistic-like form of piety without fundamentally rejecting the diversity of Hindu religious practices. And although one of the *bhakti* saints, Guru Nanak, represented a stronger break with the past in founding a new religion based on belief in one God, his message of transcending the division between Hindu and Muslim also represented a new engagement with religions from outside India that would presage further developments in Indian religious inclusivism to come.

THE HINDU RENAISSANCE AND THE EXPORTATION OF INCLUSIVISM THROUGH NEO-VEDANTA

Over the course of the eighteenth century, the Mughal Empire gradually fell apart as the English East India Company established itself in India as a colonial power. After a general Indian rebellion against Company rule in 1857, the British Crown took direct control of India, and this arrangement lasted until Independence in 1947. Although the nature of British rule was quite different from that of the Mughals, in some ways it represented a continuity with the basic situation in which Indians grappled with their religious traditions in a world that gave monotheism hegemonic power.

The period of British rule witnessed a widespread intellectual and social movement in India to rethink Hindu traditions that is now known as the Hindu Renaissance. Several "Hindu Reformers" took part in this Renaissance, the first of which was Rammohan Roy (1774–1833). Roy set the tone for the Hindu Renaissance in taking inspiration from certain Western values and using them to turn a critical eye toward Hindu traditions. In particular, he championed the idea that Hinduism is at core monotheistic and criticized the worship of multiple gods and goddesses in the form of images. He founded the Brahmo Samaj, a civic organization dedicated to "purifying" Hinduism to return it to its supposed monotheistic roots. Although this group got off to a slow start, it was revitalized into a more dynamic reformist group in 1843 by Debendranath Tagore. Another similar reformist group, the Arya Samaj, was founded by Dayananda Saraswati (1824–1883) in 1875. This group was also dedicated to returning to Hinduism's supposed original monotheism and ridding it of "idolatry," but ideologically Saraswati cast these reforms as a return to the original four Vedas, rejecting in Protestant fashion all later texts and traditions.

While much of the intellectual fervor of the Hindu Renaissance was arguably focused on accommodating Hinduism to Western mores, one particularly influential strain represented a return to traditional Indian patterns of inclusivism, adapted to a new globalized context. This strain of the Hindu Renaissance, known as Neo-Vedanta, had its roots in the life and teachings of Shri Ramakrishna (1836–1886). Ramakrishna, unlike many other Hindu Reformers, was not a highly educated intellectual; he was the son of a simple village priest who became a mystic devoted to the consciousness of God, much like the *bhakti* saints of previous centuries. In his mystical experiences, he saw the divine in a variety of manifestations—including as the Goddess, as Krishna, and as Rama, but also as Muhammad and as Jesus Christ. As he explored the presence of the divine in various religions, he even adapted his own customs to those of the other religions, including Islam, Jainism, Buddhism, and Christianity.

Shri Ramakrishna attracted several more educated disciples, including, most influentially, Narendranath Datta (1863–1902), who later took the religious name Swami Vivekananda. As we saw in chapter 5, Vivekananda became a *de facto* ambassador of Hinduism to the rest of the world when he spoke as a representative of his religion at the World Parliament of Religions in Chicago in 1893. In his teachings, both at the World Parliament of Religions and elsewhere, Vivekananda argued that Hinduism is an inherently monotheistic religion, but also that the core truths of Hinduism are found in religions around the world. Vivekananda's understanding of Hinduism and the unity of all religions is often referred to by scholars as "Neo-Vedanta." This is because it is based on a medieval Hindu philosophy called Advaita Vedanta, which emphasizes teachings in the Upanishads that equate the personal *atman* with the ultimate reality, *brahman*, thus understanding the apparent multiplicity of things in the universe as masking an inherent unity.

Vivekananda saw himself as spreading the message of his teacher Shri Ramakrishna, and he did so through a number of institutions dedicated to Ramakrishna. There are now dozens of Vedanta temples in the Ramakrishna tradition in the United States and around the world. Although culturally and stylistically quite Hindu, these temples often serve both people of Indian Hindu heritage and non-Indians, and they continue to espouse the teaching that all religions are ultimately one. This latter teaching is often displayed iconographically by the inclusion of statues of, for example, the Buddha and Jesus Christ, alongside statues of Ramakrishna and Vivekananda. The Neo-Vedanta movement that traces itself back to Ramakrishna and was spread by Vivekananda thus takes the principle of inclusivism that long was present in Indian religion and applies it to world religions writ large.

EXCLUSIVISM AND INCLUSIVISM IN RELIGIONS AROUND THE WORLD

As we have seen in this chapter, religious culture in India does not work quite the same way as in China, where a person can practice three religions at once, but it also does not follow the same principle of exclusivism that the Abrahamic traditions do. Over the course of Indian history, various religious groups have tended to find ways to *include* rival systems within their own, rather than exclude them. This has taken the form of super-enthronement, where one's own top figure is simply placed above the rival system's top figure, and it has evolved today into the global claim that all the world's religions are simply different forms of Hinduism.

To be clear, however, I don't want to imply that there is a black-and-white distinction between religions that are exclusivistic and those that are inclusivistic. It is more of a spectrum: All religions are both exclusivistic and inclusivistic to varying degrees. Even Christianity, which is largely exclusivistic, does practice inclusivism with respect to one other religion: Judaism. Christians worship the Jewish God; incorporate Jewish terminology, stories, and history into their own religious narratives; and literally *include* the Jewish scriptures within their own. Likewise, Islam, which is also largely exclusivistic, practices inclusivism with respect to both Judaism and Christianity. Muslims worship the Jewish/Christian God and see the prophet Muhammad as the last in a line of prophets that includes the prophets of the Hebrew Scriptures as well as Jesus.

I also want to make clear that although the word *inclusivism* might superficially seem to have a positive connotation compared to the word *exclusivism*, these are just technical terms about how religions conceive of their relationship to other religions. One is not necessarily better or more tolerant than the other. Consider, for example, the inclusivism that Christianity practices toward Judaism. Has that inclusivism historically made Christianity more tolerant toward Judaism and Jewish people? Of course not! Two millennia of Christian antisemitism serve as a powerful reminder that inclusivism is not the same as openness and tolerance.

The same can be said for inclusivism in India. Inclusivism may not work in the same way as exclusivism, and it might not lead to exactly the same type of rigid distinctions in identity, but it is still fundamentally a way of saying that one's own religious position is superior to another. Buddhists do not agree with Vaishnavas that the Buddha was an incarnation of Vishnu, Hindus do not believe that the Buddha was superior to the gods, Muslims and Hindus would not generally agree with Sikhs that God is neither Muslim nor Hindu, and most people around the world would not agree with Neo-Vedantins that their religions are just forms of Hinduism.

Interestingly, this last idea, which has its roots in Indian inclusivism and was popularized worldwide by Vivekananda and the Neo-Vedanta movement, has found sympathetic resonance in an intellectual movement in the Western world as well. In the West, this is known as *perennialism*. You may know the word *perennial* as referring to a type of flower that comes back every year, as opposed to an *annual* that must be replanted. The word *perennial* comes from the Latin *per annum*, meaning "every year." It implies that something keeps coming back over and over again. With respect to religion, perennialism is the idea that the same core truths have been taught repeatedly during human history and are preserved in the major world religions. Perennialists therefore say that all religions are one.

It is certainly the prerogative of a Christian, a Hindu, a Muslim, or a person who identifies as "spiritual but not religious" to take comfort in the perennialist idea that all religions point to a common truth or have a common goal. Scholars of religion, however, tend to be skeptical of perennialism and critical of its usefulness for actually understanding religion as a human phenomenon. One such scholar, Stephen Prothero, has argued quite vociferously against perennialism in his popular book *God is Not One*. He writes,

> . . . fans of Aldous Huxley's *The Perennial Philosophy* (1945) and Joseph Campbell's *The Hero with a Thousand Faces* (1949) were denouncing the longstanding human tendency to divide the world's religions into two categories: the false ones and your own. The world's religions, they argued, are different paths up the same mountain. Or, as Swami Sivananda put it, "The Koran or the Zend-Avesta or the Bible is as much a sacred book as the Bhagavad-Gita. . . . Ahuramazda, Isvara, Allah, Jehovah are different names for one God." Today this approach is the new orthodoxy, enshrined in best-selling books by Karen Armstrong and in Bill Moyers' television interviews with Joseph Campbell, Huston Smith, and other leading advocates of the "perennial philosophy."

This perennialism may seem to be quite pluralistic, but only at first glance. Catholic theologian Karl Rahner has been rightly criticized for his theory that many Buddhists, Hindus, and Jews are actually "anonymous Christians" who will make it to heaven in the world to come. Conservative Catholics see this theory as a violation of their longstanding conviction that "outside the church there is no salvation." But liberals also condemn Rahner's theology, in their case as condescending. "It would be impossible to find anywhere in the world," writes Catholic theologian Hans Küng, "a sincere Jew, Muslim or atheist who would not regard the assertion that he is an 'anonymous Christian' as presumptuous."

The perennial philosophers, however, are no less presumptuous. They, too, conscript outsiders into their tradition quite against their will. When Huxley's guru Swami Prabhavananda says that all religions lead to God, the God he is imagining is Hindu.[6]

The same came be said for any perennialist—whether they be Hindu, Christian, Muslim, or otherwise. The "God" or key truth or goal they see expressed in all religions is their own.

The religions of the world have real differences. One can only say that they are in some sense the same if one ignores those differences. And more often than not, ignoring the differences involves regarding other religions as just other forms of one's own religion (or general "spiritual" viewpoint), rather than the other way around. This strategy is fundamentally a form of inclusivism: acknowledging the validity of a rival religious system but subordinating it to one's own.

DISCUSSION QUESTIONS

1. What is inclusivism? How does it contrast to the exclusivism of Christianity with respect to most other religions?
2. How is Jainism similar to and different from Buddhism? How did both it and Buddhism practice inclusivism with respect to the religion of the Vedas?
3. How did the introduction of Islam change the religious landscape in India?
4. What are the basic teachings and practices of Sikhism? How did Sikh identity form in distinction to Islam and Hinduism?
5. What are Neo-Vedanta and perennialism, and how are they related? How can both be understood as being based on the principle of inclusivism?

NOTES

1   There is a book in German, which unfortunately has not been translated into English, that includes Hacker's own words on the concept of "inclusivism," as well as those of other scholars: Gerhardt Oberhammer, ed., *Inklusivismus: Eine indische Denkform* (Vienna: Institut für indologie der Universität Wien, 1983). I should note that Hacker contrasted inclusivism not to "exclusivism," as I have, but rather to "tolerance," which he believed Christianity to be more exemplary of. I do not accept this characterization of Hinduism vis-à-vis Christianity, nor do other scholars of South Asia who nonetheless find the concept of inclusivism to be useful.

2   You may have an uncanny recognition of this word because it was stolen by the Nazis to use as part of their racist ideology. Nazis called themselves, the supposed "Master Race," Aryans, a word that they took from ancient Indian culture. They also took and distorted the meaning of the swastika, a symbol of auspiciousness used in most Indian religions and in some Buddhist cultures elsewhere in Asia. The reason for this is that many European scholars in the nineteenth and early twentieth centuries, influenced by racist theories prevalent at the time, believed that the *aryas* referred to in ancient Indian text were white-skinned invaders related to the people who settled Europe, who then mixed with the darker-skinned indigenous people of India. Scholars have since debunked this theory and shown that the term *arya* was a cultural term of identity that had nothing to do with the modern concept of race. To be clear, neither the Indian concept of *arya* nor the swastika originally had anything to do with racism or Nazi ideology, and it is sad and outrageous that the Nazi appropriation of these cultural artifacts has transformed them into symbols of hate.

3   Controversy over this practice, called *sallekhana*, erupted in 2015 when the High Court of the Indian state of Rajasthan ruled that it is equivalent to suicide and therefore punishable under Indian law. This ruling was vigorously protested by Jains, and it was stayed a month later by the Indian Supreme Court.

4   Alexis Sanderson, "Maṇḍala and Āgamic Identity in the Trika of Kashmir," in André Padoux, ed., *Mantras et diagrammes rituels dans l'Hindouisme* (Paris: Editions du CNRS, 1986): 181–185.

5   When India gained independence in 1947, Muslims led by Muhammad Ali Jinnah, fearing that they would be mistreated in a Hindu-majority Indian state, petitioned the British to create a separate country called Pakistan, carved out of those parts of British India whose population was majority Muslim. The British granted this request, and the result was an event known as "Partition": millions of Hindus and Muslims who found themselves on the wrong side of the line that was drawn between India and Pakistan migrated to the other side of the border, and in the process about one million died through general hardships and violence. Originally Pakistan consisted of the northwestern part of South Asia around the Indus River, which was close to the border of the original Islamic Empire going back to the seventh century, as well as a smaller portion in the eastern half of the state of Bengal. The geographical distance from the rest of Pakistan, as well as major cultural differences, led East Pakistan to declare independence in 1971, and it is now the independent country of Bangladesh.

6   Stephen Prothero, *God is Not One: The Eight Rival Religions That Run the World—And Why Their Differences Matter* (New York: HarperOne, 2010), 5.

8
Tibetan Buddhism
Is It Still Buddhism?

If you want to understand a religion, what is the most important part of its history? The beginning, right? Muslims consider the Qur'an to be the perfect revelation from God; they look to Muhammad as the best example of submission to God; and they consider events from the early history of Islam to be uniquely important in defining the life of a Muslim today. Christians are the same way. They literally worship the founder of their religion as God. The events of Jesus' life are reenacted over the course of the Christian ritual calendar. And Jesus is considered the best exemplar for living an ideal Christian life. Likewise, Buddhists look to the Buddha as the example they want to follow in their path to Awakening. They, like Christians and Muslims, commemorate events from their founder's life over the course of every year. For many Buddhists, the goal is in fact to become a Buddha yourself.

The beginning clearly has a unique importance for religions like Christianity, Islam, and Buddhism, because those religions have founders that they look to as authoritative. There may be many types of Christians, many types of Muslims, and many types of Buddhists, but members of each of these religions are united by the importance they attach to Jesus, Muhammad, or the Buddha, respectively. What about religions that don't have a founder, however—religions like Judaism and Hinduism? If the beginning is the most important part of a religion's history, then what does that mean in the case of such religions? Even in these cases, there is usually an appeal to the origins of the religion in the past, although those origins may not be instantiated in a particular person. For example, Jews place great importance in the Torah and the story of how the Jewish people came to be "chosen" by God

DOI: 10.4324/9781032646428-10

and given the Torah as part of his covenant with them. Likewise, Hindus place great importance, at least rhetorically, in the Vedas as a legitimizing authority for the scriptures, stories, and practices that came afterward.

Seeking legitimacy in origins plays an important role in many religions, although doing so may take different forms or be practiced to varying degrees in different traditions. What I want to show you in this chapter, however, is that if we want to understand religious traditions in their fullness, it is important *not* to focus only on their origins or use their origins as the standard by which to judge the rest of their history. To see why this is, we will look at a particular branch of Buddhism, called Vajrayana Buddhism, that is most well known as the form of Buddhism practiced in Tibet. This form of Buddhism, in fundamental ways, is radically different from the earliest form of Buddhism we have evidence for—so much so that some have even asked whether this form of Buddhism is still Buddhism at all.

MAINSTREAM BUDDHIST MORALITY

As we learned in chapter 4, Buddhism was founded by the Buddha, an actual man who lived about 2,400 years ago in what is now northern India and Nepal. The word *Buddha* is a title, meaning "Awakened"; the man's actual name, according to tradition, was Siddhartha Gautama. He was given the title *Buddha* because, as a young adult, he attained the state of Awakening. Awakening is the ultimate goal of Buddhism. When one attains Awakening, one enters *nirvana*, a state that completely transcends all suffering. With *nirvana*, one ends the cycle of rebirth, called *samsara*. To show people the way to end this cycle of rebirth, the Buddha taught the Four Noble Truths, which explain (1) suffering, (2) its origin in craving, (3) the end of suffering, and (4) the path to the end of suffering, which is the Noble Eightfold Path.

According to Buddhist tradition, the Buddha's most important act other than the attainment of Awakening itself was to establish a community, the *sangha*, which consists of four parts: monks, nuns, laymen, and laywomen. Laymen and laywomen do not strive for *nirvana* in the short term; instead, they provide material support to the monks and nuns to make merit (good karma) that will help them attain a good rebirth. In addition, there is a basic standard of morality that laypeople are expected to follow, which is encapsulated in the five precepts. These five precepts are (1) not to take life, (2) not to take what is not given, (3) not to engage in wrongful speech (such as lying), (4) not to engage in sexual misconduct, and (5) not to drink intoxicants.

Monks and nuns, on the other hand, are, at least in theory, committed to striving for *nirvana*. For this reason, they are expected to follow a long list of rules called the *Patimokkha* that regulate their behavior. These rules are found in a scripture known as the Vinaya, which deals with monastic discipline in general. Different Buddhist traditions have different numbers of rules in the *Patimokkha*, but a large portion of the rules are roughly the same and clearly go back to the time of the Buddha or shortly thereafter. The rules of the *Patimokkha* include and go beyond the five precepts that laypeople follow. In particular, monks are nuns are not only prohibited from engaging in sexual misconduct (such as adultery); they are enjoined to maintain total celibacy. Engaging in sexual intercourse, according to the monastic rules, results in automatic expulsion from the *sangha*. Celibacy was clearly seen as key to the Buddhist path from the earliest days of Buddhism, most likely by the Buddha himself as well. According to one early Buddhist text, the Buddha said that various desires can be used to overcome themselves, with the exception of sex: "in regard to the sexual act the Blessed One has advised the destruction of the bridge."[1]

The Buddhist institutionalization of celibacy is understandable given the logic of the Four Noble Truths. According to the second noble truth, the cause of the entire problem in living existence is craving. Ancient Indian society, like many human societies (including Western society through much of its history), saw sexual lust as *the* epitome of craving. Indeed, Buddhist art—including in Tibet—has often symbolized craving by a man and woman having sex. Sex also obviously plays an important role in rebirth, insofar as it is required for a new being to be born. Buddhist descriptions of the rebirth process say that two things must happen for a birth to take place. First, the sexual fluids of the father and mother must combine through sexual intercourse. Second, there must be a consciousness[2] from a recently deceased being that enters the mother's womb and animates the embryo.[3] Both of these factors are characterized by craving—by the father and mother to enjoy each other sexually, and by the consciousness for renewed existence, which is what draws it to enter the mother's womb. The Buddhist valorization of celibacy is therefore closely tied to its teaching that craving is the source of suffering and must be eliminated to attain *nirvana*.

TIBETAN BUDDHISM AND BUDDHIST TANTRA

As we saw in chapter 4, there are three major branches of Buddhism: Theravada, Mahayana, and Vajrayana. Tibetan Buddhists belong to the third branch: Vajrayana. Vajrayana Buddhism is basically just Mahayana Buddhism with a twist. That is, like other Mahayana Buddhists, Vajrayana Buddhists believe in the Bodhisattva Path in which one strives for full Buddhahood, and as such their Buddhist universe is filled with Bodhisattvas such as Avalokiteshvara and Pure Land Buddhas such as Amitabha. The extra twist that Vajrayana Buddhist involves is Tantra.

It is possible that you have heard of Tantra, since so-called Tantra is one of the hottest trends in New Age spirituality today. The thing that people call Tantra nowadays, however, is mostly made-up. Tantra was a religious movement that arose in India in the early Middle Ages and influenced nearly all Indian religions, but especially Hinduism and Buddhism. The core of Tantra is ritual. Modern people tend not to value ritual, so modern Western appropriations of Tantra usually ignore that part, even though it is central to traditional Indian Tantra's identity. Instead, they have focused on a more titillating aspect of Tantra: sex. Modern "Tantric" sex coaches offer their services to people to help them have mind-blowing orgasms or a more spiritual sexual connection with their partners. Sex was indeed a part (although only a part) of traditional Indian Tantra, including the Vajrayana Buddhism that spread to Tibet, but its purpose was by no means to help couples have better sex lives. A key reason for this is that Tantric sex, in a traditional context, is inseparable from Tantric ritual. We'll get back to that point in a moment. First, we need to see how Buddhist Tantra, including Tantric sex, represents a real departure from what was taught in early Buddhism.

Tantra is first and foremost about ritual. Indeed, the word *Tantra* comes from the word that was used in medieval India to refer to a genre of texts that were about ritual. Nearly every religious group in medieval India wrote *tantras*, all of which are about ritual and share certain general features, but which are tailored to the particular worldview of that religious group. Among them, the two groups that were most active in writing *tantras* and developing Tantric traditions were Mahayana Buddhists and Shaivas (Hindus who worship Shiva as the Supreme Deity). Because these two groups were in competition for royal patronage, they developed their Tantric traditions in similar directions that often borrowed from one another's texts, mythological motifs, and philosophy. In the process, the Mahayana Buddhist Tantric tradition became sufficiently distinct from mainstream Mahayana Buddhism that it gave rise to a new branch of Buddhism, called the Vajrayana ("thunderbolt vehicle").

Buddhism spread to Tibet, which is just to the north of India (across the Himalayas), at around the same time that Tantra was popular in India and that the Vajrayana Buddhist tradition was developing. Tibetans engaged with the new developments in Indian Buddhism and thus developed a Vajrayana Buddhist culture of their own. As they translated various Indian Buddhist scriptures into Tibetan, they found it convenient to classify the *tantras* into four groups: Action, Performance, Yoga, and Unexcelled Yoga Tantras. The first two of these, the Action and Performance Tantras, simply give instructions on basic rituals for worshipping the Buddha, preparing for meditation, and other worldly purposes such as protection from and elimination of dangers. Buddhism always involved rituals of this sort, so the Action and Performance Tantras were mostly in continuity with earlier forms of Buddhism.

The other two classes of Buddhist *tantras* also describe rituals, but in their case the rituals they describe are specifically designed to provide a shortcut to Awakening. Although there is some overlap, they are generally distinguished from one another by how radical the rituals they describe are. Yoga Tantras are less radical: They describe meditations that involve visualizing oneself as a Buddha, as is often depicted in a special visual representation known as a *mandala*. Buddhist *mandalas* usually depict a Buddha in the center, seated in a palace which is being viewed from above (like a floorplan), surrounded by a circle of other Buddhas or Bodhisattvas. (The word *mandala* itself means "circle.") *Mandalas* are represented in many different media, but one particularly beautiful medium used in the Tibetan tradition is sand. Tibetan monks will spend several days painstakingly drawing a *mandala* using colored sand. Then, when they are done, they ritually dismantle the *mandala*, representing the Buddhist teaching of impermanence.

Visualizing oneself as a Buddha might seem odd at first, but it makes sense in light of a form of Mahayana Buddhist philosophy that we learned about in chapter 4 called Yogachara. According to Yogachara philosophy, everything in reality is simply a projection of consciousness. There is no world "out there" beyond our senses; everything is simply mind. Following this way of thinking, it makes sense that we can become Buddhas by *visualizing* ourselves as Buddhas. To be clear, however, this is not some casual act of imagination. It is a rigorous meditation exercise that involves visualizing oneself as a Buddha in minute detail in order to make it a reality. Indeed, even modern scientific studies have found that accomplishing things in the real world can be aided by visualizing ourselves doing them successfully. For example, visualizing yourself making baskets can help you actually perform better in basketball.

The fourth and most radical class of Buddhist *tantras* is the Unexcelled Yoga Tantras. An example of the radical nature of these *tantras* can be seen in a "secret empowerment" described by some *tantras* of this class.

This secret empowerment is a ritual initiation that allows one to advance more quickly toward the Buddhist goal of Awakening. According to the texts, the man[4] who wishes to receive this initiation must first find a woman to serve as his sexual partner and take her to the Vajra-master, a teacher who has already been initiated into the lineage and is qualified to teach Tantric rituals. First, the Vajra-master engages in sexual intercourse with the women. Then he collects the combined sexual fluids from her vagina and places them on the tongue of the man being initiated. These sexual fluids are equated with *bodhichitta*, literally meaning "mind of Awakening"—the state of mind considered by all Mahayana Buddhists to be the seed for attaining full Buddhahood. The initiate must swallow the semen and vaginal fluid without hesitation and exclaim, "O Bliss!" He then engages in sexual intercourse with the woman himself. As he does so, he experiences four progressive levels of bliss. According to the texts, these arise as a result of the unification of two key Buddhist principles—wisdom and skillful means—which are physically embodied in the ritual by the man's penis (skillful means) and the woman's vagina (wisdom).[5]

Clearly, this is not the Buddhism of the Buddha portrayed in the early Buddhist scriptures—the Buddha who left his wife to become a religious wanderer, established a celibate order of monks and nuns, and recommended "burning the bridge" when it came to the desire for sex.

Figure 8.1 A Tibetan painting of the Buddha Chakrasamvara in sexual union with his consort. © Getty Images

Tibetan Buddhism: Is It Still Buddhism?

Here sex is itself a means for attaining liberation—the bliss of orgasm becomes equated with the bliss of Awakening. This contradiction of the mainstream Buddhist suspicion of sex is by design. Certain Unexcelled Yoga Tantras recommend not only engaging in sexual intercourse, but also a host of things that would be considered sinful according to ordinary Buddhist morality. According to one such text, the *Hevajra Tantra*, "You should kill living beings, speak lying words, take what is not given, consort with the women of others."[6] This is an instruction to break the first four of the five precepts. Similarly, Tantric texts instruct those on the path to drink alcohol and blood, eat meat, and ingest any number of disgusting or impure substances, including pus, urine, feces, and—as we have seen—sexual fluids.

So what gives? Why would an entire Buddhist tradition advocate practices that go so clearly against basic Buddhist morality? Why would they advocate using sex to attain *nirvana* when Buddhism thitherto had taught that sex was the biggest obstacle on the path to Awakening? Is this tradition of Buddhism really Buddhism at all? Naturally, given the ways in which Vajrayana Buddhism contradicts other forms of Buddhism, it has had its critics within Buddhism even from its inception in the Middle Ages in India. Likewise, many of the earliest European scholars who studied Buddhism, including Eugène Burnouf, a nineteenth century French scholar widely considered the father of modern Buddhist Studies, were simply aghast when they learned of the contents of the Buddhist Tantric texts preserved in Tibet and neighboring Nepal.[7] They were not only repelled by the sexual elements—just as offensive to Victorian morality as they were to non-Vajrayana Buddhists—and other transgressive practices. They also were turned off by the pervasive practice of elaborate rituals in Tibetan Buddhism and Vajrayana Buddhism more broadly, since, as I explained above, ritual is quite central to Tantra. Some early European scholars called Tibetan Buddhism "Lamaism"—a reference to the importance of *lamas* (the Tibetan word for *guru* or teacher) in the tradition—and went so far as to deny that this religion was really Buddhism at all.

Although the transgressive practices of the Unexcelled Yoga Tantras may be shocking, we understand Buddhism a lot less if we simply dismiss these practices, and Vajrayana Buddhism as a whole along with them, out of hand. To begin with, Tibetan and other Vajrayana Buddhists have for centuries offered deeply philosophical arguments, rooted in the Buddhist tradition, for why transgressive rituals work. One type of explanation sees transgressive rituals as taking the Yogachara "mind-only" view of the world to its logical conclusion. If everything is just a manifestation of our consciousness, and Awakening consists of realizing that there are no distinctions between different things in the universe, then even distinctions between such things as "virtue" and "sin" or "pure" and "impure" are illusions and must ultimately be overcome in order to attain Buddhahood. One engages in transgressive practices, according to this interpretation, to attain a nondual state of consciousness that is equivalent to Awakening. To be clear, this is not open license to throw morality out the window and do whatever one wants. Rather, it is a controlled ritual technique to achieve a higher state of consciousness in which one transcends simple dualistic thinking about morality. Buddhist Tantric texts all emphasize that the transgressive practices they teach are incredibly dangerous and should only be performed under the tutelage of a qualified teacher (in Tibetan, a *lama*), because doing them improperly will simply lead to rebirth in hell, just as mainstream Buddhism teaches.

This is an important point because, while the distinctive scriptures and teachings of Vajrayana Buddhism are significant, they can easily give an erroneous impression about what Vajrayana Buddhism looks like in practice. To be clear, most Vajrayana Buddhists throughout history have not engaged in *any* transgressive practices, sexual or otherwise. Tibetan and other Vajrayana Buddhists generally live lives not all that different from Buddhists in non-Vajrayana Buddhist traditions. They follow basic Buddhist morality, make merit, and (in the case of specialists) engage in study of Buddhist philosophy and meditation. Many Tibetan teachers throughout history, while fully embracing Tantra, have understood the most radical Tantric practices as things to be visualized rather than actually performed. Indeed, some scholars today regard the transgressive practices advocated in Buddhist Tantric texts as being placed there more for their shock value—that is, to make a point about the nondual consciousness required for Awakening—than for anything else. At the same time, their shock value resides in the very *possibility* of their being performed, so there have always been some who have taken the texts literally, even if most have not.[8]

Vajrayana Buddhists have taken many philosophical approaches to explaining Unexcelled Yoga Tantras, and the *tantras* themselves are incredibly diverse in what practices they advocate, so there is no one explanation for whether or how they can be considered acceptably Buddhist. Indeed, many Buddhists from other traditions would not find any such explanations acceptable. But that does not make Vajrayana Buddhism, or Buddhism as a whole, different from any other religion and its subbranches. Every religion, over time, divides into sects or branches that disagree among themselves, sometimes radically, about what it means, in terms of belief and practice, to be a member of that religion. What matters is that Vajrayana Buddhists identify as Buddhists and make use of

Tibetan Buddhism: Is It Still Buddhism?

Buddhist principles, as they understand them, to explain, interpret, and reflect upon the practices they engage in.

If we simply take Tibetan Buddhism seriously on its own terms, we find that it has in fact produced one of the most vibrant Buddhist cultures in the world. According to Tibetan tradition, Buddhism was first transmitted to Tibet in the seventh century under the king Songtsen Gampo. In the centuries that followed, Tibet engaged in a massive cultural exchange with North India in which Indian Buddhist teachers and Tantric masters journeyed north to found monasteries, do battle with demons, and ordain and teach students; and Tibetan translators known as *lotsawa*s engaged in the painstaking process of translating Buddhist scriptures and other texts from Sanskrit into Tibetan. This intercultural exchange would prove crucial to the preservation of medieval Indian Buddhist texts, philosophy, and culture, as institutionalized Buddhism mostly died out in India in the first half of the second millennium.

As Buddhism took root in Tibetan society, it developed sophisticated institutions that reflected those of North India but also adapted to their Tibetan context. One key aspect of this institutionalization was the establishment of extremely large monastic universities in which thousands of monks live together and engage in rigorous study of the

Figure 8.2 Tibetan monks engaging in philosophical debate at Sera Monastery. The debate format is highly ritualized; what you see here is the challenger about to clap his hands and stomp his left foot to mark the end of his question. © Getty Images

Buddhist scriptures. They follow a standardized curriculum that takes many years to master, and they hone their understanding of Buddhist philosophy by engaging in formalized debate, in which two monks competitively argue about fine points of Buddhist doctrine to see who has best mastered what they have learned from their textual studies. Tibetan monasteries do not have a centralized structure but instead are divided into four major schools or lineages: Nyingma, Kagyu, Sakya, and Gelug. Each of these schools has its own history, leaders, unique teachings, and internal institutional structure.

An important aspect of Buddhist culture that developed in Tibet is the institution of *tulkus*. *Tulkus* are formalized offices whose holders are understood to be successive reincarnations of a being of high Buddhist attainment. When a *tulku* with a particular title dies, he is not replaced by his son as is the case with kings. That would often be impossible because many (though not all) *tulkus* are celibate monks. Nor is he replaced by his deputy or other person based on merit. Instead, he is replaced (according to the Tibetan understanding) by himself. Other *lamas* with a traditional role in the transition for that particular *tulku* will use various techniques, such as consulting oracles, to determine who the recently deceased *tulku* reincarnated as. They then recognize that small child as the reincarnation of the *tulku* and may (depending on the *tulku* in question) raise him as such, giving him all the education and acculturation he needs to assume his identity, which in many cases may go back centuries.

The oldest *tulku* lineage is the Karmapa, who is the leader of the Karma Kagyu (a subsect of the Kagyu school). His lineage is traced back to the twelfth century. The most important and widely visible *tulku* lineage in Tibetan Buddhism, however, is the Dalai Lama. He is understood to be an incarnation of the Bodhisattva Avalokiteshvara and is the leader of the Gelug school. In 1578, the Mongol leader Altan Khan bestowed the title "Dalai Lama" on Sonam Gyatso, the leader of the Gelug school at the time, in appreciation for receiving Buddhist teachings from him. Sonam Gyatso was already recognized as part of a *tulku* lineage, so the title was posthumously bestowed on his two predecessors, with Sonam Gyatso himself being recognized as the third Dalai Lama. The first few Dalai Lamas were simply monks who led the Gelug school, but in the 1640s, the fifth Dalai Lama rose to power as the king of a unified Tibet. He also established the Nechung oracle, whom high ranking *lamas* since have consulted for information to help them find the Dalai Lama's reincarnation upon his death.[9] This oracle is understood to be a spirit who possesses a particular man and dispenses advice for use by the Tibetan government.

The current Dalai Lama is the fourteenth Dalai Lama, Tenzin Gyatso, who was born in 1935 and recognized as the reincarnation of the thirteenth

Dalai Lama two years later. He almost immediately inherited a precarious political situation for Tibet. The Chinese Qing Dynasty had claimed Tibet as a vassal state since 1720, but Tibet remained semi-autonomous under the rule of the Dalai Lamas. As the Qing Dynasty weakened under the threat of Western colonialism, Chinese rule over Tibet, such as it was, increasingly came to exist in name only. When the Qing Dynasty fell in a revolution in 1912, the thirteenth Dalai Lama declared Tibet to be completely independent. Although the new Chinese government did not renounce China's claim to Tibet, civil war and the Japanese invasion that led in part to World War Two prevented the Chinese government from doing anything about its claim for several decades.

When the Second World War ended in 1945, the Communists and Nationalists in China resumed fighting one another in earnest. In 1949, the Chinese Communist Party, under the leadership of Mao Zedong, finally won the Chinese Civil War, forcing the Nationalist forces, under the leadership of Chiang Kai-shek, to flee to Taiwan. The newly founded People's Republic of China then set about consolidating its rule over the entire territory of mainland China that had previously been claimed by the Qing Dynasty, including Tibet. To this end, the People's Liberation Army invaded Tibet in 1950. In response to this crisis, the fourteenth Dalai Lama took over his full political powers from the regent early, at the age of only fifteen. The Tibetan government then signed the Seventeen Point Agreement with China in 1951, which stipulated that Tibet would become part of China but retain its local government under the Dalai Lama's leadership. This situation would only last for a few years, however. In 1959, a Tibetan uprising against Chinese rule broke out in Tibet. As Chinese forces moved in to crush the uprising, the Dalai Lama and other prominent members of his government fled, going south across the Himalayas into India, where they sought political asylum.

The failure of the Tibetan uprising and the flight of the Dalai Lama to India led to a more complete Chinese takeover of Tibet that continues to this day. The Dalai Lama repudiated the Seventeen Point Agreement and in 1960 established a Tibetan government in exile, with its headquarters in Dharamsala. In the years and decades that followed, many other Tibetans fled Tibet or otherwise went into exile, many of them settling in India. Tibetan exiles reestablished many of the great monastic universities, including the three great Gelug monasteries Drepung, Ganden, and Sera, in various places around India. These monasteries in exile have proven crucial for the continuation of Tibetan Buddhist culture, as much of institutionalized Buddhism in Tibet itself was destroyed during the Cultural Revolution from 1966 to 1976. For his part, the fourteenth Dalai Lama has become an internationally recognized spiritual and political figure—arguably the most recognizable Buddhist leader in the world. In 1989, he was awarded the Nobel Peace Prize in recognition of his advocacy for the plight of the Tibetans and his support for peaceful solutions to the status of Tibet.

CONCLUSION: SCRIPTURES AND THE QUEST FOR ORIGINS

In this chapter, we have seen that although we tend to place "real religion" in origins, we cannot understand religion in its fullness unless we take all periods of a religion seriously. Religions change, and there is no reason to privilege the teachings and practices of a religion at its inception over what people in that religion say, teach, and do in later periods of time. Early European scholars of Buddhism were frankly prejudiced against Tibetan Buddhism because they saw it as being too different from early Buddhism to be authentic. But how did they even know what early Buddhism was supposedly like, in order to judge Tibetan Buddhism and find it lacking? Tibetan Buddhists, after all, would say that they are practicing Buddhism exactly how the Buddha intended. They even have a whole host of scriptures, the Tantric texts I have been talking about in this chapter, to back up their claims.

The answer is that European scholars in the nineteenth century studied a whole host of Buddhist scriptures, gathered from various countries across Asia, and quickly came to the conclusion (which historians of religion today still accept) that the texts of the Vajrayana are among the youngest of the Buddhist scriptures. In fact, they did not even begin to be written until nearly one thousand years after the lifetime of the Buddha. The oldest Buddhist scriptures are found in the *Tipitaka*—a collection of texts written in Pali that are considered authoritative by the Theravada Buddhists of Sri Lanka, Burma, Thailand, Laos, and Cambodia. Indeed, if you read texts from this *Tipitaka*, you will find nothing about transgressive practices, visualizing yourself as a Buddha, or using sex to attain *nirvana*. You will instead find clear articulations of moral principles that should not be broken, including an insistence that monks and nuns *must not* engage in sexual intercourse. It is in this collection that you find the Buddha's "burning bridges" comment about sex that I cited above.

Nineteenth-century European scholars, once they discovered the Pali texts of the *Tipitaka*, immediately latched on to them as embodying "true Buddhism" and the "authentic" teaching of the Buddha. Given the extent to which the later Tantric texts of the Vajrayana differ from them, it was easy for scholars to dismiss them as not truly Buddhist—thus their disparagement of Tibetan Buddhism as mere "Lamaism." Now, you might say that in spite of everything I have shown you in this chapter—that we need to take Tibetan Buddhism seriously as a form of Buddhism, and that the innovative teachings of Vajrayana Buddhism in fact make sense in the context of the development of Buddhist thought—nevertheless it is only natural to look to the earliest scriptures of a religion to understand what it is really about. After all, isn't that what you would do with Christianity? If you want to understand Christianity, isn't the absolute first stop none other than the Bible?

Of course, I don't want to argue that the Bible isn't important for understanding Christianity. (Indeed, I wouldn't want to argue that the *Tipitaka* isn't important for understanding Buddhism either.) But imagine that you knew nothing about Christianity in the real world. You had never seen a church; had never looked upon Christian art, whether in a cathedral or in a museum; had never heard of the pope or the Vatican; had never met, read, or heard about priests, bishops, cardinals, ministers, or televangelists; had never heard of St. Francis or Mother Theresa; and had never (if indeed you come from a Christian background) attended a church service. Imagine then that you read the Bible and thought that that told you all you needed to know about what Christianity is. What would you find? Well, especially if you primarily focus on the Gospels that actually talk about Jesus' life, you would find stories about a bunch of guys wandering around peacefully with few possessions, healing the sick, and proclaiming the imminent arrival of the kingdom of God. Would you be able to deduce simply by reading the Bible what Christianity is like today? Probably not. The Bible doesn't talk about churches with steeples and altars and stained-glass windows—or in fact about churches as permanent buildings at all. It doesn't say anything about the pope, or priests, or ministers in the modern senses of those words. How would you know about any of those things?

Moreover, you might come to some ridiculous conclusions about Christianity if you based your understanding of it simply on reading the Bible. You might think that all Christians are pacifists because Jesus said to turn the other cheek (Matthew 5:38–42; Luke 6:27–31). You might think Christians are never rich and never want to be rich because Jesus told a rich man to give up his possessions and said, "It is easier for a camel to pass through the eye of a needle than for one who is rich to enter the kingdom of God."[10] You might think that Christians never make long-term plans because Jesus told his disciples not to worry about tomorrow (Matthew 6:34) and also proclaimed that God was about to destroy all the earthly powers and establish his kingdom on earth (e.g., Mark 13). So, based on just reading the Bible, Christians never engage in violence, completely reject wealth, and are eagerly waiting for God to establish his kingdom on earth.

Obviously, this is absurd, and anyone who has any experience with Christian culture (which now, because of colonialism and globalization, includes much of humanity) would find it unrecognizable. Of course, there are some Christians who are pacifists, there are some Christians who embrace poverty as a virtue, there are some Christians who think the kingdom of God is coming any day now, and there are even some Christians who are some combination thereof—but generally they are a minority. Christians, as anyone with any real-world familiarity with Christianity knows, have engaged in war (think of the Crusades, the Wars of Religion, even bellicose discourse from some Christians today), they have embraced and ostentatiously accumulated wealth (think of the Vatican or of the mansions of modern-day televangelists and megachurch pastors), and in most cases they are not too concerned about the imminence of the Apocalypse.

Another way of looking at this is to say that if you just look at the Bible, you aren't going to have a very deep understanding of Christianity. You can of course argue that the Bible teaches us what Christianity is *supposed* to be about—but that doesn't tell us about how it actually is in practice. To fully understand Christianity as a human, cultural, and historical phenomenon, you have to actually *look* at it in the real world and describe it. There are indeed continuities between all forms of Christianity today and what is written in the Bible—after all, history is not simply a series of random events—but you cannot simply *deduce* Christianity today and throughout history by reading the Bible. You cannot *understand* Christianity and Christians fully by reading the Bible alone. The same is true of Buddhism and other religions. You can't just read the scriptures that were written when they began and hope to truly understand them.

This is not simply an academic problem. It's not just that it is intellectually problematic to judge a religion solely on its earliest scripture or scriptures. Western people often go online or to a bookstore or to Amazon and read Buddhist *sutras*, the *Daode Jing*, the *Bhagavad Gita*, or else a modern book based mostly on one of those ancient Asian scriptures, and then they think that they know what Buddhism or Daoism or Hinduism is really about. They aren't concerned about what these religions mean or practically involve for people who live in Asia or come from an Asian background, whose ancestors have been practicing these religions for hundreds or thousands of years. The Tantric sex that gets marketed to Westerners these days is a case in point. As we have seen in this chapter, Tantra in its original context was mostly about ritual and only in certain very specialized circumstances about sex. It certainly was not about having better orgasms or cultivating a more spiritual sexual connection with one's romantic partner. But the modern Western appropriation of Tantra is catering to modern Western tastes, which show little interest in ritual but great interest in sexual exploration.

Western reactions to Tibetan Buddhism and Tantra therefore exemplify the Jekyll-and-Hyde nature of Orientalism we learned about in chapter 2. On the one hand, rejecting Tibetan Buddhism as not really Buddhism because it is so different from original Buddhism is overtly negative. On the other hand, engaging uncritically in modern practices of Tantric sex without a deeper awareness of the Tantric tradition exotifies Tantra and therefore is superficially positive. But both are forms of Orientalism.

DISCUSSION QUESTIONS

1. What is Tantra and how does it relate to the Buddhist tradition?
2. Why have some modern interpreters been quick to denounce Vajrayana Buddhism (Buddhist Tantra) as not real Buddhism?
3. How might Vajrayana Buddhism be seen as surprising in light of the early teachings of Buddhism?
4. How does the Vajrayana tradition explain the transgressive rituals of the Unexcelled Yoga Tantras in Buddhist terms?
5. Why is it problematic to focus solely on the origins of a religious tradition?

NOTES

1   *Anguttara Nikaya* 4.80: see Nyanaponika Thera and Bhikkhu Bodhi, trans., *Numerican Discourses of the Buddha: An Anthology of Suttas from the Aṅguttara Nikāya* (Walnut Creek: Alta Mira Press, 1999), 111.
2   The consciousness acts functionally like a soul that goes from one body to the next, but the Buddhist tradition is at pains to say that it is an impermanent process rather than a permanent entity, which is how the soul is usually understood in the West. There *was* a concept in India of a permanent entity that transmigrates from body to body, known as the *atman*, or "self." This concept is used in Hinduism to explain rebirth. Buddhism, conversely, rejects the concept of the *atman* through its teaching of *anatman*, or "not-self." See chapter 4.
3   The addition of this second requirement provided, prior to the advent of modern medicine, a convenient explanation in Buddhist societies of miscarriage and stillbirth. These would take place because, although fertilization had happened through sexual intercourse, no consciousness had entered the mother's womb to animate the embryo.

4 Although there is a rhetoric of transcending boundaries, including those of gender, in Vajrayana Buddhism, texts that describe sexual rituals are generally speaking andocentric (they assume a male practitioner) and heteronormative (involve sexual union with a female partner).
5 Paul Williams and Anthony Tribe, *Buddhist Thought* (London: Routledge, 2000), 233.
6 Williams and Tribe, *Buddhist Thought*, 237.
7 For Burnouf's disdainful reaction to Tantra, see Eugène Burnouf, *Introduction to the History of Indian Buddhism*, trans. Katia Buffetrille and Donald S. Lopez, Jr. (Chicago: University of Chicago Press, 2010), 479–480.
8 This theory has been advanced, to some controversy, by Christian K. Wedemeyer, *Making Sense of Tantric Buddhism: History, Semiology, and Transgression in the Indian Traditions* (New York: Columbia University Press, 2013).
9 The movie *Kundun*, directed by Martin Scorsese, provides a vivid dramatization of the process by which the current reincarnation of the Dalai Lama was found.
10 Mark 10:25 (New American Bible); see also Matthew 19:24 and Luke 18:25.

9
Judaism
A Religion or an Ethnicity?

Often people talk about five major world religions: Judaism, Christianity, Islam, Hinduism, and Buddhism. Judaism, however, is a bit of an outlier within this list. It might seem logical that numbers would dictate which religions are major, and for the other four this is definitely the case. Christianity has over two billion adherents, Islam has nearly two billion, Hinduism has over one billion, and Buddhism has over half a billion. Judaism, on the other hand, has only about sixteen million adherents, accounting for a mere fraction of a percent of the world's population. It is in fact only about half the size of Sikhism, itself a relatively small religion. Compared to the other four major world religions, Judaism is tiny, on a completely different order of magnitude.

Despite its small numbers, however, Judaism is arguably the most influential religion in the history of the world. Its basic worldview—of a singular, all-powerful God who created the world and has sent prophets throughout history—inspired two offshoots, Christianity and Islam, that today are the two biggest world religions and together account for nearly half of the world's population. Nearly half of the world's population, in other words, worships the Jewish God and sees the story of the Jewish people as central to their own story. The core concept of monotheism that Judaism pioneered has had an even wider reach. Through Islam, it has had an indirect influence on conceptions of monotheism in Hinduism and Sikhism (see chapter 7). And through Christianity, it has shaped the modern conception of religion that increasingly affects all people around the world—the central theme of this book.

I do not want to give the impression, however, that Judaism is important primarily as a fossilized artifact that has had influence only through its (numerically) more successful offshoots, Christianity and Islam. Judaism is a vibrant, living tradition with its own autonomous existence and influence, and it deserves to be treated as such. Moreover, in part because of its special relationship with Christianity, it has played a particularly large role in the construction of modern conceptions of religion and nationhood. Indeed, Judaism itself has been the locus of many of the modern anxieties over what these two concepts mean and how they relate to one another.

The modern concept of religion usually entails the assumption that a religion is something that one, in theory, can freely enter or renounce. Even when a person is born into a religion or when religious nationalists tie a nation's identity with a particular religion, there is still the sense that religion is, in principle, something one chooses. This is what allows a person to convert from one religion to another and what allows religions to spread and grow—or, alternatively, shrink and disappear. No religion challenges this assumption more than Judaism. On the one hand, Judaism is undeniably a religion, insofar as it is the source from which came Christianity and Islam—two religions that very much fit the paradigm of religious conversion, spread, and growth. On the other hand, Jewish identity is tied to a sense of nationhood and ethnicity. One can be Jewish even if one does not practice the Jewish religion or even if one is an atheist.

The ethnic component to Jewish identity that transcends religious belief or practice is in part a result of Jewish self-understandings and in part a result of the way these self-understandings have morphed into (often sinister) forces in the surrounding culture. On the one hand, Jewish identity is (with some exceptions for conversion) usually based on biological descent and the idea that Jews are God's "chosen people" set apart from "the nations." On the other hand, surrounding cultures, especially in the Christian world, have frequently targeted Jews with stereotyping, prejudice, abuse, and violence, a pattern of behavior that is now known as antisemitism. In the modern world, antisemitism was racialized. That is to say, antisemites weaponized modern concepts of nationhood and ethnicity with roots in the Hebrew Bible and turned them against the Jews, painting them as an incorrigible race who poison the blood of any nation they are found in and must, therefore, for the sake of the nation be expunged. This logic found its culmination in the Holocaust, during which a racist German nationalist party, the Nazis, attempted to exterminate the Jewish people and ultimately succeeded in killing six million Jews, or well over one-third of all Jews in the world at the time.

This chapter will tell the story of the Jewish people, roughly chronologically, with particular attention to the evolution of Jewish identity. It is divided into five parts. The first part retells the story of the origins of

Israel and the Jewish people as told in the Bible. The second part then explains how modern scholars understand the ancient origins of Judaism. Next, the third part addresses the split that took place in the Roman Empire between Christianity and Judaism and how a Rabbinic Jewish identity arose as part of this split and in response to the destruction of the Jewish Temple. In the fourth part, I examine the rise of intra-Jewish ethnic identities, based on the settlement patterns of Jews in the diaspora in the Middle Ages, as well as the rise of antisemitism, particularly in Christian lands. Finally, in the fifth part, we will see how Jewish identity has shaped and been shaped by modernity, through the rise of movement Judaism, Zionism, the Holocaust, and the foundation of the modern state of Israel.

THE BIBLICAL STORY OF THE FOUNDATION OF ISRAEL

Jewish identity, no matter in what sense it is construed, is rooted either directly or indirectly in the Torah. The Hebrew word *Torah* means "teaching," and it is the basis for Jewish Law, known as *halakhah*. The Torah corresponds to the first five books (also known as the Pentateuch: Genesis, Exodus, Leviticus, Numbers, and Deuteronomy) of all versions of the Bible, whether Jewish or Christian. According to a Jewish and Christian tradition that has only come to be questioned in modern times, the five books of the Torah were written by Moses, who received the commandments of Jewish Law directly from God. The Torah also includes, particularly in its first two books, Genesis and Exodus, the foundational myth of the people of Israel. Because all forms of Jewish identity (even those of modern atheists) are based on the recognition of Jews as a distinct people (a "nation" or an "ethnicity"), all are derived in one way or another from this Biblical account.

In the beginning, according to the book of Genesis, God created the world in six days. He then rested on the seventh day, providing the model for the seven-day week and the Jewish observance of the sabbath,[1] which is also observed in modified form (on Sunday instead of Saturday) by Christians. During this week of creation, God created the first human man, Adam, and the first human woman, Eve, placing them in a paradisical garden called Eden. Because they disobeyed him, however, he drove them from the garden to prevent them from eating from the Tree of Life and becoming immortal. The descendants of these first two human beings then multiplied and spread over the earth. Much of the book of Genesis chronicles God's attempts to deal with the spreading wickedness of humanity. In one particularly well-known episode, God decides to wipe the slate clean, sending a flood to wipe out all but a small remnant of life on earth. He warns Noah, who builds a large boat (the "ark") to save himself, his family, and a male and female couple of every animal species. After the flood ends, the survivors from the ark repopulate the earth. The descendants of Noah and his family give rise to all the "nations" (in Hebrew, *goyim*) of the world—the different ethnic groups of humanity—which Genesis specifies as being seventy in total.

Wickedness continues to spread after the flood, however, and God decides to confuse the speech of human beings so that they can no longer communicate with one another to create structures like the Tower of Babel to reach the heavens. He then calls on one man, Abram (whom he later renames Abraham) to move from his home city of Ur (in modern Iraq) to the land of Canaan (modern-day Israel/Palestine).[2] Abraham's wife Sarah had been unable to bear him a son, but God blesses them with a son named Isaac. He then tests Abraham's faith by demanding that he sacrifice Isaac to him. Only at the last minute, after Abraham shows he is willing to make the sacrifice, does God send an angel to stop him and sacrifice a ram instead. As a reward for his faithfulness, God promises Abraham that he will have many descendants who will be blessed.

Abraham's son Isaac has a son named Jacob. In a particularly enigmatic episode, Jacob wrestles with an angel, resulting in God bestowing him with the new name Israel, meaning "contends with God." Jacob/Israel in turn has twelve sons, who are the progenitors of the twelve tribes of Israel. These twelve tribes were likely historical social identities during the time of the ancient kingdom of Israel, with the story of Jacob, his renaming, and his twelve sons serving as a legendary story tying the twelve tribes to a common ancestor. Abraham, Isaac, and Jacob are collectively known as the three patriarchs, to signify that the Israelites traced their lineage back to them.

Jacob favors his son Joseph over the rest, and out of jealousy, the other brothers sell him into slavery in Egypt. Over time, however, Joseph becomes a confidant of the Pharaoh, ultimately rising to the position of his vizier. Using his newfound wealth and influence, Joseph moves his entire family to Egypt, including his father Jacob, who dies there. The people of Israel—that is, the descendants of Jacob's twelve sons—are thus established with prosperous lives in the land of Egypt. Unfortunately, over the course of the next few centuries, their position falls, and they are reduced to the status of slaves.

The second book of the Bible, Exodus, picks up the story with a much later generation, when a new Pharaoh subjects the descendants of Jacob's twelve sons to hard labor. Pharaoh, fearful of the Israelites (often referred to in the book of Exodus as "Hebrews"), orders the killing of all their newborn sons. One Hebrew woman saves her son by setting him adrift in a basket on the Nile. Pharaoh's daughter finds the baby, names him Moses, and adopts him as her own. When Moses grows up, he witnesses an Egyptian overseer abusing a Hebrew slave and kills the overseer. Knowing that this will get him in trouble with Pharaoh, he flees Egypt. While he is gone, he encounters God in the form of a bush that miraculously burns without being consumed. God tells Moses of his true parentage and tasks him with freeing the Hebrews from their captivity. Moses then returns to Egypt and demands that Pharaoh release the people of Israel. When Pharaoh refuses, Moses (speaking for God) sends ten plagues to prod him to change his mind. The last of these plagues is a selective killing of all firstborn sons in Egypt. To protect the firstborn sons of the Israelites, God tells Moses to have them smear lambs' blood on the lintels of their doors. This then serves as a signal to God to "pass over" those households as he kills the firstborn sons in Egypt. Jews celebrate this event, and with it their freedom from captivity in Egypt, to this day with the annual festival of Passover (celebrated in late March or April).

After the killing of the firstborn sons, Pharaoh is finally convinced to let the Hebrews go. He immediately regrets doing so, however, and sends an army to pursue them as they leave Egypt. To escape, Moses calls on God's power to part the waters of the Red Sea so that the Israelites can pass to safety on the other side. The waters part, allowing the Israelites to pass, but when Pharaoh's army tries to follow them, the waters crash back down, drowning them and allowing for the Israelites' escape.

The Israelites then spend the next forty years wandering in the desert in search of the "Promised Land": the land of Canaan where their patriarch Jacob once lived. The exodus from Egypt is commemorated to this day by the annual Jewish festival of Sukkot (the Feast of Booths, celebrated in September or October). As part of this festival, Jews perform certain rituals in temporary outdoor structures ("booths") that represent the temporary structures their ancestors lived in while wandering through the desert.

During their wandering through the desert, the Israelites stop at Mt. Sinai. Moses goes up alone to meet with God, from whom he receives two stone tablets engraved with the Ten Commandments, which are the most important and foundational commandments of Jewish Law. When he descends from the mountain, however, he finds that the Hebrews have gotten impatient in his absence, thinking that he has died and left them leaderless. They have melted down all their gold jewelry to create a golden calf—an image of a god for them to worship and ask for guidance out of the desert. Moses becomes enraged at their faithlessness, which is now particularly acute because the first two commandments on the twin tablets specify that they should have no other gods before God and that they should not make "graven images." He throws down the tablets, breaking them, and orders the destruction of the golden calf. After restoring the Hebrews' allegiance to God, Moses returns to Mt. Sinai to receive from God a new set of tablets engraved with the Ten Commandments. Later Rabbinical tradition would hold that yet another annual Jewish festival, Shavuot (Pentecost, celebrated in May or June), which was originally a harvest festival, also marks the date when Moses received the Ten Commandments.

At the end of the forty years, Moses leads the Israelites to the Jordan River and climbs a mountain that allows him to see the other side, but God punishes him for an earlier act of faithlessness by having him die there without entering the Promised Land himself. This marks the end of the story as recorded in the Torah. The other books of the Torah (Leviticus, Numbers, and Deuteronomy) enumerate in detail the commandments of Jewish Law.

The story is taken up in other books that are included in a larger collection of Jewish scriptures known as the *Tanakh*. The Tanakh is the Jewish Bible, or what Christians refer to as the "Old Testament."[3] The word *Tanakh* is an acronym that refers to its three divisions. The first is the Torah, the first five books that contain the Law of Moses. The second is the *Nevi'im*, the Prophets. These are books that either purport to be written by various prophets sent by God to Israel and Judah or otherwise record their words and stories. The third is the *Ketuvim*, or Writings, which is a miscellaneous collection of other books. The story of the people of Israel is continued in the first four books of the Prophets, the books of Joshua, Judges, Samuel, and Kings.

After Moses' death, his appointed successor, Joshua, leads the Israelites in a military campaign to conquer the major cities of Canaan. After doing so, he parcels out the land to the twelve tribes of Israel, which correspond to the descendants of the twelve sons of Jacob. For a time after Joshua's death, the tribes live in the Promised Land as a loose confederation, with *ad hoc* leaders known as judges, which are appointed by God to lead in times of crisis. Eventually, however, the Israelites express the desire for a king. God sees this as an act of faithlessness (since he is already their king), but he accedes, and his prophet Samuel assists in establishing Saul as the first king of Israel.

According to the Biblical account, Saul and his immediate successors ruled over all twelve tribes as a unified kingdom in about the tenth century BCE. The greatest of these kings was David, who became a symbol of Israelite kingship and a paradigm in later aspirations for a Messiah—a king sent by God to restore Israel to its former glory. David's son Solomon was celebrated as a wise king, and he was also significant for building the first permanent temple to the God of Israel in Jerusalem. After Solomon's death, however, there was a dispute in the royal succession, leading to a split between a northern kingdom, which retained the name Israel, and a southern kingdom in the area around Jerusalem called Judah.

The northern kingdom was destroyed by the Assyrians in 722 BCE and its people scattered. Because the people of the northern kingdom of Israel were never reconstituted, the tribes that the northern kingdom was comprised of are often referred to as the "lost tribes of Israel." This left only the southern kingdom of Judah, from which all Jews since then trace their descent. Indeed, the words *Jew* and *Jewish* are derived from the name *Judah* and therefore only really apply from the time of the split between Israel and Judah.[4]

The Babylonian Empire conquered the kingdom of Judah in 586 BCE, destroying Solomon's Temple and taking the Jews into exile. They remained there until the Persian king Cyrus the Great conquered Babylon and enacted a policy allowing and encouraging exiled Jews to return to their Judean homeland starting around 538 BCE. Shortly after the Jews returned to their homeland, the Persian-appointed governor Zerubbabel rebuilt the Temple (usually referred to as the "Second Temple") on the site of the old temple in Jerusalem. Judah was then reconstituted as a client state of the Persian Empire, under which it existed in relative peace for two hundred years, until the Persian Empire was conquered by Alexander the Great.

The Hebrew Scriptures include a variety of books that deal with historical events up to and including the period under Persian rule. Some of these books are straightforward historical books that give a detailed chronicle of events, especially for the period of the monarchies before the Babylonian exile. Many other books purport to be written by or record the teachings of a number of prophets, who were sent by God to set the Jewish people straight when they strayed from faithfulness to God and their covenant with him, often by worshipping other gods. These prophets lived in various time periods, including the monarchical period, the Babylonian exile, and the Persian period. Alexander's conquest thus closes the period covered by the books of the Hebrew Bible,[5] although some books, like the Book of Daniel, were actually *written* a bit later.

ANCIENT ISRAEL AND THE RISE OF MONOTHEISM

Modern historians and archaeologists can find corroborating evidence for the kingdoms of Israel and Judah and many of the events that followed. What is less clear is whether Israel and Judah were ever a truly unified kingdom or how these kingdoms came about. The general consensus among modern scholars is that the events preceding the kingdoms of Israel and Judah are mostly mythical (the stories of Genesis up to and including the three patriarchs and Jacob's twelve sons) or at best are highly embellished accounts of vaguely remembered historical events (the story of Moses, the Exodus, Joshua, the period of Judges, the unified monarchy). It is in the period of the twin monarchies that we enter verifiable history with roughly contemporaneous accounts outside of those in the Bible.

Scholars of both Jewish and Christian background began rethinking the historicity of the first few books of the Bible during the Enlightenment, with critical study of the Bible picking up particularly in the eighteenth century. Biblical criticism[6] began in large part by questioning the traditional Jewish and Christian assumption that the first five books of the Bible (known to Jews as the Torah) were written by Moses. This is now generally accepted, even by many religiously observant Jews and Christians, as unlikely because of inconsistencies between and within the five books and because they frequently refer to Moses in the third person. From those beginnings, the critical study of the Bible has advanced in the last two hundred years or so to develop an entirely different narrative for how Judaism and Abrahamic monotheism began.

Although there is still much debate about how the events related in the Hebrew Scriptures relate to actual history, some general contours of a consensus have emerged. The kingdoms of Israel and Judah probably emerged from the broader Semitic cultural sphere of the Levant. This cultural sphere was polytheistic, with a hierarchy of gods and goddesses like those found in most ancient cultures. However, the kingdom of Israel/Judah developed a particularly focused cult around a national god and built a temple for him in Jerusalem. This god was a fusion of a god named 'El, the high god of the broader Semitic pantheon, and Yahweh,[7] a warrior god that may have been of a more southerly origin. Some of the legal, cultural, and mythical traditions later recorded in the Bible may have had origins in this period, but the people of monarchical Israel and Judah were not strict monotheists. 'El/Yahweh was their national god, and they cultivated a strong relationship with him through a cult center in Jerusalem, but that does not mean that they did not think other gods and goddesses existed or were worthy of worship.

Strict monotheism,[8] which would have been an unusual innovation in the ancient world, was developed by Jews living in exile in Babylon in the sixth century. Their national god had, by the logic of polytheism, been humiliated. His temple had been destroyed, the kingdom he protected had been conquered, and his people had been taken into exile. Did this not imply that the gods of the Babylonians were greater than the god of Judah? Jewish thinkers in exile, in particular those from the priestly families that had once served at the Temple in Jerusalem, developed a different solution to the situation they found themselves in: 'El/Yahweh was not simply the national god of Israel or the Jews; he was *the* God of the entire universe. Seen in this light, the conquest of Judah and the exile were not signs of his humiliation; instead, they were signs that he must have a larger plan and that his people need only keep faith in him. This idea that God works in mysterious ways and may subject even his most faithful servants to great suffering would become central to Jewish self-understanding right up to the present day.

The new way of thinking about 'El/Yahweh as a monotheistic God appeared to be vindicated when the Persian king Cyrus the Great ended the exile and allowed the Jews to return to their homeland. Indeed, the Biblical book of Isaiah states that Cyrus was anointed by God to conquer the Babylonians and free the Jews from their exile, thus reflecting the new understanding of a monotheistic God who orchestrates all human events. It was around this time that much of the Hebrew Scriptures was written or redacted to reflect the new monotheistic worldview. In particular, the book of Genesis was created by reworking myths from the broader Semitic culture to explain the creation of the world by one God and the origins of the people of Israel as having a special relationship with him, and biblical narratives in other books were written or reworked to create a fairly consistent narrative of the history of the people of Israel through the monarchical period.

This revised understanding of the history of ancient Israel explains many of the inconsistencies found within the books of the Hebrew Scriptures as well as their relationship with independent historical and archaeological evidence. In particular, it explains a curious feature of many of the books of the Hebrew Bible: the fact that so many prophets over the course of hundreds of years criticized the peoples of Israel and Judah for worshiping other gods or for lacking faithfulness to 'El/Yahweh. This narrative was later weaponized in antisemitic rhetoric as exemplifying the "faithlessness of the Jews." Our new understanding of Biblical history throws these stories about the prophets into a different light: The people of ancient Israel and Judah simply were not monotheists in the strict sense it would later have. Judaism *innovated* monotheism, and it was a process that took many hundreds of years.

THE HELLENISTIC PERIOD: THE DESTRUCTION OF THE SECOND TEMPLE, THE SPLIT WITH CHRISTIANITY, AND THE RISE OF RABBINIC JUDAISM

In 332 BCE, the Persian Empire was conquered by Alexander the Great. Although Alexander was Macedonian, his empire spread Greek language and culture over a vast swath of the eastern Mediterranean. Scholars refer to this Greek-influenced culture spread by Alexander as *Hellenism*. After Alexander's death in 323 BCE, his empire split into several smaller Hellenistic kingdoms. The province of Judea (the land of the Jews) was ruled first by the Ptolemies, Hellenistic kings based in Egypt, then later by the Seleucids, Hellenistic kings based in Mesopotamia. Jews lived under Hellenistic rule fairly peacefully at first, with Jewish elites themselves becoming assimilated into Hellenistic culture. However, tensions between Hellenizing Jews and anti-Hellenists led to a civil war in the second century BCE. The Seleucid king Antiochus IV intervened in this war by banning certain traditional Jewish practices and imposing a more aggressive campaign of Hellenization in Judea. This transformed the civil war into a revolt in 167 BCE, which was led by a Jewish priest named Matthias. After Matthias' death the next year, the revolt was continued by his son Judas, who received the nickname Maccabee ("the Hammer"). One of Judas Maccabee's most important victories in the revolt, in which he captured Jerusalem and purified and rededicated the Temple, is commemorated to this day in the Jewish festival of Hanukkah (usually celebrated in December).[9]

The Maccabean revolt was long and protracted, and it had mixed results. The revolt did lead eventually to the establishment of a Jewish dynasty, the Hasmoneans, who ruled independently of the Seleucids from 110–63 BCE. Little was done, however, to stem the tide of Hellenization, and the Hasmoneans themselves continued to participate in the broader Hellenistic culture of the region. Their reign ended in 63 BCE, when the Romans conquered Judea. They later installed a vassal king, Herod the Great, who greatly refurbished and expanded the Temple in Jerusalem, bringing it to the greatest splendor it would have in its history.

Hellenism had an enormous impact on Judaism, one that had until recently been largely forgotten because of events that would follow, especially with respect to the rise of Christianity. During the second century BCE, Jewish scholars translated the books of the Jewish Bible into Greek, a translation known as the Septuagint.[10] This brought Jewish writings to a broader Greek-reading public and the Jewish concept of monotheism into conversation with Greek philosophical thought and broader learned thought, especially in the Roman Empire. In particular, Philo of Alexandria, a Hellenized Jew who lived in Egypt in the late first century BCE and early first century CE, wrote philosophical works that explored the commonalities between Jewish and Greek thought. Philo was also an example of a new trend in the Hellenistic period: the beginnings of a Jewish diaspora,[11] as Jews, equipped with Greek, moved and settled around the Mediterranean world. This era therefore also saw the rise of a new Jewish institution: the *synagogue* (another Greek word), a meeting place for Jews wherever they might live, however far from Jerusalem, to pray and discuss the teachings of the sacred writings that were beginning to coalesce into a Jewish Bible.

The intellectual ferment of the Hellenistic period, and especially the mobility around the Mediterranean that the Roman Empire brought, also led to a proliferation of Jewish sects. By the late first century CE, there were three major sects: the Sadducees, the Pharisees, and the Essenes. These sects were defined in large part by their differences. The Sadducees and Pharisees differed in their approach to the Jewish Law. Pharisees believed in the validity of what they called the "oral law"—a set of traditions surrounding the interpretation of the Torah—while the Sadducees rejected the concept of oral law and accepted only the written Torah as valid. This led to differences of opinion on issues left ambiguous by the Torah, most famously whether there is resurrection of the dead, which Sadducees rejected and Pharisees accepted. On the other hand, both Sadducees and Essenes were priestly in their orientation, but while Sadducees dominated the administration of the Temple cult in Jerusalem, Essenes were separatists, living in isolated communities that preserved priestly traditions separately from what they saw as a corrupted priestly lineage in Jerusalem.

In addition to these sects, there was, beginning in the first century, a small group that came to be known, in Greek, as Christians. They were not *per se* a significant Jewish sect in the first century, but they would become incredibly significant in subsequent centuries as Christianity grew into an independent religion. Christians were messianists, which is the literal meaning of their Greek name. Messianism was one of the significant contributions of the Hellenistic Age to Judaism. The Hebrew word *mashiah* means "anointed" and thus refers to a king, as people were made kings in ancient Israel by being anointed with oil. Messianism drew from a large body of apocalyptic literature—literature that offered "revelations" (the meaning of the word *apocalypse* in Greek) of what was going to come in the future. One of the most important apocalypses was the biblical book of Daniel, written in the second century BCE at the time of the Maccabean revolt, but there were other such books that later Jewish tradition deemed apocryphal. Messianic ideas varied widely, but they usually involved one or more messiahs being sent by God to restore Israel to its former glory. Often the Messiah was predicted to come from the lineage of the ancient king David, thus implying that David's dynasty would be restored in a final event of history in which God's glory would be fully revealed to the world.

Christianity had its roots in the life and teachings of Jesus, a Jewish man with apocalyptic teachings who was executed by the Roman authorities in Jerusalem in the early first century CE. The Christian sect that grew after his death claimed, somewhat idiosyncratically, that Jesus was, in spite of his death, the foretold Messiah, that he had been resurrected from the dead, and that he would soon return to usher in the kingdom of God on earth. It grew rapidly because, following the pioneering work of the apostle Paul, it actively sought converts among Gentiles around the Roman world. The word *Gentiles* refers to non-Jews, and it had by the Hellenistic period become part of a dichotomy that was central to Jewish identity and important to many messianic hopes. Gentiles encompassed all the nations that Israel had been set apart from as a chosen people, and a common messianic hope was that the coming of the Messiah would not only restore Israel's independence but also establish God's visible rule over the entire world, including over the Gentiles.[12]

Jews of other sects in the Hellenistic period accepted Gentile converts, but they did not necessarily actively missionize for them, and conversion would involve (for men) being circumcised and living according to Jewish Law—that is, *becoming* Jewish. Such a conversion was effectively both a religious and an ethnic conversion. Paul, on the other hand, made the argument, which was controversial at first even among Christians but eventually won the day, that the imminent coming of God's kingdom meant that there was no need for Gentiles to become Jews by being circumcised and following the strictures of Jewish Law that were meant specifically for the Jewish people. Indeed, the fact that Gentiles were turning to the worship of the one true God *as Gentiles* was a sign of the impending kingdom of God, in which God would rule over all nations.

Messianism was not confined to the Christian sect, however, and as a pan-Jewish movement it also contributed to events in the late first and early second centuries CE that would lead to one of the most calamitous events in Jewish history: the destruction of the Temple and the expulsion of the Jews from their homeland. There was periodic unrest throughout the period of Roman rule over Judea, with riots and sporadic uprisings in response to general oppression and specific violations of Jewish religious sensitivities. This unrest boiled over in the year 66 when the Jews, egged on by a radical party known as the Zealots, began a full-scale revolt against Roman rule. The Roman emperor Nero sent Vespasian to put down the revolt, but before completing the task, Nero's death and chaos surrounding the succession led Vespasian to return to Rome to become emperor himself. Vespasian left his son Titus (who himself would later become emperor) to finish the job, which he did in the year 70, when he reconquered Jerusalem and destroyed the Jewish Temple. The Temple has, to this day, never been rebuilt. All that remains is part of the retaining wall for the Temple Mount, known as the "Western Wall" or "Wailing Wall," where Jews now go to pray and lament the destruction of the Temple.

The brutal suppression of the Jewish revolt and the destruction of the Temple did not immediately end Jewish life in Judea, however. Jews continued to live in and around Jerusalem until, in the year 132, they again revolted against Roman rule. The leader of this second revolt was a man named Simon bar Kochba, who was widely believed by his followers to

Figure 9.1 People praying at the Western Wall in Jerusalem. Photo by the author.

be the promised Messiah. The Romans killed bar Kochba in 135 and fully suppressed the revolt shortly thereafter. This time, the human destruction was far greater than in the first revolt. Many thousands of Jews were killed or enslaved. As punishment for the rebellion, the Roman emperor Hadrian banned Jews from Jerusalem, built a new temple to Jupiter on the Temple Mount, and had copies of the Torah publicly burned there. Those Jews who survived mostly migrated out of Judea, some to Galilee (the far northern part of modern-day Israel) but others far beyond. This marked the pivotal moment of what is known as the *diaspora*—a Greek word that means "dispersion" and refers to the migration of Jews around the world.

The differences between Jews and Christians quickly became too great to coexist under a single religious identity. There were Jewish Christians at the time of the Bar Kochba Revolt, but they did not support Bar Kochba as Messiah since they believed the Messiah had already come in the form of Jesus. At the same time, Christianity was, demographically speaking, increasingly a Gentile movement. Non-Christian Jewish teachers, known as rabbis, did not jettison the concept of a Messiah, but they became much more cautious about it. They rejected previous messianic figures, including both Jesus and Bar Kochba, as "false messiahs," and they reformulated the concept of the Messiah as a more spiritual figure to come in the far future rather than an immediate revolutionary leader.

Over the centuries that followed, elites on both sides—Christian theologians, known as the Church Fathers, and the Jewish Rabbis—reworked their traditions in such a way as to make them increasingly mutually exclusive. The Church Fathers painted "the Jews" as having "rejected Christ" and used the slur of being "too Jewish" as a boogeyman to criticize their internal Christian enemies. On the other side, the Rabbis worked to distance their tradition from Christianity, both through their careful reformulation of the concept of the Messiah and through a general process of de-Hellenization and valorization of Hebrew traditions.

The type of Judaism that emerged after the revolts of the first and second centuries is known as Rabbinic Judaism. It accounts for the vast majority of self-identifying Jews since that time.[13] Like the Pharisaic sect of the first century, Rabbinic Juidaism places authority not only in the Torah but in a vast corpus of oral law, which together are known as the *halakhah*. In Hebrew, this word means "the way to behave," but it is often referred to in English as the "Jewish Law." It is one of several examples of religious law (see chapter 11) among the world religions, including Islamic Law, on which it had a direct influence. In the early centuries of the diaspora, Jewish Rabbis began writing down their oral traditions, which included commentaries on Biblical texts, debates between famous rabbis, and specific legal regulations that went beyond the particular *mitzvahs* (commandments) of the Torah but were intended to prevent accidental violations of those commandments.[14] The most important collection of writings on the oral law is the Babylonian Talmud, which was made in the fifth century. The Talmud has since then defined the Rabbinical Jewish tradition, being second in importance only to the Bible itself. Over the course of many centuries living as minorities among Gentiles, Rabbinic Jews have studied and practiced the halakhic traditions of the Talmud to show their devotion to God, their commitment to the Torah, and their distinctiveness from their Gentile (or *goy*[15]) neighbors.

ETHNIC IDENTITIES AND ANTISEMITISM IN THE MIDDLE AGES

Jews of the diaspora initially found themselves a minority in a pagan world. After the Roman Empire rapidly Christianized in the fourth century, they found themselves a minority in a Christian world. Then, after the Arab conquest in the seventh century, some Jews found themselves a minority in an Islamic world. Although there have been migrations of Jews to areas outside of these two civilizational spheres, especially in modern times, the bulk of Jewish experience since the early Middle Ages has been as a minority among either Christians or Muslims.

The settlement patterns of Jews have led to their differentiation into several intra-Jewish ethnic groups. Although there are other smaller groups, the majority of Jews today come from one of three major ethnic groups. The largest of these groups, accounting for the majority of Jews today, are the Ashkenazis. They are descended from Jews who settled in the Holy Roman Empire in central Europe in the late first millennium. Ashkenazis developed a common culture and a specific language called Yiddish, which is based on an old Germanic dialect and incorporates a great deal of Hebrew vocabulary. Although Ashkenazis have come to dominate the worldwide Jewish population in modern times, they were dwarfed in the Middle Ages by more prosperous Jewish communities in the Islamic world.

The other major ethnic group with its origins in Europe is the Sephardis. Sephardis are descended from Jews who settled in the Iberian Peninsula (modern Spain and Portugal) and flourished there during the period of Islamic rule. The Islamic kingdom of al-Andalus was a major center of Jewish learning, culminating in the work of the twelfth-century figure Maimonides, who is considered one of the greatest Jewish scholars in all of history. A succession of changes in regime, however, progressively forced Sephardic Jews to leave Spain. This began in the early second millennium as new Islamic rulers in al-Andalus forced Jews (including Maimonides himself) to leave if they wanted to avoid converting to Islam. It culminated in 1492, when Catholics completed their *Reconquista* of Spain by defeating the last remaining Islamic kingdom in al-Andalus. The new Catholic rulers, Ferdinand and Isabella, ordered all Jews in their kingdom to either convert to Catholicism or be expelled. Those who did convert were known as *conversios* and were subject to harassment by the Spanish Inquisition. Many *conversios* ended up settling in the Spanish colonies, and their descendants make up a considerable proportion of Latin Americans today. Those who did not convert mostly settled in North Africa and other parts of the Ottoman Empire.

The third major ethnic group is the Mizrahis. The Hebrew word *Mizrahi* means "Easterner," and it refers to those Jews who settled in the lands of the Islamic Empire, most of which are to the east of Europe. Although the Sephardic and Mizrahic ethnic groups are in theory distinct, that distinction is in modern times a bit fuzzy. The reason for this is that Sephardic Jews mixed with Mizrahic Jews, especially after their expulsion from Spain in 1492 and resettlement around the Ottoman Empire. The major cultural, ethnic, and religious divide in Judaism today is between Ashkenazis, on the one hand, and Sephardis/Mizrahis, on the other. It plays a significant role in the society and politics of the modern state of Israel, where Sephardis/Mizrahis now outnumber Ashkenazis.

Antisemitism—that is, prejudice against and oppression of Jews—has, as we have seen, roots in the ancient world, but it became particularly pronounced during the Middle Ages. Jews faced oppression and marginalization in both Christian and Islamic countries, but it tended to be worse in Christian ones. The reason for the relative tolerance of the Jewish minority in Islamic countries was the Islamic concept of "People of the Book." This refers to religious communities that possess an authentic (if, from the Islamic perspective, corrupted) revealed scripture. The Qur'an specifically refers to Jews and Christians as "People of the Book" because they possess the Torah and the Gospel, respectively. Under Islamic Law, People of the Book were eligible for "protection," or *dhimma*, which meant that they were allowed to maintain their communities and traditions as long as they paid a special tax called the *jizya*.

Things worked out a bit differently for Jews in the theology of Christianity. Christianity began as a Jewish sect, but the apostle Paul won a debate in its earliest decades over whether Gentiles who became Christian (i.e., turned away from idolatry and became loyal to Jesus as the Messiah) also needed to become Jewish by being circumcised and taking on the commandments of Torah intended specifically for Jews. This meant that Christianity preserved the Gentile-Jewish distinction within its own ranks, and very quickly Jews were a tiny minority within them. Subsequent generations of Christians then twisted certain rhetoric in the Bible—much of it from Paul's own words, some of it from other New Testament writers, but also from the original Hebrew Scriptures—to paint the Jews, God's "chosen people," as in fact faithless and cursed.

Many of the common tropes of modern antisemitism had their origins in the oppressive conditions Jews faced in medieval Europe. The Church taught that the Jews were responsible for killing Jesus Christ, thus making them intrinsically opposed to God. This theological demonization of Jews led to all sorts of popular conspiracy theories among the Christian populace. One of the most significant of these was the "blood libel." According to this calumny, Jews supposedly would abduct and ritually murder Christian children so that they could use their blood to bake matzah (unleavened bread) for Passover.

At the same time that they were subject to these religiously based prejudices, some Jews were able to accumulate wealth by lending money on interest. Christian monarchs and other elites found it useful to use Jews as bankers because the Church forbade Christians to lend money on interest, calling it the sin of "usury." This led to the rather hypocritical stereotyping of Jews as rich and greedy—hypocritical because loans on interest were economically useful to Christians and because Christians themselves often found ways to surreptitiously charge interest on loans. Although Christians generally abandoned the ban on lending money on interest around the sixteenth century, redefining usury to mean charging *excessive* interest, the stereotype of the "greedy Jew" with its origins in medieval finance has lived on.

Throughout the Middle Ages, Jews in Europe were periodically killed in outbursts of Christian mob violence known as *pogroms*. Pogroms were typically sparked by a variety of conspiracy theories deriving from the antisemitic prejudices of the day. For example, the discovery of a murdered Christian child might lead to scapegoating of Jews based on the "blood libel" calumny. Resentment among poor and indebted Christians might lead to scapegoating of Jews for their supposed "greed." Or natural disasters such as plagues might be blamed on the Jews because of their status as "Christ-killers." Christian monarchs could also manipulate popular sentiment against Jews to "keep them in line" while also using them to their own benefit.

JEWISH IDENTITY IN MODERNITY

Although the Protestant Reformation that is often seen as ushering in Western modernity did not immediately improve conditions for Jews in Europe (Martin Luther was himself a virulent antisemite), the Enlightenment that followed sowed the seeds for a reconsideration of the status of Jews in European society. It did so through the questioning of Christian traditions, through the valorization of rationality, and through a shift from communal to individual values. Prominent Jewish thinkers participated in the Enlightenment as well, in large part by questioning and rethinking their own Jewish traditions. This movement, known as the Jewish Enlightenment, or *Haskalah* in Hebrew, began among Ashkenazi communities in the eighteenth century and would come to have lasting influence on Jewish culture worldwide. Members of this movement, known as *Maskilim*, sought to improve the station of Jews in their societies and the state of Judaism in general. They did so by challenging the authority of the traditional rabbis, encouraging Jews to engage with their surrounding societies, and promoting the study of the Bible directly without deference to Talmudic interpretation. Moses Mendelssohn, one of the most influential Maskilim, was compared to Martin Luther for his role in overthrowing tradition in his religion (in this case the Talmudic learning of the Rabbis rather than the traditions of the Church).

The Jewish Enlightenment led to a split of Ashkenazi Jews into different religious movements in the nineteenth century. The first split was between Orthodox Judaism and Reform Judaism. Orthodox Jews did not necessarily completely reject the reforms advocated by the Haskalah (although some did), but they represented those who sought to preserve traditional Talmudic study and practice of *halakhah*. Reform Jews, on the other hand, sought to take the reforms of the Haskalah to their logical conclusion, emphasizing personal and innovative interpretation of the Bible instead of traditional Talmudic study and valuing a progressive interpretation of Jewish ethical teachings over the fastidious practice of the ritual aspects of Jewish Law. Conservative Judaism then arose as a third movement, seeking a compromise between these two extremes. It sought to embrace some of the progressive reforms of the Reform movement while also preserving more of the traditional practices of *halakhah*.

To be clear, the Haskalah, just like the broader European Enlightenment, did not spur Jewish thinkers only in religious directions but also in new intellectual directions that either rejected or sidelined religion. Indeed, the entire European Enlightenment had in part been sparked in the seventeenth century by the work of the Jewish philosopher Spinoza, who questioned the divine origin of the Bible and traditional interpretation

Figure 9.2 A girl reading from the Torah at her bat mitzvah. The bar mitzvah developed in the Middle Ages as a coming-of-age ceremony for thirteen-year-old boys, in which they read from the Torah in front of the congregation. The bat mitzvah developed in modern times as an equivalent ceremony for girls. It is observed by Reform Jews, Conservative Jews, and certain Orthodox Jews. © Getty Images

of God as a transcendent being. In the nineteenth century, many Jewish intellectuals contributed to or even became founding figures of secular disciplines of knowledge. Likewise, just as increasing numbers of Christians came to reject religion and identify as secular, many Jews began assuming a nonreligious and secular identity. The main difference is that secular Jews then and now typically (though not always) continue to identify as Jewish. This speaks to the ambiguity in Jewish identity: Is it a religion, or is it an ethnicity?

Insofar as Judaism was considered a religion, the secularization of the late nineteenth and early twentieth centuries led to a rapid improvement in conditions for European Jews. New concepts of liberty and equality led European governments to lift the restrictions that had historically been placed upon them. Jews were no longer required to live in ghettos, specific neighborhoods reserved for Jews in cities; they were freed from discriminatory laws; and they were integrated into the full civic life of their countries as citizens. These changes did not bring an end to antisemitism, however. Instead, they caused it to morph. The term *antisemitism* was created in the nineteenth century, in fact, to describe this new type of hatred for Jews.

Earlier types of European antisemitism (which scholars sometimes prefer to call "anti-Judaism") were ideologically undergirded by a religious claim: that Jews "rejected Christ." This does not mean that medieval Christians did not see Jews as an ethnicity: The entire concept of ethnicity had roots in the Bible and was tied up intimately with Jewish identity; likewise, Jews could potentially face persecution even after conversion, as they did under the Spanish Inquisition. Nevertheless, anti-Jewish sentiment was usually tied rhetorically to their perceived religious fault.

As secularism and religious toleration spread throughout the Western world in the nineteenth and early twentieth centuries, however, these sorts of arguments against Jews became moot. Instead, the new antisemites focused *specifically* on Jews' ethnicity. Given the prevailing racist attitudes at the time, they began to argue that the "problem" with Jews was biological: They were "racially" inferior. Ashkenazi Jews had been living alongside European Christians for well over a thousand years and did not necessarily look that different from Gentiles in their respective countries, but antisemites hyperfocused on physical characteristics perceived as "Jewish." Exaggerated caricatures of Jews, often sporting an oversized, hooked nose, became a staple of antisemitic literature. As antisemitism became increasingly racialized, it dovetailed with emerging European nationalism in volatile ways. The movement to establish state boundaries that corresponded with the supposed homelands of distinct "nations" did not fit well with the existence of ethnic minorities. Insofar as Jews were considered an ethnic group, antisemites argued that they were a "contagion" that ruined the "purity" of the nation.

One significant way in which antisemites tried to demonstrate that a Jewish minority was a threat to national purity was through the myth of an international Jewish conspiracy. The idea of such a conspiracy was spread rapidly in the early twentieth century through the publication of the *Protocols of the Elders of Zion*. This book, first published in 1905 in Russia and then translated and reprinted in many other languages, was a hoax, actually written by antisemites but pretending to be written by a secret Jewish cabal (the "Elders of Zion") who were planning to take over the world by manipulating the economy and controlling the media.

Judaism: A Religion or an Ethnicity?

Although the *Protocols* has since been shown to be a deliberate work of fabrication, its influence in spreading the antisemitic idea of an international Jewish conspiracy has been deep, broad, and enduring.

The convergence of antisemitism, right-wing nationalism, and conspiracy theories culminated in the Holocaust, or Shoah,[16] one of greatest tragedies to befall the Jewish people and one of the most shocking perpetrations of evil in the history of humanity. Adolf Hitler rose to power in Germany in the early 1930s as a right-wing German nationalist who leveraged antisemitism to blame Jews for Germany's ills at the time, in particular its perceived humiliation for having lost World War I. During his push to conquer much of Europe, the Nazi government planned and enacted what it called the "Final Solution" to the "Jewish Question": the mass extermination of all of Europe's Jews. In the end, the Nazis managed to kill six million Jews (about two-thirds of the total in Europe) as well as several million other minorities.

Even among those who are educated about the Holocaust, certain misconceptions are common. One is that the Holocaust came out of nowhere, that it was simply a unique act of madness. This ignores the long history of antisemitism, stretching back thousands of years, that was intimately tied up with Christianity throughout most of its history. Hitler could not have come to power, much less attempted to exterminate the Jewish people, were it not for this deep bedrock of antisemitism that permeated European society.

The second misconception about the Holocaust is that it was an aberration—a throwback to premodern barbarism that was but a blip in the inevitable march of modern progress. Although it is true that the antisemitism that led to the Holocaust had deep premodern roots, the Holocaust itself was very much a modern phenomenon. It was based on modern conceptions of nationhood and racialized antisemitism. It also was, logistically, a modern, industrialized process. Although Jews faced periodic pogroms during the Middle Ages, none of them were nearly as destructive as the Holocaust. It would have been simply impossible for anyone to kill six million Jews prior to the invention of modern, industrial technology. The Holocaust depended on modern planning and logistics, as well as massive train systems to transport Jews to concentration camps and factory-like facilities to murder and cremate Jews at an industrialized pace.

At the same time that antisemites were arguing that Jews posed a threat to national purity in the nineteenth century, many Jews[17] began to argue that Jews themselves needed a national homeland where they could live in safety as a majority. This movement, known as *Zionism*, was a product of the Haskalah insofar as it questioned traditional rabbinical teachings about the diaspora. There were initially different proposals about where that homeland should be established, but a consensus was quickly reached that it should be in Palestine, the region of the ancient kingdoms of Israel and Judah, which was at that time part of the Ottoman Empire. Many Jews then began emigrating to Palestine, and this emigration accelerated when the Ottoman Empire was dismantled after World War I and Great Britain took over administration of the province (a period known as the "British Mandate").

In 1917, just before the end of World War I, Great Britain had issued the Balfour Declaration, stating its support for the creation of a Jewish homeland in Palestine. However, under the British Mandate, tensions between the growing Jewish population, local Palestinians (who were Arab Muslims and Christians), and the British administration grew. The end of World War II and the worldwide realization of the extent of the Holocaust lent greater urgency to the establishment of a Jewish state. In 1947, the United Nations passed a resolution proposing the partition of Palestine into a Jewish state, an Arab state, and a special international zone for the holy cities of Jerusalem and Bethlehem. Palestinian Arabs did not accept the proposal envisioned by this resolution, but Zionist leaders declared the creation of an independent state of Israel on May 14, 1948. The next day, the British terminated their administration of Palestine, and a coalition of surrounding Arab states invaded to prevent the establishment of a Jewish state on terms that they saw as unfavorable to Palestinian Arabs.

What followed was ten months of warfare to determine who would control the former British Mandate of Palestine. The result of this war was an Israeli victory, with borders for the new state of Israel larger than proposed by the UN resolution. About 700,000 Palestinians fled or were forced from their homes in what they refer to in Arabic as the *Nakba*, or "catastrophe." Another war with the surrounding Arab countries, the Six-Day War of 1967, resulted in Israel occupying further Palestinian lands, most importantly the Gaza Strip and West Bank, that in the interim had been administered by Egypt and Jordan, respectively. The international community does not recognize these territories as being part of Israel, and the still unresolved issue of the Palestinians in the Occupied Territories continues to be a major source of conflict and international tension.

The Holocaust and creation of the state of Israel have had a transformative effect on the lives of Jewish people in the twentieth and twenty-first centuries. Over 85% of all Jews in the world today live in one of two countries: the United States and Israel. This is in part due to the mass emigration of Jews out of Europe as the Nazis rose to power and in the wake of the Holocaust, mostly to the United States and Israel. In addition, most of the Jewish minorities of Arab countries, many of them with roots going back over a thousand years, emigrated to Israel in the years after its establishment, in part because of worsening conditions in their home countries and in part out of a desire to participate in the Zionist project.

This latter aspect of migration to Israel is related to another phenomenon: a sharp rise in antisemitism in the Islamic world. In this chapter, I have focused on antisemitism in the Christian world because that is where it historically was most virulent. Jews enjoyed relatively greater toleration in the Islamic world in the Middle Ages and early modernity, but they did at times experience oppression and violence, as when Maimonides was forced to leave Spain in the eleventh century to avoid converting to Islam. When much of the Islamic world was colonized by European powers in the late nineteenth and early twentieth centuries, Muslims were exposed to more systematic, virulent, and modern forms of antisemitism with origins in Europe. This included, in particular, the ideas found in the *Protocols of the Elders of Zion*, which was translated into Arabic in 1920. Some Muslims wove European antisemitism together with Islamic traditions, such as *hadith* about Muhammad's interactions with Jews, to express antisemitic ideas in a more "Islamic" idiom. Antisemitism became further entrenched after the establishment of the state of Israel, feeding off of both political anti-Zionist sentiment and legitimate empathy for the continuing plight of the Palestinian people.

In this chapter, I have been particularly attentive to giving a detailed history of the Jewish people, in part because that is what antisemitism so often denies them, but also because Judaism confounds the Christian paradigm of religion in a particularly unique way. Throughout this book, I have been showing that we tend to see the religions of the world through Christian-tinted glasses. In most cases, the distortion of a particular tradition by the glasses of religion started in the colonial period. Not so in the case of Judaism. In the case of Judaism, this process started with the birth of Christianity itself. Moreover, the distortion of Judaism, which is felt most acutely in the form of antisemitism, is not simply a matter of being seen through a Christian lens. Judaism gave birth to Christianity, so it is, paradoxically, part of the lens itself.

Modern antisemitism capitalizes on a unique ambiguity: Judaism is simultaneously a religion and an ethnicity. To be clear, this ambiguity is not a product of antisemitism (which in fact tries to reduce Jewishness to a biological race); it derives from the Jewish tradition itself. The Biblical concept of the Jewish people being a chosen people from among the nations led to a dichotomy between Jews and Gentiles that is central to Jewish identity. This tight bond between religion and ethnicity was originally not unique to Judaism; as we saw in chapter 1, it was quite common in the ancient world. Each ethnic group (or "nation") had its own gods and traditions for worshiping those gods. The inversion of the Jewish dichotomy between Jews and Gentiles in Christianity, however, ultimately broke the link between religion and ethnicity, leaving Judaism an outlier. That is, when Christianity tipped from being mostly Jewish to being mostly Gentile, it became a "religion" that was no longer tied to an ethnicity. Insofar as Christianity is the implicit paradigm for religion today, religion is assumed to be something unrelated to ethnicity, thus rendering Judaism uncanny, *even though Christianity came from Judaism in the first place*. Ironically, nationalism as a modern political movement is conversely based on romanticized visions of the nation inspired by the Biblical account of the Jewish people (Israelites as "nation"), and religious nationalists take this romanticism to the extreme of trying to restore the link between religion and the nation. Thus, ideas that had their origin in the Jewish tradition are repeatedly twisted and weaponized against Jews through antisemitism.

I will close by addressing one final form of antisemitism, which is perhaps the most insidious of all. According to this line of antisemitic thinking, popular among some antireligious secularists, the evils of Western civilization come from Christianity, but since Christianity comes from Judaism, those evils ultimately come from Judaism. This is a particularly perverse form of antisemitism because it blames Jews for their own suffering. It is true that the Jewish people have, throughout their long history, had the misfortune to repeatedly suffer at the hands of people whose own culture, religion, and ideology was inspired by Jewish culture, religion, and ideology. But that does not make Jews responsible for their own suffering. It simply makes the many antisemites who have oppressed them hypocrites.

DISCUSSION QUESTIONS

1. Where do the words *Jew* and *Jewish* come from? How do they relate to other Biblical terms of identity such as *Hebrew* and *Israelite*? Be sure to explain the Biblical story of the origins of Israel that led to these identities.
2. What were the major sects of Judaism in the first century, and what were their differences? What distinctive ideas do most modern forms of Judaism inherit from first-century Judaism?

3. How did the split between Judaism and Christianity take place from the second century on? What differences did their elites emphasize to mark their difference? What do they nevertheless share in common?
4. What significant changes did the Haskalah bring to modern Jewish conceptions of their own identity?
5. Why is Judaism simultaneously a religion and an ethnicity? In what ways has modern antisemitism capitalized on this ambiguity to promote racist conspiracy theories about Jewish people?

NOTES

1 The Jewish sabbath begins at sundown on Friday and ends at sundown on Saturday. According to the dictates of the Torah, Jews should refrain from work on the sabbath. This is interpreted and observed differently by the different movements of Judaism today, but traditional Rabbinic Judaism has elaborate and strict rules about what activities Jews must refrain from on the sabbath, which Orthodox Jews still observe today.
2 Although the Genesis account does not say so, later Jewish tradition held that in leaving his home, Abraham rejected his father's worship of many gods in the form of idols. This tradition would later become important to Islam, which holds that Abraham was an important prophet sent by God who built the Kaaba in Mecca to worship him.
3 The word *Bible* comes from the Greek word *biblia*, which simply means "books." It was first used by Jews during the Hellenistic period, when Greek was the lingua franca, to refer to their scriptures. However, because the far more numerous Christians use the word *Bible* to refer to a larger collection of "books" (adding to them the New Testament), it is customary in English to refer to the Jewish Bible as the Hebrew Bible or Hebrew Scriptures, in reference to the language they were written in.
4 There is a proliferation of words of identity in the Hebrew Scriptures that can be confusing. The word *Israelite* refers to any descendant of one of the twelve sons of Jacob (who was given the name Israel). The word *Hebrew* (in reference to people) is sometimes used as a synonym for Israelites, especially during the narrative of the Exodus from Egypt. The word *Jew*, on the other hand, comes from *Judah*, the name of the southern kingdom after the kingdom of Israel split into two. The northern kingdom of Israel was destroyed by the Assyrian Empire in the eighth century BCE, so Jews since then trace their lineage specifically back to the kingdom of Judah. Today, *Jew* refers

to any member of the religion/ethnicity of Judaism; *Israeli* refers to a citizen of the modern state of Israel; and *Hebrew* is used (in English) only to refer to the language, with reference to people reserved for the ancient Biblical usage. Note also that the word *Jew* is a noun, referring to Jewish people, and the word *Jewish* is an adjective, referring to anything having to do with Judaism, including but not limited to people.

5 By this I mean the canonical Jewish Tanakh. Catholic and Orthodox Christian versions of the Old Testament contain additional books that describe events in the later Hellenistic period.

6 The phrase "Biblical criticism" is a standard academic term, but it can be confusing to nonspecialists. It does not mean "criticizing the Bible" in a hostile sense. Instead, it refers to the modern study of the Bible as a set of literary and historical documents, using rational, critical thinking to understand the way in which the books of the Bible were written. Many, probably most, scholars who have engaged in Biblical criticism were and are committed Christians and Jews.

7 *Yahweh* is a modern scholarly reconstruction of the name of the ancient Israelite god. All existing manuscripts of the Hebrew Scriptures retain the consonants of that name (YHWH) but replace the vowels with those of the word *Adonai*, which is Hebrew for "Lord." This is because there arose, very early on in Jewish history, a taboo against pronouncing the name of God. The hybrid form found in Hebrew manuscripts indicates that the word intended is the name of God but should be pronounced with the replacement word *Lord*. English translations of the Hebrew Scriptures usually indicate this by using the word Lord in small caps.

8 To be clear, strict monotheism in the ancient world did not mean exactly the same thing as many people in the modern world understand it to mean. Today, people often understand monotheism as being the belief that there is one God who exists, period. Ancient Jewish and Christian monotheism, however, existed in a world in which most people worshiped many gods. Jews and Christians in the ancient world did not necessarily believe that those other gods did not exist. Rather, they denied that they were worthy of worship as gods. Only the one God was worthy of worship as such. There were different ways of indicating this distinction. One common way, in Greek, was to use the word *daimones*, a term for supernatural beings of low rank, to refer to the other gods. This is where we get the word *demons*, which by the Middle Ages had come to be considered a class of specifically *evil* supernatural beings, in league with the devil.

9 Hanukkah is a relatively minor festival in the Jewish religious calendar, but it has taken on a higher cultural significance, especially in the United States, because it happens to fall at about the same time as Christmas every year.

10 Actually, the Septuagint is a bit larger than what later Jews would consider as "canonical"—that is, as properly belonging to the Tanakh. The extra books are known as the "apocrypha." Some books of the apocrypha are considered by Catholic and Orthodox Christians as canonical parts of the Old Testament. Protestants, conversely, rejected these "apocryphal" books as uncanonical.

11 The word *diaspora* comes from Greek, in which it literally means "dispersion." It is used in English today to refer to communities of any ethnic group that are found around the world outside of their homeland. The English usage, however, comes specifically from its use in the Hellenistic world to refer to communities of Jews outside of Judea.

12 The English words Gentile, ethnic, and nation are all related both to each other and, historically, to the Biblical concept of "the nations" (Hebrew *goyim*) and thus the Jewish-Gentile dichotomy. The word *ethnic* comes from the Greek word *ethne*, which was used in the Hellenistic period to translate *goyim*. The words Gentile and nation both come from Latin words that refer to groups of people with common ancestry, what can also be referred to, using the Greek word, an "ethnic" group. The original concept of *goyim*, later translated into Greek as *ethne*, is best rendered into English as "the nations." The word Gentiles is used slightly differently to refer to non-Jews, whether individually or in the aggregate.

13 The two major groups of non-Rabbinic Jews today are Karaite Jews and Ethiopian Jews (Beta Israel), both of whom reject the Talmud and the concept of oral law.

14 For example, a commandment in the Torah states, "You shall not boil a kid [i.e., a young goat] in its mother's milk." To prevent even accidental violation of this commandment, kosher food—food that is prepared properly according to Jewish dietary regulations—does not mix meat and dairy, and kosher kitchens keep separate sets of utensils for meat and dairy products.

15 The word *goy* is often used by Jews today to refer to Gentiles, non-Jewish culture, and so forth. It comes, via Yiddish, from the original Hebrew word for "the nations," *goyim*.

16 *Shoah* is Hebrew for "destruction," and many Jews prefer to use this term to refer specifically to the Nazi genocide of Jewish people, as opposed to other groups (e.g., homosexuals, Roma, political dissidents, etc.).

17 But not all. It has been a common antisemitic trope since the foundation of the state of Israel to conflate Judaism with Zionism. Not all Jews are Zionists. In fact, some ultra-Orthodox Jews reject the state of Israel because, according to their reading of the Jewish tradition, Israel cannot and should not be reconstituted until the coming of the Messiah.

10
Indigenous Traditions
What Gets Counted as a Religion?

So far in this book we have been looking at religions that can be named and identified. It may seem too obvious to even mention, but one of the characteristics that we typically associate religion with is that there are, in fact, discrete religions: things out there in the world that we identify as religions, like Christianity, Islam, Hinduism, Buddhism, and so forth. But I want you to notice two things about these religions we have been learning about. The first is that, if we look at their historical areas of influence (that is, prior to modern colonialism), they come from a fairly narrow band in a specific part of the world. That band stretches from Europe and North Africa in the West; through the Middle East, Central Asia, and South Asia; and on to East Asia and Southeast Asia in the East. Sub-Saharan Africa, Australia and Oceania, and the Americas are outside of this zone.[1] The second thing I would like you to notice is that, even within the geographical zone we have looked at, certain religions have predominated over others. Often people speak about five world religions: Judaism, Christianity, Islam, Hinduism, and Buddhism. But we have also learned about additional religions: Confucianism, Daoism, Sikhism, and Jainism. Are these world religions? What counts as a world religion anyway?

To answer these questions, it is useful to start with the second question first, since the geographical zone we have been concentrated on in this book in a sense contains the oldest historical roots of the *concept* of religion (see chapter 1). In the first section, we will therefore look more closely at the relationships between the religions we have learned about so far to gain greater insight into how certain things gain the features that lead them to be labeled religions. In doing so, we will have occasion to learn about two additional religions we have not learned about yet: Shinto and Bön.

In the second section, we will return to the issue of colonialism and see how it brought the Western concept of religion into conversation not only within the geographical zone from Europe to East Asia but also with the world as a whole. This will help us to explain the first observation given above, and it will also give us occasion to learn about a third religion we have not encountered yet: Yoruba religion. We will also learn about the Native American Church, which in a similar way represents an organization of indigenous practices as religious in the face of colonialism.

Finally, in the third section, we will examine a modern academic concept, *animism*, that has been used to dismiss the religious traditions of huge swaths of humanity. In the end, we will see that the question of what counts as a religion is not objective or value-neutral. There are very specific, and in many cases recent, historical reasons for why certain things get identified as religions and others do not—or, in a related vein, why the vast majority of "religions" come from a particular geographical band from Europe to East Asia.

WHAT DOES IT MEAN TO BE A WORLD RELIGION?

What do we mean when we call something a world religion? This phrase "world religion" is relatively new, at least as new as, if not newer than, the modern concept of religion itself. The addition of the qualifier "world" is interesting. It implies that the religion in question is not simply local; it has a worldwide significance. But what counts as worldwide significance? To answer this question, it is useful to look at those religions that frequently get called world religions. The shortest and most common list that is given when talking about world religions is the following five: Judaism, Christianity, Islam, Hinduism, and Buddhism. These five happen to correspond to the four largest religions by population, plus Judaism. The four religions of Christianity, Islam, Hinduism, and Buddhism are the only religions that can be counted on the order of billions, with the smallest, Buddhism, coming in at half a billion.

There is something a bit arbitrary, however, about how one counts the number of adherents of a particular religion, depending on, as we saw in chapters 6 and 7, how that religion polices its boundaries. I think it is useful to look first at a shorter list of three that have more in common than just numbers: Christianity, Islam, and Buddhism. These three religions, structurally speaking, have a great deal in common. They are all religions that were founded at a particular point in history by a particular person (Jesus, Muhammad, and the Buddha, respectively). They all articulate a universal worldview that promises some sort of salvation (a soteriology) equally to all of humanity. For Christians and Muslims, salvation consists of eternal life with God in heaven as opposed to eternal damnation in hell, with somewhat different conceptions of how that salvation can be achieved. For Buddhists, salvation consists of ending the cycle of rebirth, which can be attained by following the Eightfold Path. Finally, all three actively seek to bring their universal soteriology to as many people as possible. To use a Christian term, they are missionary religions. In sum, Christianity, Islam, and Buddhism can be considered world religions insofar as they attempt to speak to, and therefore have become of relevance to, the entire world.

How do Judaism and Hinduism fit into this conception of world religions? In chapter 9, I noted that Judaism is tiny when compared to the other four commonly cited world religions. Likewise, although it is possible to convert to Judaism, Jews have not typically actively sought to convert outsiders. It is difficult to identify a particular founder because Judaism is fundamentally tied up with the entire history of a particular group of people, the Jewish people. Judaism is, apparently in opposition to the concept of *world* religion, an *ethnic* religion. Nevertheless, Judaism is arguably the most influential religion in the world via its two offshoots, Christianity and Islam. And it is influential through those offshoots precisely because of the universal claims it makes about the world and all of humanity. Its unique contribution to religion is the concept of one universal God who is the creator of and ruler over the entire world. This God may be the God of Israel, and Israel may be his chosen people, but he is still the one, universal God that all people are ultimately subject to.

Similarly, Hinduism is not a religion that was founded by a particular person at a particular point in history. Rather, it is defined by the entire religious history of a particular group of people, the people of India. This happens to be a very large group of people, so numbers alone can account for why Hinduism always gets counted among the world religions. But its relationship to Buddhism also helps to account for this inclusion. Hinduism represents the religious matrix out of which Buddhism emerged, just as Judaism represents the religious matrix out of which Christianity and Islam emerged. Indeed, Hindu religious culture gave rise to the worldview of a cycle of reincarnation that one might want to escape from, and Buddhism provides a specific universal answer to how escape from the cycle of reincarnation can be achieved. Insofar as Buddhism is considered a world religion, it makes sense to consider Hinduism a world religion as well.

This strategy of pursuing family relationships between religions is also useful for understanding why other religions beyond the "main five" are identified as such, as well as why they sometimes get included in longer lists of world religions. In the context of India, we learned about Sikhism and Jainism. Jainism arose in parallel with Buddhism out of the same ancient religious speculations about reincarnation; it simply offers a different understanding of why we are trapped in the cycle of rebirth and how to escape from it. In theory, it is a universal religion, offering a universal soteriology to all of humankind, but, because of strict rules placed on its monks, it did not spread far beyond its early geographical origins and gain worldwide influence in the same way as did Buddhism. Sikhism likewise arose out of an interaction sphere between Hinduism and Islam in the Punjab. Like Christianity and Islam, it offers a worldview of a monotheistic God, and in theory its message of salvation is valid for all of humankind. Historically, it has been mostly limited to a single ethnic group—the Punjabis—but it is also a relatively young religion and has the potential to grow into more global influence in the future, especially as Sikhs emigrate to countries around the world.

In the context of China, we also learned about two additional religions: Confucianism and Daoism. As we saw in chapter 6, these two, together with Buddhism, are typically practiced together, even though they have distinct identities. This special relationship with Buddhism alone accounts for their frequent inclusion in lists of important religions. In addition, Confucianism and Daoism have been directly influenced by Buddhism, even if their origins predate the coming of Buddhism to China. In particular, Daoism became institutionally organized largely in response to the entrance of a foreign institution, the Buddhist monastic community. What might have remained an amorphous set of ideas about the Dao, *qi*, and *yin* and *yang* became the basis for institutionalized lineages of priests offering rituals in parallel to those of Buddhist monks. Daoism, in other words, looks more like a religion today because it organized itself in response to Buddhism, which in turn is recognized as a world religion because of its close structural parallels to Christianity.

This phenomenon of local traditions organizing themselves in response to Buddhism was not limited to Daoism in China. Two other religions can be cited as examples of the same phenomenon: Shinto and Bön. Shinto is sometimes given in lists of world religions even though it is relatively small and confined to the single cultural sphere of Japan. It is often described as the "indigenous" religion of Japan, meaning the religion of Japan that preceded the introduction of Buddhism in the sixth century. The word *Shinto* means "way of the gods," and it is focused on the worship of supernatural beings that are known in Japanese as *kami*. This can therefore give the impression that the *kami* are the local gods of Japan and that Shinto is therefore Japan's "original" religion.

This impression, however, does not take into account the way Buddhism works or the specific relationship it has had to the *kami* in Japan. Belief in supernatural beings of all sorts was nearly universal among human cultures until modern times. Buddhism does not deny the existence of such beings; it simply ranks them according to their karmic value within the realm of *samsara*. Whenever it enters a new culture, it must contend with supernatural beings as a part of the landscape and using the local language. In the case of Japan and the *kami*, this took different forms. Early in the history of Japanese Buddhism, Buddhists would often speak of the "subjugation" of local *kami*, basically converting these local beings so that they would not impede the spread of Buddhism but would instead protect it. Many of the *kami* that came to be popular in Japan,

Figure 10.1 The entrance to the Fushimi Inari Shrine in Kyoto, Japan. The gate, known as a torii, is typical at Shinto shrines and is one of the most recognizable symbols of Shinto. © Getty Images

however, were brought to Japan from elsewhere. These included supernatural beings of Indian, Chinese, and Korean origin that were brought to Japan by Buddhists and were simply referred to in Japanese as *kami*. Throughout most of Japanese history, the worship of *kami* was therefore intimately tied up with Buddhism. The individual stories about these *kami* were sometimes of local origin, but often they came from elsewhere, brought to Japan through Buddhist networks. Shrines to *kami* were typically attached to Buddhist monasteries because the *kami* were understood to be protectors of Buddhism.

The existence of Shinto as something separate from Buddhism is quite recent. It was in fact artificially manufactured by an anti-Buddhist government in the nineteenth century. There had been some attempts since the fifteenth century, mostly centered at the Yoshida Shrine in Kyoto, to give a more nativist interpretation of the *kami*, by reinterpreting Buddhist figures of foreign origin as manifestations of Japanese *kami*, instead of the other way around. After the Meiji Restoration in 1868, the government took this nativist program to a whole new level.[2] It pursued a policy of forcibly separating Shinto and Buddhism, to elevate Shinto, purified of "foreign" (i.e., Buddhist) elements, as the national religion. To accomplish this goal, the government arbitrarily defined what counted as Shinto and Buddhist, destroyed many local *kami* shrines, and systematized a standard model of Shinto shrine architecture and worship. It also elevated the *Kojiki*, an eighth-century text about *kami*, as the "Bible" of this newly defined Shinto religion. This text includes myths about the origin of the world and the early history of the Japanese Empire. Although this text had had limited influence on the heavily Buddhist-inflected understanding of *kami* for a millennium, it proved useful in providing a mythology for the newly invented Shinto religion and a blueprint for its rituals. Shinto, therefore, exists today as an autonomous religion largely because of its historical ties with Buddhism and recent efforts to distinguish it from Buddhism by reshaping it into a similarly organized but separate institution.

Another example of a local tradition organizing itself in response to Buddhism is Bön in Tibet. Again, as with nearly every human culture, early Tibet had beliefs about supernatural beings. Early sources from the cusp of the introduction of Buddhism indicate that there were ritual specialists called *bonpo*s who engaged in funerary rituals, animal sacrifice, and royal consecrations. One of the first Buddhist kings of Tibet, Trisong Detsen (r. 755–797), suppressed many of these practices, and early Tibetan narratives speak of monks from India "subjugating" the local spirits of Tibet, thus transforming them into Buddhist guardian spirits. The situation was thus like Japan in that local supernatural beings were incorporated into a coherent Buddhist worldview in the same way as were any other living beings trapped in *samsara*. However, in the early second millennium there was a concerted effort to build up a Bön institution in parallel to the great Buddhist monastic institutions that had by that point become dominant in Tibet. This effort was spearheaded by a man named Shenchen Luga (996–1035), who "rediscovered" a trove of supposedly old Bön texts. These became the basis for a Bön scriptural canon, which was fixed by about 1450.

Although incorporating some elements of ancient Tibetan cultural practice, Bön did so no more than did Buddhism itself, and in institutionalizing itself in the early second millennium, it also created new traditions that clearly mimicked Buddhist teachings, albeit in a subtly subversive way. According to the Bön scriptures, their religion was founded by a Buddha named Tonpa Shenrab. Tonpa Shenrab lived in a mythical land to the west called Olmo Lungring, and he attained Awakening hundreds of years before the Buddha of the Buddhists, Shakyamuni. Like Shakyamuni, he showed people how to escape from the cycle of rebirth. However, unlike Shakyamuni, he lived as a layperson and eventually became king, having many wives and children. Only later in life did he adopt the lifestyle of a celibate ascetic.

Bön has developed various traditions over the centuries, including a tradition of celibate monasticism. The most important monastery is Menri, which was established in 1405. Indeed, the parallelism between institutionalized Bön and Tibetan Buddhism is so great that some have likened it to being a fifth school of Tibetan Buddhism in addition to the four primary monastic schools. Although this is probably an exaggeration given Bön's (from a Buddhist perspective) unorthodox beliefs, it does reflect the fact that Bön is less a pure indigenous religion of Tibet than it is a deliberate construction of a putative original Tibetan religion that is structured on Buddhist models.

SETTLER COLONIALISM, THE SLAVE TRADE, AND THE DEVALUATION OF INDIGENOUS TRADITIONS IN THE AMERICAS, AFRICA, AND AUSTRALIA

As we saw in chapter 2, colonialism remade the world and gave rise to the modern concept of religion. In chapter 1, I argued that this process happened through a set of implicit comparisons to Christianity. That is, as Europeans encountered other cultures around the world, they discovered cultural systems that shared certain characteristics with Christianity, and they labelled them religions. By the height of the colonial period in the late nineteenth and early twentieth centuries, European powers had colonized most of the world—so why did most of the religions they identified end up in a narrow swath of land from Europe to East Asia?

There are two related ways of answering this question. The first is what we saw in the last section: that all the religions identified in this geographical zone are related to one another in some way. Judaism and Islam are both related to Christianity as fellow Abrahamic traditions, and they had always been known to European Christians due to their proximity. The real key to the modern construction of a unified category of world religions was the "discovery" of Buddhism during the colonial period. Once Europeans learned enough about Buddhism to see that it had strong structural parallels to Christianity, the idea of a universal category of religion going beyond the immediate Abrahamic family took shape. European knowledge about Buddhism was driven in large part by the British colonial experience in its land of origin, India, so it was natural to extend the category of religion to Hinduism, which was related to Buddhism and had come to largely replace it in its land of origin. From there, the network of family connections and resemblances in the Asian cultural sphere of Buddhism could be extended to include Sikhism, Jainism, Confucianism, Daoism, Shinto, and Bön.

At a certain point, however, this network of religious relationships could go no further in the world as it existed at the cusp of colonialism. Islam, which had dominated North Africa for over a millennium, had penetrated only so far into sub-Saharan Africa. Meanwhile, Australia, Oceania, and the Americas were separated by oceans from the Eurasian home of the newly dubbed religions. Although the precolonial links between the cultures of these lands and those of Eurasia were not nonexistent, they had not been deep enough for the non-Eurasian cultures to enter into the network of family relationships between the Eurasian religions. As it happened, cultures in Europe had little *direct* contact with the cultures of East Asia prior to the colonial period, but cultures in the *middle* of the Eurasian zone had always had contact with the cultures at both geographical extremes because Eurasia had long been integrated by strong networks of trade. Colonialism simply made Europeans aware of the longstanding, if also long-distance, relationships between the cultures of this geographical zone.

This brings us to the second way of answering the question why most of the religions that were identified were in a narrow zone from Europe to East Asia. As Europe colonized the world and mobilized Orientalist justifications for its colonial project, it did not treat all human cultures it encountered equally. It created a distinct hierarchy between them. Orientalism posited that West was superior to East, but there was still a certain relative respect that European colonizers accorded to Asian cultures. After all, colonialism had been motivated in large part by a desire to gain access to the fabulous riches of faraway Asian kingdoms that Europeans had heard about in exotified tales of "the Orient." Throughout much of the colonial period, colonialism in Asia consisted primarily of establishing outposts that would allow a country to dominate the trade with Asia—a status that was won first by Portugal, then by the Dutch. Even when European powers began establishing direct colonial administrations over Asian countries later in the colonial period, the program was not to replace or eliminate those Asian cultures. Rather, it was to refine them by bringing the supposed virtues of Western civilization to them.

The colonial experience in the rest of the world was quite different. It did not begin with establishing trading networks, nor did it include a begrudging respect for local cultures. Instead, it frequently involved the labeling of local populations as uncivilized and primitive. Nowadays, we may understand these words as meaningless slurs, which they are, but it is also important to recognize that there is a (flawed) logic to these terms that motivated early European colonizers to use them. The word *civilized* comes from the Latin word *civis*, which referred to a citizen of a *civitas*, or city. The word *civilization*, in its original, technical sense, means a culture that has cities.

Urbanization is a relatively recent phenomenon in the history of the human species. When colonizers referred to certain cultures as uncivilized, they meant that they did not have cities. But they did not mean only that. They meant it as a pejorative, because they assumed that having cities was a sign of human advancement. They assumed that civilized cultures (cultures with cities) were better than uncivilized cultures (cultures without cities). For this reason, they referred to uncivilized people as "primitive"—because they saw them as representing a less developed form of humanity. When the theory of evolution was developed in the nineteenth century, this devaluation of so-called primitive peoples became more starkly twisted into the racist notion that such peoples are sub-human, closer to our non-human animal ancestors, which incidentally were called "primates."

Of course, some of the human cultures outside of the Eurasian belt *did* have cities, so the racist hierarchy that European colonizers developed was more complex than simply a threefold scheme of (1) superior Western civilization, (2) inferior Asian civilizations, and (3) primitive people in the rest of the world. Generally, the colonial encounter with the world outside of Eurasia took three forms. In some cases, Europeans conquered and culturally assimilated existing urbanized empires. In other cases, they established settler colonies with genocidal policies against the local populations. Finally, they used certain countries as a source of human beings for the slave trade, which enabled them to exploit the land of their other colonies with enslaved labor.

One of the first encounters of the colonial era was of the first type. Shortly after Columbus "discovered" the Americas in 1492, Spanish *conquistadores* conquered the two major urbanized empires that existed there: Hernán Cortés conquered the Aztec Empire in 1521, and Francisco Pizarro conquered the Inca Empire in 1533. The Spanish did not demographically displace the local populations, but they did forcibly impose Spanish culture, language, and religion on them. The religious valences of this forcible inculturation were quite direct and brutal. For example, in the Aztec capital of Tenochtitlán, which they renamed Mexico City, the Spanish dismantled the Aztec temple and used its stones to build a Catholic cathedral. In the conquered Incan lands, they repurposed a legendary image of St. James miraculously appearing to aid in the *Reconquista* against the Muslim rulers in Spain to instead represent St. James trampling the Inca.

The *conquistadores* also married into and took mistresses from among the Aztec and Inca elite, thus creating the basis for a hybrid culture. As Spanish colonial rule solidified throughout a vast territory of the Americas, a class structure emerged that served as the paradigm for racist theories of humanity throughout the world as colonialism progressed. At the top was a small elite who claimed to possess "pure" Spanish "blood" (i.e., people descended only from Spaniards) who dominated the colonial administration. At the bottom were *indios*—"Indians" or local populations that spoke their indigenous languages, followed old customs, and had little or no genealogical mixing with the Spanish conquerors. In the middle were *mestizos*—people of "mixed blood" (i.e., both Spanish and indigenous) who spoke Spanish, practiced Catholicism, and were the bedrock of a new "Hispanic" culture—one that implicitly took European cultural norms, including religion, as superior to indigenous ones.

The second form of colonization that took place outside of the Eurasian zone was settler colonialism. The largest of these were the British colonies that became the United States, Canada (which also incorporated the French settler colony of Quebec), Australia, and New Zealand. There were also projects of settler colonialism in parts of Latin America and Africa. This form of colonialism typically took place in areas with little or no indigenous urbanization. The lack of urbanization was of both practical and ideological importance to the settler colonial project. From a practical standpoint, it was simply easier to dispossess indigenous peoples of their lands if they did not have large cities and urban networks with large populations like those of the Aztecs and Incas that had to be conquered and then administered as subject peoples. But there was an important ideological aspect to this as well. Settler colonists felt *justified* in dispossessing indigenous peoples of their lands specifically because they were "uncivilized" (i.e., not urbanized) and therefore "primitive." The combination of land dispossession, disruption of traditional ways of life, introduction of European diseases, and policies of genocidal violence led over time to sharp decreases in indigenous populations that were then demographically swamped by white settlers. What indigenous populations remained were subject to Christian missionary activity and policies of forced acculturation by settler governments.[3]

Finally, the third form that colonialism took in the area outside the Eurasian zone was the slave trade. European colonizers made early attempts to enslave indigenous populations in the Americas, but they soon turned to sub-Saharan Africa as a source of people to enslave, who were then shipped by boat across the Atlantic—with great loss of life in the process—to work in the American colonies. Although slavery was common in many cultures around the world in premodern times, this particular form of chattel slavery was uniquely brutal in its global, commercialized scale and methods. Enslaved persons were ripped from their families, cultures, and traditions in Africa to be treated as property in completely foreign cultures on the other side of the planet.

The net effect of all three of these forms of colonialism outside of the Eurasian zone was cultural effacement on a truly staggering scale. Settler colonialism effaced cultures directly through genocide. Spanish colonialism in much of Latin America effaced cultures through Hispanification: the imposition of Spanish culture, language, and religion. And the slave trade effaced cultures by ripping enslaved persons from their cultural networks and transporting them to a completely new cultural context in which they were forced to accommodate to the culture, language, and religion of their owners.

It is important to remember, however, that this cultural effacement has not ever been nor is it now complete. The peoples affected by these types of colonialism survive to this day and often thrive in spite of the tremendous violence colonialism has inflicted upon them. Moreover, the new circumstances wrought by colonialism have often led certain indigenous traditions to organize themselves in parallel to Christianity, in ways that make them more legible to the lens of the modern concept of religion. In this way, the rapid spread of Christianity during the colonial era has created circumstances similar to the earlier spread of Buddhism in Asia, which, as we saw in the last section, led to the self-organization of traditions such as Daoism, Shinto, and Bön in its wake.

There are countless examples of this phenomenon throughout the Americas, sub-Saharan Africa, and Australia/Oceania, displaying an enormous variety depending on their indigenous cultural roots, the particular colonial conditions they have contended with, and their size and geographical spread. One of the largest, however, both in terms of number of adherents and global influence, is the Yoruba religion, or perhaps better put, the Yoruba family of religions. The Yoruba are an ethnic group with origins in West Africa, in an area informally known as Yorubaland that spans parts of Togo, Benin and southwestern Nigeria. There are, moreover, many people of Yoruba ancestry in the Americas (particularly the Caribbean and Brazil) because of the slave trade. The Yoruba have a common set of beliefs and practices that have long had to contend with major world religions—Catholicism in the Americas, Islam and various forms of missionary Christianity in Africa—that constrain, mold, and structure Yoruba customs into what the modern world recognizes as "religion."

The basic Yoruba worldview is as follows. Human being can reincarnate—and unlike in India, where reincarnation is considered a bad thing, here it is something to be desired because it takes place within families and serves to preserve family continuity. The world is moreover inhabited by supernatural beings called *orishas*. *Orishas* are of different types: Many are akin to what in English are called gods in various religious traditions, while others are ancestors. Indeed, maintaining ties with the ancestors was and is an important part of Yoruba religion in Africa, although it is less so in the Americas because of the disruptive effect slavery had on family networks. There is also a supreme being called Olodumare. He is the ultimate source of *ashe*, a fundamental power that drives what happens in the universe. Yoruba practitioners do not typically worship or interact with Olodumare directly, however. Instead, they worship *orishas*, who dispense *ashe* and help practitioners with everyday, practical concerns.

One of the primary ways in which Yoruba practitioners interact with *orishas* is with the help of a trained diviner known as a *Babalawo*. A Babalawo is trained in a vast corpus of oral knowledge known as Ifa, which is considered to be the manifestation of the *orisha* Orunmila. In the original system still practiced in Africa (but simplified in the Americas), the divination can result in 256 numerologically possible outcomes. Depending on the particular outcome, the Babalawo then recites four poems, and the practitioner picks one out of the four that best fits their situation. The Babalawo then usually prescribes an animal sacrifice for the practitioner to perform as an act of generosity to the *orisha* that was invoked in making the divinatory request.

Yoruba religion lacks any centralizing institution or even a common name beyond the term Yoruba. Yoruba-inspired religious practices are known by a variety of names in the Americas. Among the more common are Santería in Cuba, Candomblé and Umbanda in Brazil, and Trinidad Orisha in Trinidad and Tobago. These forms of Yoruba religion typically make extensive use of Roman Catholic symbols and sacred images. The original reason for this was practical: When slaves of Yoruba origin were brought to Latin America from the fifteenth to the nineteenth centuries, they were not allowed to openly practice their Yoruba customs and were forced to adopt Catholic Christianity. To continue their traditional practices, therefore, they established correspondences between *orishas* and Catholic saints. They might appear to be praying to a particular Catholic saint when in fact they were worshiping the *orisha* they considered that saint to be a manifestation of. This practice became so widespread that Catholic imagery is a commonplace in Yoruba-derived religious practices in the Americas. Likewise, Yoruba religion is so widespread in the Caribbean and Brazil that it is often difficult to determine whether a practice is "really" Catholic or Yoruba, or whether that distinction even makes sense. In recent years, there have been some efforts to "purify" Yoruba religion of Catholic elements, returning it to a more open expression of its African roots. This effort seeks to create a separate religious identity

Figure 10.2 An altar in Brazil with statues of Catholic saints mixed with statues that more overtly depict *orisha*s. © Getty Images

for Yoruba practices in much the same way as the Meiji government did for Shinto in Japan in the nineteenth century.

Another example of the self-organization of indigenous religious practices in the face of colonialism is the Native American Church. This religious organization was founded in 1918 in Oklahoma and is now the largest Native American religious organization. It was founded specifically to circumvent efforts by the US government to outlaw the use of peyote by indigenous people in the United States. As such, it does not correspond to any specific precolonial religion or indigenous nation. Indeed, pre-colonial use of peyote in traditional rituals appears to have been centered far to the south in the Aztec realms of modern Mexico, although it was also known to the Apache, whose ancestral lands were along the northernmost habitat of the peyote cactus. When the Apache were forcibly removed to the Indian Territory in Oklahoma, they shared their knowledge of peyote's power to bring visions and healing with members of other indigenous nations who had also been forcibly removed to Oklahoma. By the time the Native American Church was founded, it included members from many indigenous nations, not all of whom had traditional cultural practices involving peyote. The Church was also heavily influenced by Christianity, not least of all in its name, and most members identify as Christians who see peyote as a special sacrament given by God to Native Americans. The Native American Church thus represents another way in which Christianity under the aegis of colonialism has shaped the organization of indigenous cultural practices into a form recognizable in the modern world as religious.

ANIMISM IN THE EYE OF THE (NON-) BEHOLDER

The variety of beliefs and practices that could be deemed religious across the full gamut of human cultures is far too great to be covered in a single book, much less a single chapter. What is important to understand is that, although the modern concept of world religions tends to focus on a narrow geographical band across Eurasia, *all* human cultures bear features that fit a common polythetic definition of religion. All human cultures have stories about the nature of the world, how it came to be, and the place of human beings within it. All human cultures include within their worldview higher powers that influence the lives of human beings. And all human cultures engage in ritualistic practices, often pertaining to stages of life, social structure, and death. Not all cultures, however, attribute such practices to a founder or codify them in written texts, making them less legible in the modern world as discrete religions.

The modern academic field of anthropology arose in the nineteenth century in part out of the attempts of Western scholars to grapple with how to understand religion within its full human context, rather than just within the Eurasian context of the world religions. One of the founders of anthropology, Edward Tylor, coined the word *animism* to refer to the religion of cultures outside the realm of world religions in his 1871 book *Primitive Culture*. According to Tylor, animism is the belief that human beings have "souls" (the Latin word for which is *anima*) that give us life and that such souls also "animate" natural things such as animals, rocks, and trees. Tylor argued that animism is ubiquitous among primitive peoples and is the starting point for all religion. That is, the belief in gods, spirits, an immortal soul that survives death, and so forth all are relics of animism, which Tylor regarded as resulting from a primitive human tendency to (erroneously) anthropomorphize objects in the natural world. Unsurprisingly, given his use of the word *primitive*, Tylor had an evolutionary understanding of human culture. That is, he understood human cultures as evolving from a primitive state toward civilization. Primitive animists were, from his standpoint, a throwback to an earlier stage of human evolution.

Scholars today generally recognize that animism, as it was originally articulated by Tylor, is a deeply problematic and even racist concept.[4] It assumes, as the Western elites of Tylor's day did, that civilized (i.e., urbanized) societies are superior to uncivilized (i.e., non-urbanized) societies. Likewise, it posits that so-called uncivilized peoples are primitive because they supposedly represent an earlier stage of human evolution. Scholars now recognize that there are a multitude of ways in which human societies today and throughout history have organized themselves. None of them is inherently superior, and there is no inevitable linear progression from "primitive" societies to more "advanced" societies. These ideas were simply Western conceits that were used to justify the brutal domination of other societies around the world during the era of colonialism.

Although *animism* is not necessarily a commonplace term outside of academia, the idea it represents continues to influence the popular perception of religion in the modern world. I bring it up because (1) you may see the word if you look up information about the religious practices of indigenous peoples and, (2) even when it is not used explicitly, the word *animism* distorts our understanding of the world in two serious ways. First, it leads us to assume that a wide variety of indigenous human cultures, from the Americas to Africa to Australia to Papua New Guinea to Siberia, all follow essentially the same religion. Second, it leads us to assume that the religion of indigenous peoples in some fundamental way makes them different from "us."

Both assumptions are backwards. First, there is incredible variety in the cultures that were affected by colonialism. There are currently 574 federally recognized indigenous nations in the United States alone. The idea that this diverse array of indigenous nations—which includes, for example, the Navajo of the Southwest, the Inuit of Alaska, and the Lakota of the Plains—all are religiously the same is absurd. Now expand this to include all the indigenous peoples of Latin America, Africa, Australia, and beyond. We are talking about thousands of human cultures, each with their own particular history, geographical context, and experiences with other human cultures (indigenous and colonial).

Whenever you read or hear about human cultures that can be considered indigenous to lands that were colonized, be on the lookout for words that try to force them into a single paradigm. One of those words, of course, is *animism*. Another word with a similar pedigree is *shamanism*. The word *shaman* originally comes from a language spoken by indigenous people in Siberia. Modern Western scholars, however, applied the term to a variety of indigenous cultures around the world that have no connection to Siberia, using it vaguely to refer to any ritual specialist who helps members of their community to contact spirits. Especially when transformed into the abstract noun *shamanism*, it gives the sense that all of these ritual specialists in widely separated societies with no connection to each other basically are the same thing.[5]

When studying different cultures, I personally follow a rule of thumb that I think is useful to avoid falling into the trap of treating all indigenous cultures as the same. Whenever possible, I try to learn and understand the meaning of the words people in those individual cultures *themselves* use to refer to roles in their community, different types of beings that inhabit the universe, and other concepts that inform their worldview. Anthropologists usefully make a distinction between *emic* and *etic* terms. An *emic* term is used *within* the culture being studied. An *etic* term is used by scholars to describe that culture from the outside. There is nothing inherently wrong with etic terms; in fact, we need them to be able to create a common vocabulary to talk about and compare human cultures. Nevertheless, etic terms can become a problem when they are applied too early in learning about a culture, without making the effort to learn and understand the emic terms within that culture first. Moreover, some etic terms reflect old, problematic attitudes and have arguably outlived their usefulness.

Another thing to look out for whenever you read or hear about indigenous cultures is anything that smacks of the two faces of Orientalism. On the one hand, there is the overtly negative. Does the portrayal of that culture imply, even subtly, that it is primitive? On the other hand, there is the superficially positive. Does the portrayal of that culture exotify it? One common example of exotification is the trope of the "noble savage." This is a very old and still common motif in which a character belonging to an indigenous culture is portrayed as noble and admirable because he or she is "uncorrupted" by civilization. This motif reinforces the idea that certain cultures are primitive; it simply turns the idea on its head by suggesting that maybe that is a good thing. Exotifying portrayals of indigenous peoples also ignore the ways in which they have long engaged quite actively and often ingeniously with the cultures and technology of their colonizers. The idea of certain cultures being pure because they are untouched by civilization, aside from being patronizing, is also largely a figment of the imagination.

The concept of animism not only flattens the diversity of indigenous cultures; it also falsely implies a gaping chasm between the people of those cultures and "us"—whether "we" are conceived of as civilized, modern, the West, or what have you. As I have already mentioned, *all* human cultures talk about powers greater than the human, engage in storytelling ("mythmaking") about the world around them, and practice ritualistic behaviors that structure their societies. These are not things that set "animists" apart as primitive or exotic; they are things that we all share as part of our common humanity.

But there is another, more specific, way in which "we" are not so different from so-called animists that is worth mentioning because it has a bearing on how we understand all the religions we have studied in this book. The basic premise of animism—that there are spirits or souls that animate human beings, animals, and other natural objects—is not unique to animism; it is found historically even in the major world religions. For example, throughout most of the history of Christianity, it was commonplace for people to talk about, fret about, appease, and take precautions against ghosts, goblins, elves, gnomes, ogres, and the like. They were just as much a part of the world those Christians lived in as human beings and animals. Today Western society preserves reminiscences of this enchanted world in fairy tales.

What changed—or more to the point, did it change? Yes and no. Western intellectual life has followed a particular trajectory since the High Middle Ages that scholars call "disenchantment." The history of disenchantment is long and complex, but the upshot of it is that the efforts of medieval scholars to create a more orderly conception of spiritual beings based on the philosophy of Aristotle, followed later by Protestant polemics against

Catholic "superstition," gave way in the Enlightenment to a progressive questioning of the very existence of such beings. The emergence of the modern scientific worldview has banished talk of spiritual beings from academic and normative public discourse.

Recently, however, scholars of religion and modern culture have come to question whether modern culture really is so disenchanted after all. On the one hand, polls consistently show that large proportions of people continue to believe in ghosts, spirits, and the supernatural. On the other hand, even self-consciously "rational" discourse consistently anthropomorphizes the world around us. We regularly talk about the economy, the country, and society as if they are living entities. Environmentalists practically worship Mother Nature, and atheists revere Science with as much fervor as fundamentalist Christians have for Jesus. What if animism, insofar as the word has any meaning, is not so much the religion of "primitive" people as it is a basic modality of human thought?

Why then did Tylor and other scholars of the late nineteenth and early twentieth centuries find the concept of animism so compelling? I would argue that it was precisely because they were living at the height of the Western narrative of disenchantment. They were the intellectual heirs of a long tradition of Western thinkers that had, by that point, for centuries questioned the nature and existence of spirits, and they prided themselves on their rationality as conceived of within that intellectual discourse. They therefore found cultures that avidly believed in and engaged with such beings to be uncanny and took this, given their sense of cultural superiority, as further evidence that people in those cultures were primitive. We would all do well to set aside this outmoded and racist way of thinking and instead take human cultures seriously on their own terms, both in their remarkable diversity and in their common humanity.

DISCUSSION QUESTIONS

1. Why do most of the religions we have studied in this book come from a narrow geographical band in Eurasia?
2. In what ways have Bön's and Shinto's relationship with Buddhism contributed to their modern identification as religions?
3. What are the three major forms that colonialism took outside of the Eurasian zone? How did these modes of colonialism affect indigenous cultures and their religious traditions in different ways?
4. In what ways does Yoruba religion exemplify the interface between the slave trade, Roman Catholicism, and indigenous traditions?
5. What is animism? Why was the concept of animism so compelling to Western scholars at the height of the colonial period, and how does it distort perceptions of indigenous traditions?

NOTES

1. Sub-Saharan Africa is a bit of an exception insofar as Islam and to a lesser extent Christianity were practiced in parts of it prior to modern colonialism, especially further to the north. My reasons for including it in this list will become apparent later in the chapter.
2. The "Meiji Restoration" was a political revolution in Japan, largely in response to pressure from Western imperialism, that consolidated political power under the rule of Emperor Meiji, ending centuries of rule by military leaders called *shoguns*. The new Meiji government enacted sweeping reforms meant to modernize Japan in the face of the Western imperialistic threat.
3. One of the most significant ways by which this forced acculturation was accomplished was through boarding schools run by Christian organizations for indigenous children, which their parents were either forced or heavily pressured to send them to. In recent years there has been a reckoning in Canada, the United States, and Australia over the abuses suffered by indigenous youth in these boarding schools, which included physical and sexual abuse, not to mention forced acculturation through the suppression of all signs of their indigenous language and culture.
4. In recent years, however, there has been an effort by some scholars and indigenous activists to reclaim the term *animism*, a movement called "the new animism." This movement seeks to embrace the sort of respect for nonhuman beings cultivated in many indigenous cultures, seeing it as a virtue rather than as an "intellectual error" as Tylor dubbed it.
5. Note, however, that some indigenous communities have embraced the term *shamanism* to refer to their religious tradition and/or the term *shaman* to refer to specialists within their community. This can be a practical strategy to make indigenous concepts legible to a wider audience when the indigenous culture and language are little known to outsiders.

11

Secularism

Can We Put Religion in a Box?

If you have grown up in the modern Western world, you probably see religion as a discrete aspect of life. This may seem so natural that you just take it for granted. Think of it this way: Can you distinguish between aspects of life that are religious and those that are not religious? Probably the answer is yes. Going to church and praying are religious; doing the dishes, driving your car, and shopping are not. Can you distinguish between people who are religious and those who are not? You might also say yes to this: People who go to church (or a synagogue, mosque, or temple), believe in God, and/or pray are religious; those people who don't do any of these things are not religious.

Is it so simple, though? Can we really draw a hard and fast line between those aspects of life that are religious and those that are not? Maybe it seems easy to categorize things like doing the dishes (not religious) and praying (religious), but what about something like voting? At first blush, you might think that this is not religious. After all, it has to do with government, not church. But what if you attend a church that teaches that abortion is murder, one of the greatest moral evils of our time? What if your pastor tells you that you should only vote for politicians who advocate outlawing abortion? In that case, voting certainly is a religious act, is it not?

But what if you are pro-choice? Probably you will only vote for politicians who promise to protect a woman's right to get an abortion. Is your act of voting any less religious than that of the pro-life voter? From your perspective, perhaps it is, and in fact that may be a large factor influencing your vote: You believe that the pro-life position is rooted in religious convictions (for example, about the existence of a

DOI: 10.4324/9781032646428-13

soul that is infused in the embryo at the moment of conception) that should not be codified into the law and trump a woman's individual right to determine what happens to her own body. Paradoxically, though, this means that even the pro-choice person's vote *does* have something to do with religion, insofar as it is contributing to a broader debate about the influence that a religion (usually the dominant religion of a country, which in the case of the US is Christianity), or a particular interpretation of that religion, should have over public life.

This is not simply a semantic sleight-of-hand. First, many pro-choice voters are *themselves* religious. They may be motivated to vote for a woman's right to choose because they don't think their own religious convictions should affect the choices of others about what to do with their own bodies. That is, they may *personally* object to abortion but not want to impose their moral choice on others. (After all, there are many moral choices that people, including deeply religious people, make without feeling the need to impose them on others.) Or they may be motivated to vote for a woman's right to choose because they feel that their religious convictions *require* women to have the right to choose what happens to their own bodies.

Moreover, there are many laws to which basically no one, whether religious or nonreligious, would object, even though one could (and many do) point to religious justifications for those laws. Generally, legal systems outlaw murder and theft, as do the moral codes of most religions. A conservative Christian voter might point to the Ten Commandments as a justification for laws against murder and theft, but this will not lead nonreligious voters to object to laws against murder and theft. They simply see such laws as promoting the common good, without recourse to a divine origin.

The debate over abortion in the United States thus reveals a paradox within most modern societies. Many countries today, to varying degrees, follow a system called *secularism*: a system that separates religion and government. But secularism does not eliminate religion. It simply says that government should not sponsor any particular religion, or religion in general. When a secular government is also democratic, and many of the people who vote are themselves religious—or, even if they are not, are influenced by a dominant religious culture—it is inevitable that religion will be a part of public discourse, at the very least to determine what should count as religion and therefore not have a place in public life. In other words, even secularism, a system that is premised on a separation between the religious and the secular—religion and nonreligion—must perpetually engage with religion to define this separation!

SECULARISM

The United States was historically at the vanguard of creating the modern secular form of government. The Constitution of the United States, which was ratified in 1788, states, "No religious Test shall ever be required as a Qualification of any Office or public Trust under the United States." In addition, the First Amendment to the Constitution, ratified as part of the Bill of Rights in 1791, states further, "Congress shall make no law respecting an establishment of religion, or prohibiting the free exercise thereof." Although certain Christian nationalists delight in pointing out that such language is not actually found in the Constitution, no less a Founding Father than Thomas Jefferson himself asserted that the First Amendment served as a "wall of separation between church and state." Since then, "separation of church and state" has become a catchword for secular government.

In a secular form of government, such as that found in the United States since the beginning, and now many other countries as well, government and religion are kept separate. People are allowed to follow any religion they want, and the government does not get involved. It doesn't force people to be members of one particular religion, but it doesn't discourage people from being religious either. In effect, government ends up being nonreligious—not in the sense of being *antireligious*, but simply in the sense of being separate from religion. The word usually used to refer to such a nonreligious entity is *secular*. That is why we say that the United States has a secular form of government.

Secularism has a lot of advantages. First, it allows for greater individual freedom. It allows people to follow their conscience in practicing the religion of their choice. This was important to many settlers in the American colonies, especially the northern colonies, since they had left England precisely because they didn't want to be forced to be members of the Church of England. The Pilgrims celebrated during the American Thanksgiving holiday were Puritans who founded the Plymouth Colony to escape persecution in England. When Roger Williams was expelled from another Puritan colony, the Massachusetts Bay Colony, for his dissenting religious beliefs, he founded Providence Plantations, which would become Rhode Island. William Penn founded Pennsylvania as a haven for Quakers, and Lord Baltimore founded Maryland as a haven for Catholics. Many of the English colonies that would later form the United States were founded by religious dissidents escaping persecution back home.[1]

A second advantage of secularism is, quite bluntly, that it discourages people from killing each other over religion. Christianity has a long history of contention, which sometimes has spilled over into violence, between centralizing forces that attempted to impose their vision of orthodoxy and those whom they deemed to be heretics. When the Protestant Reformation shattered centralized religious authority in Western Europe, the potential for state violence against religious minorities was transformed into a potential for all-out warfare. This potential was realized in the Thirty Years' War, fought mostly in Central Europe between 1618 and 1648. It began as a fight between Protestants and Catholics and was the bloodiest war that Europe had ever seen up to that time. The Peace of Westphalia that ended this war represented a first step toward secularism in allowing princes to determine the religion of their state and dissidents within each state to practice their own religion freely within certain limits.

The third advantage of secularism, some would argue, is that it actually *promotes* religiosity. Whether you think this is an advantage or not obviously depends on whether you consider religion to be a good thing. There does seem to be truth to it either way, however. The United States has had freedom of religion since the beginning, and the rates of religious participation there are relatively high. This contrasts with Europe, where there were enforced state religions until relatively recently, and rates of religious participation are now relatively low. There is a certain logic to this: Religious freedom creates a sort of free market for religion and thus promotes religious growth and innovation, just like a capitalist market. When there is a single state religion, many people become disillusioned and drop out as soon as the law allows them. When there are many options, however, if you are dissatisfied with one religion, you can try out another. If you don't like any of the options out there, you can create your own. American Christian nationalists who oppose secularism like to point to the vibrant Christian traditions of American society but are sadly oblivious to the role religious freedom has played in that vibrancy.

So, there is a lot to be said for secularism. There is one irony inherent to it, however. When you get down to it, secularism is based on an assumed distinction that is not clearly defined. That distinction is between religion and the secular, between religion and nonreligion. After all, if you are going to keep government separate from religion, you must be able to distinguish between what is religious and what isn't, do you not? You have to be able to relegate religion and the state to separate spheres. The usual way of thinking about this in a secular society is that the state pertains to the public sphere, while religion should stay in the private sphere. (We will learn more about why this is in Part III.)

There is a problem here. Society is made up of human individuals, and each human individual participates in both private and public spheres.

Where are you supposed to draw the line between public and private? If a human individual is religious, how are they supposed to compartmentalize those two parts of their being? And if a majority of people in a country belong to the same religion, or are influenced by similar religious ideas, what is to prevent them, in a democracy, from imposing their religious convictions, whether overt or covert, on those who do not share them?

In practice, a secular society like the United States is not a static entity in which religion simply stays in the private sphere and the state is unproblematically secular. It is instead a dynamic system in which there is a constant battle over where to draw two lines: the line between religion and nonreligion and the line between the private and public spheres. The debate over abortion in the United States is an example of such a battle. To nonreligious people who are pro-choice, it *seems* like the pro-life crowd is simply confusing the natural order of things by injecting religion into politics. That is because secularism beguiles us into thinking that there is a natural division between religion and politics.

In fact, there is no such thing. One of the primary purposes of politics in a secular society, in fact, is precisely to decide where the division between religion and politics should be. There is a paradox here because the individuals who collectively decide where to divide religion and politics must inevitably do so based on their own religious (or "religious") convictions. People who are pro-life can no more turn off their conservative Christian convictions when they vote than can those who are pro-choice turn off their feminism (or other motivations) when they vote. The former only seem to be injecting religion into their decision more because, for historical reasons, we call Christianity a religion and feminism not a religion.

Deciding how to maintain Jefferson's "wall of separation" is actually a recurring political question in secular societies. Does Obamacare, with its mandate for birth control coverage, violate the religious freedom of employers who are opposed to birth control? Does forcing a cakeshop owner to make a wedding cake for a gay couple violate his religious freedom if he considers homosexuality a sin? Can there be prayer in public schools? If not, then what about afterschool events? Can the Bible specifically, or religion in general, be taught in public schools? If so, then in what capacity? What about evolution and creationism? And what about yoga and meditation? Are these religious exercises like Christian prayer that should be banned from schools? What about state drug laws? Should Native Americans be allowed to consume peyote as part of their religious ceremonies, or should it be banned like any other controlled substance? Secular countries other than the United States sometimes end up asking very different questions. For example, in France, there are raging debates about whether wearing conspicuous religious symbols, such as yarmulkes and hijabs, in public schools should be allowed. If you live in a secular society, you probably have strong opinions about whatever questions concerning the separation of religion and the public sphere are being debated where you live. That is completely normal. What I want to point out is that there is no obvious answer to any of these questions because a natural division between religion and nonreligion simply does not exist. Secular politics is a process of *creating* that distinction.

This finally brings me to the thesis of this chapter. What I want to show you now is that secularism—putting religion and nonreligion into separate boxes—is not a natural state of affairs, and thinking that it is can often obscure our understanding of the religions of the world. In fact, I want to go a step further. My thesis is this: Secularism, as an institution, has deep Christian roots. As such, it is tied up with the same Christian assumptions that we have been talking about in this book—the assumptions that give the Christian tint to the glasses of religion. This thesis may seem ridiculous on its face because we associate the secular with nonreligion, and Christianity is, well, a religion. Of course, this is a very secular, and therefore Christian, way of looking at things. Confused? Not to worry, I promise that what I am saying will make sense by the time you get to the end of this chapter.

SHARI'A AND THE ROHINGYA: THE JEKYLL AND HYDE OF ORIENTALISM

To see how the assumption that there is a natural distinction between religion and the secular distorts the way we see religion, I'd like for us to consider two cases that pertain to Asian religions and the way they are perceived in the West. The first is Shari'a, or Islamic Law, and the hysteria over it now in the United States. The second is the plight of the Rohingya, a Muslim minority in majority-Buddhist Burma. These two cases will not only help us to better understand the issue of secularism; they also happen to illustrate the two seemingly opposite ways in which Orientalism operates.

First, let us consider Shari'a. As we learned in chapter 3, *Shari'a* is an Arabic word that means "path" and refers to the Law of God. Ultimately, it is an abstract principle, an ideal that all Muslims strive to follow, just as people in all monotheistic religions strive to follow some ideal set by God. In the years since September 11, 2001, however, a certain hysteria has arisen over Shari'a in the United States. According to the Southern Poverty Law Center, between 2010 and 2018, 201 bills designed to ban Shari'a were introduced in forty-three states.[2] These bills are usually pushed by Islamophobic hate groups who claim that there is a threat Shari'a will be allowed to influence American legal decisions and eventually be imposed on all Americans. To drum up fear of Shari'a, these groups typically point to Shari'a "laws" that they know many Americans will find scary or barbaric. For example, one anti-Shari'a website lists supposed laws found in Shari'a that include the following: amputating the hands for theft, stoning for various religious crimes, the need for multiple male witnesses to prove rape, the allowance of polygamy, unequal rules of inheritance for men and women, allowance of wife-beating, and other laws treating men and women unequally.[3]

This hysteria over Shari'a misrepresents what Shari'a is and concocts a threat from it where none exists. First, anti-Shari'a Islamophobes scare Americans who otherwise would have no interest in the finer points of Islamic theology by conflating Shari'a and *fiqh*. Shari'a is an abstract principle: God's eternal Law. Muslims aspire to adhere to God's Law, making them no different from Christians. *Fiqh*, on the other hand, is a body of legal judgments as to how God's Law should apply in specific situations. It is not eternal; it changes over time, and even at any given time two *muftis* (jurists) might have totally different opinions about the same case. It is true that historically over the over 1,000 years of Islamic jurisprudence since the early Middle Ages, *fatwas* (legal opinions) have periodically been made that many modern Western people today would consider draconian, unfair, or sexist. This is hardly surprising. The reason for it is that such *fatwas* are generally *old*. If you look at any premodern legal code, you will find laws that you, as a modern person, will consider draconian, unfair, and sexist. Ever heard of drawing and quartering people, or of burning people at the stake? These are parts of the European legal tradition. In fact, if you look at medieval European laws, you will find any number of horrifying corporal punishments that are enough to turn your stomach. Standards of justice and punishment changed in the modern era, and that is why we see such older laws as "barbaric."

On top of this, there is a particular hypocrisy to Western people, often themselves practicing Christians, criticizing what they consider the barbaric laws of Shari'a. Do you know where else you can find laws calling for amputation, stoning, and unequal treatment of women? The Bible. You've probably heard of "an eye for an eye and a tooth for a tooth." That's straight from the Bible (e.g., Exodus 21:24). Often the judgments associated with Shari'a are quite similar to those found in the Torah, the first five books of the Hebrew Scriptures (what Christians call the Old Testament). This is no accident. Not only do Islam and Judaism come from similar cultural spheres in the Middle East, but Islamic Law, as it developed, clearly mirrored aspects of Jewish Law. That is why, even today, both Jews and Muslims abstain from pork and practice circumcision.

In any case, the draconian punishments found in historical Islamic jurisprudence do not generally form the basis of criminal law in Islamic countries today. During the modern era, most Islamic countries adopted criminal codes based on Western models, with similar concepts of humane punishment and justice. In the process, traditional Islamic jurisprudence was relegated primarily to personal Islamic practice and family law among Muslims (marriage, divorce, inheritance, etc.). There are certain exceptions among more repressive regimes, and Islamists (Islamic religious nationalists) have at times successfully lobbied for at least a nominal renewal of the use of certain corporal forms of criminal punishment even in countries with secular systems of criminal law. In this respect, debates between more conservative and more progressive groups over crime and punishment parallel those found in Western countries, albeit drawing from a different historical tradition.

Aside from the fact that anti-Shari'a activists erroneously equate Shari'a with historical legal judgments that lack applicability even in most Islamic countries today, they also conjure a threat posed by Shari'a in the US that is simply a mirage. Most Muslims around the world have a positive view of Shari'a, in the ideal sense of God's Law, but they differ widely in their opinions about if and how it should be applied in the modern world. That is true in traditionally Islamic countries, and it is certainly true of Muslims who live in the United States.[4] Moreover, even if most American Muslims wanted to "impose Shari'a Law"—which, again, they don't—they are in no position to do so. Muslims represent a tiny minority of the US population—about one percent. American Muslims are by no means in a position of power; quite the contrary, they are in an extremely vulnerable position because they are such a tiny minority and subject to violence, harassment, and general mistrust and hatred on the part of the majority.

Why then is there so much fear of Shari'a Law in the United States? The obvious answer is Islamophobia. But why focus on Shari'a specifically? Yes, many Americans are fearful of and bigoted toward Muslims, especially since September 11th, but what is it about Shari'a, of all the different aspects of Islam, that gets people so riled up? This has to do with the secular mentality of modern people. Shari'a historically is an example of religious law. Even people who are not Islamophobic may see "religious law" as having a negative connotation. There are many reasons for this, but the most important is that the very juxtaposition of the words *religious* and *law* grates against modern ears. This is simply how secularism teaches us to think. Religion is religion. It belongs in the private sphere. Law is associated with government; it is in the public sphere. The very idea of mixing the two seems repugnant.

Let us now turn to a second case that exemplifies the intersection between secularism and the perception of Asian religions in the West: the plight of the Rohingya. The Rohingya are a Muslim minority who live in Burma, which is a majority Buddhist country. Although the Rohingya have been living in Burma for many generations, the Burmese government claims that they are illegal immigrants from neighboring Bangladesh and denies them citizenship. In addition, the Burmese government has severely cracked down on the Rohingya, burning their villages and torturing and raping civilians. Rohingya have also been subject to violence from Buddhist mobs. As a result, hundreds of thousands of Rohingya have become refugees, many of them fleeing to Bangladesh. Those who remain in Burma are confined to camps whose conditions are so abysmal that they have been compared to concentration camps. The journalist Nicholas Kristof, who works for the *New York Times*, made a short documentary about the Rohingya crisis, which you can watch on YouTube.[5]

When I show this documentary to my students, many are shocked, not only by the cruelty that is being inflicted on the Rohingya, but by the fact that the people inflicting it are Buddhists. Isn't Buddhism a religion of peace? In the West, we associate Buddhism with blissed out monks meditating, not angry, murderous mobs. In fact, the violence against the Rohingya is not limited just to the army or civilian mobs; they are often egged on by prominent Buddhist monks. The most infamous of these is Wirathu, the leader of the 969 Movement, which claims to work for the protection of Buddhism in Burma against Islam. Although Wirathu claims that he does not advocate violence, his frequently bigoted Islamophobic rhetoric serves to stir up public sentiment against the Rohingya. Using a trope similar to that used by American anti-Catholic bigots in the nineteenth century, he says that Muslims "breed rapidly like African catfish," which is why Burmese Buddhists should be afraid of them "taking over" even though they represent a tiny minority. And like Islamophobes everywhere, he claims that Muslims spread *jihad* wherever they go, thus conflating the violent acts committed by a small number of extremists with Islam as a whole.

How can this be? How can Buddhists support and even participate in the violent persecution of a religious minority? After all, the common perception of Buddhism as being a religion of peace is not entirely baseless;

it derives from principles found in the Buddhist scriptures. Wirathu and others like him like to say that, although Buddhism is a religion of peace, Buddhists must defend themselves when they are threatened. But according to the very scriptures revered by Buddhists in Burma, the Buddha once said, "Monks, even if bandits were to carve you up savagely, limb by limb, with a two-handled saw, he among you who let his heart get angered even at that would not be doing my bidding."[6]

We cannot, however, truly understand Buddhism simply on the basis of its scriptures. Scriptures are *normative* texts; they tell us what their authors think people in a religion *should* do. To better understand a religion, we need a *descriptive* account, which we can arrive at only by looking at the words and actions of actual people in the religion, and for Buddhism in Burma, that includes people like Wirathu, the angry Buddhist mobs, and Buddhists in the Burmese army who torture Rohingya civilians and burn their villages.

Of course, most Western people would instinctively realize that even though Jesus said to turn the other cheek, that is just an ideal; in reality, Christians over the centuries have often engaged in violence. Why then is it so easy for people to believe that the peaceful normative ideal of Buddhism is indicative of Buddhism in the real world? The plight of the Rohingya, after all, does not suddenly prove that Buddhists are uniquely hateful and violent; it just shows that *some* Buddhists are hateful, bigoted, and violent—*which makes Buddhism no different from any other religion on the planet*. Why would anyone have ever thought that Buddhism should, uniquely of all religions, be free of bigotry and intolerance? This is an example, strange as it may seem at first, of Orientalism, just as much as Islamophobia itself is. You'll recall that, at the end of chapter 2, I said that Orientalism has a Dr. Jekyll-and-Mr. Hyde personality. Sometimes it is overtly negative. Islamophobia is an example of overtly negative Orientalism. But sometimes it is superficially positive. It exotifies. Buddhism comes from the "mystical East," so it must be uniquely cool, spiritual, peaceful, and awesome. This attitude may not seem as hateful as Islamophobia, but it is certainly patronizing and dangerous in its own way.

Now let us return to the topic of this chapter, secularism. What specifically would drive Burmese Buddhists to perceive a Muslim minority as a threat when it clearly is not? The answer is *religious nationalism*. Religious nationalism is a type of political movement whose adherents understand the nation—that is, the people of a certain country—to be tied to one specific religion, usually in defiance of pre-existing secular norms. Religious nationalism is common in the political right wing around the world and is manifested in just about every religion. There is Christian nationalism in several Western countries, especially the US;

Hindu nationalism in India; Islamic nationalism in majority-Muslim countries; and Jewish nationalism in Israel. Likewise, there is Buddhist nationalism in majority-Buddhist countries like Burma. When taken to an extreme, religious nationalism can easily lead to the persecution of religious minorities. A classic example is Nazi Germany. Jews, as a religious minority, were viewed as not truly German; they were instead a "contagion" that needed to be expunged from the German nation. A very similar logic seems to be operative in Burma today.

Religious nationalism intrinsically militates against secularism. It is a reactionary protest against secularism's attempt to create a sharp divide between religion and politics. Although the type of state and society it wants to create is thoroughly modern, it is born out of a nostalgia for a pre-secular past when religion and politics were not separated. Buddhism is no different in this respect. Contrary to the Orientalist fantasy of Buddhism as apolitical, traditional Buddhist cultures prior to the modern period did not see a division between religion and politics. According to the traditional life story of the Buddha, when the Buddha was born, Brahmans (priests) skilled in divination examined his body and determined that he had thirty-two distinguishing marks that destined him to become a Great Man. That meant that his life would take one of two courses. Either he would become a world-conquering monarch, or he would abandon his home and become a great religious leader. His father was a king and wanted his son to follow in his footsteps. So, he took extreme steps to make sure his son would never become interested in spiritual matters. He kept his son in the palace and prevented him from seeing any signs of old age, sickness, and death. Eventually his son was overcome with curiosity, so he went out of the palace and, despite his father's best efforts to sanitize the capital city, came across an old man, a sick man, and a corpse. This led him to become disenchanted with the life of luxury he had grown up in, so he abandoned his home and eventually attained *nirvana*, becoming the Buddha.

At first glance this story might seem to advocate a division between religion and politics. The Buddha, as a great man, had two courses open to him, one political and the other religious. He chose the religious path. But this is not how Buddhists have traditionally interpreted the story. Instead, they have interpreted it to mean that kings and Buddhas are intrinsically similar. The Buddha was a religious leader, but he could just as easily have become a king. That means the Buddha is like a king, and indeed much of the rhetoric around the Buddha in traditional Buddhist societies treats him as such (very similar to the royal terminology surrounding Jesus—"Christ the King"—in Christianity). But if you flip this idea on its head, it also means that kings are like Buddhas.

Now, Burma no longer has a monarchy because the British abolished it when they colonized the country in the nineteenth century. Right next door to Burma, however, is another Buddhist country, Thailand, that still has a king because it was never colonized. The king of Thailand is treated as a near-sacred figure, and he is seen as not only the head of the state but also the protector and defender of Buddhism. Back when Burma had a king, he was viewed in very much the same way. And even though Burma no longer has a king, the unity of religion and politics that traditional Buddhist kingship represented still lives on in the minds of many Burmese Buddhists. This is why Buddhist nationalism is such a potent force in Burma today.

SECULARISM IS NOT THE NORM

Orientalism has led to a demonization of Islam and an exotification of Buddhism. Insofar as secularism is a modern ideal, it maps onto Islam and Buddhism in popular perception in a very predictable way. People in the West often perceive Islam as having trouble respecting the boundary between religion and politics. That is why there is so much anxiety over Shari'a. Buddhism, on the other hand, is often assumed by Westerners to naturally fit modern secular norms because it is more of a philosophy or way of life for the individual than a religion. That is why the persecution of the Rohingya in Burma, and the religious nationalism that fuels it, seems so shocking. The truth is, Buddhism and Islam are not really all that different in this respect. Moreover, they are perfectly representative of most religions in the history of the world. When looking at the grand scheme of human history, it is simply not normal to separate religion from politics or even to think of them as separate things. Secularism is an extremely new idea, with its origins in Europe. Mixing religion and politics is the norm, not the exception.

To begin with, Islam is hardly unique in having a body of religious law. I already mentioned that many of the outdated *fatwas* that are found in old Islamic jurisprudence have close parallels in the Bible. That is because the Bible contains the Torah, which is the basis of Jewish Law, or *halakhah* (see chapter 9). Like the Shari'a, Jewish Law deals with an extremely wide variety of topics. These include personal ethics and morality (love your neighbor), dietary restrictions (which is why many Jews do not eat pork or shellfish), ritual prescriptions, and crime and punishment. As it was originally written, it does not respect any division between the private and the public, between the religious and the secular. It is a holistic vision for realizing God's will in all aspects of life, public and private, social and domestic.

Another important example of religious law is found in Hinduism. There are many books of what can be considered "Hindu Law" that were written in India, but the most famous is the *Laws of Manu*, which was probably written sometime in the first couple centuries CE. It covers a variety of topics, including the system of social classes, the proper course of life for upper-class males, marriage, study of the Vedas, proper and improper food, purity, restrictions on women, kingship, public justice, and litigation. All these laws are said to have been handed down by the first man, Manu, who was created by the god Brahma. Again, there is no separation between public law and private morality, between religion and the secular.

Although not associated with a defined corpus of religious law akin to those found in Judaism, Islam, and Hinduism, Confucianism is another religion that historically did not respect a line between the religious and the secular. Confucius was essentially a political philosopher who wanted to create the ideal state, and he spent his life looking (in vain) for a ruler who would put his ideas into practice. The means by which Confucius sought to accomplish his clearly political goal, however, respected no distinction between the public and the private. You will recall that one of the central concepts in Confucius' thought was *li*, or ritual. Confucius wanted people to conform to the rituals as they were practiced at the beginning of the Zhou Dynasty, and he thought that would restore China to its former glory. But this "ritual" included everything from personal ethics to norms of comportment to public ceremonies. In modern terms, it was both secular and religious. And although Confucius was unable to find a ruler to put his ideas into practice in his own lifetime, Confucianism was adopted as the ideology of the state in the Han Dynasty, founded in 206 BCE. From then until the revolution that toppled the last imperial dynasty, the Qing, in 1911, civil servants in the imperial bureaucracy were required to study and master the Confucian classics, and Confucian principles were the basis of Chinese law and statecraft.

Finally, as we just saw in the last section, even Buddhism did not historically respect a differentiation between religion and the secular. One of the most important institutions of traditional Buddhism was in fact the monarchy, the pinnacle of political power. The king was understood to be Buddha-like, just as the Buddha is king-like, and he was the supreme protector and patron of the order of Buddhist monks. That is why, even today in Burma, a country where the traditional monarchy no longer exists, ordinary Buddhists are quick to conflate Buddhism with the Burmese nation.

THE CHRISTIAN ROOTS OF SECULARISM

To the list of religions that historically have not respected a distinction between religion and the secular, we can also add Christianity. Secularism, after all, is a modern phenomenon. During the Middle Ages and even well into the modern period, Church and State were allied. Kings were understood to rule by divine right and often were crowned by the pope. Even after the Reformation, there typically was a state-sponsored Church. The United States was a true trailblazer when it set up a secular system of government—and in the grand scheme of things, that was not very long ago, only a little over two hundred years.

Why then did I make the surprising claim earlier in this chapter that secularism has its roots in Christianity? To be clear, in making this claim, I am not saying that Christianity was always secular in the modern sense of the term. That would obviously not be true, for the reasons I just mentioned. What I mean is that Christianity gave birth to secularism, and the seeds of secularism were always present within Christianity. It's not just that Christianity fractured during the Reformation, and the ensuing violence forced Christians to create secularism to be able to live with one another in peace—although that is also true. What I mean is that there is something peculiar about the structure of Christianity as a religion, going all the way back to its beginning, that served as the basis for the very idea of secularism in the first place.

To understand this, let's look at the word *secularism*. It is derived from a Latin word, *saeculum*, which means "age." *Age* here means a long period of time—like the Middle *Ages* or the Modern *Age*. So, what do ages have to do with secularism? Think of it this way: The word *secular* means "having to do with the ages," or to put it more simply, "having to do with time." In certain Christian contexts, in fact, the words *secular* and *temporal* are used as synonyms.

What does the secular, which we now think of as nonreligion, have to do with time? Well, what is the opposite of something that is temporal? Something that is eternal, of course. And what is eternal? God. This distinction is very important to Christianity. Although today we may associate traditional Christianity with a mixture of religion and politics, that association comes mostly from the Middle Ages. We must remember that in its earliest centuries, Christianity was in no position to mix religion and politics for the simple reason that it lacked any political power. Prior to Constantine's conversion in the early fourth century, Christianity not only lacked political power; it was actively persecuted by the state.

Early Christians, therefore, lived under a sort of siege mentality. They had faith in the ultimate power of God, but in the world around them, they lacked power themselves and were subject to the power of a hostile regime. This is reflected in an aspect of Christianity that nowadays has become somewhat marginal but originally was quite central to the Christian message: the faith that Jesus Christ will return, wipe out the worldly powers, and establish the kingdom of God on Earth. Most mainstream Christians today think little of this aspect of their religion, but they continue to refer to it in their Creed: "He will come again in glory to judge the living and the dead, and his kingdom will have no end." In the first century or so, however, Christians believed that this event was quite imminent, likely to take place in their own lifetime. We might be persecuted now by the powers here on Earth, but they are only *temporary*; soon, Jesus will return and establish God's rule directly, which is *eternal*.

Of course, even though Jesus didn't come back, the situation of Christians desperately waiting for God to relieve them from their suffering under earthly powers did not last forever. Instead, the primary earthly power of their day, the Roman Empire, *itself* became Christian in the fourth century. From then on, Christianity and the state were allied. And so things remained in the Western world for well over a thousand years, until the process of secularization slowly began after the Reformation, finding its culmination in the adoption of a fully secular government by the United States in 1788, with other countries adopting secularism to varying degrees since then.

But even during the long Middle Ages in between, a conceptual *distinction* between religion and the secular was recognized, though the two were mixed and European society was by no means secularist in the modern sense. An example of this distinction can be seen in the way that heretics were burned at the stake. Often people today associate this practice with the Catholic Church, and with good reason, since such executions were the result of trials conducted by clerics under the auspices of the Inquisition, a Church institution for rooting out heresy. Once a person was found guilty of heresy, however, the Church did not execute them directly. It instead handed the supposedly guilty party over to the local political authorities, who would then execute them. This was a recognition of a division of powers: The Church had the religious authority to determine heresy, and the king had the temporal authority to put someone to death.

An exception to the general pattern of Church and monarchical authorities working side-by-side in complementary roles was the Papal States. Throughout the Middle Ages, the pope was not only the religious leader of the Catholic Church throughout Western Europe (and later the world); he was also the king of a significant territory in central Italy, with its capital in Rome. But even then, the pope was understood to hold two distinct authorities: his temporal authority as king of the Papal States and his religious authority as supreme pontiff of the Catholic Church. When most of the Papal States were conquered by forces seeking to unify Italy in 1861, and then the city of Rome itself in 1870, the pope, from a Catholic perspective, lost his temporal authority but retained his religious authority.

Modern secularism didn't just appear out of nowhere. It took a long-standing distinction that had been maintained from Christianity's very inception and made it the basis for a novel governing principle. Religious and political power had always been recognized as distinct in Christianity, even when they were allied (as in most of medieval Europe) or even invested in the same person (the pope). The only significant change was to create a "wall of separation" between the two, as Thomas Jefferson put it. But to separate two things, you first have to recognize them as two distinct things. This was possible within Western societies precisely because of the long-standing differentiation between secular and religious power.

THE PARADOX OF SECULARISM

We are thus left with a strange state of affairs. Secularism is designed to allow people of different religions to live together harmoniously in a single society, without any religion privileged above any other. Secularism supposedly clears a public space that is free from religion so that all individuals will be treated equally and will be able to practice the religion of their choice privately. But secularism is not a neutral arbiter because it itself comes from a particular religious background. The very idea of a distinction between religion and politics is a Christian one. It is not an obvious distinction, and it is not one that has typically been made throughout human history. Moreover, as we will see in more detail in chapter 12, the idea that religion most properly belongs in the private sphere comes from a particular branch of Christianity, Protestantism. Secularism allows different religions to flourish side-by-side, but only insofar as they agree to conform to (1) the Christian distinction between religion and politics and (2) the Protestant relegation of religion to the private sphere.

This was not a major problem in the early United States. The vast majority of citizens were Christian, and most of them were not only Christian, but Protestant. The different religions whose coexistence secularism sought to safeguard shared in the same intellectual heritage that secularism presupposed. But now that American demographics are changing, one can no longer rely on this shared heritage. After well over a century of immigration from Catholic countries in Europe and now Latin America, Catholicism is the religious identity of nearly a quarter of Americans. Catholicism at least shares the basic Christian heritage presupposed by secularism, but with its strong roots in the medieval social order, it has historically been more resistant to the modernizing trends associated with secularism than the various Protestant denominations. Indeed, a common trope of American anti-Catholicism has been a fear of the mixture of religion and politics represented by the papacy. When John F. Kennedy ran for President, many of his opponents tried to stir up anti-Catholic hysteria by claiming that Kennedy would take marching orders from the pope.

In addition, although they are still found in far lower numbers, members of non-Christian religions play an increasingly large and important role in American life. These include most importantly Jews, but also Muslims, Hindus, Buddhists, Sikhs, and others. The vast majority of Americans who practice these religions are more than happy to conform to American social expectations, but their religions are changed in the process. They are forced to conform to Christian, and often specifically Protestant, norms to "make sense" within America's secular order. This entails artificially limiting one's religiosity to a "private sphere" defined on American, and therefore mostly Protestant Christian, terms. Perhaps most adversely affected by this constraint are Native Americans, who, as we saw in chapter 10, had their entire way of life destroyed by white settlement, and who now can only fight in the courts to maintain their religious practices, often in vain because those practices do not map easily onto a secular conception of what properly should be protected as religious.

Nor is this problem confined to the United States or even the Western world. Under Western hegemony, Western political norms, including secularism, have been adopted by a wide variety of countries around the world. Countries that are predominantly non-Christian have found ways to accommodate themselves to secularism. This has two outcomes. First, it means that secularism must be reformulated in Islamic, Buddhist, Hindu, or some other religious terms to work in a particular country. As a result, minority religions must find some way to accommodate themselves to the paradigm set by the majority religion in order to make sense within that country's particular secular framework.

But in addition to that, even the majority religions are changed in the process. The majority religion of a particular country may have a certain amount of wiggle room to maintain a secular regime on its own terms, but it must in any case adopt the Christian distinction between religion and politics, no matter how foreign that is to the tradition. This is having a real effect on Islam, Hinduism, Judaism, Buddhism, and other religions in the world today. As I have said before, *religion*, as a hegemonic category, is like a pair of Christian-tinted glasses that makes the things we apply it to look like different shades of Christianity. But in this case, it is not only affecting the way we *perceive* religions; it is also restructuring them in the real world. It is like a pair of magic red-tinted glasses that not only make all the paintings in a gallery look red, but also, over time, actually make them red.

So, with secularism, we're basically trying to foster tolerance and harmony between all religions using an ideology whose structure and assumptions derive from the history of a particular religion, Christianity. It's like playing with loaded dice. I wish I could propose an alternative to you, but I can't. So far, secularism seems the best system we have for fostering interreligious harmony and preventing religious violence. I certainly do not want Christian nationalists taking over the United States and creating something like Margaret Atwood's Gilead any more than I like the fact that Buddhist nationalists are persecuting the Rohingya in Burma, that Hindu nationalists make life miserable for Muslims in India, or that Islamists persecute Coptic Christians in Egypt.[7] But I do think that those of us who support secularism should do so with a bit of humility. Secularism is not a natural state of affairs, and we must be open to each other's differences—not just privately, but publicly—in order to make secularism work for everyone. We certainly should not be deluded into thinking that "secular" is a neutral, nonreligious position from which we can judge religious people.

DISCUSSION QUESTIONS

1. What is secularism? What is its purpose, and how does it work?
2. Can you name any public debates in the United States (or whatever country you may live in) that involve an adjudication of the line between religion and the state?
3. What is Shari'a? How does modern secularism contribute to the particular fixation of Islamophobes on Shari'a?
4. What is religious nationalism, and how can the treatment of the Rohingya in Burma be seen as an example of religious nationalism?
5. In what ways does secularism have its roots in Christianity?

NOTES

1. To be clear, these dissidents did not always want *others* to have the freedom to choose their own religion—as was the case with the Puritans, who were intolerant of dissent. Nevertheless, the immigration of so many different religious groups to the American colonies set the stage for a religiously pluralistic country.
2. https://www.splcenter.org/hatewatch/2018/02/05/anti-sharia-law-bills-united-states
3. www.billionbibles.org.
4. See Pew Research Center, "The World's Muslims: Religion, Politics, and Society," Chapter 1: Beliefs about Sharia," https://www.pewresearch.org/religion/2013/04/30/the-worlds-muslims-religion-politics-society-beliefs-about-sharia/; Appendix A: US Muslims—Views on Religion and Society in a Global Context, https://www.pewresearch.org/religion/2013/04/30/the-worlds-muslims-religion-politics-society-app-a/.
5. Nicholas Kristof, "Twenty-First Century Concentration Camps," https://www.youtube.com/watch?v=hqMSfT9eI6o.
6. Thanissaro Bhikkhu, trans., "*Majjhima Nikaya* 21, *Kakacupama Sutta*: The Simile of the Saw," https://www.accesstoinsight.org/tipitaka/mn/mn.021x.than.html.
7. A brilliant study of the situation faced by Egyptian Coptic Christians in the context of secularism can be found in Saba Mahmood, *Religious Difference in a Secular Age: A Minority Report* (Princeton: Princeton University Press, 2016). The theoretical discussions of secularism in this book, Prof. Mahmood's last before her far-too-early death in 2018, were extremely helpful to me in thinking through the themes of this chapter.

Part III
Learn How the Glasses Work

12
You Are Martin Luther

I began this book by asking you what religion is. We saw that it is stubbornly difficult to define, and I argued that to really understand religion, we have to see it not merely as some thing out there in the world, but as a way of looking at the world. I compared it to a pair of glasses, which I have called Christian-tinted because the whole concept of religion is tied up with the history of the West and therefore Christianity. In Part II, we saw the many ways in which these Christian-tinted glasses distort our perception of the world's religions. Now, in Part III, we are going to examine precisely *why* the Christian-tinted glasses distort our perception of the world's religions in the ways that they do. We will do so in detail in the next chapter. But before we do, we need to learn a bit about one specific Christian: Martin Luther.

Our modern perception of the world's religions is profoundly influenced, through the concept of religion itself, by Christianity. But Christianity, as we will see in more detail in chapter 14, is not just one thing. Nevertheless, certain forms of Christianity have, for various historical reasons, exercised greater hegemony than others. Martin Luther was the first of many Reformers in a revolution in Western Christianity that took place in the sixteenth century, known as the Protestant Reformation. In the course of his fight with the Catholic Church, Luther developed new ideas about Christian authority and salvation that would become the basis for Protestant theology. Protestant Christian theology would in turn, through the Enlightenment and other associated social movements, shape the course of modern ways of thinking about the world that were globalized by colonialism. The modern concept of religion, therefore, is not only a pair of glasses that are tinted by Christianity; it is, in many respects, tinted specifically by *Protestant* Christianity.

DOI: 10.4324/9781032646428-15

It might seem hard to believe that an old and obscure theological dispute could produce a person or event of such world-historical importance as Martin Luther or the Protestant Reformation. Yet I cannot emphasize this enough: *Martin Luther and the Reformation he sparked were pivotal in creating the modern world*. Not only that, but insofar as you are a product of the modern world, Martin Luther created *you*. *You*, in a very real sense, channel the ghost of Martin Luther. If you are Lutheran or grew up in the Lutheran Church, then this might not seem so surprising. But it is true even if you are Catholic. It is true even if you are Jewish or Muslim or a member of some other non-Christian religion. It is even true if you are an atheist or reject religion altogether. The way you think about the world, no matter what your religious background, is without a doubt deeply influenced by the ideas of this one man.

THE STORY OF MARTIN LUTHER

On Halloween in 1517, or so the story goes, a German monk named Martin Luther walked up to All Saints' Church in Wittenberg and nailed to the front door a list of ninety-five theses, thus inaugurating the Protestant Reformation and setting in motion an epochal change that destroyed the hold of the Catholic Church over Western Europe and ushered in the modern world. Many scholars today question whether the nailing of the *Ninety-Five Theses* to the door of the church in Wittenberg ever happened (it may have been a story invented later to make the event sound more dramatic), but the document and the man who wrote it are very much real and did indeed set in motion a series of events that destroyed the unity of the Catholic Church and played a pivotal role in creating the modern world. Martin Luther was a member of the Augustinian order who was highly educated and worked as a professional theologian, teaching at the University of Wittenberg. He wrote the *Ninety-Five Theses* to protest the sale of indulgences by the Catholic Church, originally sending it in a letter to his local bishop. Shortly thereafter, the document was printed throughout Germany, and within a couple years it had spread throughout Western Europe, creating a sensation in the Church.

An indulgence is an official dispensation from the pope granting a Christian remission from a certain amount of punishment in purgatory for their sins. According to Catholic theology, there are three possible destinations one may go after one dies—hell, purgatory, or heaven. The concept of purgatory is not found in the Bible—and for this reason it is rejected and criticized by Protestants—but Catholic theologians proposed it as a logical necessity to explain how the vast majority of Christians can

Figure 12.1 A portrait of Martin Luther, painted during his lifetime by Lucas Cranach the Elder. © Getty Images

go to heaven. Aside from Jesus, all human beings, even saints, are sinful, but God wants to save people from the fires of hell and indeed does so through his grace. The soul still needs to be purified before entering heaven, so after death, it makes a temporary stop in purgatory to be purged of its sins before being allowed into heaven. Indulgences—which incidentally still are granted by the Catholic Church, although not in the same way as in Luther's day—basically shorten your time being punished in purgatory. It's a little bit like a court reducing a criminal's sentence in prison.

Luther ended up making an extended theological argument against the granting of indulgences by the Church in general, but the immediate precipitating cause that led him to write his *Theses* was the *sale* of indulgences to raise funds for the Church. In particular, he was incensed by the ostentatious selling of indulgences by Johann Tetzel, a Dominican monk who was sent to Germany in 1516 to raise funds to rebuild St. Peter's Basilica in Rome. (Indeed, if you have ever been to St. Peter's Basilica, which is the largest and arguably the most beautiful church in the world, then you know that this fund-raising campaign was incredibly successful.) Tetzel's aggressive fund-raising tactics struck Luther and others (including many Christians, even Catholics, today) as outrageous since he was effectively telling people they could buy their way into heaven. Moreover, he was taking advantage of devout poor people to enrich the coffers of the already wealthy pope and cardinals in Rome.

Luther was certainly not the first Catholic to protest Church policies, and his criticism of what in the grand scheme of things was a relatively minor practice could easily have resulted in one of the three fates of earlier such critics: being accommodated and co-opted by the Church (like St. Francis), being burned at the stake as a heretic (like Savonarola in Florence or Jan Hus in Bohemia), or simply being ignored and falling into obscurity. That Martin Luther did not become a Catholic saint, get killed, or end up forgotten, but rather sparked a veritable revolution that transformed Western Europe and created an entirely new form of Christianity (Protestantism), was due to a fortuitous confluence of circumstances.

The first and most important of these circumstances was that Luther lived shortly after the invention of the printing press in Europe. Johannes Gutenberg created the first European printing press with movable type (the first such press in the world had been invented in China centuries earlier), and by the time Luther wrote his *Theses*, printing had become common enough in Europe that texts such as his could be easily printed and disseminated to a wide reading public. We take the rapid dissemination of information for granted today because there are so many tools for it—newspapers, books, phones, television, and the internet, to name a few—so it is easy to forget that this was not always the case. The printing press was the first technology that allowed information to be spread rapidly and widely. Prior to that time, monks working with pens and parchment would spend weeks or months just to create a single copy of a book. If it had not been for the printing press, Martin Luther would likely have fallen into obscurity. His *Theses* would probably have rankled the local bishop and potentially have caused career repercussions for Luther, but few outside of that diocese would have ever heard about it. With the printing press, Luther's *Theses* became an international sensation; Luther himself became a celebrity, and for the rest of the career he was able to disseminate his ideas to a broad Western European public.

Also important to Luther's success as a Reformer was a combination of *chutzpah* and dumb luck. When Luther's criticism of the sale of indulgences ran into resistance in the Church hierarchy, he did not submit to correction like a good son of the Church but, rather, doubled down. As a result, he was excommunicated by Pope Leo X on January 3, 1521. Excommunication is an official act whereby a person is barred from receiving the sacraments and exercising any ministry in the Church. Luther had come to reject the Catholic Church's claim to be God's representative on Earth; he was not swayed by the excommunication but instead continued to preach his newly emerging theology of Christianity that was in key ways at odds with those of the Church.

This easily could have been the end of Luther; in the past, when critics of the Church were deemed too dangerous by the Church and therefore excommunicated, they were executed as heretics. This is where Luther proved exceptionally lucky. The Catholic Church, although during the Middle Ages extending throughout Western Europe (and today the world), was not an empire that directly controlled the lands over which it held influence. It relied on local kings and princes to exercise its will, especially in the realm of executions. Luther might very well have been executed for defying the Church, but he was protected by a powerful patron, Frederick III, the Elector of Saxony. Shortly after his excommunication, Luther was summoned to an imperial council summoned by the Holy Roman Emperor, Charles V. During this Diet of Worms, Luther refused to recant his writings, and as a result, the emperor declared him an outlaw and decreed that anyone could kill him with impunity. On his way back to Wittenberg, Luther was, by the arrangement of his patron Frederick III, "abducted" for his own protection and whisked away to Wartburg Castle in Eisenach. He remained there for about a year, until it was safe enough for him to return to Wittenberg. Until his death in 1546, Luther was able to preach, write, and live freely according to his new interpretation of Christianity because of the protection of Frederick III and then the outright patronage of Lutheranism by Frederick's successor as Elector of Saxony, John.

LUTHER'S THEOLOGY

The theology that Luther developed after making the break from the Catholic Church includes three basic principles that became highly influential over all Protestant thought thereafter. The first is that the Bible is the sole source of authority for Christians in determining the will of God. The second and third are that salvation is attained by the faith of the individual Christian alone and by the grace of God alone; it cannot be earned through works (i.e., what a person does). These three principles are closely related both to one another and to the controversy about indulgences that led to Luther's excommunication. I will begin with the issue of the Bible since it sets the scene for the principles of salvation by faith alone and by grace alone.

Many people today, especially in English-speaking countries, take it for granted that Christians look to the Bible as a unique source of authority. They consider it the Word of God, they read it, they discuss it, and they model their lives on its teachings. This is a relatively recent phenomenon, however. Throughout most of Christianity's history, ordinary Christians would not have owned a Bible, much less would they have read it; in fact, in most cases, they would not have been able to read it. Partly this was a technological problem: Prior to the fifteenth century when Gutenberg invented (for Europe) the printing press, books had to be painstakingly copied by hand, usually by monks in monasteries. As a result, books were precious and rare; ordinary peasants certainly could not afford them, not even a Bible. Even if they could, though, they would not be able to read it. In many cases, they simply were not able to read at all, but even more importantly, if they (in Western Europe) wanted to read it, they would need to know Latin since the Bible was only generally accessible in a Latin translation known as the Vulgate. During the Middle Ages, Latin was no longer a language spoken by ordinary people, but it was a lingua franca used by scholars in Western Europe to communicate with one another. Thus, the study of the Bible was effectively restricted to a relatively small number of elites who were educated, usually under the auspices of the Church. This does not mean that ordinary people did not know about stories and teachings found in the Bible. They would know about them by looking at artwork in churches, by listening to the sermons of priests during Mass, and through popular entertainment that dramatized Biblical themes. But they would not have been able to read what the Bible says *directly*.

The restriction of direct access to the Bible to a small number of highly educated people was not an accident. The Catholic Church actively fought against efforts to make the Bible more widely accessible, such as by translating it into vernacular languages. It simply did not want ordinary people to read the Bible. Why do you think this might be? When I ask my students this question, often the first answer I get is that the Church wanted to maintain its power, and therefore it had to control the message. This is of course a cynical way of looking at the matter—which is not to say that it is wrong—but I think it is worthwhile to consider the issue from the Church's perspective as well. The Catholic Church was indeed interested in controlling the message, and it could only do so if it restricted access to the Bible to those trained by the Church in its interpretation. If ordinary people read the Bible, it reasoned, then there would arise a multitude of conflicting interpretations. On this point, the Church was objectively correct, as was quickly proven after the Reformation—the Reformation did not result in simply one non-Catholic Church, but rather an ever-growing proliferation of Churches who each had their own interpretation of the Truth of Christianity. (To this day, there is only one Roman Catholic Church, but Protestantism is divided into hundreds or even thousands of denominations.) From the Church's point of view—which has generally been shared by most Christians, even Protestants—there is only one *correct* interpretation, known as *orthodoxy* ("right teaching"); all other interpretations would be false teachings, or *heresies*. Adhering to a heretical teaching would lead a person to eternal damnation in hell. So, by controlling the message, the Catholic Church was, again from its point of view, not simply maintaining its power, but in fact saving souls.

The Catholic Church, like all Christian Churches, recognizes the Bible as the Word of God, divinely inspired scripture, which is therefore one of the most important authorities for determining the will of God. According to the Catholic Church, however—both in the Middle Ages and still today—the Bible is not the *sole* authority for a Christian. The Church itself is another authority. The Bible is the Word of God, but it is the Church's job to *interpret* the Word of God so that ordinary Christians understand it correctly. The Church claims this authority based on particular verses in the Bible that it interprets as saying (1) that Jesus founded his Church on St. Peter, whom Catholics consider to be the first pope and (2) that the Holy Spirit guides the Church throughout the ages so that it represents God's authority on Earth. According to the Catholic Church, then, there are two sources of authority for understanding the will of God: the Bible (scripture) and the Church. Since the Church is a dynamic institution embedded in history, this second authority is also referred to as Tradition (with a capital *T*)—referring to the traditions of the Church that it draws upon in interpreting the Bible and pronouncing on the proper Christian life.

Since Luther was excommunicated from the Catholic Church, he obviously could not accept this twofold model of Christian authority. Indeed, because the Catholic Church in his day took positions (e.g., on indulgences) that he considered clearly at odds with the Word of God in the Bible, he concluded that the Catholic Church could not be considered an authority at all for Christians. It had become utterly corrupt and represented not God, but rather the Devil. He pointed to the Bible itself, which predicted the coming of an Antichrist who would attempt to mislead Christians during the End Times. Luther concluded that the pope himself was the Antichrist.

So how is a Christian to know the will of God? Luther's solution—followed by all other Protestants afterward—was to simply remove the Church as an authority and retain the Bible alone as an authority. This principle is known in Latin as *sola scriptura*—"by scripture alone." Protestants to this day put an enormous emphasis on the Bible. Driving around the United States, for example, you will often find so-called Bible churches (which are generally nondenominational Protestant), and the word *evangelical*, which comes from the Greek and Latin terms for gospel, is a popular term of identity for many Protestants.[1] Luther himself called his new Church *evangelisch*, and this is the term used in German to this day to refer to Protestants. The implication in all these terms is that the person who identifies with them follows the Bible, as opposed to Catholics who supposedly do not, or other Protestants who are supposedly too much like Catholics.

An important cultural shift that resulted from Luther's dictum of *sola scriptura* is an increasing emphasis on the individual. The modern world, especially the modern Western world, puts great emphasis on the individual and individualism. You probably take for granted that you have rights as an individual, dignity as an individual, and freedom to make choices on a great deal of issues (including religion) as an individual. What you may not realize is that this emphasis on the individual is largely the product of the Protestant Reformation; it is, in effect, a theological position. The Catholic Church teaches that it serves as a mediator between individual Christians and God. Indeed, the whole Catholic worldview is characterized by mediators between the individual and God. The Church as an institution mediates between individual Christians and God by guiding Christians and even dispensing God's grace (his gift of salvation) through certain rituals known as the sacraments (baptism, communion, confirmation, etc.). In addition, when Catholics pray, they do not necessarily pray directly to God; in many cases, they pray "through" a saint or the Virgin Mary to intercede with God on their behalf. This model is reflective (and at one time was partly constitutive) of medieval society, in which elaborate hierarchies of rank and patronage would separate ordinary peasants from the king.

Luther himself, and increasingly the more radical Reformers who followed him, rejected this system in favor of a more direct relationship between individual Christians and God. Since the Church was corrupt, it could not serve as an intermediary between individual Christians and God. In addition, Protestants increasingly came to view the practice of praying through (which can often seem like praying *to*) saints and the Virgin Mary as being paganism with a thin Christian veneer. They therefore sharply deemphasized Mary, the saints, and the sacraments in favor of a model whereby individual Christians read the Bible for themselves and cultivate a *personal* relationship with God. If you have ever had an evangelical Christian ask you, "Have you accepted Jesus Christ as your personal Savior?" (or have yourself asked it!) then you have witnessed the modern theological expression of this emphasis on the individual. The point being made with this question is that you must cultivate a personal relationship with God in order to be saved, rather than relying on a Church to mediate that relationship for you.

The second principle that is central to Luther's and all subsequent Protestant theology is known in Latin as *sola fide*, which means "by faith alone." It is the principle that Christians are saved by having faith in Jesus Christ, not by doing anything to earn salvation. The issue that sparked the Reformation was the so-called sale of indulgences, but this practice was in fact simply the logical extension of a broader principle that even today many people without in-depth theological training take for granted: the idea that people go to heaven because of the good deeds they do in this life. Think about it: An indulgence is simply a document stating that you can go to heaven faster. If good deeds are what get you into heaven, then wouldn't it make sense to get an indulgence when you do a good deed? And is it not a good deed to give money to God's Church? After all, all Christians support their respective Churches financially, even Protestants. Members of other religions also support their religious institutions in this way; without such financial support, no religious institution could survive. So, from the Church's perspective, it was not selling indulgences; it was instead granting indulgences to those individuals who engaged in the meritorious act of donating to the Church. Of course, this practice became increasingly scandalous as Church officials like the infamous monk Tetzel raised exorbitant sums of money to fund the building of St. Peter's Basilica by convincing poor peasants to donate what little they had to the Church. But the practice still technically made sense if you understood good deeds as getting you into heaven.

It was this understanding of the mechanism of salvation, rather than simply the practice of selling indulgences, that Luther attacked as he developed his theology. Recall that because he considered the Catholic Church to be corrupt and led by the Antichrist, he rejected the Church and its teaching as an authority for Christians and turned instead to the Bible itself for guidance. In reading the Bible closely, especially St. Paul's Letter to the Romans, he became convinced that the idea that good deeds get you into heaven is wrong. The Letter to the Romans is St. Paul's longest letter, and in it he develops an extended argument over the relative importance of two things: faith and works. The issue in the context of which Paul developed this argument was of course not indulgences but rather whether Gentile (non-Jewish) Christians need to follow the Jewish Law. Paul considered himself to be "apostle to the Gentiles," sent by God to spread the good news that Jesus was the Messiah, not to his fellow Jews, but rather to Gentiles. He travelled extensively throughout the eastern part of the Roman Empire, especially in what are now Greece and Turkey, converting Gentiles to worship of the one true God and founding churches. To communicate with the churches he had founded or visited, he wrote letters, which were preserved by later Christians who considered them so authoritative that they made them part of the New Testament of the Christian Bible. Several times in his letters, Paul touches on the issue of whether Gentiles need to become Jews and thus follow the Jewish Law. While other Christian missionaries (who, like Paul, were born Jewish) argued that Gentiles must follow at least some aspects of Jewish Law, Paul argued strongly that they do not and should not.

From the second century onward, as Christianity and Judaism solidified into separate identities, Gentile Christians interpreted Paul's writings about the Jewish Law in a new way to argue that Jesus Christ had superseded the Law and that Christian faith in Jesus was therefore superior to Jewish devotion to fulfilling the Law. Paul's argument, as a Jew, against other Jewish apostles about whether Gentiles should follow the Jewish Law was thus transformed into a Christian argument against Jews about the value of the Law in general. Luther took this reinterpretation of Paul's argument and reinterpreted it once again to use against the Catholic Church. He argued that Paul's letter (which of course he considered sacred scripture) proves that one is saved by having faith in Jesus Christ, not by anything one does ("works")—whether those works were specific to the Jewish Law or not. In fact, Luther was quite adamant that it is impossible for you to *do* anything to earn your way into heaven.

Luther had been haunted for his entire life by the fear that he was not good enough to be saved. His solution was simple: He finally admitted that in fact he was *not* good enough to go to heaven, and that no human being is. The reason for this, according to Luther, was something called original sin. Original sin is the concept, developed early in the history of Christianity, that because Adam (the first human being) disobeyed God by eating the forbidden fruit of the tree of knowledge, all human beings have inherited a state of intrinsic sinfulness. This is a point that Luther and subsequent Protestants particularly emphasize: Human beings are complete reprobates. We are congenitally prone to evil and cannot possibly do anything to earn salvation. All of us, in other words, deserve to go to hell.

Luckily, God devised a solution. He sent his only son, Jesus Christ, to Earth to die on behalf of his people. By dying on the cross, even though he was blameless, Jesus took on the sin of all believers and thus earned salvation for them. Christians may not be able to save themselves by doing good deeds, but God saves them freely as a gift, which is known in Christian theology as grace. This is the third principle of Luther's theology, known in Latin as *sola gratia*, which means "by grace alone."

The principles of *sola fide* and *sola gratia* are closely related because, according to Luther and later Protestant theologians, God dispenses his grace through faith. In other words, a person need only accept God's gift of salvation by having faith that Jesus Christ died for their sins. (Otherwise, there would be no distinction between Christians and non-Christians.) Now, this might sound at first glance like a cheap way to get to heaven—you can do whatever we want, as long as you say that you believe in Jesus—but Luther and subsequent Reformers argued, following their interpretation of the words of the apostle Paul, that true faith results in a transformation of the individual, purifying them in preparation for eternal life—a process known as justification. Good people go to heaven, in other words, but they don't earn heaven by doing good things; rather, God saves them as a gift and makes them good (or just) in preparation for heaven.[2]

The Protestant understanding of *sola gratia* can be seen, for example, in the popular hymn "Amazing Grace." You've probably heard this song even if you are not Christian—President Obama famously sang it while giving a eulogy for a black pastor who was killed by a racist gunman in Charleston, SC. Many people have been moved by the words of the hymn: "Amazing Grace! How sweet the sound / That saved a wretch like me! / I once was lost, but now am found; / Was blind, but now I see." What you may not know is why these words were written. John Newton, an English clergyman who had previously worked in the slave trade, wrote them in 1779 after he had a conversion experience, realized that slavery was evil, and became an abolitionist; it is this that he refers to as "Amazing Grace" in his hymn. Like a good Protestant, he did not consider himself to have done anything to become a good person; rather, God made him a better person as a gift.

Just as the principle of *sola scriptura* leads as a corollary to an emphasis on the individual, so too do the principles of *sola fide* and *sola gratia* lead to another corollary: a *deemphasis* of ritual. If you have ever been to both a Catholic Mass and a Protestant service, then you know the difference. A Catholic Mass[3] is highly ritualized. Almost every moment of the Mass, except for the part in the middle when the priest gives his homily (sermon), is highly scripted. The priest says things according to a set script, and the congregation responds according to a set script. At certain points in the Mass, people stand, at other points they sit, and at still other points they kneel. Catholics who attend Mass regularly know by heart what they are supposed to say and do at each point, not because they have studied it, but simply through sheer repetition. The culmination of the Mass is an elaborate ritual whereby bread and wine are transformed—and this is understood quite literally according to Catholic Church doctrine—into the body and blood of Christ, which is then consumed by the priest and congregation. This process, like any ritual, involves the priest using precise words and hand gestures to effect the transformation (known technically in Catholic theology as transubstantiation) of the bread and wine into Jesus' body and blood.

Many Protestant church services[4] display a stark contrast from the ritualism of the Catholic Mass. Although there may be a set liturgy that is followed, there is far less of the prescribed words and postures that one would find in a Catholic Mass. The focal point is usually the minister's sermon, which can in some churches be quite emotive and spontaneous. Most Protestant churches do not have communion (the eating of the bread and wine) every week, and even when they do have communion, they generally do not precede it with an elaborate ritual to transform it into the body and blood of Christ. This is because most Protestant Churches do not accept the Catholic doctrine of transubstantiation. They instead understand the bread and wine to symbolize the body and blood of Christ and thus take communion to be simply a memorial of the Last Supper before Jesus died.

Although the degree of ritualization can vary across Protestant denominations, generally the trend in the history of Protestantism has been toward ever-less ritual. The Catholic Church teaches that the Bible gives precedent for seven sacraments—special rituals performed by the Church whereby God dispenses his grace to ordinary Christians. These are baptism, communion (the consumption of the body and blood of Christ), reconciliation (in which one confesses one's sins to a priest), confirmation, matrimony (marriage), holy orders (ordination as a deacon, priest, or bishop), and anointing of the sick. Luther reduced this number to the first two or three, arguing that the others lacked Biblical basis to be considered sacramental. Later Protestant Reformers rejected the concept of sacrament altogether, arguing that if one is saved, as Luther had argued, by faith instead of works, then there is no need for rituals to dispense God's grace. God instead dispenses his grace directly to individual Christians who have faith.

Since the centerpiece of the Catholic Mass had always been the sacrament of communion, the rejection of this sacrament by Reformers after Luther, as well as the rejection of the related doctrine of transubstantiation, led to a rapid de-ritualization of Christian worship. Even today, movements within Protestantism innovate in finding ways to make worship less ritualistic than it already is. The Pentecostal movement, for example, puts an emphasis on the spontaneity of the Holy Spirit, expressed in such practices as speaking in tongues. The Evangelical movement likewise puts great emphasis on the need for each individual to be "born again" by accepting Jesus Christ as their "personal savior"—outside of any communal church protocol. And many Protestant churches today—especially nondenominational churches, but also some within established congregations—try to attract larger and larger flocks by abandoning traditional church liturgies and replacing them with hip, contemporary music and raw, spontaneous preaching.

HOW THE REFORMATION CREATED THE MODERN WORLD—AND YOU

The principle of *sola scriptura* had profound implications for Protestant culture and, as a result, the culture of the modern world as a whole. The fact that you are reading this book, in fact, is in part a result of Luther's rejection of the Church as an authority for Christians. Luther wanted ordinary people to see the truth of the gospel, which he felt was being hidden by the Catholic Church to maintain its own power. He seems to have naively thought that if people read the Bible, they would see that the Catholic Church was lying to them and turn to the true gospel. I say "naively" because Luther did not believe any less than the Catholic Church that there was only one correct interpretation of the Bible; he just believed that the Catholic Church's was not it. But as I already pointed out, whatever you think of the Catholic Church's policy of restricting access to the Bible, it was certainly correct that opening access would lead to a proliferation of different interpretations. That is indeed what happened, and although most of us today would consider that to be a good thing—it led to freedom of thought, which led to the Enlightenment, which led to the Scientific Revolution, democracy, and so forth—Luther did not. Already in his lifetime he found himself fighting against other, more radical Protestants whose varying interpretations of the Bible had been unleashed by his own rejection of the Church's authority.

In any case, the Protestant emphasis on the Bible as the sole authority for Christians led to several important cultural shifts. Luther and other Protestant Reformers wanted ordinary people to read the Bible. Luckily, that was becoming a technological possibility in the sixteenth century because the invention of the printing press allowed for the mass production of Bibles and thus increasingly made it possible for ordinary people to own one (even if, as was often the case, that was the only book they owned). It was not practical (or necessary) to expect ordinary people to know Latin, so Luther translated the Bible into his own mother tongue of German, and Reformers in other countries quickly translated it into other Western European vernacular languages as well. It *was* necessary, however, for ordinary people to be literate to read the Bible. Protestants therefore became promoters of mass literacy, laying the foundation for universal education, which we take for granted today. As I said, you have Luther to thank for the fact that you are able to read this book.

In addition, nearly all of modern culture, especially in the West, and especially in the most *progressive* (and often non- or even anti-Christian) corners of Western culture, is predicated on this Protestant emphasis on the individual that arose out of *sola scriptura*. This emphasis on the individual was first cultivated in a firmly Christian context: the Protestant rejection of the authority the Church and its dispensation of grace through the sacraments in favor of individuals cultivating a personal relationship with God by reading the Bible. Nevertheless, it quickly broke free of the specific issue of authority and salvation or even Christianity in general and took on a life of its own.

Democracy, universal education, and science all are based on the idea, which would have seemed absurd during the Middle Ages, that human individuals have the ability, right, and responsibility to think and decide things for themselves. We take it for granted now that human individuals can and should think for themselves and choose their own leaders. And though many conservative Protestants today are outraged at such developments, even such things as feminism, secularism, and the fight for LGBTQ rights are natural outgrowths of the Protestant emphasis on the individual. Feminism is at core the principle that women should have the right as individuals to control their own bodies and destinies.

Secularism is at core the principle that human individuals should be able to choose their own religion—or no religion at all—without interference from the state. And the LGBTQ movement has at its core the principle that human individuals should be able to choose for themselves whom to love, whom to have sex with, and how to express their gender identity. If we think of the last five hundred years as a progressive unfolding of principles established by Luther and the other Reformers, then feminists, secularists, and the LGBTQ community are all at the vanguard of a "Reformation" that continues to this day—even if the reforms being contemplated are far beyond anything Martin Luther would have recognized.

DISCUSSION QUESTIONS

1. Who was Martin Luther? What background gave him the stature to ignite the Reformation, and what special circumstances allowed his message to spread and allowed him to avoid execution?
2. What does the Catholic Church teach are the two sources of authority for Christians? Why is it important, from the Church's perspective, to have both of those sources of authority?
3. Explain briefly the three cornerstone principles of Luther's theology: scripture alone (*sola scriptura*), faith alone (*sola fide*) and grace alone (*sola gratia*). How are the three related?
4. What were some of the broader implications of Protestant theology for the modern understanding of religion?
5. In what way can many modern movements (the Enlightenment, the Scientific Revolution, democracy, women's rights, etc.) be understood to have their roots in changes brought about by the Protestant Reformation?

NOTES

1 *Evangelical* is used in two slightly different senses in English today, which can be confusing. First, there is the generic meaning of *evangelical* as "having to do with the gospel," which is sometimes generically used by Protestants to emphasize their adherence to the principle of *sola scriptura*. An example is in the name of the Evangelical Lutheran Church, which is the largest Lutheran denomination in the United States. But when people use the word *Evangelical* today, they are usually referring to a specific interdenominational movement within Protestant Christianity that has its roots in religious revivals in Britain and the United States beginning in the eighteenth century. Because

Evangelical in this latter sense is not tied to any single denomination, it is often adopted by individuals to characterize the nature of their Christian commitments or by various Protestant churches who wish to ally their congregations with the movement. The Evangelical Lutheran Church is *not* Evangelical in this latter sense.

2. Technically speaking, the principle of *sola gratia* was not an innovation of Luther; by itself, it is also accepted by the Catholic Church. That is, Catholic teaching also holds that one is saved by the freely given gift (grace) of God, not by one's own efforts. The difference between Catholic and Protestant theology lies more specifically in the understanding of this concept of justification. According to Catholic teaching, one must actively engage one's faith through good works in order for it to truly be faith; only then can one receive God's grace and be justified. Luther, conversely, argued that justification happens automatically to the person who has faith; God's grace itself brings about the transformation of the individual without their active participation.

3. The word *Mass* refers to a Catholic church service. It has two parts. First, the Liturgy of the Word consists of introductory prayers, a set of readings from the Bible, and the priest's homily (sermon) on them. Second, the Liturgy of the Eucharist consists of a ritual in which the priest is believed to turn ordinary bread and wine into the literal body and blood of Christ, which members of the congregation then consume. Prior to a decision by the Second Vatican Council in the 1960s to switch to local languages, the ritualized prayers of the Catholic Mass around the world were recited in Latin. At the end of the Latin Mass as it was celebrated for centuries, the priest would dismiss the congregation by saying "*Ite, missa est,*" which means, "Go, it is the dismissal." The Latin word *missa* was adopted in Catholic cultures as a colloquial way to refer to the entire church service, and it entered into English as *Mass*.

4. Though not all. Certain Protestant denominations, such as Lutherans and Episcopalians/Anglicans, have church services that are fairly ritualistic, like the Catholic Mass. That is because those denominations were created early in the Reformation and were less radical in their reforms than other denominations. Where one will see a starker contrast with the ritual of the Catholic Mass is in the church services of Baptists, Methodists, Presbyterians, and various nondenominational churches.

13
How the Glasses Work

Throughout this book, I have been introducing religious traditions by emphasizing the disconnect between stereotypes about those traditions and the reality. But where have the stereotypes come from? Why does popular culture so consistently misunderstand and misrepresent religions around the world? And why do specific religions get misrepresented in the specific ways that they do, often seemingly in very different ways from each other? We are now equipped with the intellectual tools to answer these questions.

At the beginning of the book, I argued that religion is not so much a thing out there in the world as it is a lens through which we see the world. It is an ideological construct with its origins in the West, tied up through most of its history with Christianity, that was then imposed on the rest of the world through colonialism. We can think of the very concept of religion as being like a pair of tinted glasses. Just as red-tinted glasses make everything look like a different shade of red, so too does the concept of religion act like a pair of Christian-tinted glasses, making everything look like a different shade of Christianity.

Christianity in general has certain distinguishing features that contribute to how these glasses work. One of these, of course, is **monotheism**, which it also shares with some other traditions. In addition, as we saw in chapter 1, Christianity is unique among religions in its extreme **emphasis on orthodoxy**, which dictates in relatively minute detail what Christians are supposed to believe. Moreover, Christianity is a **universalizing** religion: That is, it addresses itself to all of humanity and actively attempts to convert people around the world.

Not all forms of Christianity had an equal influence on the formation of the modern concept of religion, however. Because colonialism took place on the heels of the Protestant Reformation, *Protestant*

DOI: 10.4324/9781032646428-16

Christianity in particular had an outsized influence on how religion has come to be understood in the modern world.[1] The particular claims and emphases made by Protestant Christianity that we learned about in the last chapter, therefore, are particularly relevant to understanding why religion is understood in the particular way it is today.

Martin Luther introduced certain theological principles that formed the bedrock of Protestant thought afterwards. Among these was *sola scriptura*: scripture alone. As a result, the modern concept of religion tends to put an enormous **emphasis on scripture**. Another theological principle introduced by Luther was *sola fide*: faith alone. As a result, the modern concept of religion tends to put an enormous **emphasis on belief**, often paying more attention to what religious people believe than what they do. As I mentioned in chapter 1, I have been asking my students for many years to come up with their own definitions of religion, and invariably the word *belief* is one of the first words most students use in their definition. Perhaps *belief* showed up in your definition as well. This is not an accident. We are conditioned in the modern world to think that religion is mostly about belief.

There are also several downstream effects of these core Protestant principles on modern thinking about religion. One is an emphasis on origins. This comes from the Protestant rejection of the Church and its Tradition, as well as its emphasis on the Bible alone as a source of authority for Christians. The latest books of the Bible were written within less than a hundred years after the death of Jesus, so the emphasis on the Bible equates to an **emphasis on the origins** of Christianity. If we extend this principle to religion in general, it implies that the origins of any religion are what is most important; anything coming later is not authoritative and maybe even suspect.

Another downstream effect is a deemphasis of or even outright **disdain for ritual**. Luther himself was not opposed to ritual, but Reformers after him increasingly came to question the value of ritual, especially as embodied by the Catholic Mass. After all, if faith is what saves you, and not what you do, what do you need rituals for? The more radical Protestant reformers ridiculed the rituals of the Catholic Church and in particular the claim that the priest transforms ordinary bread and wine into the body and blood of Christ. This way of thinking had an influence on Enlightenment intellectuals, and as a result the modern world has little interest in or patience for rituals. Modern people often see rituals as empty or meaningless.

A practical effect of the Protestant Reformation was to deepen the assumption that religions are **mutually exclusive**. This was already implicit within the monotheism of Christianity as a whole: From the very beginning, to become a Christian was to acknowledge the one true God and give up worship of any other gods. The Protestant Reformation, however, fractured Christian identity insofar as it led to the formation of hundreds of new Christian denominations. For the most part, these denominations were treated as mutually exclusive: to be a Baptist was *not* to be a Catholic or a Lutheran or a Presbyterian, and so forth. Western experience in the modern era has therefore been thoroughly suffused with the practical experience of religious identity being mutually exclusive.

Another downstream effect of the Protestant Reformation is **iconoclasm**. Luther himself was not particularly opposed to the traditional Catholic use of religious images, but later, more radical Reformers were. These Reformers ridiculed the Catholic cult of the saints and veneration of the Virgin Mary, which they regarded as paganism with a thin Christian veneer. In some cases, Reformers deliberately tore down statues and frescoes in old cathedrals to put an end to what they saw as Catholic idolatry. Protestant iconoclasm has arguably had a profound effect on the aesthetics of modernity in general, especially in historically Protestant countries. More importantly, it has shaped modern conceptions of normal or acceptable forms of religious worship.

Finally, an overall downstream effect of the Protestant Reformation is an **emphasis on the individual**. Individualism has become such a widespread value in the modern world that it can be easy to forget that it has specific origins in and relevance to religion. Because Protestants rejected the authority of the Church, they encouraged individual Christians to read the Bible for themselves and cultivate a personal relationship with God. This, together with the practical necessity to prevent religious conflict that the Reformation unleashed, provided the basis for modern secularism, which relegates religion to the private sphere and ultimately to the sovereignty of the individual conscience. We take it for granted today that religion is something deeply personal, but this has not generally been the case throughout human history.

To summarize, then, there are ten features of Christianity—the first three of Christianity in general and the other seven coming more specifically from Protestantism—that contribute in significant ways to the modern perception of religion: (1) monotheism, (2) an emphasis on orthodoxy, (3) universalism, (4) an emphasis on belief, (5) an emphasis on scripture, (6) an emphasis on origins, (7) disdain for ritual, (8) mutual exclusivity, (9) iconoclasm, and (10) an emphasis on the individual. To be clear, there is some overlap between some of the elements of this list (e.g., number 4 is basically a Protestant doubling down on number 2), and many of the elements are related to each other (e.g., number 6 comes from number 5, and number 7 comes from number 4). But this list gives a useful framework for understanding what it is about Christianity specifically that gives the glasses we call religion their Christian tint.

The structure of (Protestant) Christianity alone, however, does not fully determine how the modern concept of religion works. It provides the tint, but Orientalism determines how the image of a particular religion is refracted. As we saw in chapter 2, Orientalism has two faces: the overtly negative and the superficially positive. (Protestant) Christian assumptions can, on the one hand, lead to an overtly negative image of a particular religion. Or they can, conversely, lead to an exotified image of a particular religion. In the latter case, the image of the religion in question is essentially a projection of modernist fantasies that draw from the downstream effects of the Protestant Reformation.

In this chapter, we will apply this framework to the religions we have studied in this book. We'll begin with three religions that often suffer from negative stereotypes: Judaism, Islam, and Hinduism. We'll then turn to two religions that often are portrayed in an exotified way in the West: Buddhism and Daoism.[2] Next, we'll turn to issues that are of more global importance for the way we perceive religions: religious boundaries and what counts as real religion. Finally, I'll wrap things up by explaining how all this fits together and why understanding how the modern concept of religion works is so important for understanding our world.

OVERTLY NEGATIVE STEREOTYPES: JUDAISM, ISLAM, AND HINDUISM

Three of the religions we have studied in this book often have overtly negative stereotypes attached to them: Judaism, Islam, and Hinduism. These stereotypes have deep roots in the Christian experience of Europe in the Middle Ages. During that period, European Christians had a much simpler taxonomy of religions than the modern conception of world religions. There was the "true" religion, Christianity. Then there were Judaism and Islam, both of which were traditions that, like Christianity, worshiped the God of Abraham but were deemed false because they did not recognize the divinity of Jesus Christ. Antisemitism and Islamophobia therefore both have deep roots in the Middle Ages. Beyond Judaism and Islam, medieval Christians knew little about other religions, lumping them together as a vast mass of "heathens." Heathens were presumed to be polytheists who did not know the one true God and therefore were quite beyond the pale of salvation. Although medieval European Christians knew little to nothing about Hindus, their disdain for heathens led to negative stereotypes of Hinduism once they did learn about it during the colonial period.

As we saw in chapter 3, Islamophobia is ironic because, of all the major religions, Islam is the most similar to Christianity. Yet it is the small differences that have led to fear and hatred of Islam. Indeed, some of the earliest Christian accounts of Islam refer to Muhammad as a heretic—a word usually reserved for *Christians* who deviate in some way from orthodoxy. The emphasis on orthodoxy is thus the seed from which Islamophobia has grown. Christian orthodoxy holds that God is a Trinity—three in one—with the important corollary that Jesus is divine. Islam denies the Trinity and the divinity of Christ and thus drew (orthodox) Christian ire from the very beginning. This grew into the full-blown Islamophobic narrative that continues (even among non-Christians) to this day. Because Islam is so similar to Christianity, it is a prime candidate for the projection of Christian anxieties about their own culture. The two main themes of Islamophobia—that Islam is inherently violent and that it is misogynistic—can just as easily be applied to Christianity and Western culture in general and thus are emblematic of this sort of projection.

Antisemitism in a sense has the same root as Islamophobia: the Christian emphasis on orthodoxy. Judaism is obviously closely related to Christianity insofar as Christianity arose out of Judaism, but it deviates from Christian orthodoxy insofar as it denies that Jesus is the Messiah. As we saw in chapter 9, however, the gap between Christian orthodoxy and Judaism is more the result of the split between Christian and Jewish identities than the cause of it. Another aspect of Christianity—its universalism—helps to explain not only why Christian antisemitism arose in the first place but also specifically how modern antisemitism negatively stereotypes Jews. Though Christianity was originally a Jewish sect, its mission to Gentiles ultimately created a movement that was predominantly non-Jewish. The widespread success of Christianity as a *universalizing* religion ultimately rendered Judaism uncanny insofar as it was tied to a specific ethnic group. Modern antisemitism has capitalized on this ambiguity in Jewish identity—both a religion and an ethnicity—to create a racist narrative of Jews as a biologically constituted threat to the purity of any and all other nations.

Finally, negative stereotypes about Hinduism are rooted in Christian monotheism. As we saw in chapter 5, many Hindus today regard themselves as monotheists, and "polytheism" is a simplistic label for a complex and diverse religious culture. Because Hinduism does involve the worship of many gods (even if they are regarded by many Hindus as manifestations of one God or the Goddess), it appears as polytheistic from the binary perspective of Abrahamic monotheism. Protestant iconoclasm has also contributed to the negative perception of Hinduism. Not only do Hindus worship many gods; they worship them in the form of images. This served as a double indicator of their perceived deviation from monotheism as Christian missionaries began working in India under the auspices of British colonial rule. Indeed, to this day negative portrayals of Hinduism in popular media often involve mockery of the imagery of Hindu gods. Christian monotheism and specifically Protestant iconoclasm have had a deep impact on modern perceptions of what is reasonable in religion—even to those who are not religious—rendering myths about multiple gods and the use of statues of gods in worship uncanny or even ridiculous.

BUDDHISM, DAOISM, AND THE PROJECTION OF POST-PROTESTANT FANTASIES

What about the flip side of the Orientalist coin? How does Orientalism refract the image of religions through the tint of Christian assumptions to create an *exotified* image, rather than an overtly negative one? Popular conceptions of Buddhism and Daoism in the West today are prime examples of this exotification. Both are treated as screens on which to project modern fantasies about religion that have their roots in Protestant theology.

Let us begin with Buddhism, which in many ways represents the antithesis of Islam in the Western imagination. Although at one time many Westerners had negative views of Buddhism as pessimistic and atheistic (and today some Christian conservatives still hold these views), nowadays Western popular culture is populated by "positive" stereotypes of Buddhism as much as by negative stereotypes of Islam. Buddhism is focused on the individual; it allows you to follow your own path instead of obeying a bunch of rules. It's not about ritual and prayer, but about inner spiritual cultivation. It is egalitarian, democratic, and supportive of women. It is rational—scientific even!—and doesn't have God, gods, miracles, or the supernatural. Buddhism is, in short, the perfect religion—not so much a religion, in fact, as a philosophy or way of life.

As we have seen, though, none of these things that so many people in the West "know" about Buddhism is really true of Buddhism as it is and has for millennia been traditionally practiced in Asia. Buddhists do not exist in isolation or "follow their own path"; Buddhism is institutionalized with a monastic order, which is the focus of communal life for both monks and laypeople. Every traditional form of Buddhism has elaborate rituals and prayers, just like Christianity. And traditional Buddhism is hardly "rational" or "scientific" to the point of eschewing gods, miracles, or the supernatural—Buddhists believe in rebirth, including the possibility of rebirth as a god or other supernatural being, and traditional Buddhists engage in the worship/propitiation of these beings just like in any other religion. And far from being egalitarian or feminist, traditional Buddhist societies are highly hierarchical and patriarchal.

Where, then, does the modern Western image of Buddhism come from, if it bears so little resemblance to the reality of traditional Buddhist practice? The answer is that it is largely a projection of modern Western fantasies onto Buddhism. The Protestant Reformation created a modern focus on the individual, as well as a sharp devaluation of ritual. As a result, modern people tend to value individualism, especially when it comes to religion, and look upon rituals as antiquated. Likewise, the Reformation set into motion a series of events that led to the Enlightenment, the Scientific Revolution, democratization, and various movements for equality such as feminism. Modern Western people therefore tend to value rationality, science, and equality. All these modern values are projected onto Buddhism in popular Western discourse. Even though a cursory knowledge of actual Buddhist *practice* shows that these values are not nearly as operative in traditional contexts as Westerners believe, the (Protestant) Christian emphasis on religion as being about belief embodied in scripture enabled Westerners to project their modern fantasies onto Buddhism, nonetheless. Through a selective reading of early Buddhist scriptures, one could argue that Buddhism is really individualistic, anti-ritual, rational, scientific, and egalitarian. Once Westerners constructed this image of true Buddhism, their Orientalism allowed them to ignore the actual practices of Asian Buddhists on the basis that they supposedly did not understand their own religion and had therefore corrupted it.

A similar projection of Western fantasies onto the East is seen in the case of Daoism. Based on little more than a superficial reading of a single text, the *Daode Jing*, people in the West often have the impression that Daoism is all about going with the flow, following your own path, being spiritual and spontaneous, not having to follow any set rules. But as we have seen, this image of Daoism would scarcely be recognizable to anyone raised in a traditional Chinese context in which Daoism is actually practiced. Daoism has an elaborate pantheon of gods and supernatural beings, lineages of priests, and elaborate rituals performed by these priests to interact with the gods and manipulate supernatural forces that govern the universe. Historically, Daoist masters have sought the goal of immortality by a variety of means, including meditation and "internal alchemy." Concepts such as the Dao, *wuwei*, and *yin* and *yang* are not just cool ideas that you can tattoo to your body and think about as suggesting the need for balance; they were once an integral part of premodern scientific thinking in China that informed the way in which Chinese scholars understood and interacted with the world around them. One of the most important legacies of this premodern Chinese science is traditional Chinese medicine, which is still practiced and patronized in the Chinese world alongside Western medicine today.

So then where did the no-rules, go-with-the-flow version of Daoism come from? Again, it is a projection of modern Western fantasies onto a foreign culture. The Protestant emphasis on the individual led to the fierce individualism of modernity, to the point that institutionalized religion in general (even Protestant) has become anathema to many people in the modern world. When Westerners discovered the *Daode Jing*, certain ideas within it, particularly the Dao and *wuwei* ("nonaction," but effectively meaning "spontaneous action") satisfied this yearning for an individualized spirituality. The *Daode Jing* also had two fortuitous characteristics that enabled it to catapult to the status of an Eastern classic in the eyes of the West: It is (supposedly) the oldest Daoist text, and it makes no reference to the gods, rituals, and priesthood of institutionalized Daoism. Christianity has long delegitimized the worship of and belief in multiple gods in the West, and the Protestant Reformation delegitimized rituals and priesthood, so modern Western people had no use for those aspects of Daoism. The fact that the *Daode Jing* is the "original scripture" luckily made it easy to ignore those aspects because the Reformation valorized the Bible as the true expression of Christianity and rejected later tradition as corrupt—by extension, the earliest scripture of any other religion supposedly tells us what that religion is really about, later tradition be damned.

BOUNDARIES INTERNAL AND EXTERNAL TO RELIGION

Judaism, Islam, Hinduism, Buddhism, and Daoism are all viewed through the glasses of religion—some in a more overtly negative way, some in a more exotified way—because we categorize them as religions. But the modern conception of religion does not only affect the way we see certain discrete things out there in the world that we happen to call religions. It also affects the way we divide the world up into discrete things to apply the religion label to in the first place. We have seen the effects of how the modern conception of religion reckons the boundaries of religion—both internal and external—in several chapters of this book. The boundaries we have examined respond to two questions: (1) How are the lines drawn between one religion and another? (2) What is the difference between religion and nonreligion? The answers to both questions have been conditioned by Christian assumptions and the way in which specifically Protestant Christian polemics have shaped modern values and understandings of the world.

First, the question of how lines are drawn between different religions is informed by the Christian assumption of mutual exclusivity. Christianity, as a monotheistic tradition, polices its boundaries primarily by exclusion: To be a Christian is to not be a member of another religion. The Protestant Reformation created hundreds of denominations within Christianity, and these have historically operated according to the same mutually exclusive logic. But as we saw in chapters 6 and 7, not all religions police their boundaries in the same way. In China there are three major religions—Buddhism, Confucianism, and Daoism—but many people practice all three at once. In India, religions police their boundaries vis-à-vis one another not through *exclusion* but through *inclusion*. Indian inclusivism involves the incorporation of elements of a rival religious tradition within one's own but in a subordinated role.

Second, in chapter 11 we examined the boundary between religion and nonreligion. We saw that this distinction is ultimately arbitrary and can only be perceived because of the modern ideology of secularism. Secularism is crucial to the coexistence of people of multiple religions in the modern world, but it is paradoxically predicated on an old Christian distinction between religious power and temporal (or "secular") power. The Protestant Reformation both brought about the modern need for secularism and provided the ideological basis for it. To begin with, the Reformation unleashed such violent religious strife in Europe that it created the need for a new paradigm for religious coexistence, one that was first fully realized in the Constitution of the United States in the late eighteenth century. The way it accomplished this, however, was through a privatization of religion that grew out of the Protestant rejection of the authority of the Church and concomitant emphasis on cultivating a personal, individual relationship with God.

Modern secularism considers religion a matter of the individual conscience, which should be exercised in the private sphere, and thus creates a secular public sphere that (in theory) does not favor or hinder any particular religion. Throughout most of history, however, the things that we call religions have not worked like this. Religion was often very much part of the public sphere, and it would have been difficult to point to any element of life as either religious or not religious. Although secularism has become the norm across much of the world, in countries with populations of nearly every religious tradition, nostalgia for a pre-secular past continues to play a role in contemporary politics in the form of religious nationalism.

THE MODERN DEVALUATION OF RITUAL AND THE PERCEPTION OF "REAL" RELIGION

In addition to the way we perceive individual religions, and in addition to the way that we draw boundaries between religions and around religion as a whole, Protestant Christian assumptions have also had a profound effect on what we perceive as "real" religion. It's as if, even within the realm of religion, some ways of being religious count more than others. We have seen examples of this in our examination of Tibetan Buddhism in chapter 8 and of indigenous religions in chapter 10. These two cases are related on a deeper level once we examine the particular way in which they are both affected by the distorting effect of the glasses of religion.

In chapter 8, we saw that Tibetan Buddhism has often been maligned in the West as not real Buddhism because Tibetans practice a form of Buddhism, Vajrayana, that is not the oldest form of Buddhism—in fact, its foundational scriptures, the *tantras*, were not written until almost 1,000 years after the time of the historical Buddha. We now have the tools to see why the first Western scholars to study Buddhism were inclined to view this late form of Buddhism as inauthentic. Protestant Christianity was predicated on a rejection of centuries of Catholic tradition in favor of returning to the "authentic" Christianity outlined in the Bible. This impulse was abstracted in the modern concept of world religions as a general assumption that *real* religion, *authentic* religion, is found in origins, and that later developments within a religion's history are suspect.

The Vajrayana Buddhism practiced by Tibetans was particularly vulnerable to this preference for original religion because, at least on the surface, it is quite different from older forms of Buddhism. But as we saw, there was another aspect of Vajrayana Buddhism that reinforced the idea that it was not real Buddhism: It is heavily ritualistic. Indeed, the entire genre of texts that form its foundational scriptures, the *tantras*, is dedicated to outlining rituals. The ritualism of Vajrayana Buddhism flew in the face of the modernist fantasy that Buddhism is a religion without rituals, which in turn is based on the Protestant disdain for rituals. Indeed, many early Western accounts of Tibetan Buddhism compared it to Catholicism and disparaged it using typical anti-Catholic rhetoric.

The anti-Catholic Protestant rhetoric that informed the disparagement of Tibetan Buddhism, however, was just part of a much longer trend in Western intellectual discourse that has a profound effect on the way we see the world, and the place of religion within it, today. To illustrate this, I'd like for you to indulge in a thought experiment with me. I want you to think of these three things: magic, religion, and science. Try to visualize them in your mind. For magic, I'm not talking about modern-day illusionists. I'm talking about *real* magic, with wizards and witches, potions and spells, and the like. Think Merlin, not Houdini. For religion, it's useful to focus on ritual. Lots of religions have rituals, but for our purpose it is useful to think about the Catholic ritual of the Mass. Think of a Catholic priest making special hand gestures over the bread and wine and pronouncing the words of consecration to transform them into the body and blood of Christ. Finally, for science, think of scientists in a lab, performing an experiment.

Now, ask yourself, what is the difference between these three things—magic, religion, and science? Consider the following definition: "Performing a series of actions in a prescribed way so as to accomplish some goal." This definition, if we are being impartial, could equally describe (1) what magicians like Merlin do, (2) what religious people (like Catholic priests) do when they perform rituals, and (3) what scientists do. So then what is the difference between these three words? The answer lies in their *connotation*. Magic, religion, and science are not different so much in their substance, but in our *attitude* towards them.

Words are not just tools for talking about the world around us. They are also weapons we use to collectively bully one another into thinking a certain way. Magic, religious ritual, and science may all consist of "performing a series of actions in a prescribed way so as to accomplish some goal," but we think of them very differently. Different people may think of these words in different ways, but let me describe what I take to be the generally prevalent attitude toward these three things in modern society.

Magic, to begin with, is complete nonsense. Many modern people—with notable exceptions such as Wiccans who deliberately embrace it and conservative Christians who demonize it—do not consider magic to be real, and claiming that magic is real in the public sphere will likely get you laughed out of the room. Magic survives mostly as a form of entertainment—in the shows of illusionists like David Copperfield and in works of fiction like *Harry Potter*—but its entertainment value lies precisely in the assumption that it is not real.

Religion and religious ritual have a somewhat more ambiguous position. Modern people tend not to be big fans of ritual, but ritual is generally considered to be okay if it is done privately in a religious context. In other words, *you* can perform your own religious rituals and even believe that they are efficacious, so long as you keep them to yourself and don't expect *me* to believe in them.

Finally, science is generally accepted as real. It has a prominent position in the public sphere; scientific research is funded by governments, and people learn about science in public schools. Acceptance of science is generally taken for granted in the public sphere, except for certain politicians who question well-established science because it conflicts with prominent corporate interests (e.g., climate change) or religious interests (e.g., evolution).

This hierarchy—magic is nonsense, religion and its associated rituals are okay if you keep them to yourself, and science is real—is so embedded in modern consciousness that most of us simply take it for granted that it is rooted in some fundamental difference between the three. I think there is a better way of looking at the matter, however, one that takes a historical perspective.[3] The word *magic* was already used in ancient Greece to refer to exotic and/or suspect religious practices. It was derived from the Persian word *magus*, which referred to a priest within Zoroastrianism, the religion of pre-Islamic Persia. As such, it reflected a very early form of Orientalism, by appropriating a term from a foreign and "exotic" culture to the east to refer to any religious practice one regarded as strange and exotic.

When the Roman empire became Christian, the word *magic* was used by Christians to refer to *all* pagan practices, even those traditionally practiced by the ethnic groups of the Roman Empire. By using a derogatory term to refer to the various polytheistic religions of the ancient world, their priests and priestesses, and their practices, Christians created a contrast between those practices, which they deemed false, and their own practices, which they considered to be true and legitimate. As Christianity became increasingly institutionalized, it established formalized procedures for its religious practices, including but not limited to the celebration of church services on Sundays. Within the Western (Catholic) church, these formalized procedures came to be known as *rites* (from the Latin *ritus*). The word *ritual*, which literally means "pertaining to the rites," is derived from this term. By the end of the Middle Ages, it had been ingrained in Western consciousness that the Catholic Church had a monopoly on authorized rituals like the Mass; the religious practices of pagans or anyone acting outside of the authority of the Church were simply magic.

It is important to realize, however, that the distinction between ritual and magic that was thus created was more rhetorical than substantive. After all, what really is the difference between magic and ritual? In both cases, a person who has specialized knowledge manipulates specific substances with hand gestures and verbal formulas to transform them. In the Catholic Mass, the priest uses hand gestures and specific words to transform the bread and wine into the body and blood of Christ. How is this not magic? The difference lies in our attitude towards it. Catholics, of course, would be scandalized to hear that the priest is performing magic, and non-Catholics tend not to refer to the Mass as magic because they grant it a certain degree of legitimacy (even if they don't believe in it) as religious. But this attitude was fostered by the history of Christianity. Just as much as Catholic ritual can be considered magic, so too can magic be considered ritual. *Magic* is just a nasty word that Christians used over many centuries to delegitimize the rituals of non-Christian ("pagan") priests and priestesses as Christianity spread across Europe in late antiquity and the early Middle Ages.

During the Reformation, the Protestant Reformers took this logic a step further and condemned Catholic ritual as well. As we saw in chapter 12, Protestant Reformers after Luther increasingly came to deemphasize ritual, especially the ritual of the Mass, because of their doctrine of justification by faith alone. Just as earlier Christians had rejected the rituals of non-Christian polytheists, so too did the Reformers reject the rituals of the Catholic Church. This led to the attitude we see among modern people today: general disdain for ritual, but a certain grudging tolerance so long as it is done within some "legitimate" religious context. Anything else is considered ridiculous (i.e., magic). The disdain for ritual is a legacy of Protestantism, the grudging tolerance of it in religion is a legacy of Catholicism, and the utter contempt for magic is a legacy of the destruction of European polytheism by Christianity.

The Protestant rejection of Catholic ritual created a problem, however. Protestants offered a nonritual means to attain salvation, but how do you get things done in the world? Modern science emerged to fill this void. Contrary to popular belief, the early modern scientists and scientific thinkers of Europe were not antireligious or opposed to Christianity; indeed, in many cases they were deeply motivated by their belief in God. They wanted to understand *how* God's will works in his creation.

For complex theological and philosophical reasons that we need not get into here,[4] the paradigm that emerged was of a homogeneous world filled with discrete and separate bodies whose motion and interaction with one another is governed by predictable laws of causality. The task of science then became to ascertain what sorts of bodies exist in the universe and the rules of causality that govern their motion and interaction with one another. Scientists harness this knowledge to accomplish real things in the real world: building buildings, roads, and bridges; developing powerful weapons; curing diseases; and so forth. All these technological marvels are made possible by the elaborate rules developed by scientists to describe the causal processes governing fundamental bodies (organs, cells, molecules, atoms, and subatomic particles) in the universe. Indeed, these rules are far more elaborate than those of even the most elaborate magic spell or religious ritual, requiring ever-more specialized technical expertise. The fundamental worldview governing the development of these rules might have changed, but as with magic and religious ritual before it, science still consists of "performing a series of actions in a prescribed way so as to accomplish some goal."[5]

Even though modern science had its origins in theological concerns around the time of the Reformation, in time it came to be seen by many[6] as completely autonomous of religion. Instead of understanding the causal interaction between physical bodies as the manifestation of God's will in his creation, one could simply remove God from the picture entirely and understand the universe as existing and operating autonomously of any first cause. In the nineteenth century, the emergence of a science autonomous of religion fed into early anthropologists' evolutionary theories about humanity. In chapter 10, we learned about Edward Tylor, whose theory of animism was that there was a fundamental intellectual error at the heart of religion that science had rectified. The implication was that so-called primitive people were primitive not only because they lacked cities (i.e., were "uncivilized") but because they had not transcended this supposed intellectual error, which Tylor imagined Western culture had transcended through science.

Not long after Tylor published his work, another anthropologist, James Frazer, codified this implied theory of cultural evolution with his own theory, which stated that human beings have evolved from primitive magic to modern science, with religion as an intermediate stage. Interestingly, this theory of a three-step evolution—from magic to religion to science—objectifies the very three terms that I have been arguing in this section are relics of a long history of Christian rhetoric. The Catholic Church in the Middle Ages disparaged pagan practices as magic. During the Reformation, Protestants disparaged Catholic rituals as *themselves* magical, and this led to the modern devaluation of ritual. Frazer took these terms, which were originally just ways of disparaging one's rivals, as objective realities. As a result, many people in the modern world do as well. The public consensus is that magic is nonsense, religion (which preferably has as little ritual as possible) is respectable as long as you keep it to yourself, and science constitutes true knowledge.

Unfortunately, this way of looking at the world has been disastrous for indigenous traditions. As I pointed out at the beginning of chapter 10, most of the commonly identified world religions lie in a narrow geographical band from Europe to East Asia. We saw that this is in part because of the perceived similarity between traditions that historically have family relationships with one another, but also because colonialism created a racist hierarchy that regarded the indigenous peoples of much of the world, especially outside this zone, as uncivilized and primitive. Anthropologists beginning with Edward Tylor created the concept of animism to label the amorphous mass of religious practices among these "primitive" peoples. The category of animism served a dual purpose. On the one hand, it allowed for the study of indigenous cultures as part of the study of religion, primarily in service of evolutionary theories of religion that saw religion in general as emerging out of primitive animism. On the other hand, it served to distance the cultures of indigenous peoples from the world religions. Within the threefold scheme of magic-religion-science, animism smacked of magic, and thus the traditions of so-called animists rarely inspired Western scholars to elevate them to the level of world religions. This led to a vicious cycle: The more a particular indigenous people was perceived as primitive, the more its traditions were perceived as animistic or magical and therefore unworthy of being taken seriously as a world religion. And the more the traditions of an indigenous people were not taken seriously as a world religion, the more they were perceived as primitive and therefore justifiably subject to colonial policies of genocide, both cultural and literal.

SO WHAT IS RELIGION, ANYWAY?

I began this book by asking you to define *religion*, to show you that doing so is extremely difficult, if not impossible. By now, I hope that I have thoroughly confused your previous understanding of what religion is. The fundamental problem is that we take religion for granted; we assume that religions are things that exist in the world out there, like rocks or trees. But that's not what religion is at all. Religion is not a word for objective things in the world; it is a cultural artifact, and increasingly a powerful ideology. By a series of historical accidents, a particular Latin word became a big deal in European civilization and inextricably tied up with Christianity—an ideological system that inherited the relatively small cult of a national god, the God of Israel, and took it global, having world-historical implications for other cultures in the process.

At first, Christianity's import was mostly limited to the Mediterranean and, a bit later, northern Europe, wiping out the various polytheistic cults in that fairly limited corner of the world. But colonialism gave Europe a theretofore unheard-of power over the entire planet, spreading the concept of religion, tied up as it was with Christianity, to every human culture. As it happened, Christianity itself was at the same time going through a major transformation, and the debates within Christianity unleashed by the Reformation echoed throughout the newly global conceptual sphere of religion.

The ramifications of this globalization have been profound. *Religion* has become universalized, with aspects of nearly every human culture being suddenly subsumed under it. I have asked you to think of the word *religion* as being like a pair of glasses that lead you to see the world in a certain way. But these glasses are magic[7] glasses: They don't just affect the way the wearer sees the world; they cause things in the real world to morph in conformity with the image the lenses produce. So, all of the Orientalist anxieties and fantasies projected onto religions that I detailed in this chapter are not just fantasies; increasingly they are causing real changes within the practice of the religions themselves.

In the end, you might say, "Who cares?" After all, times change; why shouldn't religions change with them? But religions are not simply things out there that change with the times. Rather, the world's religions have, in a sense, been brought into being in recent times. Naturally, the raw material of these religions is old and traditional to each of the cultures they belong to, but they have been brought into being *as religions* to conform to a Western model, which in turn dictates the changes taking place within them. Religion and religions are the locus of an ongoing colonial project, in which Western norms wield hegemonic power over the entire world. And ironically, because the Western concept of religion is so tied up with Christianity, *Christian* norms hold a hegemonic power over the entire world, even in the absence of actual Christians to police them!

Hindus feel pressure to represent themselves as monotheists and to apologize for or minimize image worship, not so much because Christians are telling them that they are heathens or idolaters, but because modernity, itself a legacy of Christianity, programs people in such a way as to make them see polytheism and the worship of images as ridiculous or superstitious. Cultures around the world, including but by no means limited to Islamic cultures, are grappling with setting up boundaries between private religion and the public sphere not because such a division is natural, but because the idiosyncratic theology of a sixteenth century Christian monk has gained unprecedented hegemonic power and made it seem like it is. Once-obscure texts such as the *Daode Jing* are gaining new life as the arbiters of what is correct in the newly minted religions, often at the expense of centuries of tradition, simply because they have been deemed the original scripture of the religion in question.

Practices deemed to be at best rituals and at worst magic are increasingly looked down upon as obsolete because modernity is the product of a Western/Christian theological process that has used these words to define, judge, and malign rival practices and ultimately practice as such. Instead, religions increasingly must define themselves in intellectual terms, in terms of what they believe. Thus, we find, for example, the modernist portrayal of Buddhism as a philosophy rather than a religion, not only in the West, but increasingly in traditional Buddhist cultures in Asia as well.

And finally, the worldviews and social structures of the world's religions are forced to adapt themselves under the full weight of concepts of democracy, freedom, egalitarianism, feminism, and rationality that are rooted in the theological assumptions of the Reformation and have become constitutive of modernity. Depending on which way the Orientalism blows, this can play out in different ways: Islam is maligned for its oppression of women, while Buddhism's history of patriarchy, sexism, and inegalitarian hierarchy is frequently ignored.

To be clear, I am not saying that all the changes being wrought by the modern concept of religion are necessarily bad. As a modern person, I unequivocally support democracy and equality. Secularism is the best system we have so far for maintaining religious harmony, and it is unquestionably preferable to the imposition of a rigid religious ideology on an entire society. I think public policy should be supported by science rather than special corporate interests or reactionary religious anxieties. The world we live in is irreducibly modern, and to a certain extent we must accept that regardless of where modernity came from.

Nevertheless, I think we should have some humility about this process we call modernity. First, what is being lost in this process? How is secularism changing cultures around the world? What are its contradictions, and how are they playing out on the ground? What aspects of traditional cultures are being cast aside because science and the modern disdain for ritual and magic have deemed them obsolete or, worse, ridiculous? Do they make sense on their own terms? Do they not have value? In what ways are the world's religions being cheapened by their need to fit the hegemonic mold of what a religion is supposed to be like?

Second, why do *Western* norms dictate the changes that are happening in the world today? And why do the theological concerns of Christianity, and in particular Protestant Christianity, dictate what happens to what we now call religions—and in fact the very structure of social life—all around the world? Is that fair? And how uncanny is it that many people—perhaps you are among them—who would swear up and down that they are not Christian, that they are not even religious, think in ways largely determined by Protestant Christian theology and unwittingly impose that theology on the world at large? We modern people like to think of ourselves as so enlightened, as so tolerant, as so progressive, as the protectors of the oppressed around the world, but the fact remains that colonialism, the Reformation, and the Christian mission to convert the world continue apace—*and we are their agents.*

DISCUSSION

Rather than several discrete questions for this chapter, I recommend one large discussion project. Create a table of three columns. In the first column, list each of the chapters from Part II of the book (or those that you studied in your class). Many of these will correspond to discrete religions, but others will correspond to regions or themes in the study of religion. The second column should be labelled "stereotype vs. reality." In this column, you should try to identify what major stereotype, misunderstanding, or misperception of religion we learned about in that chapter and how it contrasts with the reality. The third column should be labelled "Christian assumptions." In this column, you should use what you have learned from this chapter to identify what Christian assumptions lead to the stereotype/misperception you have identified for the chapter corresponding to each row. As a reminder, the ten Christian assumptions we identified in this chapter are (1) monotheism, (2) an emphasis on orthodoxy, (3) universalism, (4) an emphasis on belief, (5) an emphasis on scripture, (6) an emphasis on origins, (7) disdain for ritual, (8) mutual exclusivity, (9) iconoclasm, and (10) an emphasis on the individual. (The first three come from Christianity in general; the other seven come more specifically from Protestant Christianity.) There may be many ways to fill out this third column, which will be productive for discussion. In filling out column two, you may also consider exploring stereotypes and misperceptions that you are aware of from pop culture that go beyond those discussed in this book.

NOTES

1 The astute observer will note that of the five major European colonial powers, three were Catholic countries (Portugal, Spain, and France), while only two were Protestant (Britain and the Netherlands). Why then would Protestant Christianity have had an outsized influence on the modern concept of religion? It is important not to have an overly simplistic understanding of how colonialism led to the modern concept of religion. It was not simply the case that colonizers went out into the world, observed various cultures, and then created a concept of religion in their own image (Catholic or Protestant). Rather, reports from the colonies informed intellectual discourse in Europe (and the Western world in general), and it was within this intellectual discourse that the modern concept of religion was formed. Due to the Enlightenment, Western intellectual discourse had become autonomous of the Church, but insofar as the Enlightenment was made possible by the Reformation, it was heavily inflected by Protestant assumptions and norms. Thus, scholars in the three intellectual powerhouses of Europe in the nineteenth century—Great Britain, France, and Germany—were all influenced by Protestant ways of thinking about religion, regardless of their personal religious background.

2 In this book, I have focused on a particular *type* of Orientalism (either overtly negative or superficially positive) that I think is particularly relevant to the popular perception of each religion in the world today. Please note, however, that *every* religion has historically been, and to a certain extent still is, the object of *both* overtly negative *and* superficially positive Orientalism. Antisemitism, for example, has a patronizingly pro-Jewish counterpart known as philosemitism. Popular perceptions of Islam today are often Islamophoboic (i.e., overtly negative), but Orientalism has also created exotified pictures of Islamic culture, often focusing on harems, belly dancers, and hookahs. Hinduism is often ridiculed in popular culture for its supposed polytheism, but it is also exotified as being more "spiritual" than the "materialistic" West, as being a source of yoga and meditation, and so forth. And although exotified portraits of Buddhism and Daoism are prevalent today, there have historically been quite overtly negative portrayals of both—of Buddhism as atheistic, corrupt, or fanciful with its elaborate cosmologies; of Daoism as involving necromancy and superstition. Indeed, it is important to call out Orientalist exotification just as much as its overtly negative counterpart because often such exotification belies an underlying contempt for certain realities of the tradition in question.

3 My own insight into this historical perspective is indebted to an important article by the anthropologist Talal Asad: "Toward a Genealogy of the Concept of Ritual," in *Genealogies of Religion: Discipline and Reasons of Power in Christianity and Islam* (Baltimore: The Johns Hopkins University Press, 1993), 55–79.

4 For details, see Michael Allen Gillespie, *The Theological Origins of Modernity* (Chicago: University of Chicago Press, 2008).

5 You might object that the difference between science, on the one hand, and magic and ritual, on the other, is that science *actually* accomplishes its goals, while the other two do not. But this is only true if you apply science's standards to the other two. By the standards of modern science, magic and ritual do not accomplish anything. But by their own standards, the things we call magic and ritual are indeed efficacious. Their standards of proof are simply not accepted by modern science.

6 But certainly not all. Not only do many nonscientists continue to embrace religion even while enjoying the fruits of scientific endeavor; many *scientists* themselves are religious and believe in God. There are, to be sure, militant atheists in the scientific community, perhaps most famous among them being Richard Dawkins, who see religion as completely outmoded and dangerous insofar as it (supposedly) impedes scientific progress, but other scientists, surely more true to the example of Sir Isaac Newton, Copernicus, and other early scientists, see no contradiction between their practice of science and belief in God. In keeping with the spirit of an increasingly secularizing modernity, however, these latter scientists keep their religious beliefs to themselves and engage in a scientific discourse that (for the most part) simply does not refer to God one way or the other.

7 A reviewer suggested that I change my word choice here because of the irony it creates when juxtaposed with my earlier discussion of the word *magic* in this chapter. I've decided to keep it because it expresses exactly what I want to say, and although the irony was unintended when I first wrote these words—in fact, *because* the irony was unintended when I first wrote these words—I think it perfectly exemplifies how language deeply structures the way all of us see the world. Even scholars like me who think deeply about such things are not exempt from this!

14

Christianity

Does It Look Different with the Glasses Off?

We've had a lot to say about Christianity in this book. We saw in chapter 1 that the very concept of religion is tied up with the history of the West and therefore Christianity. I've compared the word *religion* to a pair of Christian-tinted glasses that affects the way we perceive all the things we call religions in the modern world. We learned in chapter 12 about a particularly influential form of Christianity, Protestantism, and in chapter 13, we saw how Christian assumptions, and in particular *Protestant* Christian assumptions, have led to various misperceptions about each of the major world religions we learned about in Part II.

So far, however, we haven't had occasion to talk about Christianity in the same way as the other major world religions we have studied. We've had a lot to say about how Christianity is built into the structure of the glasses of religion, but we haven't said anything yet about Christianity apart from the glasses. We've seen how taking off these glasses helps us to see the other major world religions more clearly. But what does Christianity *itself* look like if we take the Christian-tinted glasses off?

I already hinted at an answer to this question in chapter 12 when I said that we needed to learn about Protestant theology because certain types of Christianity have historically had more hegemonic power than others. The tint of the glasses of religion does not actually come from Christianity *per se*. Christianity, as we will see in this chapter, is simply too diverse for that to be possible. Rather, the Christian tint comes from specific Christian *norms*—not the norms of all Christians, which again have been quite diverse—but rather those that have historically been the most influential.

DOI: 10.4324/9781032646428-17

There is a common narrative about the history of Christianity that is both constitutive of the Christian tint of the glasses of religion and the product of viewing Christianity through those glasses. Jesus was an itinerant Jewish preacher in the early first century CE who was executed by the Roman governor Pontius Pilate for potentially seditious behavior as a purported messiah. His followers claimed to see him raised from the dead and expressed hope that he would return soon to establish the kingdom of God on earth. Apostles, or "messengers," spread this "good news," first to other Jews and then to Gentiles (non-Jews) around the Roman Empire. The most important of these was Paul, who saw it as his special mission to convert Gentiles. For centuries, the early Christians, as they were called, were forced to meet and worship secretly because they were persecuted by the Roman authorities. Martyrs, of whom Paul was an early example, preferred death rather than renouncing their faith in Jesus Christ.

This situation all changed in the early fourth century when the emperor Constantine converted to Christianity. Constantine called a council of Church leaders at Nicaea, which defined Christian orthodoxy ("right teaching") as based on the theology of the Trinity—one God in three persons (the Father, Son, and Holy Spirit). The empire rapidly Christianized, and even after the fall of Rome and the western half of the empire in the fifth century, Christian missionaries spread the faith north throughout Europe. The Christian world organized itself into a system of districts known as dioceses that were each led by a bishop, but disagreements about the relative eminence of the bishops eventually led to a schism in the Church in 1054. The patriarch of Constantinople, the capital of the still surviving Eastern Roman Empire (Byzantine Empire), refused to recognize the supremacy of the pope, the bishop of Rome. The result of the split was the Roman Catholic Church, consisting of western dioceses who paid allegiance to the pope, and the Eastern Orthodox Church, consisting of eastern dioceses who recognized the preeminence of the patriarch of Constantinople.

In the sixteenth century, a revolt took place in the Roman Catholic Church that was known as the Protestant Reformation. A series of reformers, beginning with the German monk and theologian Martin Luther, rejected the authority of the pope and the traditions of the Catholic Church, arguing that they had strayed from the Word of God as expressed in the Bible. The values of the Reformation, as we saw in chapter 12, led inadvertently, over the course of the centuries that followed, to mass literacy, the Enlightenment, the Scientific Revolution, democracy, secularism, and—as I have been arguing in this book—to the modern concept of religion.

This narrative is not exactly wrong, but by focusing on the most powerful and influential people and ideas in the course of Christian history, it can make it look like Christianity is a monolithic entity that only acts in certain ways and not in others. In fact, Christians at all points of history have been incredibly diverse, and for each of the Christian assumptions that we worked with in chapter 13, there are numerous counterexamples. It turns out that the Christian-tinted glasses distort our view not only of *non-Christian* religions, but also of *Christianity itself*.

How can this be? Shouldn't an object that is red look exactly the same when viewed through red-tinted glasses? Yes, in theory, but keep in mind that even the color red comes in many shades and varieties. Only the shade or variety of red that is found in the lenses themselves will be left unchanged when viewed through the glasses. Christianity is no different. It comes in many varieties, but these differences are effaced when viewed through the glasses of the modern concept of religion. That is because the modern concept of religion is based on the most dominant Christian narrative—one that is European rather than Asian or African, based in Tridentine orthodoxy as opposed to any "heresy," Western as opposed to Eastern, Protestant as opposed to Catholic, and ultimately committed to a faith in rational modern progress.

In this chapter, I'm going to give a broad sketch of the variety of Christianities throughout history by retelling the history of Christianity with an emphasis on how the dominant voices emerged from much more variegated landscapes. Another way of thinking about this is to say that, as we learned in chapter 1, yes, Christians are obsessed with orthodoxy, but they are obsessed with it precisely because they so rarely have agreed on what Christian orthodoxy is. It is impossible to cover every aspect of Christian history in a small chapter, so I will focus on three broad themes within it: Christian origins, the imperialization of Christianity, and the spread of Christianity in modernity. I will then close with a reflection on the academic discipline introduced by this book, Religious Studies, and how its core methodology is related to the traditional practice of Christian theology.

THE ORIGINS OF CHRISTIANITY

One thing that you probably know about Christianity whether you have any personal connection to it or not is this: Christianity is centered on a man named Jesus, whom most Christians worship as God incarnate ("in the flesh"). Jesus was a Jew who lived in the first century CE in a region known as the Galilee, which is the northernmost part of modern-day

Israel. We do not know much about Jesus' life. The best historical sources for his life are four short texts written in Greek, which are known in English as *Gospels* and form the first part of the New Testament of the Christian Bible.[1] These Gospels unfortunately have two shortcomings as historical documents. The first is that they were not written by eyewitnesses; they were written several decades after Jesus' death by followers who appear not to have known Jesus in person. As such, they have irreconcilable differences between them, sometimes in small details, and other times in quite significant ways.[2] The second shortcoming is that, for the most part, they tell us only about the last one to three years of Jesus' life.[3] And within that one to three years, the bulk of the focus is on the very last week of Jesus' life, during which Jesus entered Jerusalem; was arrested; was executed by crucifixion; and, according to Christians, then rose from the dead. This particular focus of the Gospels tells us a lot about what early Christians saw as significant about Jesus' life but little about his life as a whole.

Since the eighteenth century, countless scholars have been obsessed with trying to reconstruct the life of the "historical Jesus." The basic premise behind this quest has been to get past the many centuries of accumulated Christian dogma to figure out what the actual human being Jesus was like. Not surprisingly, there have been as many reconstructions of the historical Jesus as there have been people doing the reconstructing. To this day, there is not much consensus about what Jesus really said or did. The brief account I offer here follows some of the most commonly accepted themes about Jesus' life and avoids reading too much of our modern concerns into the very different situation that was found in first century Galilee and Judea.

As noted above, Jesus was Jewish. Judaism in the first century was quite diverse. While united by a belief in one God, there were several Jewish sects that differed over questions of belief, practice, and how to deal with the Romans. In addition, there were several loosely affiliated millenarian figures, prophets who proclaimed an imminent intervention by God in human events. Jews had by this time been ruled over by Gentiles (non-Jews) for several hundred years, with only a brief period of independence under the Hasmoneans. Since this seemed incongruent with the omnipotence of the Jewish God, the idea had arisen that God would send a king or *messiah* (Hebrew for "anointed," since the kings of Israel had been anointed with oil rather than crowned) to defeat the pagan powers, redeem Israel, and establish God's rule directly on Earth. In the early first century, there was a prophet named John who lived in the wilderness and urged people to repent of their sins and purify themselves in preparation for the coming of the kingdom of God on Earth. His signature practice was ritually bathing ("baptizing") people in the Jordan Riven to purify them of their sins.[4] Two of the Gospels state that Jesus was baptized in the river Jordan by John, with the other two obliquely implying the same event.[5] It thus appears that Jesus was drawn to John's message and then became an apocalyptic prophet in his own right.

It is difficult to know what exactly Jesus' message was because all our sources were written by Christians who had developed different understandings of who Jesus was after his death. Almost certainly Jesus proclaimed the imminent arrival of the kingdom of God on Earth. It is not clear whether Jesus considered himself to be the promised Messiah, but it is likely that enthusiasm among people in Jerusalem that he might be the Messiah led to his execution by the Romans. In any case, the Christian authors of all our documentary evidence of Jesus' life understood him to be the Messiah. It is for this reason that Jesus is referred to as Jesus Christ. *Christ* is not a name but rather a title. It is a Greek word that means "anointed," and thus is a translation of the Hebrew word *messiah*. All the books of the Christian New Testament were written in Greek,[6] and thus it became common to refer to Jesus as Christ, from which the religion of Christianity gets its name as well.

All four Gospels agree that in the week before he died, Jesus and his followers entered Jerusalem to celebrate the Jewish feast of Passover, which celebrates the liberation of the Israelites from slavery in Egypt. On Thursday night of that week, the temple guards arrested Jesus, apparently with the collaboration of one of Jesus' disciples, named Judas. They then handed Jesus over to the Roman governor, Pontius Pilate, who had him executed by crucifixion on Friday. The charge that, according to the Gospels, was posted on his cross was "Jesus of Nazareth, King of the Jews." This would seem to imply that Jesus was executed as a potentially seditious figure, presumably because of messianic claims that were being made about him.

This might have been the end of Jesus—another failed messiah forgotten to history—had it not been for the fact that many of his followers then claimed to have seen him risen from the dead. The accounts of these encounters with the risen Christ are quite varied. Nevertheless, the belief arose early on that Jesus rose from the dead "on the third day, in accordance with the scriptures"—that is, the Jewish scriptures. Counting Friday, the day Jesus died, as the first, the third day is Sunday. It is for this reason that Easter, the celebration of Jesus' resurrection, is always celebrated on a Sunday; for the same reason, most Christians hold their church services once a week on Sunday.

Many scholars would agree that the most important person to the history of Christianity after Jesus himself was a contemporary of his named

Figure 14.1 A mosaic bearing the image of Jesus in the dome of the Church of the Holy Sepulcher in Jerusalem. This church marks the spots where Jesus is believed by Christians, since at least the time of Constantine, to have been crucified and buried. Photo by the author.

Paul. Paul was a Jew who did not live in the land of Israel but rather came from Tarsus in what is now Turkey. Paul was a cosmopolitan man who was able to write in Greek and who traveled throughout much of the eastern half of the Roman Empire. Paul never knew Jesus personally. By his own account, he was a fierce opponent of the fledgling community that grew among those who claimed to have seen Jesus risen from the dead in Jerusalem after Jesus' death. This completely changed, however, when Paul *himself* had a vision of Jesus risen from the dead. Paul was converted: He came to believe that Jesus indeed *was* the Messiah, that he was alive, and that he would return soon in power and glory to establish God's kingdom on Earth. Moreover, he believed that Jesus had given him a mission to spread the gospel, the "good news" of his imminent return to establish the kingdom of God. For this reason, Paul is known as an *apostle*, a Greek word that means "emissary." There were many apostles in early Christianity, since those who had visions of the risen Jesus Christ felt they were thus chosen to spread the "good news" to others. We know this because Paul himself refers to other apostles and sometimes complains about them—indicating that even the earliest missionaries of the Christian message did not speak with one voice.

We know more about Paul than we know about any other person in the first century Christian movement, including Jesus, because the Christian New Testament preserves at least seven texts that were written by Paul himself. Paul travelled all around the Mediterranean, establishing churches (assemblies of the Christian faithful) in various cities. To keep in contact with the Christian communities he founded or was in contact with, he wrote them letters. These letters, and letters written by others, were preserved by early Christians and came to be revered as authoritative scripture. In his letters, Paul has a lot to say about Jesus Christ as the risen Lord, but very little to say about what Jesus said and did before he died. In fact, given that Paul never knew Jesus personally, it is unclear how much he actually knew about what Jesus did or said. What was important to Paul was that God had really raised Jesus from the dead. For Paul, this proved that Jesus truly was the Messiah and that the coming of the kingdom of God was imminent.

According to Paul, Jesus' death on the cross was a salvific act. Humanity had entered a sinful state due to the disobedience of Adam at the beginning of humanity. This explained why the world was under the dominion of demonic powers. God then sent his Son, Jesus, as the Messiah to redeem humanity. Jesus' death was not a failure, as it might appear in the eyes of the world, but rather the first step in the salvation of humanity. God sacrificed his Son in place of all of humanity, to redeem people from their sins. Since sin brings about death, this redemption allows the possibility, for all of humanity, of eternal life. Jesus' own resurrection was the precursor of a more general resurrection to come. When Jesus returned—an event Paul seemed to think would come quite soon—there would be a final judgment of the living and the dead. Those who had faith in God would be given eternal life. Paul focused his missionary activity on Gentiles (non-Jews), and he saw the turning of Gentiles to worship of the one true God as a key component of the end times that would culminate with Jesus' return and the establishment of the kingdom of God on earth.

Paul was executed in Rome before having a chance to see the return of Jesus Christ. Nevertheless, Paul's ideas about the nature of Jesus Christ, his role in history, and his future return (although this last point is often deemphasized in practice), laid the foundation for the basic theology that most Christians adhere to even today. Indeed, Paul's influence was so profound that we have little knowledge of the diversity of viewpoints in the first-century Christian movement except indirectly through Paul's references to them and their possible influence on later Christian authors. Why Paul of all the early apostles was so influential—why his letters were preserved and why they were seen as authoritative by such a wide variety of later Christians—is unclear. One reason may be that the center of the early Church's power structure in Jerusalem, originally led by Jesus' brother James—an authority that Paul himself recognized—was irrevocably disrupted when the Romans razed Jerusalem in 70 CE. This would have shifted the balance of influence in the early Christian world from a Jewish center to the sort of Gentile communities that Paul catered to. But another reason was probably that Paul was simply an impactful figure within the early Christian movement—both through his personal missionary activity across the eastern Mediterranean and through his penchant for letter-writing, which allowed his voice to be preserved for posterity.

THE IMPERIALIZATION OF CHRISTIANITY

One of the most common motifs of the story of Christianity is that, during its first three centuries, it spread underground, through networks of downtrodden converts throughout the Roman Empire who had to worship in secret because of harsh persecution by the Roman authorities. This narrative, while based on the real situation of Christianity before the fourth century, is misleading. Christians were persecuted from time to time by Roman authorities during the first three centuries of the Common Era, but these persecutions were sporadic and unsystematic. The worst and most systematic persecution of Christians, the so-called Great Persecution, actually came quite late, starting in the year 303 when Diocletian and his co-emperors issued edicts against Christianity. But even this persecution was enforced unevenly around the empire, and it was brought fully to an end with the Edict of Milan in 313, issued by Constantine (himself a new convert to Christianity) and his co-emperor Licinius.

In many ways, Christianity flourished even prior to Constantine's conversion and the Edict of Milan. Christianity, as it spread in the Roman Empire, did not enter a completely hostile "polytheistic" vacuum. As far back as the fourth and fifth centuries BCE, the classical Greek philosophers Plato and Aristotle had already been speculating about a single God behind the multiplicity of gods worshiped by ancient peoples. By the time Christianity arose in the first century CE, the Jewish philosopher Philo of Alexandria was promoting the compatibility of Judaism with Greek philosophy, and a significant number of Gentiles took an interest in the God of Israel without necessarily giving up their "pagan" customs. Beginning in the second century CE, several learned Christians, known retrospectively as the Church Fathers, took up Philo's mantle to write philosophically informed texts about the nature of God from a Christian perspective. By the third century, the Christian Church—or rather Churches, as they were not united by a central authority—had accumulated significant property and developed a hierarchical clergy with bishops (from Greek *episkopos*, "overseer"), priests (from Greek *presbyter*, "elder"), and deacons (from Greek *diakonos*, "servant"). Indeed, it was Christianity's very success and visibility that motivated the Great Persecution at the beginning of the fourth century.

When the emperor Constantine became a Christian and ended the Great Persecution, he inherited not a single Church but a vast, variegated movement that had many competing teachings about the Christian message. For example, the second-century Christian Valentinus taught that the Jewish scriptures should be read allegorically, and on that basis he argued that Jesus' Father was an ultimate, immaterial being who was distinct from the creator of the material universe, a lower being who created the world by mistake. Jesus, according to Valentinus, taught the knowledge (Greek *gnosis*) necessary to transcend the material world and dwell with God in immaterial form. Another second century teacher, Marcion, rejected the Jewish scriptures altogether, saying that the god they spoke of was an evil, vengeful being who created the material world and was completely distinct from the good God revealed by Jesus.[7] In the third century, a Persian visionary named Mani drew upon Zoroastrianism, Buddhism, and the teachings of Marcion to preach a Christian message in which light/goodness and darkness/evil are locked in a cosmic battle, with particles of light entrapped in dark matter. Following the model of the Buddhist *sangha*, he organized his community into two tiers, with a celibate and vegetarian elite called the "elect" supported by laity known as "hearers."

Of course, many Christian teachers of the second and third centuries saw the Jewish scriptures as authoritative and Jesus as the Son of God—the same God who created the world in the book of Genesis. They did not necessarily have full agreement about the nature of Jesus' relationship to God the Father. A particularly significant dispute on this point erupted at around the same time as Constantine converted to Christianity in the early fourth century. A priest in Alexandria named Arius got into an argument with his bishop, Alexander, because Arius held that Jesus, though divine, was subordinate to and contingent upon God the Father, while Alexander held that the Father, the Son (Jesus), and the Holy Spirit were united and coeval. In 324, Constantine sent another bishop, Ossius, to settle the dispute, and Ossius sided with Alexander against Arius. Realizing that disputes like this were widespread throughout the empire, in 325 Constantine convened a council of bishops in the city of

Nicaea in what is now Turkey. This council adopted an early version of the Nicene Creed, as we learned about in chapter 1, which defined the Trinity, one God who manifests in three distinct "persons": the Father, the Son, and the Holy Spirit. This Trinitarian theology became the basis for an imperially defined Christian orthodoxy, which, as we learned, means "right teaching."

Imperial efforts to create, maintain, and enforce a single catholic (universal) Church based on orthodoxy continued long after Constantine's reign. In 380, the emperor Theodosius, together with his co-emperors, issued the Edict of Thessalonica, which stated that only those who followed orthodoxy as defined by the Council of Nicaea could be considered catholic Christians. All others were considered crazy and were branded heretics.[8] In 393, a meeting of bishops at the Council of Hippo established a canon—a list of authoritative books to be included in what we now call the Bible. This canon was distinctive in two respects. First it included the Hebrew Scriptures in a so-called Old Testament, thus reflecting the orthodox position, contra Marcion, that "the Father" as spoken of by Jesus was the same God as that of the Jews. Second, it defined a New Testament of twenty-seven books, including four Gospels, twenty-one letters, the Acts of the Apostles, and the Book of Revelation. This construction of the New Testament was significant because, prior to that time, Christians had recourse to hundreds, if not thousands, of early Christian texts, including many Gospels beyond the four known to Christians today, to support their views. The act of creating a closed canon—a set list of books—enabled Church leaders to limit authoritative reference to only those books they saw as supporting an orthodox position.

Imperial efforts to create a universal Church based on right teaching, though influential for the future development of Christianity, were never fully successful, for several reasons. First, pre-Christian religion was not simply snuffed out overnight. Rather, Christian identity gained cultural cachet under imperial patronage and the increased visibility and largesse of Church institutions. As is often the case with cultural novelties, Christianity gained traction first in cities and only more slowly in the countryside. The word *pagan*, which in Western culture has long referred to non-Christian polytheists, comes from the Latin word *paganus*, which was used in late antiquity to refer derisively to unsophisticated country dwellers—something akin to "country bumpkin."

Second, political developments made centralized imperial control of the Church across the Mediterranean basin increasingly impossible. When Theodosius died in 395, his sons split the empire into a western and an eastern half. The eastern half, with its capital in Constantinople, survived for another millennium, until Constantinople was conquered by the Ottoman Turks in 1453. The western half, however, lasted for less than a century, until 476, when the Germanic warlord Odoacer (who himself was an "unorthodox" Arian Christian) deposed the last Roman emperor, Romulus Augustulus. Although the Eastern Roman Empire (often referred to in modern histories as the *Byzantine* Empire, after the original name of the city on which Constantinople was founded) did make some attempts to regain western territories that had been lost, these were short-lived, and it never regained the full territorial extent of the Roman Empire at its height. Indeed, during the Arab conquest of the seventh century, it lost many of its eastern lands in North Africa and the Levant.

Third, although the emperor in Constantinople continued to have political control over his eastern territories and a certain amount of influence through Church networks to the west as well, efforts to find or forge unity among the Church's elites, its bishops, always fell short because orthodoxy itself was a moving target. In 431, the Council of Ephesus addressed a dispute between Nestorius, patriarch of Constantinople, and Cyril, patriarch of Alexandria, over the relationship between Christ's human and divine natures. The council ruled that Nestorius's position was heresy, but dissenters from the council's decision survive to this day as the Church of the East. Likewise, the Council of Chalcedon in 451, which sought to further clarify the decision of the Council of Ephesus, created more dissenters, which survive to this day as the Oriental Orthodox Churches, which include the Syriac Orthodox Church, the Coptic Orthodox Church, the Armenian Orthodox Church, the Ethiopian Orthodox Tewahedo Church, the Eritrean Orthodox Tewahedo Church, and the Indian Orthodox Church. Although neither the Church of the East nor the Oriental Orthodox Churches became as large as other Christian branches, many of their adherents comprised a significant portion of the Christian minorities who lived under Islamic rule from the seventh century on.

Even within the "orthodox" Church as defined after the Council of Chalcedon, unity remained precarious. This was because Christianity had an old, hierarchical structure of clergy led by bishops, but no central authority. In the sixth century, the emperor Justinian tried to codify a higher leadership among bishops by referring to the bishops of Rome, Constantinople, Antioch, Jerusalem, and Alexandria as *patriarchs*. This concept of *pentarchy* (literally "five leaders") did not meet with universal acceptance, however, and even in theory it was subject to rivalry among the five patriarchs. The rivalry between the bishops of Rome and Constantinople was particularly significant, especially after the Arab conquests reduced

Christian communities in the other three cities to minority status. Their rivalry led to the Great Schism in 1054. In that year, a delegation sent by the bishop of Rome (by then known as the "pope") to Constantinople demanded that the patriarch of Constantinople submit to his authority. When the patriarch refused, they excommunicated him—that is, they declared him to no longer be in communion with the Church. In retaliation, the patriarch of Constantinople excommunicated them. This led to a series of breaches between the Western and Eastern Churches that have never healed to this day and resulted in two major branches of Christianity in Europe: the Roman Catholic Church and the Eastern Orthodox Churches.

Although the official split between the Roman Catholic and Eastern Orthodox Churches did not take place until the eleventh century, it ratified a cultural split that had long existed in European Christianity. When the peoples of Northern Europe were Christianized in late antiquity and the Middle Ages, some were Christianized by missionaries from Western dioceses that looked to the Roman pope as preeminent. This included Britain and Ireland, the various Germanic peoples of mainland Europe and Scandinavia, and the Poles. Others were Christianized by missionaries from the Byzantine empire who looked to the patriarch of Constantinople as preeminent. This included various Slavic peoples in Eastern Europe, most importantly the Russians. These two groups of missionaries introduced two different manners of worship. The Western missionaries introduced the Roman rite, which was based on the style of church services in Rome and was conducted in Latin. The Eastern missionaries introduced the Byzantine rite, which was based on the style of church services in Constantinople. The Byzantine rite was originally written in Greek, but it was translated into Slavic languages during the missionary process. After the Great Schism brought finality to the East-West Split, the Western (Roman Catholic) Church grew in a more centralizing direction, with the pope emerging as the supreme authority above all bishops in his Church. The Eastern Orthodox Churches, conversely, maintained, as they do to this day, a more traditional structure in which autonomous Churches that are in communion with one another look to the patriarch of Constantinople as a "first among equals" rather than a direct leader.

THE SPREAD OF CHRISTIANITY IN MODERNITY

The Western Church that emerged from the Great Schism served as the seedbed for most of the vast expansion of Christianity in the modern era and as the cultural matrix that informs most global forms of Christianity today. The reasons for this, however, are a matter of historical accident. When new European technologies made global colonial ventures possible beginning in the fifteenth century, the countries that became colonial powers—Portugal, Spain, the Netherlands, France, and England—all had easy access to the Atlantic and were therefore within the cultural sphere of the Western Church. Meanwhile, the seat of the patriarch of Constantinople had been conquered by Muslims, the Ottoman Turks, in 1453. The only Eastern Orthodox country that was able to spread its form of Christianity over a large territory in the modern period was Russia, but it did so mostly through land-based imperialism across sparsely inhabited territories in Siberia and Central Asia.

It is important to recognize, however, that although the Western Church inherited the mantle of imperializing Christianity, it never effectively established the long-sought unity of Theodosius' catholic (universal) ideal. This was true long before the Reformation shattered any pretense of unity in the sixteenth century. Even before the fall of Rome in the fifth century, there was a large disconnect between the elite ideals of bishops and popular Christian practice. In ancient times popular enthusiasm for the martyrs—Christians who had died during the era of persecution—was often exuberant and at odds with bishops' ideas of proper Christian piety. Church elites sought to channel these popular practices into the cult of the saints—exemplary Christian men and women—and eventually the Roman Catholic Church would centralize decision-making power over who counts as a saint under the authority of the pope.

Likewise, in late antiquity a significant number of people demonstrated their Christian piety through various forms of asceticism—religious self-discipline—which involved such practices as celibacy, fasting, voluntary poverty, itinerancy, and seclusion from society. As such practices tended to attract popular attention to charismatic figures outside of the official Church hierarchy, there were early elite efforts to institutionalize and regulate ascetic practice. This involved establishing settled communities, known as monasteries, that were gender-segregated and governed by a community rule. The most important monastic reformer for Western Christianity was Benedict of Nursia, who established several monasteries in central Italy and wrote a series of regulations for them to follow, known as the *Rule of St. Benedict*, that became a template for monastic practice in Western Christianity thereafter.

Even in its institutionalized form, monasticism served as a powerful engine for Christian diversity in the Middle Ages. As monasteries became larger and richer, they drew criticism, which led to the establishment of new monastic orders by charismatic leaders, such as Dominic de Guzmán and Francis of Assisi. Both men, who were later recognized as saints by the Catholic Church, founded mendicant orders (the Dominicans and the Franciscans, respectively) in the early thirteenth century that, at least in theory, returned to an earlier ascetic model of itineracy. Even when given the blessing of the pope, however, the dynamism of the monastic orders and the example provided by their asceticism threatened the authority of secular[9] clergy—the old hierarchy of deacons, priests, and bishops that was led in the Western Church by the pope. In an effort, in part, to imitate the ascetic charisma of the monastic orders, as well as to maintain the dignity of the secular clergy in the eyes of the laity, papal directives increasingly sought to regulate the behavior of ordained priests, in particular by enjoining universal celibacy in the priesthood during the first few centuries of the second millennium. Prior to this time, clerical celibacy, while often held up as an ideal, was not universal; to this day, priests within the Eastern Orthodox Churches (which were unaffected by Western papal reforms) can be married.

Monasticism, however, represented only one facet of diversity within Christianity in the Middle Ages, one that was relatively controlled through institutionalization and (in the West) by the legitimizing authority of the pope. There were many other reform movements and popular practices that did *not* receive the blessing of local bishops or the pope and therefore were branded heresies. One of the most significant of these groups was the Cathars, who flourished in southern France and northern Italy in the twelfth to fourteenth centuries. They were loosely organized around charismatic ascetic teachers and had eclectic beliefs that often harkened back to the ideas found in pre-Nicene Christianity, such as that the creator of the world described in the Old Testament was a bad god in distinction to the good God of the New Testament. To root out beliefs, practices, and organized movements that it deemed heretical, the Catholic Church developed an organized set of procedures and personnel known as the Inquisition. Clerical and monastic agents of the Inquisition would interrogate people suspected of heresy to determine their guilt and then hand them over to secular authorities of the local monarch for punishment, which included the infamous practice of burning at the stake.

Efforts by the Roman Catholic Church to root out perceived heresy and impose papally authorized orthodoxy were never fully successful and failed spectacularly in the sixteenth century with the Protestant Reformation. In chapter 12, we learned about Martin Luther, whose writings and actions served as its catalyst, but the Reformation as a whole was a much broader revolution in Western Christianity that both reflected and contributed to changes in Western Europe that historians typically point to as marking the emergence of the modern era. During the early Middle Ages, Western Europe had been a cultural backwater, with the focus of cosmopolitan culture and patronage of elite learning having shifted east to the Byzantine and Islamic Empires. However, during the eleventh to thirteenth centuries, the Crusades—military efforts spearheaded by Roman popes to retake the Holy Land around Jerusalem from Muslims—brought Western Europeans into closer contact with cultures to the east. Many texts from classical antiquity had been better preserved in Byzantine and Islamic lands, and their rediscovery and translation into Latin by Western scholars led to an intellectual revival in the West that in turn sparked a cultural movement known as the Renaissance in the fifteenth and sixteenth centuries.

The Reformation shared with the broader Renaissance a perception that a certain wisdom from classical antiquity had been lost during the Middle Ages. For the Reformers, however, this wisdom was contained not in secular texts of philosophy and science that had been preserved in faraway Eastern lands; rather, it was found in the books of the Bible, which had never been lost to Western scholars but had been hidden away (according to the Reformers) in Latin and behind the traditions of the Catholic Church. As we saw in chapter 12, Martin Luther was not the first person to challenge Church-sanctioned orthodoxy, but by a fortuitous set of circumstances, he managed to stake a position outside of the normal bounds of Church cooption (monastic reform and sainthood) while also avoiding the fate enjoyed by other radicals: execution as a heretic. Pivotal to Luther's success in this regard was protection from a political leader, Frederick the elector of Saxony. Indeed, as the Reformation progressed, the desire of various kings and princes throughout Western Europe to assert independence from the pope and greater control over their local clergy was just as important as the ideas and charisma of the Reformers themselves.

Martin Luther's theological ideas, which became influential over Protestantism as a whole through the principles of *sola scriptura*, *sola fide*, and *sola gratia*, were rooted in the old imperialistic Christian concept of orthodoxy, even while Luther claimed that that orthodoxy was being misrepresented rather than defended by the Roman Catholic Church. If we look past the rhetoric of the Reformers to the practical consequences of their actions, however, a different picture emerges. The Reformation did not restore a lost orthodoxy; rather, it reacted against the centralizing tendencies of the late medieval Catholic Church to reassert what had always been characteristic of Christianity: its fundamental diversity and lack of consensus. The new branch of Christianity that emerged from the Reformation, Protestantism, simply provided a new channel for the inherent lack of consensus among Christians that the Catholic Church, in the imperial Christian tradition, had been attempting to dam up through enforcement of orthodoxy.

This tendency was already apparent within the lifetime of Martin Luther himself. He became embroiled in bitter arguments with other Reformers whose ideas conflicted not only with the teachings of the Catholic Church but also with his own understanding of the clear meaning of scripture. The German cleric Thomas Müntzer, for example, took Luther's ideas in a radical direction to argue for a revolt by ordinary Christians not only against corrupt Church authority but also against corrupt secular authorities. This led, in 1524 and 1525, to a widespread uprising of German peasants against their feudal overlords known as the German Peasants' War. Luther sided with the aristocrats and argued vociferously for the use of violence against the peasants. In the end, close to 100,000 rebels, including Thomas Müntzer, were killed.

A more theological feud that Luther had in his lifetime was with Ulrich Zwingli, a Reformer in Zürich, Switzerland. Zwingli rejected the Catholic teaching of transubstantiation, which holds that the ritual of the Mass transforms bread and wine into the literal body and blood of Christ. The idea that communion is nothing more than a commemorative meal would become widely influential in later Protestantism, but Luther held to a position, closer to that of the Catholic Church, that the words of Jesus at the last supper ("This is my body") must be taken literally as indicating his presence in the bread and wine. Theological differences between Protestants more closely aligned with Luther and those more closely aligned with Zwingli led to an early split between Lutheran and Reformed branches of the Protestant movement.[10]

John Calvin, a French lawyer who became a theocratic leader of the Swiss city of Geneva, was the most influential Reformer of the Reformed branch and the second most influential Reformer of the entire Reformation after Luther himself. His *Institutes of Christian Religion*, published in 1536, provided a detailed exposition of Reformed Protestant theology that built upon but also went beyond the principles articulated by Luther. In particular, Calvin would become known for his adherence to a strong form of predestination—the idea that God has already decided and predestined before all time which human beings will be saved and which will be damned, leaving little or no room for human free will. This teaching would have a deep influence on Protestant piety for centuries that followed. In 1904, Max Weber, one of the founding figures of modern sociology, argued that Calvinist culture played a role in the rise of modern capitalism. He supported this conclusion with data showing correlations between Calvinist societies and a higher rate of capitalist

Figure 14.2 A bishop in Brazil elevates a chalice of wine during a Roman Catholic Mass. The Catholic teaching that the ritual of the Mass transforms the bread and wine of communion into the literal body and blood of Christ became a major point of contention during the Reformation in what led to a progressive devaluation of ritual in the modern world. © Shutterstock

development, and he argued that it was due to Calvinists' ethic of austerity, which, combined with anxiety over whether they were saved, led them to throw themselves into their work in the hope that worldly success would serve as a sign that they had been chosen by God for salvation.

The spread of Protestant ideas, and the decisions of various kings, clerics, and ordinary Christians over which side to take over the course of the sixteenth century, led to a major destabilization of the medieval social order in Western Europe. The Thirty Years' War, fought from 1618 to 1648, was driven in large part by conflicts between Catholics and Protestants in the German-speaking Holy Roman Empire, with external kingdoms intervening as well. It was the bloodiest conflict in European history prior to the Napoleonic wars. The Peace of Westphalia that ended the war established that rulers within the Holy Roman Empire could choose between Catholicism, Lutheranism, and Reformed (Calvinist) Christianity, but their subjects would also have freedom to worship differently.

The Thirty Years' War and Peace of Westphalia were but a harbinger of how the Reformation would continue to play out. Various monarchs in Western Europe attempted, on a national scale, to carry forward the unifying mission of imperial Christianity within their chosen Church, but they inevitably faced dissent among their subjects from Protestants (in the case of Catholic monarchs), Protestants of a different or more radical persuasion (in the case of Protestant monarchs), or even Catholics (in the case again of Protestant monarchs).

This phenomenon was particularly prevalent in England, which had established its own independent national Church in 1534 in the wake of conflicts between King Henry VIII and the pope. The Church of England faced dissenters from both sides—Catholics who maintained allegiance to Rome and Protestants who felt that the national Church was not sufficiently reformed and therefore too "Catholic." Many of these dissenting religious groups, in an effort to escape persecution at home, settled in the English colonies in North America, especially in New England and the Mid-Atlantic. The resulting religious diversity of the thirteen colonies that broke away from England in the American Revolution led the framers of the US Constitution to create a full separation of Church and State, setting the template, as we saw in chapter 11, for modern secularism.

The settlement of the United States by Christians of an ever-proliferating number of different denominations was but an example of a broader global phenomenon: the massive expansion of Christianity, or rather Christianities, under colonialism. To a certain extent, this expansion took place under the logic of the old imperializing ethos, especially within the early colonial empires of Catholic Portugal and Spain. But as Christianity continued to spread globally during the colonial period, its spread came to reflect the inherently creative diversity of Christianity as a whole. In part, this was due to competition between different colonial powers, some Catholic and some Protestant, and their associated missionaries. Even within the Catholic colonies of Latin America, however, the interaction with indigenous and African religious traditions led, as we saw in chapter 10, to new ways of interpreting, engaging with, and expressing Catholic traditions. Moreover, near the end of the colonial period, in the late nineteenth and early twentieth centuries, missionaries from a variety of Protestant denominations found fertile ground for spreading their various versions of the Christian gospel in colonies around the world, especially those that were part of the British Empire.

The globalized Christianity that has emerged in the postcolonial period manifests quite vividly the diversity of thought and expression that was always present in Christianity from its earliest centuries but suppressed by the imperializing mission to centralize and unify the Church that began in the fourth century and continued in various forms for well over a millennium. Roman Catholicism is now the largest single Christian denomination, accounting for approximately half of the worldwide Christian population. It is, therefore, more global and, in a sense, more universal (catholic) than it ever pretended to be during the Middle Ages. But the truly global extent of the Catholic Church today is also fueling significant changes within it. The old European core of the Catholic Church that informs many of its traditions is now a minority within it, and the regions where Catholicism spread during colonialism, while providing much of its dynamism, also provide challenges to the imperializing ethos of the Catholic Church through the diversity of local expressions of Catholicism they represent, as well as through local competition with Protestants and other non-Christian religions.

At the same time, the increasing global embrace of modern secularism has allowed for the dynamic growth of many non-Catholic forms of Christianity, including the full gamut of Protestant denominations and new forms of Christianity that are difficult to categorize. The United States, as the country with the oldest system of fully secular government, has been a particular hotbed for Christian innovation. A wide variety of Protestant denominations with their roots in Europe are well represented in the United States, but much of the dynamism within American Protestantism today is among nondenominational churches and non- or interdenominational movements. Examples include the Evangelical movement, which emphasizes spreading Christianity through conversion (the concept of being "born again" in Christ), and the Pentecostal movement, which emphasizes the reception of special gifts of the Holy Spirit, such as speaking in tongues, that are referred to in the Bible but had fallen out of practice in mainstream Christianity.

Another significant movement within American Christianity has been Restorationism, which refers to a loose array of new Churches that claim to represent the original essence of Christianity that has been corrupted not only by the Catholic Church but by all existing Churches. The largest and most influential new Church to emerge from this movement is the Church of Jesus Christ of Latter-Day Saints (LDS Church), more commonly known to outsiders as Mormonism. It was founded in 1830 by the charismatic prophet Joseph Smith, who claimed to have discovered a set of golden plates that he then "translated" into the Book of Mormon, which his followers regard as scripture alongside the Bible. The Mormons split into different groups after Joseph Smith was murdered by a mob in Illinois in 1844, but the majority followed the leadership of Brigham Young and settled in Utah, where the mainstream LDS Church now has its headquarters. Mormonism developed several theological innovations that rethink some of the basic orthodox positions of post-Nicene Christianity, such as the Trinity. Its global missionary efforts have made the LDS Church a rapidly growing new form of Christianity.

The end of colonialism and global spread of secular norms has brought Christian innovation to the entire postcolonial world. Evangelical Christianity is attracting large numbers of converts in the traditionally Catholic countries of Latin America. Likewise, as Christianity is becoming well established and even traditional among many populations in the Americas, Africa, and Asia, new Christian denominations and movements are emerging that speak to local concerns and incorporate local forms of religious expression. The imperializing ethos of medieval European Christianity may have motivated, in part, the colonialism that enabled Christianity's global spread, but the result has been a reassertion of Christian diversity on a truly global scale.

THE RELATIONSHIP BETWEEN RELIGIOUS STUDIES AND CHRISTIAN THEOLOGY

We have now come full circle. I began this book by asking, "What is Religion?" and I suggested that the best way to answer to question is to recognize that religion is not simply something out there in the world. It is a way of seeing the world, like a pair of glasses. Because the concept of religion comes from the West, which has historically been dominated by Christianity, these are Christian-tinted glasses. They distort our view of the things we call religions by filtering them through a set of Christian assumptions. In Part II, we explored different world religions to see the contrast between popular misconceptions about them—a result of the Christian-tinted glasses—and the reality of how they are practiced. Then, in chapters 12 and 13, we saw how specific Christian assumptions, and in particular *Protestant* Christian assumptions, have led to the various misconceptions about different world religions.

But what about Christianity itself? Does it look the same when we take the Christian-tinted glasses off? As we have seen in this chapter, the answer is no. The Christian tinting of the glasses of religion does not represent Christianity in its fulness but rather a specific understanding of Christianity, determined by late Roman imperial orthodoxy and modern Protestant theology, that has historically enjoyed the greatest hegemony. Once we take the glasses off, we see that Christianity is anything but a single orthodoxy; it is and has been throughout its history a wide variety of understandings of God, Jesus, the world, and their relevance for human beings' lives.

Christianity: Does It Look Different with the Glasses Off?

In this book, I have introduced you to a specific academic field of study called Religious Studies. From the name, it is obvious that this field of study involves the study of religion, but after reading this book, you may have found the approach to studying religion different from approaches you have seen before. Often, when people think about studying religion, they think of people studying in a seminary or other religious school, often to become a priest, minister, rabbi, imam, or other clergy member. That is, they think of studying religion as a way of *being religious*. But that is not the approach to studying religion we have followed in this book. Instead, we have been studying religion in order to simply *understand* it as an aspect of the world, in the same way that sociologists study society, historians study history, or chemists study matter.

But how do we go about simply understanding religion as an aspect of the world? And how do we do so in such a way that makes it distinct from studying religion to be religious? Every field of academic study has a particular way of engaging in academic inquiry, which is referred to as its *methodology*. What is the methodology of Religious Studies, and how is that methodology distinct from that of *theology*—in other words, studying religion as part of being religious?

It turns out that this is not an easy question to answer, in part because Religious Studies has a historical connection to Christian theology. The concept of theology—literally, the "study of God"—goes back to Plato, and it was included within ancient Greek and Roman lists of the "liberal arts," fields of study suitable for free men. Medieval Christians included specifically *Christian* theology within the liberal arts, and thus Christian theology was enshrined as an academic field of study as the Western academy developed over the centuries after the founding of the first European universities in the eleventh century. In the wake of the Enlightenment and the Scientific Revolution, Western academic inquiry expanded greatly, with most modern academic fields being established by the end of the nineteenth century. This resulted in the now familiar grouping of the liberal arts into four branches: the fine arts, the humanities, the social sciences, and the natural sciences. Theology was categorized under the humanities.

The late nineteenth and early-to-mid twentieth centuries saw the progressive opening of academic inquiry to all people, regardless of gender or class. In part, this was accomplished by the founding of state-funded universities. Public universities, as well as the system of secularism in general, posed a problem for the place of theology within the academy. Insofar as theology is the study of religion from a particular religious perspective (historically, in the West, a form of Christianity), it cannot be considered secular. This posed a particular problem in the United States, whose Constitution mandates a separation between Church and State. Throughout the history of the United States, the Supreme Court has routinely been called on to rule on this separation, including, at times, as it pertains to public schools. One particularly significant decision in this regard was *Abington School District v. Schempp*, made in 1963. The major purport of this decision was to declare school-sponsored Bible readings and prayers in public schools unconstitutional. But it also made clear that teaching about religion "objectively" as a part of secular education was not prohibited.

Religious Studies as a secular field of inquiry was emerging at around the same time as the Schempp decision. It responded in part to the needs of secular education but also to the practical academic desire to understand religion objectively as a significant part of the human world. In 1963, the same year as the Schempp decision, the National Association of Bible Instructors changed its name to the American Academy of Religion to reflect the need for such a shift, and it is now the largest professional society for the academic study of religion in the world. In a similar reflection of the shift away from pure theology, Religious Studies departments have been established at many public universities, and the methodology of Religious Studies has also become increasingly influential in departments at private universities that historically focused only on Christian theology.

How exactly to distinguish Religious Studies methodologically as a secular field of inquiry from Christian or any other religious theology is a matter of continuing debate among scholars. But a common way of articulating this methodology is as follows. Theology takes a *normative* or *prescriptive* approach to studying religion. That is, its goal is to articulate what people *should* do or believe, from a particular religious perspective. It is so called because it prescribes behavior and beliefs; it sets norms. Religious Studies, by contrast, takes a *descriptive* approach. It *describes* what religious people do and believe—in their fullness and variety—without taking a stand as to whether any particular belief or practice is "correct." If someone says that they identify with a particular religion, and they believe or act in a certain way, then Religious Studies sees them as important to describing that religion—even if other members of that religion reject those people, their beliefs, or their practices.

Considering what we have learned in this chapter, the methodology of Religious Studies can be understood as taking the Christian concept of orthodoxy and turning it on its head. Throughout Christian history, many Christians have understood there to be only one correct Christian teaching, which needed to be determined by the proper authority and enforced to maintain unity in the Church. Any deviations from this orthodoxy were heresy. But as we saw in this chapter, if we look at Christianity as a broad human phenomenon, there has been little consensus as to what it should mean to be a Christian. To see this, however, we need to stop asking the question of what Christianity is supposed to be and instead simply describe what self-identifying Christians believe and do. This is what taking the glasses off looks like.

In fact, the whole metaphor of religion as glasses that I have been using throughout this book is simply a way of dramatizing what the Religious Studies methodology of taking a descriptive rather than a normative approach to studying religion looks like. Avoiding a normative approach is easier said than done. You cannot simply say, "I will study religions objectively without following the norms of my own religious perspective," and expect to have a fully descriptive approach. That is because the very concept of religion has a history that has baked assumptions within it, many taken from the most hegemonic conceptions of Christian orthodoxy. As I have been arguing in this book, all of us in the modern world, regardless of our particular religious background, if any, are already influenced by these assumptions, even if subconsciously.

I should make clear that nothing about the methodology of Religious Studies should be construed to mean that there is something wrong with making normative judgments or with being religious. If you identify with a particular religion, you will certainly make and adhere to judgments about what a member of that religion should do or believe. And whether you are religious or not, you will certainly make normative judgments as an ordinary part of life. Normative judgments have a place—an important place—in being a human being in a society. A person who does not ever make a judgment as to what people should or should not do is a sociopath.

That said, the opposite of a sociopathic lack of a moral compass is equally problematic. If we constantly rush to judgment, then our judgments have no meaning. We need to be able to step back and view a particular issue dispassionately to come to a meaningful conclusion about what one should do or not do. This is precisely the advantage of Religious Studies methodology with respect to religion. We can understand religion better as a human phenomenon if we set aside normative judgments about religion long enough to describe what religious people actually think and do. Understanding religions in their fulness then enables us to make better normative judgments, whether from a particular religious perspective or simply as a human being. We all see the world through religion. But understanding that we do so, as well as how and why, enables us to see the world, and make judgments about it, more clearly.

DISCUSSION QUESTIONS

1. Who was Jesus? What were the historical circumstances in which he lived? What did he teach? How/why did he die?
2. What was the significance of the apostle Paul for the early spread of Christianity?
3. What are the major branches of Christianity? What disagreements led to the splits between them, and when did those splits occur?
4. Take a close look at the full text of the Nicene Creed on p. 21. The bulk of it (the first three paragraphs) deals with the Trinity, a central concept within Christian theology. Who are the three persons of the Trinity? How do they relate to one another? What do Trinitarian Christians believe about the nature of God and the nature of Jesus Christ?
5. What is Religious Studies, and how is it distinct from theology? Explain the methodological distinction between normative and descriptive approaches to studying religion.

NOTES

1 A great deal of Christian literature, including many more than four Gospels, was written in the first few centuries CE. However, modern scholars consider the four Gospels that were made canonical, all written in the late first century to early second century CE, to be among the oldest Gospel texts.
2 The Gospels of Mark, Matthew, and Luke are similar to one another. For this reason, scholars refer to them as the *Synoptic* Gospels, which means that they can be "looked at together." Nevertheless, there are small irreconcilable differences between them. The leading scholarly theory is that Mark was written first, then Matthew and Luke independently wrote their Gospels using Mark as a source, adding material from another (now lost) source that modern scholars refer to as "Q." The fourth Gospel, the Gospel of John, is radically different from the other three and cannot be easily reconciled with them.
3 All four Gospels purport to recount Jesus' preaching career from his encounter with John the Baptist to his death, but they differ on how long it lasted. In the Synoptic Gospels, it appears to have lasted only one year, while in John, it appears to have lasted three. In addition, Luke and Matthew begin their Gospels with a short account of Jesus' birth. These two accounts do not agree with one another, but they are often synthesized by Christians into a single narrative that incorporates the major elements of both.
4 Because of the prominence of Jesus' baptism in the Gospel narratives, later Christians adopted baptism as a rite of initiation. In fully

Christianized societies, baptism became a beginning of life ritual, performed on newborns, and for practical reasons full immersion in water was replaced with a simple ritual of pouring water over the forehead. During the Protestant Reformation, the Anabaptist movement argued that baptism is only valid if the person in question is old enough to choose it freely. Certain Christian groups today therefore have revived adult baptism and full-immersion baptism.

5 Luke (3:21) states that Jesus was baptized in the Jordan, but it illogically says this after saying that John had been put in prison. John (1:29–34) says that Jesus went to John while he was baptizing in the Jordan, but it does not specifically say that John baptized him. It is likely that early Christian authors were reluctant to portray Jesus as in any way subordinate to another figure.

6 Prior to Roman rule, the land of Israel had been conquered by Alexander the Great and thus entered a Hellenistic (Greek-speaking) cultural sphere. Greek remained the lingua franca of the eastern Mediterranean even under the Roman Empire.

7 Although Marcion's version of Christianity would later be rejected by imperial authorities, he played a significant role in the history of Christianity by proposing the first list of authoritative Christian scriptures, which consisted of a Gospel and ten of Paul's (real and supposed) letters.

8 The English word *heresy* comes from a Greek word that means "choice." The implication is that various deviations from orthodoxy come from human choices rather than divine truth.

9 In the Roman Catholic Church, there is a distinction between secular clergy and the religious. *Secular clergy* refers to ordained ministers (deacons, priests, and bishops) who are not members of a religious order. *Religious* refers to a member of a religious order, who may or may not be an ordained member of the clergy. This distinction reflects the predominant meaning of the word *religious* in the Middle Ages, which was to refer to the intense practices of people in monastic orders, as distinct from the ordinary practices of most Christians.

10 There are some peculiarities of nomenclature in English about the Reformation that can be confusing. The entire movement that led to the split of Protestants from the Roman Catholic Church is referred to as the Reformation, and the major figures within it, including Martin Luther, are referred to as the Reformers. However, there was an early split in Protestantism between Lutheran and Reformed branches. In this sense, Luther was one of the Reformers of the Reformation, but he was not part of the Reformed branch of Protestantism that emerged from it.

For Further Reading

CHAPTER 1. WHAT IS RELIGION?

Miles, Jack. *Religion As We Know It: An Origin Story*. Norton, 2019.
Pals, Daniel L. *Ten Theories of Religion*. Oxford University Press, 2021.

CHAPTER 2. COLONIALISM AND THE TWO FACES OF ORIENTALISM

King, Richard. *Orientalism and Religion: Postcolonial Theory, India and the 'Mystic East.'* Routledge, 2013.
Said, Edward. *Orientalism*. Vintage, 2014.

CHAPTER 3. ISLAM: DOES FEAR IMPLY DIFFERENCE?

Esposito, John. *Islam: The Straight Path*. Oxford University Press, 2016.

CHAPTER 4. BUDDHISM: A PHILOSOPHY OR A RELIGION?

Gethin, Rupert. *The Foundations of Buddhism*. Oxford University Press, 1998.
Lopez, Donald. *The Scientific Buddha: His Short and Happy Life*. Yale University Press, 2012.
McMahan, David. *The Making of Buddhist Modernism*. Oxford University Press, 2008.
Williams, Paul, with Anthony Tribe. *Buddhist Thought: A Complete Introduction to the Indian Tradition*. Routledge, 2000.

CHAPTER 5. HINDUISM: A POLYTHEISTIC OR A MONOTHEISTIC RELIGION?

Flood, Gavin. *An Introduction to Hinduism*. Cambridge University Press, 1996.

CHAPTER 6. CHINESE RELIGION: WHAT IS IT, AND WHERE CAN WE FIND IT?

Komjathy, Louis. *The Daoist Tradition: An Introduction*. Bloomsbury, 2013.
Thompson, Laurence. *Chinese Religion: An Introduction*. Wadsworth, 1995.
Van Norden, Bryan W. *Introduction to Classical Chinese Philosophy*. Hackett Publishing, 2011.
Yao, Xinzhong. *An Introduction to Confucianism*. Cambridge University Press, 2000.

CHAPTER 7. INDIAN RELIGIONS: HOW CAN ONE RELIGION "INCLUDE" ANOTHER?

Dundas, Paul. *The Jains*. Routledge, 2002.
Singh, Nikky-Guninder Kaur. *Sikhism: An Introduction*. I.B. Tauris, 2011.

CHAPTER 8. TIBETAN BUDDHISM: IS IT STILL BUDDHISM?

Lopez, Donald. *Prisoners of Shangri-la: Tibetan Buddhism and the West*. University of Chicago Press, 2018.
Samuel, Geoffrey. *Introducing Tibetan Buddhism*. Routledge, 2012.
Wedemeyer, Christian. *Making Sense of Tantric Buddhism: History, Semiology, and Transgression in the Indian Traditions*. Columbia University Press, 2014.

CHAPTER 9. JUDAISM: A RELIGION OR AN ETHNICITY?

Batnitsky, Leora. *How Judaism Became a Religion: An Introduction to Modern Jewish Thought*. Princeton University Press, 2011.

Boyarin, Daniel. *Border Lines: The Partition of Judeo-Christianity*. University of Pennsylvania Press, 2006.
Goodman, Martin. *A History of Judaism*. Princeton University Press, 2018.
Smith, Mark. *The Early History of God: Yahweh and Other Deities in Ancient Israel*. Eerdmans, 2002.

CHAPTER 10. INDIGENOUS TRADITIONS: WHAT GETS COUNTED AS A RELIGION?

Bassett, Molly, and Natalie Avalos, eds. *Indigenous Religious Traditions in 5 Minutes*. Equinox, 2022.
Prothero, Stephen. "Yoruba Religion." In *God is Not One: The Eight Rival Religions that Run the World and Why their Differences Matter*. Harper Collins, 2010.
Rambelli, Fabio. "Shintō (Honji Suijaku) and Buddhism." In *Encyclopedia of Buddhism*, ed. Robert Buswell, vol. 2. 767–771. Thomson Gale, 2004.
Wedemeyer, Christian. "Bon." In *Encyclopedia of Buddhism*, ed. Robert Buswell, vol. 1, 66–68. Thomson Gale, 2004.

CHAPTER 11. SECULARISM: CAN WE PUT RELIGION IN A BOX?

Asad, Talal. *Formations of the Secular: Christianity, Islam, Modernity*. Stanford University Press, 2003.
Asad, Talal. *Secular Translations: Nation-State, Modern Self, and Calculative Reason*. Columbia University Press, 2018.
Mahmood, Saba. *Religious Difference in a Secular Age: A Minority Report*. Princeton University Press, 2016.

CHAPTER 12. YOU ARE MARTIN LUTHER

Cameron, Euan. *The European Reformation*. Oxford University Press, 2012.

CHAPTER 13. HOW THE GLASSES WORK

Cameron, Euan. *Enchanted Europe: Superstition, Reason, & Religion, 1250–1750*. Oxford University Press, 2010.

Masuzawa, Tomoko. *The Invention of World Religions: Or, How European Universalism Was Preserved in the Language of Pluralism*. University of Chicago Press, 2012.

CHAPTER 14. CHRISTIANITY: DOES IT LOOK DIFFERENT WITH THE GLASSES OFF?

Boyarin, Daniel. *The Jewish Gospels: The Story of the Jewish Christ*, New Press, 2012.
Ehrman, Bart. *Jesus: Apocalyptic Prophet for the New Millennium*. Oxford University Press, 1999.
Ehrman, Bart. *The Triumph of Christianity*. Simon and Schuster, 2018.
Fredriksen, Paula. *Jesus of Nazareth, King of the Jews: A Jewish Life and the Emergence of Christianity*. Vintage, 2012.
Fredriksen, Paula. *Paul: The Pagan's Apostle*. Yale University Press, 2017.
Fredriksen, Paula. *Ancient Christianities: The First Five Hundred Years*. Princeton University Press, 2024.

Index

969 Movement 219

Abbasids 53
abortion 211–212, 215
Abraham 57–58, 61, 168, 252
Abrahamic religions 56, 58, 61–62, 172, 199; in contrast to Hinduism 97, 99–101, 128, 145, 254
Acts of the Apostles 278
Adam 22, 58, 167, 243, 275
adhan 54–55
afterlife 4, 7, 23
Agni 95, 129
ahimsa 131, 133
Akbar 141
al-Andalus 179–180
alchemy 120–121, 256
Alexander the Great 130, 171, 174
Allah 57, 146
Altan Khan 158
"Amazing Grace" 243–244
American Academy of Religion 290
Amitabha 78, 119, 152
Analects 106–107, 109–110, 115, 123
anatman 80–81
animism 193, 205–209, 262–263
anthropology 206
Antichrist 59, 240, 242
Antiochus IV 174

antisemitism 13, 34, 44, 145, 166–167, 179–181, 184–188, 252–253
apocalyptic literature 176
apostles 270, 274
Aristotle 100, 208, 276
Arius 277
Arjan, Guru 140–141
Arya Samaj 143
asceticism 70–71, 73, 131, 133, 281–282
Ashkenazis 179–180, 182, 184
Ashoka 72
atheism 4–6, 18, 100
atman 80–81, 130, 135, 144
Aurangzeb 141–142
Australia 31–32, 192, 198–199, 201, 203, 206–207
Avalokiteshvara 78, 118, 152
avatar 90
Awakening 68, 70–73, 77–79, 84; in Chinese religion 119, 124; in comparison to Hinduism 99; in Vajrayana Buddhism 149–150, 153–156
Aztec Empire 30, 201–202, 205

Babalawo 203
Babylonian Empire 171, 173
Balfour Declaration 186
Baltimore, Lord 213
Bangladesh 138, 219
baptism 240, 244

bar Kochba, Simon 177–178
Benedict of Nursia 281
Benin 203
Bethlehem 186
Bhagavad Gita 96–98, 136, 139, 146, 162
bhakti 97, 139–140, 142, 144
Bible 4, 146, 179, 197, 215, 217, 287, 290; account of origins of world and Israel 167–173; and antisemitism 166, 181, 184; Christian expansion of 272, 278; and the concept of scripture 22; and the Enlightenment 182; and the Reformation 14, 234, 238–242, 244–246, 250–251, 256, 258, 270, 283; relationship between Jewish and Christian versions of 12, 47; relationship of Islam to 58, 61–62, 222; relevance for understanding Christianity 161–162; translation into Greek 175
Bill of Rights 213
bishops 4, 161, 234, 237, 245, 270, 277–282
blood libel 181
bodhi 70
bodhichitta 154
Bodhisattva Path 77–78, 117–118, 152
Bön 193, 195, 197–199, 203
Brahma 89–91, 93, 135–137, 139, 223
brahman 135, 144
Brahmans 18, 95–96, 130–131, 135, 139, 221
Brahmo Samaj 143
British Mandate of Palestine 186
Buddha 5, 15, 19–20, 44, 72, 99, 105, 114, 123, 149, 194, 220, 258; in Bön 198; compared to Mahavira 130–131, 134; and kingship 221, 223; in Mahayana Buddhism 72, 77–82, 117–119, 122, 152; meaning of word 68, 150; in Neo-Vedanta 144; special powers of 77; and super-enthronement 134–135, 137, 145; traditional biography of 68–71, 73–76, 150–151, 221; in Vajrayana Buddhism 153–154, 156, 160
Buddhist Modernism 73, 79, 83–85, 124
Burma 33, 72, 160, 216, 219–223, 228
Bush, George W. 66
Byzantine Empire 30, 52, 60, 270, 279–280, 283

California textbook controversy 87, 102
caliphs 52–53
Calvin, John 284
Cambodia 16, 31, 33, 72, 160
Canaan 168–170
Canada 31–32, 201
capitalism 31, 40, 284
Cathars 282
celibacy 64, 96, 131, 151, 281–282
Central Asia 65, 68, 72, 77, 79, 117, 192, 281
Charles V 237
chosen people, Jews as 120, 166, 176, 181, 187, 194
Church Fathers 178, 276
Church of England 213, 286
Church of Jesus Christ of Latter-Day Saints 287–288
Church of the East 279
circumcision 62, 176, 181, 218
clergy 4, 6, 17–18, 63, 105, 277, 282–283, 289
Columbus, Christopher 30, 201
communion 240, 244–245, 280, 284

Confucius 19, 23, 105–106, 123; compared to *Daode Jing* 110–112; his disciples 115, 117; his life and teachings 106–109, 223
conquistadores 30, 201
Conservative Judaism 182
Constantine 11, 224, 270, 276–277
Constantinople 30, 270, 278–281
Constitution of the United States 213, 257, 286, 290
conversios 180
Cortés, Hernán 30, 201
Council of Chalcedon 279
Council of Ephesus 279
Council of Hippo 278
Council of Nicaea 270, 278
Crusades 13, 16, 30, 59, 162
Cyrus the Great 171, 173

Dalai Lama 78, 158–159
Daniel, Book of 171, 176
Dao 18, 107, 109–112, 114, 120–121, 124, 195, 256
Daode Jing 106, 110–115, 119–120, 123–125, 255–256
David, King of Israel 171, 176
Dawkins, Richard 5
definitions of religion 3–4, 7–10, 18, 25, 205, 250
Delhi Sultanate 101, 137–138
democracy 40, 215, 246, 265
descriptive approach to religion 220, 290–291
Devil 240
Dhammacakkappavattana Sutta 73
dharma 15, 71–72, 78–79, 82, 84
dhikr 64
dhimma 180
diaspora 167, 175, 178–179, 186
Digambaras 133
disenchantment 208–209
Dominic de Guzmán 281–282

Dr. Jekyll and Mr. Hyde 43–44, 163, 216, 220
Durga 93–94
Dutch colonialism 15, 31, 200

East India Company: Dutch 33; English/British 33, 143; French 33
Eastern Orthodox Churches 14, 270, 280–281
Edict of Milan 11, 276
Edict of Thessalonica 278
Egypt 168–169, 174–175, 186, 228, 273
Eid al-Adha 57
Eid al-Fitr 56
'El 172–173
emic-etic distinction 207
Enlightenment: European 84, 172, 182, 209, 233, 246, 250, 255, 270, 289; Jewish 182; as synonym for Buddhist Awakening 68, 71, 84
Essenes 175
evangelical 240–241, 245, 287–288
Eve 167
excommunication 237–238
Exodus 167–169, 172, 217
exotic 37–38, 61, 87, 208, 260

fasting 4, 8, 24, 281; and the Buddhist Middle Path 70, 73; in Islam 24, 56; in Jainism 133
fatwa 63, 217, 222
feminism 215, 246, 255
Ferdinand and Isabella 180
filial piety 109, 122, 124
Final Judgment 59, 275
fiqh 62–64, 217
Five Pillars of Islam 53–57
five precepts 150–151, 155
Four Noble Truths 73–76, 79, 83, 114, 117, 150–151
Francis of Assisi 161, 236, 282

Frazer, James 262–263
Frederick III 237
French colonialism 15, 31–33, 201

Gabriel 50
Galilee 178, 271–272
Ganesh 87, 91, 93
Gautama, Siddhartha 68–69, 150; see also Buddha
Gaza Strip 186
Genesis 58, 167–168, 172–173, 277
Gentiles 179, 184, 188, 253, 272, 276; as the focus of Paul's mission 176, 180, 242, 270, 275
German Peasants' War 284
glasses metaphor for religion 17, 25, 43–45, 249, 252, 256, 258, 264; and Christianity 269–271; and Judaism 187; and Protestantism 233; and Religious Studies 288, 291; and secularism 216, 228
Gobind Singh, Guru 141–142
Goddess, in Hinduism 89, 93–94, 98–100, 137, 139, 144, 254
golden calf 169–170
Golden Temple of Amritsar 141
Gospel 161, 272–273, 278; and colonial missionary activity 286; as "good news" 274; of Luke 50; and Luther 245; recognized by Islam 180; and the word *evangelical* 240
Great Persecution 276–277
Great Schism 280
Greeks, ancient 19, 30, 35, 41, 100, 130
Guanyin 78, 118–119
gurdwara 142
Guru Granth 22, 140, 142
Gutenberg printing press 236, 238

hadith 50, 63, 187
Hagar 58
hajj 56–57
halakhah 62, 167, 178, 182, 222
Han Dynasty 107, 116–117, 119, 223
Han Feizi 116
Hanuman 87, 93
Haskalah 182, 186
Hasmoneans 174, 272
heaven 4, 6, 75, 84, 146, 194; in ancient Indian cosmology 95; in the Bible 168; in Buddhist cosmology 76, 135; in Chinese cosmology 110; in Reformation theological debates 234–236, 241–243
Hebrew Scriptures 145, 171–173, 181, 217, 278
hegemony 39–40, 42, 227, 233, 288
hell 4, 12, 75, 84, 97, 194; in Buddhist cosmology 77, 82, 156; in Reformation theological debates 14, 234–235, 239, 243
Hellenism 174–176
Henry VIII 286
heresy 225, 271, 279, 282, 291
Herod the Great 174
hijab 60–62, 216
hijra 51–52
Hindu Renaissance 143
Hindutva 101–102, 138
Hira 50
Hispanification 202
Holocaust 13, 166–167, 185–187
Holy Land 13, 30, 59, 283
Holy Roman Empire 179, 285
Holy Spirit 20, 239, 245, 270, 277, 278, 287
hungry ghost 76
Hus, Jan 236

Iberian Peninsula 52, 60, 179
iconoclasm 56, 139, 251, 254
iftar 56
ihsan 64

Index

imam 54, 289; in Shi'ite Islam 53
impermanence 74–75, 77, 80–81, 153
Inca Empire 30, 201
inclusivism 43, 128–129; of Buddhism toward the gods 134–135; in Christianity and Islam 145; of Hindu sects toward the gods 137, 139; and influence of Islam 142–143; its influence on perennialism 147; in Neo-Vedanta 143–144
individualism 240, 251, 255–256
Indra 95, 129, 134
indulgences 234–238, 240–242
Inquisition 180, 184, 225, 282
Institutes of Christian Religion 284
Isaac 58, 168
Isaiah, Book of 173
Ishmael 58
Islamic Empire 13, 52–53, 59–60, 64–65, 138, 180
Islamophobia 13, 34, 43–44, 49, 59–60, 66, 80, 220, 252–253; and controversy over Shari'a 218; and hate crimes against Sikhs 142; in Hindutva 138
Israel: abstract community 23, 167, 169–170, 176, 194, 264, 272, 276; land of 274; modern nation-state 13, 178, 180, 186–187, 221, 272; name given by God to Jacob 58, 168; northern kingdom 171–174; twelve tribes of 58, 167; united kingdom 170–171

Jacob 58, 168–170, 172
Jahangir 141
Jainism 18–19, 24, 94, 96, 129, 131, 133–134, 144, 192, 195, 199
James, brother of Jesus 276
James, St. 201

Japan 37, 72; as a colonial power 32–33, 159; and Shinto 195–197, 205
Jefferson, Thomas 213, 215, 226
Jerusalem 59, 171–173, 175–178, 186, 272–274, 276, 279, 283
Jesuits 106, 115
Jesus Christ 4–5, 13, 19–20, 22–23, 90, 99, 137, 144, 149, 161, 194, 209, 220–221, 225, 250, 252, 288; early Christian debates about nature of 277, 278; in Islam 53, 58–59, 145, 253; and Judaism 105, 176, 178, 180–181, 253; life of 270–273; and Paul 273–276; in Protestant theology 14, 235, 239, 241–245, 284
jiva 131
John, Elector of Saxony 237
John the Baptist 272–273
Joseph, son of Jacob 168
Joshua 170, 172
Journey to the West 117
Judah 170–174, 186
Judas Maccabee 174
Judea 171, 174, 177–178, 272
Jungle Book 36
junzi 107, 109
Jupiter 10, 95, 129, 178
Justinian 279

Kali 20, 94
kami 196–197
karma 76, 80, 82, 95–97, 130, 133–134, 150
Karmapa 158
Kennedy, John F. 227
Khadija 51, 61
Khalsa 141–142
Kipling, Rudyard 36
Kojiki 197
Korea 32, 72, 197
Krishna 90, 96–97, 136–137, 139, 144

Lakshmi 93
lama 155–156, 158
Laos 31, 33, 72, 160
Laozi 19, 105–106, 110–111, 119–120
Latin 15, 264; as language of Catholic Church 238, 246, 280, 283; used by Jesuits to translate names of Confucian figures 106, 115; words in 10, 20, 34, 146, 200, 206, 224, 240–241, 243, 260, 278
Latin America 32, 201–202, 204, 207, 227, 286, 288
Laws of Manu 223
Legalism 116
Leo X 237
Levant 13, 30, 52, 172, 279
LGBTQ movement 246–247
li 108–109, 223
Li Si 116
Licinius 12, 276
linga 91, 136–137
Luther, Martin 182, 233, 261, 270, 282; his impact on modernity 246–247; his life 234–237; his theology 14, 238–243, 245, 250–251, 283–284
Lutheran Church 104, 234, 237, 251, 284–285

magic 16, 259–265
Mahabharata 90, 96–98, 135–137, 139, 142
Mahavira 19, 130–134
Mahayana 72, 77–82, 117–119, 151–154
Maimonides 179–180, 187
mandala 153
Mani 277
Mao Zedong 5, 159
Marcion 277–278
martyrs 141, 270, 281

Marx, Karl 5
Mary 50, 58, 240–241, 251
Mass, Catholic 62, 238, 244–245, 250, 259, 261, 284
Mecca 24, 50–52, 54–57
Meiji Restoration 197, 205
Mencius 115, 117
Mesopotamia 174
Messiah 13, 105, 171, 253; bar Kochba as 178; Jesus as 58, 99, 176, 181, 242, 270, 272–275
mestizos 201
Mexico 30, 201, 205
Middle Ages 12–13, 16, 66, 120, 208, 224–225, 237–239, 246, 252, 261–262; and Christianity 23, 30, 280–283, 287; and Islam 60, 63, 217; and Judaism 167, 179–181, 185, 187; and Tantra 152, 155
mihrab 54
minbar 54
misogyny 36, 61–62, 66
Mizrahis 180
moksha 131, 133
monasticism: absence and parallels in Islam 54, 64; Bön 198; Buddhist 72, 117, 119, 121, 125, 151, 157–158, 195, 197, 255; Christian 12, 18, 281–283; Jain 133–134
monks 18; Buddhist 24, 71–72, 105, 117, 121–122, 150–151, 153–154, 157–158, 195, 197, 219–220, 223, 255; Christian 64, 236, 238, 241; Jain 133; Martin Luther as 234, 265, 270
monotheism 18, 216; Abrahamic 128; Christian 12, 249, 251, 257; and Hinduism 43, 87–89, 94, 97–102, 138–139, 143–144, 253–254, 264; Islamic 13, 50, 57, 59; Jewish 11, 165, 172–175; Sikh 195

Mormonism *see* Church of Jesus Christ of Latter-Day Saints
Moses 19, 58, 167, 169–170, 172
mosque 54–55, 88, 211
mufti 63, 217
Mughal Empire 101, 137–138, 141–143
Muhammad 13, 19–21, 60, 64, 105, 144–145, 149, 187, 194, 253; his life 49–52, 61, 63; and his succession within Islam 53; in Islamic doctrine 54–58, 99
Müntzer, Thomas 284
murti 139
myth 8, 19–20, 101, 184, 208, 254; in the Bible 167, 172–173; in Bön 198; in Buddhism 78, 117–118, 152; in Daoism 119, 122, 124; in Hinduism 89–91, 99; in Shinto 197

Nakba 186
Nanak, Guru 140, 142
Native American Church 193, 205
Native Americans 205, 215, 227
Nazis 13, 166, 185, 187, 221
Neo-Confucianism 116
Neo-Vedanta 143–145
Nepal 68–69, 72, 150, 155
Nestorius 279
New Age 36, 113, 124, 152
New Testament 57, 181, 242, 272–273, 275, 278, 282
New Zealand 31–32, 201
Newton, John 243
Nicene Creed 20–21, 278
Nigeria 203
Ninety-Five Theses 14, 234
nirvana 4–6, 70–71, 75–79, 115, 117, 150–151, 155, 160, 221
Noah 58, 168
Noble Eightfold Path 75, 115, 117, 123, 150, 194

noble savage 208
normative approach to religion 220, 290–291
North Africa 13, 33, 52, 180, 192, 199, 279
nuns 18; Buddhist 24, 71–72, 105, 117, 121, 150–151, 154, 160; Jain 133

Obama, Barack 34, 243
Oceania 192, 199, 203
Odoacer 279
Old Testament 22, 57–58, 170, 218, 278, 282
oral law 175, 178–179
Oriental Orthodox Churches 279
Orientalism 26, 29, 33, 200, 260; defined by Said 34–42; and exotification of Buddhism 80, 163, 254–255; Jekyll-and-Hyde nature of 43–44, 208, 216, 220, 222, 252, 265
Orientalism 34
orishas 203–204
Orthodox Judaism 182
orthodoxy 13, 20, 22, 214, 239, 249, 251, 253, 270–271, 278–279, 282–284, 287–288, 290–291
orthopraxy 21
Orunmila 203
Ottoman Empire 30, 33, 180, 186, 279, 281

pagan 20, 100, 179, 241, 251, 260–262, 272, 276, 278
Pakistan 138, 140
Papal States 225–226
Papua New Guinea 206
Parvati 91, 93
Passover 169, 181, 273
Patimokkha 151
patriarch of Constantinople 270, 279–281

patriarchy 61, 265
Paul, St. 176, 180–181, 242–243, 270, 274–276
Peace of Westphalia 16, 214, 285
Penn, William 213
pentarchy 279
Pentecost *see* Shavuot
people of the book 60, 101, 180
perennialism 145–147
Persian Empire 13, 52, 60, 171, 173–174
Persian language 94, 137–138, 260
Peter, St. 239
peyote 205, 215
Pharisees 175
Philippines 30, 32
Philo of Alexandria 175, 276
Pilate, Pontius 270, 273
pilgrimage 4, 8, 24, 56
Pilgrims 213
Pizarro, Francisco 30, 201
Plato 100, 276, 289
pogroms 13, 181, 185
polygamy 60–61, 217
polytheism 18, 50–52, 172–173, 252–253, 260–261, 264, 276, 278; and Hinduism 43, 87–89, 94, 99–102, 138, 254
pope 23, 59, 161, 224–227, 281–283; and the Great Schism 14, 270, 280; and the Reformation 234, 236–237, 239–240, 270, 286
Portuguese colonialism 30–32
Prajapati 129, 135, 139
prayer 4, 9, 12, 22, 24; in Buddhism 254–255; in Islam 54–55, 64; in public schools 215, 290
prescriptive approach to religion *see* normative approach to religion
priests 18, 260–261; Brahmans as in Hinduism 95, 134–135, 221; Christian 4, 161, 238, 259, 277, 282; Daoist 105, 120–124, 195, 256
Promised Land 169–170
Prothero, Stephen 146
Protocols of the Elders of Zion 184–185, 187
Ptolemies 174
Punjab 140, 195
Puranas 136–137
Pure Land 78, 118–119, 122–123, 152
Puritans 213

qi 113–114, 120–122, 124, 195
qibla 54
qigong 113, 122
Qin Shi Huang 107, 116
Qing Dynasty 116, 159, 223
Qingming Festival 122
Quakers 213
Qur'an 22, 50–51, 55, 57–58, 60–61, 63, 149, 180

Rabbinic Judaism 167, 170, 178–179, 186
Rama 90, 93, 144
Ramadan 24, 56
Ramakrishna 88, 143–144
Ramayana 90, 93
rebirth 19; in Bön 198; in Buddhism 23, 76–77, 80–81, 120, 124, 150–151, 156, 194, 255; development of concept in early Indian religion 95–96, 130–131, 134–135; in the *Gita* 97, 139; in Jainism 133, 195; *see also* reincarnation
Reconquista 180, 201
Reform Judaism 182
Reformation 14–16, 22–23, 249, 270; and antisemitism 182; history of 233–234, 239, 241, 281–285; legacies of 240, 245–247, 250–252, 255–257, 261–262, 264–266; and secularization 214, 224–225

reincarnation 21, 78, 95, 130, 158, 194–195, 203; *see also* rebirth
religio 10–12, 16
religious death 133
religious nationalism 220–222, 258
Religious Studies 7, 9, 22, 70, 100, 271, 288–291
ren 107–109
Restorationism 287
Revelation, book of 278
ritual 18, 21, 24, 207; in Bön 197; in Buddhism 79, 254; and the Catholic Mass 244, 284; in Confucianism 108–109, 114–115, 223; in the *Daode Jing* 110, 112; in Daoism 120, 122; in Jewish Law 182, 222; Protestant deemphasis of 250–251, 255, 258–263, 265; in Tantra 152, 154–156, 162–163; in Vedic religion 129
Rohingya 216, 219–220, 222, 228
Roman Catholic Church 14, 23, 204, 239, 270, 280–283, 286
Roman Empire 5, 10–13, 16, 65, 116, 128, 167, 175, 179, 225, 242, 260, 270, 274, 276, 279
Romans, Letter to the 242
Rome 6, 10–12, 14, 17, 23, 128–129, 177, 226, 236, 270, 275, 279–281, 286
Romulus Augustulus 279
Roy, Rammohan 143
Russia 184, 280–281

sabbath 167
sacraments 205, 237, 240–241, 244–246
Sadducees 175
sage kings 107–110
Said, Edward 34–35, 39–40
salat 54
samsara 76, 79–80, 82, 95–96, 131, 133–134, 150, 196, 198

Samuel 170
sangha 23–24, 71–72, 79, 150–151, 277
Sanskrit 96, 117, 130, 157; words in 15–16, 70, 80, 91, 93, 95, 98, 135, 139
Sarah 58, 168
Saraswati (goddess) 93
Saraswati, Dayananda 143
Saudi Arabia 50, 65
Saul 170
Savonarola 236
sawm 56
science 36, 41, 246, 255, 257, 259–263, 265, 283, 289; and atheism 6, 18, 209; and Buddhism 76, 84; premodern Chinese 256
Scientific Revolution 246, 255, 270, 289
scripture 4, 6, 8, 17–18, 22, 104–106, 115, 123–124, 160–162, 255–256, 265; in Bön 198; in Buddhism 72–73, 76–77, 79, 81, 117–119, 135, 151, 153–154, 156–158, 220, 258; in Christianity 145, 239–240, 242, 250–251, 255, 273, 275, 277, 284, 287; in Daoism 120; in Hinduism 90, 94, 97–99, 150; in Islam 57–58, 60, 63–64, 180; in Jainism 133; in Judaism 12–13, 23, 170; in Sikhism 140–142
secularism 44, 184, 246–247; Christian roots of 224–228, 251, 257–258, 265, 270, 286–287; defined 212; history and purpose of 213–216; and religious law 219; and religious nationalism 220–222; and Religious Studies 289
Sephardis 179–180
September 11, 2001 216, 218
Septuagint 175
shahada 20, 54, 139

Shaiva 98–99, 137, 152
Shakta 98, 137
shamanism 207
Shari'a 62–64, 216–218, 222
Shavuot 170
Shenchen Luga 198
Shi'ites 52–53, 104
Shinto 9, 15, 193, 195–197, 199, 203, 205
Shiva 20, 89–94, 98, 136–137, 152
Shoah see Holocaust
shramanas 95–97, 130–131, 134, 139
Shuddhodana 69
shunyata 81
Shvetambaras 133
Siberia 207, 281
Sikhism 22–24, 94, 129, 145, 165, 192, 195, 199, 227; history of 140–142
Sinai, Mt. 169–170
Six-Day War 186
Skanda 93
slavery 33, 168, 202–203, 243, 273
Smith, Joseph 287
sola fide 241, 243–244, 250, 283
sola gratia 243–244, 283
sola scriptura 240, 244–246, 250, 283
Solomon 171
Soma 129
soteriology 18, 22–23, 194–195
South Asia 138, 192
Southeast Asia 15–16, 30–32, 65, 72, 192
Spain 13, 30, 32, 179–180, 187, 201, 281, 286
Spinoza 182
St. Peter's Basilica 236, 241
sub-Saharan Africa 65, 192, 199, 202–203
Sufism 64–65, 139
Sukkot 169
Sunnis 52–54, 64, 104
super-enthronement 135–137, 145
sutras, Mahayana 72, 117–118
synagogue 175, 211

Tagore, Debendranath 143
Taiwan 32, 72, 120, 159
Talmud 179, 182
Tanakh 22, 170
Tang Dynasty 116
Tantra 43, 151–156, 162–163
tantras 72, 79, 152–156, 258
Tegh Bahadur, Guru 141
Temple, Jewish 167, 171, 173–175, 177–178
Ten Commandments 169–170, 212
Tenochtitlán 201
Tenzin Gyatso 158; see also Dalai Lama
terrorism 44, 59–60
Tetzel, Johann 236, 241
Thailand 33, 72, 160, 222
Thanksgiving 213
Theodosius I 12, 116, 278, 281
theology: as a branch of ancient Greek philosophy 100; Catholic 234; in distinction to Religious Studies 271, 288–290; general Christian 146, 180, 270, 275, 278; Hindu 137; Islamic 217; Protestant 14, 233, 237–238, 241–244, 254, 265–266, 269, 284
Theravada 72, 79, 151, 160
Thirty Years' War 16, 214, 285
Thor 129
three bodies of the Buddha 78, 82
three jewels 71–72
three patriarchs 58, 168, 172; see also Abraham; Isaac; Jacob
Three Teachings 121–122, 125
three-peaked mountain 122
Tibet 72, 78, 84, 150–163, 197–198, 258–259
Tipitaka 72, 160–161

Titus 177
Togo 203
Tonpa Shenrab 198
Torah 149–150, 167, 172, 178–179, 181, 217; as the basis for Jewish Law 62, 178; composition of and place in the Tanakh 170; and the first-century Jewish sects 175; and Islam 180, 217, 222
transubstantiation 244–245, 284
Trimurti 89–91, 93
Trinity 59, 89, 253, 270, 278, 287
Trisong Detsen 197
tulku 158
Turkey 33, 242, 274, 278
Tylor, Edward 206, 209, 262–263

Umayyads 53, 65
umma 23, 52–53, 56
Unexcelled Yoga Tantras 153, 155–156
Upanishads 130, 135, 144

Vaishnava 98–99, 101, 137, 139, 145
vajra 129
Vajrayana 72, 79, 150–153, 155–156, 160–161, 258–259
Valentinus 277
Vatican 161–162
Vedas 90, 95–97, 129–131, 135–136, 139, 143, 150, 223
Vespasian 177
Vietnam 31, 72
Vishnu 20, 87, 89–91, 93, 97–98, 129, 136–137, 145
Vivekananda 88–89, 144–145
Vulgate 238

Wailing Wall *see* Western Wall
Way of the Celestial Masters 120, 125
Weber, Max 284

West Bank 186
Western Wall 177
Williams, Roger 213
Wirathu 219–220
Wittenberg 234, 237
world religions 16, 29, 31, 84, 144, 146, 178, 203, 208; modern concept of 14, 43–44, 199, 205, 252, 258; religions included 4, 68, 96, 131, 165, 192–195, 206, 263; view of distorted by Christian assumptions 26, 269, 288
World War I 33, 185–186
World War II 32, 39–41, 186
World's Parliament of Religions 87–89, 144
wuwei 111–112, 119, 256

xian 120
Xuanzang 117
Xunzi 115–117

Yahweh 172–173
Yama 129
yin and *yang* 112–114, 121–122, 124, 195, 256
yoga 87, 97, 215
Yoga Tantras 153, 155–156
Yogachara 80–82, 153, 155
Yoruba 193, 203–205
Young, Brigham 287

zakat 56
Zealots 177
Zerubbabel 171
Zeus 10, 95, 129
Zhang Daoling 120
Zhou Dynasty 107, 109, 115, 119, 223
Zhuangzi 111, 119, 124
Zionism 167, 185–187
Zoroastrianism 60, 260, 277
Zwingli, Ulrich 284

For Product Safety Concerns and Information please contact our EU representative GPSR@taylorandfrancis.com
Taylor & Francis Verlag GmbH, Kaufingerstraße 24, 80331 München, Germany

www.ingramcontent.com/pod-product-compliance
Lightning Source LLC
Chambersburg PA
CBHW051350290426
44108CB00015B/1953